Cultures of Schooling

Cultures of Schooling:
Pedagogies for Cultural Difference and Social Access

Mary Kalantzis
Bill Cope
Greg Noble
Scott Poynting

Based on a report for the Australian Advisory Council on Languages and Multicultural Education, Canberra, commissioned as part of its contribution to the Education and Cultural and Linguistic Pluralism Project conducted by the Centre for Educational Research and Innovation, Organization for Economic Cooperation and Development, Paris.

 The Falmer Press

(A member of the Taylor & Francis Group)
London · New York · Philadelphia

UK	The Falmer Press, Rankine Road, Basingstoke, Hampshire, RG24 OPR
USA	The Falmer Press, Taylor and Francis Inc., 1900 Frost Road, Suite 101 Bristol, PA 19007

© M. Kalantzis, B. Cope,
G. Noble and S. Poynting 1990

All rights reserved. No part of this publication may be reproduced, stored in a retrieval system, or transmitted in any form or by any means, electronic, mechanical, photocopying, recording or otherwise, without permission in writing from the Publisher.

First published in 1990

British Library Cataloguing in Publication Data
Cultures of schooling : pedagogies for cultural difference and social access.
1. Australia. Multicultural education
I. Kalantzis, Mary
370.115

ISBN 1-85000-784-5
ISBN 1-85000-785-3 pbk

Library of Congress Cataloging-in-Publication Data
Cultures of schooling: pedagogies for cultural difference
  and social access/Mary Kalantzis ... [et al.].
    p. cm.
  'A draft report for the Australian Advisory Council on
Languages and Multicultural Education, Canberra, commissioned
as part of its contribution to the Education and Cultural and
Linguistic Pluralism Project conducted by the Centre for
Educational Research and Innovation, Organisation for Economic
Co-operation and Development, Paris.'
  'University of Wollongong, Australia, Centre for Multicultural
Studies.'
  'November 1989.'
  Includes index.
  ISBN 1-85000-784-5—ISBN 1-85000-785-3 (pbk.)
  1. Education, Bilingual—Australia—Case studies.
2. Intercultural education—Australia—Case studies. I. Kalantzis,
Mary. II. Australian Advisory Council on Languages and
Multicultural Education. III. Organisation for Economic Co-
operation and Development. Education and Cultural and
Linguistic Pluralism Project. IV. University of Wollongong.
Centre for Multicultural Studies.
LC3739.C85 1989   90-43996
371.97'00994—dc20   CIP

Jacket design by Caroline Archer

Typeset in 10.5/12 Caledonia
by Graphicraft Typesetters Ltd. Hong Kong.

Printed in Great Britain by Burgess Science Press, Basingstoke

Contents

Acknowledgments		vi
Foreword Joseph Lo Bianco		vii
Chapter 1	Introduction	1
Chapter 2	A Systems Perspective	15
Chapter 3	A Mission of 'Empowerment': The Community Liaison Program at MacKillop Girls' High School	40
Chapter 4	'Australian is a Wide Word': The Bilingual 'ESSPRO' and Languages Other Than English Programs at Brunswick East High School	68
Chapter 5	'Different Paths We'll Tread': The Translators' and Interpreters' Course at Burwood Girls' High School	92
Chapter 6	'Two Steps Forward, One Step Back': The Bilingual and Languages Other Than English Programmes at Collingwood Education Centre	116
Chapter 7	'A Place in the World': The Language in Learning Program and the Intensive Language Unit at Cabramatta High School	148
Chapter 8	'Culture Cocktail': The English as a Second Language and Languages Other Than English Programmes at Footscray High School	181
Chapter 9	Conclusions: Pedagogies for Cultural Difference and Social Access	215
Bibliography		251
Index		262

Acknowledgments

Special thanks to Joe Lo Bianco for his comments on an earlier draft report; the members of the Australian Advisory Council on Languages and Multicultural Education (AACLAME) steering committee who provided useful advice at the project design stage; the Organization for Economic Cooperation and Development (OECD) project organizers, particularly Allan Wagner and Jim Cummins who provided the critical impetus in the formulation of the case study protocol; and, perhaps most importantly, the educational administrators, principals, teachers, parents and students who so graciously allowed us to intrude in their lives. Needless to say, responsibility for the content of the report resides with the authors.

Foreword

Multicultural social policies in Australia have tended to gravitate between two opposing extremes, which in the past have seemed irreconcilable. On the one hand there has been a stress on the needs of minority communities to equip them with the linguistic skills and cultural knowledge so that their adjustment to the dominant societal values would be eased, and to bring about social justice, occupational mobility and educational equity for these minority groups. At the other extreme, multicultural policies have stressed the enrichment to the whole society through diversity and social pluralism. In education, multicultural policies have mirrored these emphases — occasionally stressing appropriate English language education, transitional bilingual programmes, bicultural aspects to curricula and facilitation of home-school relationships, thereby directly targeting immigrant and Aboriginal minorities and aiming to ensure educational equality for them. At other times, the stress has been on making available 'community' language programmes for all students, adding 'multicultural perspectives' across all curricula, and teaching history, Australian studies and social education generally from a pluralist perspective; in this way trying to construct a new version of Australian identity.

In recent years, a new emphasis has emerged which incorporates but transcends these two divergent tendencies. This new way of conceiving, 'naming' and talking about multicultural policies and their application to education reconciles the contradictory emphases of the past with a stress on the social and economic *functionalism* of cultural pluralism. In education, it is more common now to conceive of children's cultural and linguistic diversity not as a *problem* to be eradicated, nor necessarily as a *right* to be guaranteed, but rather, as a *resource* to be cultivated — an intellectual, social and economic resource. An essential part of this new way of viewing cultural and linguistic pluralism has to do with the construction of a vigorous and new national identity — no longer dependent and derivative but, at the same time, locally and internationally oriented.

In this respect, Australia is part of what will increasingly be a world-wide phenomenon; driven by the universalization of labour migration, increased economic interdependence among nations, the emergence of large trading blocs, greatly expanded international student mobility and the unification of the globe in a network of sophisticated, instantaneous telecommunications. Traditionally labour-exporting nations such as Italy and Greece are now immigrant-receiving nations, hosting hundreds of thousands of foreign-born workers; 'guest' workers in Northern Europe have 'stayed on', and their 'home countries' are now either in the EEC or have applied to join, and the provisions for bringing about the single European Market by 1993 would mean the free movement of labour. Japan's labour force now increasingly includes Pakistanis, Bangladeshis, Filipinos; many societies which previously regarded pluralism as a 'North American' phenomenon are having to acknowledge the issue. Race relations, pluralism, teaching national languages to domestic minorities, and cultural and linguistic preparation for international communication are on the agenda of many societies, developed and developing alike. Such changes have influenced the way in which second language learning in schools is regarded. Whereas only fifteen years ago the learning of languages in Australia (in a world then presumed by some to speak only English) was only rarely regarded as instrumentally useful, now language learning is advocated mostly in this way.

The Australian Advisory Council on Languages and Multicultural Education (AACLAME) has sought to invest considerations of cultural pluralism in Australian education with a more modern, some would say a more 'hard-nosed', economically rationalist dimension, without neglecting either the rights and opportunities of minorities or the benefits of culture to the wider society, but bringing these together into a broader discourse. The traditional mainstays of multicultural education, *viz* cultural and linguistic maintenance for minority groups, and their equal access to the socially dominant language, knowledge and values, could be revitalized by placing them in an overarching internationalist context and seeing the pluralism of our population as a resource enhancing Australia's capacity to participate in the world.

The programme which funded many of the innovations examined in this book was terminated in 1986 federal budget. The case studies in this extremely valuable book are eloquent testimony to the fact that Australian teachers and schools have been given an enormously difficult job to do, and, with only 'stop-start' and inadequate support, they have done it very well indeed. Serious problems of increasing the achievement levels of students, and the range and depth of language programmes — i.e., problems of planning to service a multilingual, multicultural population (and this increasingly within an international orientation) persist.

The book documents that the process of innovation is a long and arduous one and that the society's ever increasing expectations of schools are not matched by the appropriate support for them. Despite this, very many Australian schools have embraced the principles of cultural pluralism and fashioned them into viable and imaginative curricula.

I commend the authors for the dedicated and systematic way they have

Foreword

gone about their task, and assure them, and the schools which so generously gave of their time, that AACLAME is committed to addressing the issues they report to us — both to the OECD/CERI, of whose project on Education and Cultural and Linguistic Pluralism this research forms a part; and to the relevant Australian authorities.

Joseph Lo Bianco
Chair
Australian Advisory Council on Languages and Multicultural Education

Chapter 1

Introduction

Setting the Scene: Servicing Cultural and Linguistic Diversity in Australia

Australia is the site of a quite remarkable social experiment. In just over four decades since the post-war immigration programme began, the Australian population has more than doubled, from 7.5 million in 1947 to 16 million by the mid-1980s. Without immigration, given the birth rates of the native born, the Australian population would now be only about 11 million. This in itself is not remarkable. Mass migration has been one of the most important historical features of the era of global industrialization, from the country to the city, the developing to the developed world, from points of crisis to points of quieter affluence. But, in a half century when global mobility has been greater than ever before, Australia's immigration programme has been greater than that of any first world country relative to the size of the existing population, bar the peculiar historical phenomenon of the establishment of the state of Israel in British Mandated Palestine.[1]

The diversity of Australia's post-war immigrant intake is also remarkable. Ostensibly, the first Minister for Immigration, Arthur Calwell, intended that mainly English-speaking immigrants come from the British Isles. This fitted with the official policy of assimilation, in which those people least likely to appear different in cultural and linguistic terms were to be encouraged as ideal immigrants and non-English speakers were to become 'normal', unaccented English-speaking Australians by the second generation. In fact, this prescription for cultural and linguistic homogeneity was immediately unworkable, even in the late 1940s, and the historical evidence shows that Calwell knew it despite much of the public rhetoric.[2] As insufficient British immigrants could be recruited, a large emphasis was placed on recruiting refugees from Northern and Central Europe. During the 1950s and 1960s, recruitment was increasingly from Southern Europe — again, very much determined by the availability of suitable immigrants. During the 1970s, with the 'economic miracle' in Europe, the net had to be spread still further, to include Middle

Eastern countries, particularly Turkey and Lebanon, then South and Central America. From the mid-1970s an increasing number of Indo-Chinese came to Australia, many as refugees. This was nominally the result of an international humanitarian obligation and a by-product of Australia's involvement in the Vietnam War. In reality, considerable diplomatic pressure was brought to bear upon Australia by front-line South East Asian countries with a serious refugee problem, and the Australian government perceived a need to avert the possibility of a large-scale arrival of 'boat people' on the shores of Northern Australia.[3]

Thus, although the original official intention of Australia's post-war immigration programme had been cultural and linguistic homogeneity, the end result has been extraordinary diversity. As well as about 150 extant Aboriginal languages, there are now over 100 immigrant ethnic groups, speaking about 80 different languages. Over 25 per cent of the population in 1988 was of non-English speaking background (NESB).[4] Of the two million Australians who reported in the 1986 Census that they spoke a language other than English at home, 20.6 per cent spoke Italian, 13.6 Greek, 6.7 per cent a Chinese language, 5.6 per cent German and 5.4 per cent Arabic; Spanish, the various Yugoslav languages, Polish, Dutch, Vietnamese, Maltese, French, Macedonian, Aboriginal languages, Turkish, Hungarian and Russian each scored between 1 and 5 per cent; and a very large proportion of 14.4 per cent were 'other' languages, each with less than 1 per cent representation per language.[5]

Numbers and diversity alone, however, do not justify the claim that this continent is the site of a remarkable social experiment. Immigrants have officially been encouraged to come and become citizens, not guestworkers. Unlike other countries whose immigrant recruitment was largely for labour force reasons, Australia's immigration involved population building and thus permanent settlement. Later this reality came to be forced upon countries with temporary guestworker programmes, despite their intentions. A succession of sophisticated settlement policies were orchestrated by the Australian federal government for two purposes: to reduce the social cost of return migration and to 'sell' mass immigration to the existing population — a population which in 1947 was 90 per cent Australian born, almost exclusively Anglophone, and harbouring a vigorous history of racism.

The history of these policies — from the assimilation policy of the 1940s to the 1960s, then integration, and, most recently, multiculturalism since the late 70s — is complex, subtle, and of immense historical importance. If one overarching assessment of these programmes can be made, it is that, on their own terms, they have been extremely successful. For immigrants, there has been a degree of upward social mobility, perhaps not always commensurate with their aspirations but at least as significant as that found in any other country at a similar stage of economic development.[6] In broader social terms, one of the world's most homogeneous societies, culturally insular and racist, has been peacefully transformed into one of the most diverse. The extraordinary sense of quiet on this continent belies an experience of world historical significance in the pace and extent of population change. The fact that change on this scale was effected in so few decades and the quiet maintained, history having been made almost behind the backs of its population, itself attests to the sophistication, creativity and adaptiveness of the succession of government policies dealing with cultural and linguistic diversity.[7] Australia, in this respect, is an important place to look for lessons about social policy and practice relating to immigration and settlement.

This book documents this historical achievement on one social site only — schooling. Education, in fact, happens to be an extraordinarily significant site. It is compulsory. It is the place where the state, as nation builder and maker of national identity, can play its most deliberate, systematic and sustained socializing role. It is a place where the state can be creating the cultural conditions for peaceful social change rather than reactively patching up popular resistances to change. In fact, at each stage in the development of Australian policy, the state has always seen education this way: as one of the most important places where the real work of assimilation, or integration or multiculturalism — whatever the policy at the time happened to be — took place.

Perhaps ironically, recently vocal opponents of multicultural education cite the social mobility of immigrants as a reason to scrap specialist programmes. Immigrants do not seem to need, so these opponents argue, the special treatment and additional government expense. Ethnic minorities have their own particular sense of commitment, closely bound into the migration process itself, manifest in the 'ethnic success ethic' or 'ethnic work ethic'. It is argued that these factors, extraneous to institutionalized education, mean that specialist servicing such as multicultural education is unnecessary. These critics, in other words, advocate a *laissez faire* approach to the interaction of processes of immigration/settlement and education.[8]

Critical to the story of mobility, however, has been the success of education systems in meeting the special needs of immigrant students, in part through precisely those special programmes which the new critics of multicultural education seek to abandon. Rather ironically, it is precisely the interventionary role taken by Australian governments, not just in education but in all areas of social policy, that has made the social changes wrought upon Australian society by mass immigration so peaceful, despite the cultural proclivities of the native born population in 1947, despite the extent of the changes, and despite the inherent structural difficulties of incorporating labour migrants in such a way that they do not form a permanently ghettoized underclass. Whatever their weaknesses, federal government policies of assimilation, followed by policies of integration and then of multiculturalism, were extremely active and effective processes of state intervention, almost always ahead of public opinion in their historical vision, and taking an educative stance even in relation to 'educated', seemingly professional and 'expert' service providers, such as state education authorities and teachers. Most importantly, these policies have never been static. Assimilation, for example, was a necessary story to tell a population about to face mass labour immigration, but with a powerful, popular tradition of economically-based racism. But the architects of mass immigration knew right from the start that the immigration programme would inevitably bring with it cultural diversity which could not be erased by fiat of a policy of assimilation. Assimilation was therefore an extremely effective step in creating a culturally and linguistically diverse society, and its success was its own peaceful supersession by integration and multiculturalism.[9] Similarly, today, multiculturalism is an unfinished historical process, visionary and historically active, yet ridden with limitations and inherent difficulties upon which its practitioners work creatively in their daily activity.

Despite the effective role of education, for example, in creating lasting social, cultural and linguistic change in Australia, there are still critical issues to be tackled. The positive social effects of education are distributed unevenly among ethnic groups. And even when educational attainments are statistically positive for any one ethnic group, generalization about the performance of students of particular ethnic groups ignores the fact that each group is itself deeply divided socioeconomically and by school performance. Even if one small stratum is making it through to higher education at a rate marginally more than average, the majority may still be having difficulties specific to their minority cultural and linguistic status in Australia in which their background plays a contributing part. Moreover, first generation immigrants enjoy substantially less social mobility through education than the second generation.[10] And the cultural and linguistic content of curriculum is an issue that all Australian schools need to face all the time. These are just a few of the nagging questions that face those dealing with cultural and linguistic diversity in Australian education.

Thus this book is a critical documentation of an evolving social project. Australia might in some respects lead the world in the development of multicultural education policies and practices, yet this means more than ever that we must evaluate our ongoing failings, as lessons to be learnt before taking the next step. There are no lessons for direct export, which can be happily duplicated elsewhere. But there are experiences of partial success and a constructive approach to failure that might be very useful.

A Focus on Innovation

The research project 'Education and Cultural and Linguistic Pluralism: Innovative Schools' (ECALP), upon which this book is based, was devised by the Centre for Educational Research and Innovation (CERI) in the Organization for Economic Cooperation and Development (OECD). A number of OECD member countries is involved in a parallel programme of research, employing a common methodology centred around a case-study protocol. The Australian component of the project was initated and subsequently funded by the

Introduction

Australian Advisory Council on Languages and Multicultural Education (AACLAME) which operates under the National Policy on Languages. The Australian fieldwork and reporting has been undertaken by the Centre for Multicultural Studies at the University of Wollongong, New South Wales.

The objectives of the overall project were expressed by CERI/OECD as follows:

> The purpose of this project is to study innovation strategies which have resulted in particularly successful forms of education for the children of immigrants or ethnic minority groups. Through case studies of innovations in OECD member countries, approaches proven to be successful in a variety of settings will be identified and the common conditions under which the approaches have succeeded will be described and analysed.
>
> The detailed analysis of the innovations is likely to be of interest to all those who are involved in multicultural education. It will draw attention to some effective and exemplary practices and also identify useful criteria for the formulation of new policies in this area. In assembling case studies from a number of countries, the project seeks to go beyond the narrow circumstances reflected in a particular educational system or country setting. In this way, the conditions under which innovations succeed may be revealed more clearly, even amplified.
>
> A case study approach is especially well suited to the goals of the project, since inclusion in the sample is dictated by the uniqueness or creativity of the approach rather than on the number of such cases. The multi-site case study strategy adopted for the project is unique in that, while the case studies are guided by the overall objectives of the CERI project, the design allows for case studies of quite different types of innovations. As a result, the individual case studies will have in common those aspects necessary to permit comparisons across cases, but they will differ in striking ways according to the characteristics, settings and purposes of the innovation/approach under study.[11]

For the Australian component of the project, case studies were conducted at Brunswick East High School, Collingwood Education Centre and Footscray High School (each part of the Victorian state education system); Burwood Girls' High School and Cabramatta High School (both part of the New South Wales state education system); and MacKillop Girls' High School (a Catholic systemic school, in the Sydney Archdiocese). These secondary schools were selected by AACLAME in consultation with the Victorian Ministry of Education, the New South Wales Department of Education and Catholic Education Office, Sydney. The criteria for selection were those specified in the ECALP project guidelines:

The schools that will be singled out as candidates for a case study will be chosen from among those providing examples of approaches which have been successful in improving the performance of minority children in the following educational situations:

i) Cultural/linguistic incorporation;
ii) Community participation;
iii) Pedagogy;
iv) Assessment;
v) Use of new technologies in basic learning.

It will become clear as this book unfolds that 'innovation' in the Australian context turned out to be a somewhat different phenomenon to that evidently presupposed in the original project design. This does not imply that the focus on innovation was unfruitful or that there was no innovation to be found. On the contrary, the six Australian case-study sites were able to show off innovations in multicultural education of precisely the order of those anticipated by CERI/OECD. But, taking the liberty of 'reading into' the CERI/OECD guidelines, the rationales of seeking 'uniqueness or creativity' rather than representative national cases, and of attempting 'to go beyond the narrow circumstances reflected in a particular educational system or country setting', imply that perhaps isolated but replicable cases of excellence in multicultural education are thrown up at a grassroots level, in very specific micro-environments.

In none of the six Australian case studies were innovations found that had been developed uniquely within that school. There were no school-based innovations in this sense. Yet innovations there were, in the sense of dramatic departures from traditional curriculum and school structures. These, however, have to be viewed as systemic, structural, historico-cultural events, in which the basis of educational innovation and change, and, in some cases, the reasons for the abandonment of certain of the innovations, are to be located outside the school itself. This is not to deny that the six cases surveyed here are amongst the best to be found in Australia, but to locate the origin and sustainability of the innovations outside each school — to those broad historical phenomena, alluded to above, that make Australia an interesting place.

Further, within each school it is often not the innovatory programme or practice alone which 'works' for the school, but the institutional framework in which it is set: that cluster of leadership, sense of community, and so on, that make a good school 'work' as a whole. Sometimes, in fact, there was nothing innovatory about the programme itself (such as teaching Turkish from traditional textbooks). It was simply having Turkish in the school, as part of a compulsory core programme in languages other than English, that was innovative. Turkish would never have featured in a more traditional curriculum structure, taught to Turkish-speaking background students.

Introduction

Case-Study Methodology

The principal data sources for the six case studies were:

Education Authorities:	Policies and other documentary evidence
	Extended key informant interviews
School Staff:	Extended key informant interviews (principals, key teachers, school support staff)
	Policies and programme documentation
	Records: enrolment
	Records: achievement
	Classroom observation
Students:	Selected extended interviews
	Written questionnaires
	Observation of classroom/playground interaction
	Analysis of work produced
Parents:	Selected extended interviews
	Observation of parent-school interaction (such as meetings)
External:	Community profile data
	Community sources: local government/ethnic organizations (interviews and documentary evidence)

It is evident that there were three main means of collecting data: collecting documentary evidence, structured extended interviews and observation. The first step in analyzing each case-study situation was to examine closely all supporting documentation, particularly as it reflects systems/school/programme objectives, the sociological context of the school (such as enrolment details) and educational results. This was followed by structured oral interviews centred around the key case-study questions. The format of the interview schedule was both focused and open, allowing for responses and lines of conversation to go beyond the alternative answers presupposed in the interview format. Particular care was taken to seek out different perspectives on the multicultural education innovations, from the committed, to the uncommitted and the oppositional. Interviews ranged in length from forty-five minutes to two and a half hours and were tape-recorded with the interviewee's permission. In some cases, it was necessary to return to re-interview certain key informants when issues came up in subsequent fieldwork that required additional clarification from them. Finally, observations were made of classroom interaction, and various school meetings: staff meetings, parent-teacher evenings and school councils, for example. This involved recording observed interactions, based on semi-structured observation schedules, and was incidental to the main thrust of the interviewing and collection of documentary material.

Case-study methodology (unlike, for example, voluntary participation in an interview or laboratory work) involves the researcher peculiarly in observation of the subject's everyday world of experience. It is thus potentially much more an intrusion than other forms of research. This difficulty is compounded by the 'official' nature of this project. Accordingly, preliminary negotiations involved explaining the project in full and seeking permission from education authorities (insofar as they were not already aware of its objectives and methodology), principals, teachers, parents and students. A brief (two page) and clear description of the project was prepared, and continuous explanation provided orally as the need arose.

Given this intrusive nature of the research, the researchers' programme took second priority to the needs of individual subjects and school organization. This was the case both for time planning and the data collection itself. Interviewing, for example, had to be open-ended with no necessary assumption that the interviewee could or would want to cooperate or follow the logic of the questioning and data analysis. Data collection instruments were thus not presented as rigid or mandatory in form, but more as a structured programme of prompts in situations that had more of the feel of an extended conversation than a formal interview. The willingness of schools to give of their time and throw their activities open to public scrutiny, hiding no warts, was quite remarkable, and is reflected in the very full, complex and, at times, necessarily controversial picture that comes through in the case-study chapters.

The particular virtue of case-study methodology is that it actively seeks out the detailed dynamics of social process, rather than, as is the tendency in more traditional social research, collating results and infering causal relationships. If in a given context, certain things demonstrably work or do not work for reasons that can be traced in the details of process, then generalizations can be drawn about the transferability of this experience to a similar context.

A veritable mountain of data was interrogated for its validity and reliability according to the following criteria, adapted from Yin[12]:

i) Construct Validity: Does each case study focus on the operational issues it purports to reflect?
— Multiple sources of evidence were used.
— Agreed cause-effect relations were established both amongst the research team and in discussion with key informants.
— Key informants were asked to review case study drafts.

ii) Internal Validity: Within the case study, do purported cause-effect relations hold?
— Alternative or rival explanations were sought.
— Frequency of response, observation, and so on was checked.
— Purported cause-effect was checked against time series.
— Different types of evidence (such as oral/documentary) were cross-checked.

— All observations and interviews were attended by two researchers, and processes for the validation data discussed at the end of each interview/observation.

iii) External Validity: Can findings be generalized from one case to another?
— Case studies were compared with each other. Sometimes it was necessary to explain why generalization could or could not be made.
— The innovation was examined to find out if it replicated other comparable experiences.
— For the purposes of maximizing the validity of generalization across cases, all four researchers spent considerable stretches conducting fieldwork (in rotating pairs) in all six schools, and all contributed to the writing of this book.

iv) Reliability: Would another researcher conduct the same study, using the same case-study protocol, and arrive at the same conclusions?
— The project involved questioning from a variety of perspectives, both in terms of category of individual (e.g., parent) and having enough individuals in each category to verify observations or represent effectively the range of interpretations of the cause-effect relations stemming from the innovation.

With these emphases, data reduction has occurred throughout the data collection process, focusing on salient information in three stages. Critical evaluation has been the main basis for data reduction, from the very beginning of data collection.

Method / Analysis	Observations	Interviews	Documents
Stage one: Observe and establish hypotheses			
Stage two: Inquire further and validate hypotheses			
Stage three: Seek to explain data, construct narrative of report, identify gaps in data etc.			

Cultures of Schooling

Anticipatory data reduction had already begun before fieldwork in the formulation of the case-study propositions themselves. During stage one, the testing of hypotheses involved a dialogue between the field and the researcher which focused clearly on the salient element of the innovation and its impact. In stage two, conclusion drawing and verification began: as well as transcribing and collating the raw data, draft narratives attempting to describe patterns and irregularities were written. During stage three, this process continued, developing explanations of cause-effect relationships. A draft of the empirical narrative of the report and tentative generalization on its immediate results was ready soon after the completion of fieldwork to allow the researchers to verify ambiguous points, fill in data gaps and so on. Key informants were then asked to read and verify this narrative.

The Case-Study Propositions

The general framework of investigation for the ECALP project was spelt out by CERI/OECD as follows:

> All the OECD countries share the view that the school should prepare all pupils for active participation in the life of the society and that all children should have equal chances of success. This broad view raises a number of questions about such matters as the avoidance of underachievement and wastage of human resources; the improvement of the performance of all pupils; and the positive exploitation of diverse cultural and linguistic heritages (for example, through two-way bilingual education programmes).
>
> The work proposed here is intended to throw light on two aspects: on the one hand, what is happening in those schools that are implementing multicultural education programmes (which is the purpose of the case studies) and, on the other, what happens at the policy-making level once it is decided to allow schools greater latitude so that they are able to adapt the general aims of multicultural education policies, curricula, teaching materials, and structures of support and assistance to suit local conditions.[13]

Within this overall framework, five key case-study propositions — hypotheses to be tested in each of the six schools by the study of innovations tackling the challenge of cultural and linguistic pluralism — were formulated for the Australian research. They are broadly based on the CERI/ECALP Guidelines, but include particular pedagogical and institutional perspectives that have emerged in the Australian context.

First, schools can *incorporate* 'minority' (adopting the OECD/CERI terminological equivalence with non-majority, immigrant) students in a variety of ways, each of which might portend greater success at school. They can incorporate in the sense of bringing 'minority' students into the mainstream and providing paths to academic success (the 'ethnic disadvantage' model of specialist teaching). This may well incorporate 'minority' students successfully yet also assimilate them culturally (intentionally or unintentionally), by subsuming their 'minority' culture to the demands of the dominant culture. They can also incorporate in the sense of actively respecting and allowing the difference of 'minority' students (the cultural pluralist model). This may well succeed at the affective level (esteem, etc.), and through this, perhaps, have a bearing on student access to the mainstream. Incorporation might also take place in both of the above senses: structural equity in the context of cultural diversity. The main thrust of this proposition is that cognizance of cultural context is a necessary prerequisite to both structural incorporation (removing barriers to access to mainstream industrial society/culture) and cultural incorporation (allowing openness to cultural diversity and facing the demands of intercultural communication in the school and the community).

Second, schools can use a variety of techniques to increase the 'minority' *community participation* in education. These can range from processes which democratize decision making, to making minority parents and communities feel part of the social atmosphere of the school. Yet there are tensions between the rhetoric of participation as an ideal and, in particular circumstances, problems including: a community's capacity to participate; a potential conflict between community views on the way schools should work and the positions of authority of the school personnel; the time and material resources required to support community participation; a possible threat to teacher professionalism and control of their work; and the fact that the culturally specific liberal ideal of grassroots community participation might well be at odds with many immigrant cultural expectations. Effective school management and community participation, in other words, involves interaction in which parents and the broader community play a significant role in school life, whilst, at the same time, teacher professionalism is maintained and a mutually educative dialogue is established between school and community about the role and function of schooling in advanced industrial society.

Third, schools use a variety of *pedagogies* according to their educational philosophy; the preferred teaching styles and perceived learning styles of their students, the method that appears most effective, systems and syllabus requirements, or parental demands. Successful pedagogy reflects both the living hand of cultural tradition (cueing into culturally specific learning styles) and the particular social, linguistic and cognitive requirements of the future in a rapidly changing industrial society. This is an historically unique demand to be put upon education as a public institution and is pivotal in the articulation of private and public rites of passage or socialization. Pedagogy for 'minority' students will be most effective when it is clear about the core social linguistic and cognitive requirements of the dominant society, yet sensitive to the differential pedagogical techniques necessary to achieve that end. While addressing this core, successful multicultural education will be open to community cultural diversity in its curriculum content and social/behavioural objectives. Pedagogical strategy is thus an essential issue in this twofold endeavour: initiation to the core linguistic, cognitive and employment requirements of late industrial society, yet sensitivity to the local, the culturally specific and the particular.

Fourth, *assessment* performs a dual function in schooling: promotion from one level or class to another and final school credentialling; and diagnosis of learning needs. Assessment is frequently accused of being a process of ranking which reconstructs differential performance and achievement as reflecting inferior or superior ability. For example, low ranking in the 'majority' language early in a student's school life can affect later educational participation, self-esteem, and so on. However, 'soft' forms of assessment are often weak in their capacity for comparability, in failing to report accurately on results as they lead to the final school credential for entrance to higher education, in being often unclear and ambiguous, and involving, as they frequently do, a devaluing of the assessment process to the point where it loses much of its meaning. Notwithstanding the critique of the effect and reliability of standardized testing and IQ tests on 'minority' students, assessment is crucial. Teachers need assessment tools of broad comparability for diagnostic purposes. Parent participation requires a clear and accurate assessment and reporting procedure. Students need accurate feedback on their work. Education systems need comparable results for final school credentialling and to determine entrance into post-secondary education. Assessment, therefore, needs to be designed to be sensitive to cultural differences, not foreclosing possibilities in the fashion of standardized tests or IQ tests, yet reporting to teachers, parents, students and systems in ways which are accurate and ensure comparability.

Fifth, the use of *new technologies in basic learning* can involve learning in traditional ways (but more efficiently whilst incidentally gaining familiarity with new tools), or new ways of learning, packaging knowledge or presenting curriculum which would not otherwise be presented. In other words, new technologies in basic learning can mean both more efficient ways of teaching the 'basics' using traditional pedagogy and new ways of knowing in which, for example, memory and note-taking are less important than an ability to access information storage, use spelling programs or draft and edit on a keyboard.

The Style of Reporting

These propositions are tested in the six chapters (three to eight) which report directly on each of the case studies. The style of reporting in these chapters is not analytical in the sense of interpreting the data directly and systematically in relation to the hypotheses, and vice versa. Rather, these chapters each describe a part of the life of the institution largely 'from the horse's mouth', reporting what people say, with little or no analytical commentary other than

Introduction

the participants' own reading of the situation. This is appropriate because they say it all, anyway, albeit in various voices framed by various discourses. No perspective on the problem of education for cultural and linguistic pluralism seems to escape the critical gaze of these education professionals, parents and students. Direct engagement with the cases-study propositions, and interpretation of the whole spread of data, occurs in the concluding ninth chapter.

The book itself needs to be prefaced with a very strong statement in praise of teachers and school. It is, after all, an area of life and work which enjoys relatively low social prestige, for the length of training of its professionals, for the intensity of its working conditions, and for the high expectations that are placed upon it by communities and governments as a social cure-all. Despite this, the case studies stand, more than anything, as a testimony to teacher professionalism and commitment beyond the call of duty, social reward and remuneration. This professionalism and commitment is probably evident more in teachers' awareness of critical lessons to be learnt from the difficulties and limitations of their practice, than in their school success stories. The critical professional appraisals, in other words, are more revealing than reports of unequivocal success or statements of noble intention.

Notes

1 CASTLES, S., COPE, B., KALANTZIS, M. and MORRISSEY, M., *Mistaken Identity: Multiculturalism and the Demise of Nationalism in Australia*, Pluto Press, Sydney, pp. 24–25; AUSTRALIAN BUREAU OF SSTATISTICS, *Australian Yearbook 1988*, Canberra, 1988.

2 KIERNAN, C., *Calwell: A Personal and Political Biography*, Thomas Nelson, Melbourne, 1978, pp. 117–121; KUNZ, E.F., *Displaced Persons: Calwell's New Australians*, Australian National University Press, 1988, pp. 11–20.

3 VIVIANI, N., *The Long Journey: Vietnamese Migration and Settlement in Australia*, Melbourne University Press, Melbourne, 1984, p. 114.

4 DEPARTMENT OF IMMIGRATION AND ETHNIC AFFAIRS, *Don't Settle for Less — Report of the Committee for Stage 1 of the Review of Migrant and Multicultural Programs and Services*, (Jupp Report), Australian Government Publishing Service, Canberra, 1986, p. 42.

5 AUSTRALIAN BUREAU OF STATISTICS, *Australian Profile — Census 86*, 1988.

6 WOOD, D. and HUGO, G., *Distribution and Age Structure of the Australian Born with Overseas Born Parents*, DIEA, Canberra, 1984, pp. 254–257; KALANTZIS, M. and COPE, B., 'Why We Need Multicultural Education: A Review of the "Ethnic Disadvantage" Debate', *Journal of Intercultural Studies*, 1988, Vol. 9, No. 1, pp. 39–57.

7 The terms 'homogeneous', 'peaceful' and 'quiet' refer to the European experience in Australia only. The indigenous Aboriginal peoples suffered grievously at the hands of the British, who, from their perspective, invaded their land. The waves of new settlers remained blind to the original dispossession and unwittingly did nothing to alleviate the injustice. This work concerned as it is with immigrants does not address the issue of the indigenous peoples of Australia. The discussion

of multiculturalism and the forging of community in Australia cannot go forward however, without an integration of their concerns.

8   BIRRELL, R. and SEITZ, A., 'The Ethnic Problem in Education: The Emergence and Definition of an Issue'. Paper presented at AIMA Conference, Melbourne, 1986; BULLIVANT, B., *Getting a Fair Go; Studies of Occupational Socialisation and Perceptions of Discrimination*, Australian Government Publishing Service, Canberra, 1986; KALANTZIS, M. and COPE, B., 'Why We Need Multicultural Education: A Review of the "Ethnic Disadvantage" Debate', *Journal of Intercultural Studies*, 1988, Vol. 9, No. 1, pp. 39–57.

9   JAKUBOWICZ, A., MORRISSEY, M. and PALSER, J., *Ethnicity, Class and Social Policy in Australia*, Report No. 46, Social Welfare Research Centre, University of New South Wales, 1984, p. 27, 40.

10 HUGO, S., *Australia's Changing Population: Trend and Implications*, Melbourne, Oxford University Press, 1986; HORVATH, B.M. 'An Investigation of Class Placements in New South Wales Schools', Mimeo, NSW Ethnic Affairs Commission/Sydney University, 1986; CASTLES, S., LEWIS, MORRISSEY, M. and BLACK, J., Patterns of Disadvantage Among the Overseas Born and Their Children, Centre for Multicultural Studies, Wollongong University, 1986; AUSTRALIAN INSTITUTE OF MULTICULTURAL AFFAIRS, *Reducing the Risk; Unemployed Migrant Youth and Labour and Market Programs AIMA*, Melbourne, 1985.

11 ORGANIZATION FOR ECONOMIC CO-OPERATION AND DEVELOPMENT: CENTRE FOR EDUCATIONAL RESEARCH AND INNOVATION, Project No. 6., *Education and Cultural and Linguistic Pluralism (ECALP): Innovative Schools*, Protocol, OECD, Paris, 1989.

12 YIN, R.K., *Case Study Research: Design & Methods*, 1984, Sage, p. 30.

13 ORGANIZATION FOR ECONOMIC CO-OPERATION AND DEVELOPMENT: CENTRE FOR EDUCATIONAL RESEARCH AND INNOVATION, Project No. 6., *Education and Cultural and Linguistic Pluralism (ECALP): Innovative Schools*, Protocol, OECD, Paris, 1989.

Chapter 2

A Systems Perspective

A Brief History of Responses to Cultural and Linguistic Diversity in Australian Education Since 1947

It is a complex history that links Australian federal immigration and settlement policy to the life of schools. At first glance, it would seem that these two realms are, institutionally at least, far removed. Under the division of powers in the Australian Constitution, immigration is a federal matter and education a state matter. Yet, the connections between the two have been very close. The immigration power has given the federal government a licence to generate programmes which meet the special needs of immigrant children. The most important constitutional turning point in this regard was the passage of the federal Immigration (Education) Act of 1971. And, in the past two decades particularly, tied grants (in the distribution of federal income taxes to the states) have given the federal government an additional lever with which to influence directly state education policy and programmes.

In fact, it is possible to argue that adjustments to the cultural and linguistic policies of the federal government have been translated into education policy and practice more quickly and more effectively than they have impacted upon other realms of life more institutionally autonomous of government, including much of high culture (such as academic interpretations of Australian history and identity) and public opinion.[1] In other words, education has been an important opinion leader, a critical element in actively reshaping Australian culture and identity. It has been a central part of the project of winning over people's hearts and minds, be it to assimilation, or integration, or multiculturalism.

The brief historical sketch that follows, therefore, concentrates on federal politics as the heart of any explanation of the origins of multicultural education in Australia. The chapters of this book that document the six case-study schools are the empirical proof of the pudding — that the political debate about immigration, settlement and cultural diversity actually came to something, indeed, often wrought significant changes, in schools.

Cultures of Schooling

From the beginning of the post-war immigration programme, Australian education systems were unable to turn a totally blind eye to the presence of non-English speaking immigrant children. Special classes were set up outside school time to teach 'Elementary English and Civics'. But the main idea in the quite frequent departmental exhortations to teachers was that the 'New Australian' or 'foreign-speaking' child would fit in quickly and with a minimum of assistance. This was the advice of the New South Wales Department of Education in 1951:

> The fact that the New Australian child is eager to master the language and, indeed is forced to do so if he wishes to take his place amongst Australian children, makes the teacher's task much easier. It has been found that children with little or no command of English appreciate being given an 'adjustment period' of a fortnight or so during which they can observe their new class and 'get the feel' of the new conditions without being unduly worried by formal classwork. The adjustment process is helped by seating the migrant beside a sympathetic Australian child.[2]

It soon became obvious, however, that assimilation was not this simple. Even by the mid-1950s a New South Wales school inspector was lamenting 'the social problems of integration of Australian and Migrant Peoples'. The word describing the 'absorption' process had changed by then, as had even some of the niceties of how it was to be done, but not the fundamental historical, cultural and linguistic intent.

> The Australian way of living has for its base a magnificent [English] tradition. On this base we have grafted the material and economic fruits of our adjustment to a markedly different environment ..., [and a] preoccupation with material purposes and prospects has undoubtedly been responsible for our amazing material and scientific development.
>
> ... [T]he planners decided that 'social and cultural absorption' of migrant peoples was essential if Australia was to gain, in the limited time left, the national strength required in population and development for her protection. Fear of unabsorbed alien minorities, based on war-time experiences in other lands made 'assimilation' a fundamental issue in our mass immigration policy. But Australians have yet to realize the real meaning of assimilation in terms of mutual attitudes, appreciations, and activities. The first step to a better understanding of the problems is to substitute the term integration for assimilation, and to realize that differences cannot be 'rubbed off' merely by daily contact with Australians! Indeed, the merging together of peoples is a time process which has, as its outcome, the merging together of migrants and the local population in such a way

that the newcomers find a satisfying place in the economic and social life of their new environment.[3]

A measure of mutual cultural respect, evidently, would assist the 'absorption' process. But, at the end of the day, it was believed, there is one Australian Way of Life, materially affluent and culturally English, and immigrants will benefit from this when they integrate.

The doctrine of assimilation lasted in official rhetoric until the late 1960s, even if the terminology had cosmetically shifted to integration through that decade. As late as 1969, Billy Snedden, Liberal Minister for Immigration, could say emphatically:

> We must have a single culture. If migration implies multi-cultural activities within Australian society, then it was not the type Australia wanted. I am quite determined we should have a mono-culture with everyone living in the same way, understanding each other and sharing the same aspirations. We do not want pluralism.[4]

Assimilation, however, was a very contradictory phenomenon. There was more to it than first meets the eye. In some quite fundamental and immediately obvious ways it was racist, assuming the inherent virtue of changing one's culture and language until the ideal point is reached when one disappears into the, presumably superior, Australian crowd. Yet, it was also a rather benevolent ideology of immigrants benefiting (after an appropriate spell of hard work) from the suburban culture of the double-fronted brick veneer house with a Holden car in the garage. Assimilation did not contain the assumptions of traditional, biologically-based racism that there are unbridgeable human cultural gaps. It presumed instead that cultural change, 'becoming like us', was both possible and desirable. In the long term, in fact, the language of assimilation which assured Australians that cultural differences were not immutable, also paved the way for the softening of a racist popular culture and for a quietly successful mass immigration programme. Assimilation was so successful a public discourse that it created the conditions of its own demise: a culturally diverse society. Its rhetoric belied its real and perhaps unselfconscious historical mission.

Through to the mid-1970s, then, the project of education systems was cultural and linguistic assimilation or integration. The main medium for this was the learning of English. Yet the strategies and programmes in the teaching of English were hardly sophisticated, sustained, or at all adequately funded until the establishment of the Commonwealth-funded Child Migrant Education Program in 1971.

Even from the mid-60s, however, it was becoming obvious to many people that neither the policy of assimilation nor integration had been working quite as well as the rhetoric implied. A plethora of government reports showed, for example, that immigrant students of non-English speaking background were educationally disadvantaged. At the same time, larger concerns pressured government towards a shift in policy: assimilation or integration of a cultural and linguistic level was simply not occurring; specialist servicing (such as language services) was increasingly needed as the proportion of the population of non-English speaking background increased; return migration to the European 'economic miracle' was a serious economic drain which needed to be reduced; and 'ethnic' organizations and lobby groups were emerging and possibly even constituting a 'migrant vote'.[5] At first, however, responses to these problems, such as the Child Migrant Education Program, stayed within the paradigm of integration.

The Labor Party, under the leadership of Gough Whitlam, came to power in the federal arena in 1972, after twenty-three years of conservative government. It came with a dramatically new vision for social reform, including a massive expansion of the welfare state and government initiation of huge development projects.

In many ways, the three turbulent Labor years represent a culmination of the project of integration, even though they also laid some of the groundwork for the later emergence of a policy of multiculturalism. Al Grassby, Labor Minister for Immigration from 1972 to 1974, addressing the, by then, well-known difficulties faced by immigrants, spoke, not of cultural difference, but of a unified 'family of the nation', rid of all forms of social injustice.

> It is in our national interest to abolish discrimination. It is in the long-term interest of all Australians — and not only the many who suffer in varying degrees from discrimination — that we eradicate those things which divide us as people and strengthen and build upon those things which unite us. . . .
>
> I have spoken on other occasions of 'the family of the nation'. I shall go on speaking of 'the family of the nation' until the message implicit in that phrase is fully grasped and until it becomes the guiding principle for us all. It is not a cliché, but a fundamental objective. Unless we achieve unity of purpose, unless we are joined — all 13,000,000 of us — in a common purpose, how can we succeed as a nation?
>
> It is not only a question of ensuring equal economic opportunity for migrants, but also of providing whatever assistance is necessary to place them on an equal footing with Australian-born. The only question that should ever be asked in law is whether a person is a citizen or not. There can be, in future, no first and second-class citizens. . . .
>
> It is also a question of enabling them — indeed, encouraging them — to contribute to the social and cultural life of Australia. It is not merely a question of helping them to share what we already have, but of encouraging them to add to it, helping them to enrich our national life and to contribute towards the creation of a new and distinctive Australia.[6]

The fundamental welfare orientation of Labor was towards 'disadvantage' and lines of socioeconomic division. In fact, Grassby very rarely used the term 'multicultural' as Minister for Immigration. 'Migrants' (a word later to lose favour in the era of multiculturalism) were to be understood as a subset of the general class of those who suffered socioeconomic disadvantage and discrimination. Symptomatic of this policy stance was the break-up of the Department of Immigration and the delegation of its functions to the various 'mainstream' departments of labour, welfare, education, and so on. The problems of immigrants were considered, at root, to fit under the general rubric of social welfare and social justice.

In education, major reform initiatives, under the umbrella of the newly established Commonwealth Schools Commission, which included the Disadvantaged Schools Program, aimed at improving the standard of educational provision in poor neighbourhoods. The Child Migrant Education Program was expanded, but its fundamental orientation was still integrationist: ensuring equality of opportunity through the teaching of English.

The history of the rise of multiculturalism in Australia is often portrayed as one of progress and development, with Grassby as a founding father; progress through the period of Malcolm Fraser's conservative prime ministership (1975–83), and continuing development since the return of the Labor government under Bob Hawke in 1983. Contrary to these romantic assumptions, the movement is subtle and complex, marked by constructive political contest and changing policy directions more than steady development. Grassby's vision was one of welfare reformism. As it emerged, Fraser's was an equally brilliant, but fundamentally different, neo-conservative policy of cultural pluralism which attempted to dismantle Labor's welfare reformism, not to build upon it.[7]

But, to return to the train of the historical narrative. Losing the elections of 1972 and 1974, certain members of the conservative Liberal Party began to consider that a decisive 'migrant vote' could possibly be mobilized. Fraser, Mackellar and MacPhee, the latter two of whom were to become Ministers for Immigration in subsequent Liberal governments, were particularly important in re-orienting Liberal policy in these years. Their efforts eventually came to fruition in electoral success and government policy from 1975 to 1983. The concept of 'multiculturalism' itself and the particular programmes that emerged by the early 1980s were pre-eminently the product of the Fraser period of government, the pinnacle of which was its acceptance and implementation of the Galbally Report in 1978.[8]

Only twelve years after Billy Snedden's remarks about why Australia would never accept cultural pluralism, Malcolm Fraser, a prime minister of the same political persuasion, was to say:

> We cannot demand of people that they renounce the heritage they value, and yet expect them to feel welcome as full members of our society. ... Multiculturalism ... sees diversity as a quality to be

actively embraced, a source of social wealth and dynamism.... The [Galbally] report [has] identified multiculturalism as a key concept in formulating government policies and recognized that Australia is at a critical stage in its development as a multicultural nation.[9]

And in a statement supporting changes to the Australian Citizenship Act, the Minister for Immigration, Ian MacPhee, said,

> Acquiring Australian citizenship should not require suppression of one's cultural heritage or identity. Rather, the act of becoming a citizen is — symbolically and actually — a process of bringing one's own gift of language, culture and traditions to enrich the already diverse fabric of Australian society. Our vision of a multicultural society shares with our concept of citizenship, a strong emphasis on building a cohesive and harmonious society which is all the more tolerant and outward-looking because of the diversity of its origins.[10]

Fraser-Galbally multiculturalism, in sharp contrast to Grassby's 'family of the nation', was a clear, determined and extremely cost-effective element in pruning and re-constructing the welfare state. It actually produced a reduction in overall government expenditure, as its recommendation (which was accepted), that tax rebates for overseas dependants be abolished, more than paid for the programmes it set in motion.[11] It involved shifting migrant services from the general rhetoric of social welfare to 'ethnic specific' services. This in part involved constructing 'ethnic' communities as self-help welfare agencies and giving them basic financial support. 'Ethnic schools' and 'grants-in-aid' were typical of this approach. In multicultural education, the McNamara Report in the spirit of Galbally gave a 'lifestyles' flavour to the new Multicultural Education Program.

The new multiculturalism's manifestations were the multilingual Special Broadcasting Service (SBS), the Australian Institute of Multicultural Affairs, and the Multicultural Education Program, to name just a few bold initiatives. Typically, the change in policy represented a move away from Labor's fundamental conception of social policy for immigrants: from a social analysis based on the concept of disadvantage to one based on the concept of cultural difference. For Labor, being an immigrant had been primarily a subset of more general lines of socioeconomic division. For the new Fraser-Galbally multiculturalism, ethnicity became a critical new form of social categorization. Cultural dissonance rather than social justice was seen to be the problem that government policy most needed to address.

In the history of the Commonwealth Schools Commission, for example, one can see the distinctive move from a paradigm of disadvantage in the Whitlam Labor years to a much less interventionist celebration of ethnic differences and 'lifestyles' in the Fraser years. The Commission had been established in 1973 in a spirit of reform. The Whitlam government saw it as one of its roles to finance experimentation in education in its quest for a more equitable and just society. But the Schools Commission's language of reform in its first years of operation, in retrospect, was insensitive to what would later become the politics of pluralist multiculturalism.

The reforming role of the school, argued the first report of the Schools Commission (the Karmel Report), lay in the process of socialization and the passage of the child into social responsibility and social participation. The problem is that

> education ... has proved to be an inadequate means of changing patterns of social stratification or of *initiating* all young people *into society*. Central to ... the special functions of schools ... [is] the acquisition of skills and knowledge [and] *initiation into the cultural heritage*.... More intensive and varied efforts will be required in some schools and for some children to enable them to acquire the basic skills necessary to *participate in the society*.... [the Interim Committee] supports their right to be *initiated into the culture* through a comprehensive core curriculum ....[12] [our emphases]

The revealing thing about the Karmel Report (which was the basis for the establishment of the Schools Commission) was its use of the word 'culture'. Primarily, when talking about culture, it referred to an implicitly homogeneous Australian culture.

By the time of the Schools Commission's *Report for the 1982-4 Triennium*, full-blown multiculturalism had arrived. This was partly because it had been given a range of tasks through the Galbally Report recommendations.

> The plurality of Australian society is demonstrated by *the variety of values, lifestyles, political viewpoints, beliefs and roles* which operate. This holds true in a racial and ethnic sense: while Anglo-Celtic values and traditions continue to dominate Australian society, the social composition of Australia continues to change in terms of numbers and representation of different national groups.[13] [our emphasis]

Multiculturalism is 'an attitude of mind' and should become 'a cornerstone in our society'. This very much reflected the influence of the McNamara Report.

A very complex but profound shift has by this point occurred in the meaning the Commission gives to the word 'culture'. Whereas in the earlier reports the dominant culture in Australia had been a monolith in which groups are related by relative advantage (successful initiation) or disadvantage (unsuccessful initiation: failure to gain a participating role), now the dominant culture is Anglo-Celtic, against which minority cultures are to be perceived and respected as equals. From a programme of cultural reform (despite the limitations of its integrationist intent), the Schools Commission had now moved to a theory of cultural relativism: focusing on culture, insofar as it can be plural and relative, and celebrating its diversity. This involved narrowing the meaning of the word 'culture' since, for example, it is only the distinctive Anglo-Celticness of the dominant culture which is equal and relative to what is distinctive about minority cultures. Too often, in schools, the culture of multiculturalism was reduced to things folkloric — spaghetti and polka, or, for the dominant group, Irish ditties and Yorkshire pudding. It involved de-emphasizing the cultural prerequisites of success and power in Australian society. Yet, the move also represented a remarkable institutional transition, a whole reframing of social policy in such a way that, for the first time, cultural diversity was explicitly recognized. In some fundamental ways, however, the Karmel Report also heralded changes entirely compatible with what would later become pluralist multiculturalism — that schools were to be more flexible places, allowing 'choice and diversity' in response to local needs and reflecting particular community aspirations.

To sum up, the shift in the language for reading cultural difference and formulating settlement and welfare policy was from a unified 'family of the nation' to multiculturalism; from disadvantage to difference; from concern with general socioeconomic issues in which migrants were implicated (a Labor view of reform) to the paradigm of cultural difference in which cultural dissonance was the main problem; from a social theory of class as the primary social division to a social theory of multiple social divisions, none of which has priority. Ethnic groups in the new multiculturalism were implicitly viewed, not as class-divided, but as homogeneous. 'Leaders' of ethnic groups could thus be viewed as 'representative' and, at the same time, potentially vocal pressure groups could be incorporated into the spirit of the state and given some responsibility for the welfare provision of their own 'community'.

In education, the project of 'initiation to core culture', to caricature the change, was replaced by self-esteem programmes in which one would end up feeling good about one's cultural difference. The problem was that, however positive this granting of esteem to differences, differences are not innocent. Deeming cultures to be formally equal neglects the fact that they define each other in social relation, and through this process end up giving their members unequal access to social goods.

In the area of languages policy and practice, Fraser-Galbally multiculturalism manifested itself in a move away from almost exclusive concern in the Labor reform years with better English language provision to a new emphasis on cultural diversity and linguistic maintenance. Schools became involved in the rise of so-called 'community' language education programmes. But with limited rationales of self-esteem and cultural maintenance and inadequate funding, this, in the worst cases, meant tokenistic short-term programmes in which students often only poorly learnt a few words of domestic interchange and a little bit of 'culture'. At the same time it also often meant the removal of some educational responsibility to the semi-private sector in the form of meagre subsidies to community-run 'ethnic schools'. These schools have a history in Australia beginning from 1839. By 1980, it was estimated that there were 97,000 students studying 45 different languages in about 1,400 after hours in ethnic schools and insertion classes in day schools, managed or sponsored by some 500 ethnic school authorities. The majority of these were conducted after school hours. There were, however, 48 ethnic day schools operating at both primary and secondary level with links to Jewish, German, Lebanese, Japanese and Greek communities.[14] There has been considerable debate about the existence of separate ethnic schools and their role in Australian society at large. The issues range from the quality of the education provided to arguments for and against cultural maintenance. On the whole it appears that ethnic schools are primarily concerned with promoting aspects of cultural continuity and solidarity within the community.[15] They are increasing in number and acceptability.

Notwithstanding this critical sketch of the main debates of 1975 to 1983, the Fraser period has to be seen as one of extraordinary change, as a time when the rhetoric and programmes of the federal government came to recognize fully Australia's linguistic and cultural diversity. Moreover, the policy and funding created a new institutional space, which in turn fostered the emergence of a new cadre of professionals, committed to their field of endeavour and sufficiently aware of the structural limitations within which they were working, to become an articulate pressure group.

Bob Hawke came to power in 1983, and for three years Fraser-Galbally multicultural programmes were left basically intact. New, reformist programmes with traditional Labor underpinnings were developed beside these. So, for example, whilst the Multicultural Education Program that was a product of the Galbally Report was maintained (supporting developments in 'community languages' and sociocultural curriculum), the Commonwealth Department of Education set up the Participation and Equity Program, which was very much concerned with general disadvantage, including the disadvantage suffered by non-English speaking immigrants. The specifically multicultural programmes continued, but without any overt commitment to them being displayed by the government.

Then, in 1986, two things happened coincidentally. Budget cuts undid many of the Galbally programmes, and the Jupp Report Multicultural and Migrant Programmes and Services was released. On the funding front, the Australian Institute for Multicultural Affairs, publicly criticized for having conservative political allegiances, was closed. Despite the three reports by Campbell *et al.*, pointing to serious under-resourcing of English as a Second Language (ESL) and the relatively limited impact to date of ESL methodologies on mainstream subject teachers in contact with non-English speaking background students, Commonwealth ESL funding was almost halved.[16] The Multicultural Education Programme, which injected federal resources into languages other than English and sociocultural education, was scrapped. Further, as an 'economy' measure, it was proposed that the Special Broadcasting Service's multilingual television and radio be merged with the Australian Broadcasting Commission. Although some of these cuts were last-minute and ill-considered, they showed a symptomatic underlying uneasiness with things multicultural on the part of the Labor Party at this time. This, as it transpired, proved to be politically inept. Persistent protest led to the partial restoration of ESL funding and reversal of the decision to merge the Special Broadcasting Service with the ABC. It also led to the setting up of the Office of Multicultural Affairs, with a research and public relations function, in the Prime Minister's Department.

The Jupp Report of late 1986 represented a rhetorical return to Laborism, very much in the spirit of Grassby's welfare reformism. The term 'multiculturalism' was used very infrequently in the report and, when it was, it was less for its ideological cogency than as a mere description of a certain type of government programme. The report's catch-cry was 'equitable participation', far removed from the Galbally model of cultural dissonance.[17] In a similar spirit, a 1987 report by the National Advisory and Consultative Committee on Multicultural Education, launched on the day of its demise after a three year life, self-consciously removed itself from the former cultural pluralist approaches to ethnicity in education and stressed instead the predominant goal of social equity, albeit through a sophisticated servicing of cultural diversity.[18]

Around this time, 'mainstreaming' came to be used as a new policy concept. It originated as a critical revision of the perceived limitations of the Galbally model of multiculturalism. The general mainstreaming argument reasoned that relegating crucial social issues to specialist funding can, in effect, marginalize those issues and make them institutionally very vulnerable. Certainly, specialist funding is a significant step beyond ignoring the issues altogether — as in allowing non-English speaking background students, for example, to sink or swim according to 'ability', as was the case in the era of assimilation. Specific purpose programmes, admittedly, have the virtue of recognizing specific educational needs, targeting particular groups at risk, making teachers aware of specific needs in a concerted and clear fashion, and building up new areas of specialist pedagogical expertise. But, whatever the role of special purpose programmes as an intermediate stage in raising consciousness and in developing specialist expertise, the proponents of mainstreaming argued that such policy at the same time takes the issues off the central agenda of the institution. 'At the system level', said one of the key educational administrators interviewed as part of this project, 'you always feel very marginal; you always have to fight for support through the hierarchy'. At the school level, if there is a specialist teacher or liaison officer, mainstream teachers seem to be relieved of a great deal of the responsibility for that issue. And, at a larger political level, Commonwealth acceptance of special responsibility (linked, perhaps, to the federal immigration programme) seems to absolve the states of responsibility in their everyday service provision.

A senior member of the Victorian Ministry of Education described an historical move, over four decades, from indifference to the needs of students of non-English-speaking background, to assimilation, to multiculturalism, and now to a further stage with 'multiculturalism linked to mainstream social justice and economic strategies':

> While schools cannot create a totally just society, they have a responsibility to ensure that all students experience success in a fully comprehensive curriculum which furthers the knowledge, understanding and competencies necessary for people to participate effectively in the life of a multicultural society.... For students of non-English speaking background, specific programmes must be provided which lead to full competence in the English language, particularly those forms of discourse used in the subject areas.... There are [also] compelling reasons for maintenance of first languages ... [including the] wise husbanding of valuable linguistic resources which have been wasted in the past, despite the need to move purposefully into international trade and commerce.... Attention [is also needed] to the needs of the cultural majority in the context of heightened concern about our national identity and recurrent racism.

The institutional move away from specialist programmes towards mainstreaming was paralleled by a move from a primary concern with cultural pluralism to a primary concern with social equity in the mid-80s.

In reality, however, mainstreaming has sometimes proved to be a two-edged sword, and at worst no more than a euphemism for cutting 'ethnic specific' services in the hope that mainstream institutions will assume a multicultural stance — following the requirements of official policy and exercising a considerable degree of gracious goodwill — but often without funding to support concrete initiatives. The 1986 budget cuts, in fact, realized the worst fears of those who had reservations about what might happen in the name of mainstreaming. To quote the Minister's 1986 budget guidelines to the Commonwealth Schools Commission:

> The specific purpose programs [which included the Multicultural Education Program] have been designed to encourage new and improved methods and directions in areas of educational need. Where these objectives have been achieved, the Commonwealth can withdraw; in some areas the objectives of the programs can be integrated with its *mainstream* provisions of States and systems.[19] [our emphasis]

The most significant recent development which impacts directly on multicultural education is the 1987 *National Policy on Languages*. Written by Joe Lo Bianco, and building upon the 1984 *National Language Policy* from the Senate Standing Committee on Education and the Arts, this builds positively upon Fraser-Galbally multiculturalism, and consolidates the move towards social equity in the 1980s. It was based on the important work of the Federation Ethnic Communities Council of Australia (FECCA) in organizing a series of conferences leading to the 1982 National Language Conference and in getting together a broadly based language policy coalition.[20] The document has to cover everything from the situation of English, to the place of Aboriginal languages, to the questions of 'community' language maintenance, to learning 'foreign' languages used in Australia, to learning languages of 'economic importance', to the issue of the needs of the communication disabled. It reflects a range of interests such as government pressure to use language as means of extending economic links with Asia, to the pressure of ethnic community organizations for funding for language maintenance.

Reflecting a necessarily comprehensive approach, the broad social goals of language policy are stated by the report to be 'enrichment, economic opportunities, external relations and equality'. Establishing the status of languages in the Australian context, English/Australian English is proclaimed the national language. Aboriginal and immigrant 'community' languages other than English (including the languages of the deaf) are explicitly recognized, their use in education and service delivery advocated, and the right to their maintenance recommended. Specifically, in the teaching and learning of languages, three guiding principles are set out: English for all; support for Aboriginal and Torres Strait Islander languages; and, perhaps most dramatically, a language other than English for all. In the more general area of service delivery, the report also notes the importance and roles of interpreting and translation, public libraries, languages in relation to the media and communication technology, and the need to improve language testing procedures.[21]

On 5th June 1988, Cabinet approved $15 million for the implementation of the policy in the remainder of 1987–88 and $28 million for each of the two years 1988–89. Of this, $13 million will go in a full year to an expanded ESL programme; $7.5 million to 'community' languages and 'languages of economic importance' (through the Australian Second Language Learning Program); $1 million towards a National Aboriginal Languages policy; $2 million to Asian languages; $1.8 million to cross-cultural and community language studies in professional and para-professional training programmes; and $2 million to adult literacy. In 1989 the establishment of a Languages Institute of Australia was announced, under the *National Policy on Languages*. This will act as an agency for professional development, as an information clearing house and as a research centre on language teaching for schools.

Despite progress, however, this area is still fraught with difficulties. There are only relatively small amounts of money to be translated into concrete programmes. Some ethnic communities have already complained about the funding levels for their languages. There is also an assumption that the states will come to the party and match federal funding, in education programmes, for example, but this might not necessarily happen in all cases. Moreover, multiculturalism in education is now seen almost solely to be an element of language policy, rather than vice versa. This has meant the neglect of critical sociocultural programmes axed in 1986, such as those under the Multicultural Education Program, which aimed to reduce levels of racism in schools. Finally, there is the problem that the *National Policy on Languages* and its Australian Advisory Committee on Languages and Multicultural Education, however much it represents a positive development in the policy and practice of multicultural education, is also itself part of the ever more frequent institutional chopping and changing — the bewildering succession of reports, committees, programmes and changed funding arrangements that has characterized this field in the past two decades.

The term multiculturalism, in decline for a while in the mid-80s, recently began to enjoy a temporary respite, not just as the *National Policy on Languages* got into full swing, but also under the aegis of the Office of Multicultural Affairs in the Prime Minister's Department. No sooner had it found its way back into official discourse, however, than the 1988 FitzGerald Report on Australia's immigration policy set back the word's progress once again.[22] This report was not only anti-multicultural at the level of words. It advocated a return to some of the public policy that had preceded multiculturalism. Immigrants should know English, have skills, have entrepreneurial inclinations, and so on. And, in settlement, commitment to a singular Australian identity, it said, should come before multiculturalism.

FitzGerald identified some of the difficulties in the concept of multiculturalism and its practice. First, the Report said, it is not widely understood. Indeed, it is true that even amongst academic, welfare and public policy workers in the area, there is no consensus as to whether it primarily means ethnic maintenance or access to mainstream social institutions, or whether these two objectives are conflicting or complementary. Second, multiculturalism is, according to FitzGerald, divisive. Some multicultural activities, it is strongly implied, have tended to delineate ethnic groups iconographically and stereotypically so they appear more clearly distinct than they are in a complex and contradictory reality. This can tend to increase, rather than reduce, chauvinism, racism and social division. Third, multiculturalism has tended to neglect some non-negotiable cultural fundamentals in Australia, including non-discrimination, non-racism, non-sexism and so on. We should not, the Report argues, unproblematically respect the integrity of immigrant cultures which do not necessarily include these values. FitzGerald calls these things 'Australian', though this seems a strangely parochial way of describing some of the principles of human rights in a liberal society.

So what did FitzGerald propose as an alternative settlement policy? He suggested 'cosmopolitanism' as a more accurate description of our virtue as a relatively quiet society with a mass immigration programme. Immigration will go on, according to FitzGerald, and will inevitably include a large non-European component. But many critics of FitzGerald have asked how is this new word different from multiculturalism? Why fiddle with words so regularly? Wouldn't it be better to strengthen multiculturalism? And, what would emphasizing unitary 'Australian' identity mean in a world where national descriptors become less and less meaningful? The problem, really, is not unitary Australianness but servicing a culturally diverse society in an equitable way. The core values and practices in this exercise are not Australian but liberal-democratic.

Then there is the issue of racism. FitzGerald identified this as a real issue. But, having discarded multiculturalism as a viable settlement policy, the Report did not spell out how a non-racist cosmopolitanism might work. Certainly, there are no riots in the streets. However inter-group tensions reduce the productivity of schools. Immigrants' skills are not recognized. Racism does not even make economic sense. A society which continues to depend on mass immigration as a central element of economic and social policy, must make sure it benefits from this. But, as soon as we address racism, its complex origins and interconnections mean that anti-racist social policy has to be broader and more sophisticated that the FitzGerald Report allows. This need can be seen in reactions to a number of issues: Japanese investment and tourism; South East Asian refugee immigration; suggestions of a treaty with Aborigines; and ethnic chauvinism of immigrant groups. These issues all overlay each other in racist discourse in complex and parasitical ways.

With much fanfare and at great expense, the latest development in the history of Australian settlement and cultural policy has been the launching by Prime Minister Hawke of the *National Agenda for a Multicultural Australia*. This states that 'Australia has changed dramatically in the last generation. Our strategic relationships, trading network and investment patterns have become far more enmeshed in the Asia Pacific region; and our immigration policy has been progressively liberalised'.[23] The order of issues in this opening salvo for a revived multiculturalism is indicative of yet another shift. A multicultural outlook is essential from a regional economic point of view. It is essential if Australia is not to become the 'poor white trash' of Asia. 'The Australian Government', replied longtime critic of multiculturalism, Professor Lauchlan Chipman, 'killed multiculturalism last Wednesday — and nobody noticed. . . . If one looks at the main spending policies associated with the government's multiculturalism manifesto', he went on, 'there is little that an assimilationist or an integrationist . . . would disagree with' — more ESL, streamlined mechanisms for recognizing overseas qualifications, and so on.[24]

In conclusion, the relative social quiet of the past four decades, despite the extraordinary level and diversity of immigration, has been achieved to a significant degree through the adaptiveness and responsiveness of the cultural and linguistic policies of federal governments. During the phase of economic growth, assimilation was a viable settlement strategy. By the mid-1970s, the sheer numbers of immigrants, the rates of return migration, the obvious specific welfare and education needs of the immigrants, and the rise of ethnic organizations, seemed to challenge the quiet. Some very different political responses to this situation have emerged, such as the welfare reformism of Labor in the early 1970s and the cultural pluralism of the Fraser period. Since the return of Labor in 1983, there has been a shift back to welfare reformist rhetoric, but with a strong emphasis now on the economic benefits of immigration and multiculturalism. Meanwhile, immigration continues apace; ethnic groups organize more and more effectively to secure their rights; socioeconomic difficulties with a potential to disrupt the peace appear to be getting more serious; and the whole question of Australian identity has been made no more certain by the controversy surrounding the Bicentennial of British settlement in 1988.

This quick historical trip through the Australian history of multicultural education, focusing as it has on politics and policy, tells little of what actually happened at the school level; how much real impact multicultural education has had on the lives and destinies of Australian children. This book tries to do some of that job. It tells the grassroots stories of six schools. By the time the sixth story is told, it will be obvious that these schools have, for better and sometimes worse, revolutionized their structures, curriculum and pedagogy as an everyday response to cultural and linguistic diversity. These may well be schools which, for reason of demography, have simply had to take on multicultural education. Hundreds of other schools, for the same sorts of demographic reasons, have made similar moves.

No schools in Australia would be totally unaffected by multicultural education, not even the ones that would seem most isolated from the social impact of mass immigration. At the level of senses of Australian identity engendered in children, for example, a study of 650 history and social studies texts published since 1945 shows a fundamental paradigm shift from a homogeneous, England-oriented identity, confidently intent on assimilating Aborigines' and immigrants' differences, to an identity which centres itself on the differences themselves.[25]

This new Australia, ever more publicly aware of its cultural and linguistic multiplicity, might well harbour a self-image which is often laced with a good deal of self-doubt and which is plagued by the iconographic stereotyping characteristic of popularized cultural pluralism. Still, the surprising thing is that so much change in education should have been wrought from a centralized initiative and with such a relatively small amount of funding. The critical debates aside, something must have been happening for the past forty years.

By 1989, the Victorian state education system had 679 specialist ESL teachers in mainstream schools, 141 ESL teachers in ten English language schools for new arrivals, 149 supernumerary teachers of Languages Other Than English (LOTEs) in primary schools (secondary schools provide LOTE programmes in their normal staffing establishment), 190 ethnic teacher aides, and 32 interpreters in the Education Interpreter Service. There are 35 LOTE and ESL consultants in the newly established State Multicultural Education Coordination Unit. Multiculturalism as a principle and practice, reported several senior administrators, infuses all educational policies and syllabi. There are two main guiding documents: the 1986 *Education In, and For, a Multicultural Victoria: Policy Guidelines for School Communities* and the 1989 *Languages Action Plan* by Joe Lo Bianco.[26] Still, there was a profound sense amongst those departmental officers interviewed for this project that there was still a long way to go. 'I'm optimistic when I see progress in some schools', said one of them, 'but I despair when I see nothing happening in others.'

Cultures of Schooling

The Catholic Education Office, Sydney, conducted a census in 1988 of the language backgrounds of students. Of the 65,000 students in Sydney Archdiocese Catholic Schools, 50.42 per cent came from homes where a language other than English is spoken. The largest language groups were Arabic (11 per cent) and Italian (10.5 per cent), with twelve language groups other than English having a representation of over 1 per cent of the total student population and at least forty-six language groups being represented in all.[27] Mass immigration has transformed the old Irish-dominated Catholic Church almost beyond recognition. High on the list of priorities in the Sydney Archdiocesan Catholic Schools Board's 1989 *Vision Statement*, is that schools should 'examine critically their response to the various cultural and language needs of students who have English as a second language'.[28] The annual ESL budget, not including the new arrivals programme, is made up of $2.3 million directly from the Commonwealth and $1.4 million from the Catholic Education Office's own budget. Australian Second Language Learning Program funds go into the teaching of LOTEs, as well as initiatives within schools' general funding. There is no multicultural policy and programme as such. According to a senior Catholic Education Office administrator, 'it's difficult when there are no funds, no resources and no staff.' There is no longer a sociocultural approach to multiculturalism at the systems level, although 'the Catholic Education Office had supported the development of the Social Literacy programme for a number of years, and these materials are still used extensively in schools'.[29]

The New South Wales Department of Education, reported a senior officer, spent a total of between $30 and $40 million per year on multicultural programmes and services. The lion's share of this is from Commonwealth funding. Between 60,000 and 70,000 students have some sort of exposure to specialist ESL teaching, and 13,500 to LOTEs teaching in eleven 'community' languages. There is a *Multicultural Education Policy* which spells out mandatory guidelines about school practice and is supported by the policy documents *English as a Second Language, Community Languages, Multicultural Perspectives to the Curriculum* and *Ethnic Studies*.[30] In 1988 a *State Language Policy* was launched, aiming to elevate the role of LOTEs teaching in NSW state schools. The universal acceptance of multiculturalism in schools, according to a senior departmental administrator, despite the policy being mandatory, 'cannot happen in two, five or even ten years; the system can only change teachers' mentalities slowly, but it's hard to implement effective concrete practices in schools, especially within funding constraints'.

A Revolution in Pedagogy

Changes in pedagogy have occurred in Australian education in the past four decades which are no less momentous than the changes in official government cultural and linguistic policy. In fact, developments in pedagogy in general and in multiculturalism in wider social arenas are integrally related. For the

A Systems Perspective

purposes of characterizing an overall trend in pedagogy, the change can be summed up as a move from traditional pedagogy to progressivist pedagogy as the dominant medium of curriculum. One cannot understand the development of multicultural education outside an historical view of the rise of progressivist pedagogy.[31]

In institutional terms, the whole relationship between schools and education systems has radically changed. Departmental syllabus documents in the 1940s and 1950s spelt out a programmatic sequence of content to be followed by schools. The content of schooling was deemed both to be universalistic (the same content for all students) and something which was appropriately determined by centralized education systems in their role as an arm of government to be worth knowing. The central medium of instruction was the textbook, which followed the content and sequence of the syllabus, chapter and verse. At the end of the cycle, institutional expectations were measured by centralized examinations.

Today, curriculum is much more school-based and syllabi spell out processes of learning rather than a catalogue of content. A good deal of store is placed upon teacher professionalism in formulating curriculum relevant to the specific needs of students. Key elements of curriculum nowadays are choice (hence the proliferation of school-based courses, particularly in the secondary school), diversity (according to perceived individual or local community needs), relevance, student interest and community involvement. Even official documents which one would expect to be the most staid, often speak the language of 'democratic curriculum'. Programming of content at all levels is up to individual teachers and schools. Teachers as curriculum-developers are supported by a structure of specialist departmental curriculum 'consultants', 'inservice' training courses, 'resource centres' from which to collect materials to fill out their school-based curricula and 'seeding grants' to develop innovative curriculum practices.

Of course, the story is not quite this clear. There are still outposts of traditional pedagogy dotted throughout the education system. Nevertheless, there has been a revolution in pedagogy, not universal in the sense of transforming all the *minutiae* of every child's experience at school, but in the official view of the way curriculum should work and, in the main, in school practice. Even if it is only to pay lip-service, no teacher has escaped the move to progressivism. In this sense, it is possible to say that, whereas traditional pedagogy was dominant three decades age, progressivism is dominant today.

This huge historical change can be illustrated in virtually every curriculum area. Its effects, moreover, are not only institutional, but run to the heart of pedagogy and implicate the content and status of knowledge itself. To take literacy in English as one example, traditional pedagogy was pre-eminently concerned with the learning of formal rules, such as of spelling and grammar. The old school grammar, for example, had a primarily prescriptive function, to correct 'errors'. Writers were taught not to split infinitives, to make sure the subject agrees with the verb, to say 'better than I' instead of 'better than me',

31

and so on. Following these formal rules, however, in no way guaranteed effective communication.

In the place of traditional literacy pedagogy, 'process' writing has emerged as the most influential way of teaching writing. It is based on the assumption that children learn writing conventions 'naturally' through use. If they are in an environment in which they want to write and write for a purpose, so the argument goes, effective writing will develop in much the same way that young children develop oral language. The role of the teacher now is to facilitate students in the processes of writing — drafting, editing, and so on. Whilst the imparting of formal knowledge was at the centre of traditional pedagogy, student motivation is at the centre of progressivism. Imposing formal rules can inhibit students' desire to express themselves. Encouraging the will to communicate takes precedence over 'correct' English.

In the teaching of languages other than English, a directly parallel move has occurred, away from language learning as a formal academic exercise, symbolized most powerfully by the chanting of conjugations and declensions. Now, the emphasis is more strongly on communicative competence and learning a 'foreign' language through contextualized 'real' use rather than abstract rules. In a similar spirit, even the range of languages on offer has changed somewhat, away from 'academic' Latin-French-German, and towards 'relevant', 'Asian' languages of 'economic importance' to Australia and Australian 'community' languages. By the end of the 1980s, over thirty languages were examined at the school leaving certificates across Australia, compared to the handful a decade or two before.

To examine, also, the important case of how cultural identity is transmitted through history and the social sciences, the purpose of these subjects in the era of traditional curriculum was almost exclusively to impart social content. Textbooks religiously followed the syllabus, chapter by chapter, and both were a list of content areas to be covered sequentially: the peopling of the ostensibly 'empty' land of Australia in fourth class and 'our' deep links with the English 'Mother Country' in sixth, to take the example of the NSW 1959 Primary Social Studies Syllabus. This content-ladenness and the syllabus-textbook relation embodied an unconscious or semi-conscious pedagogy: of social prescription. The nature and purpose of history and society were centrally defined truths, to be accepted and learnt by all. At the bottom of this pedagogy was a profound sense that the story of history and society could be told through a singular, universal narrative. 'Facts', to be learnt and regurgitated by students, gave this story a universal truthfulness. There was no concession to students' diversity; to culture, gender or ethnicity. It was the one story for all.[32]

With the rise of progressivism, no longer are there the lists of social contents as there had been the past. Since its radical 1975 revision, the NSW Primary Social Studies Syllabus, to stay with the same example, has gone no further than to advocate child-centred 'inquiry' learning processes. The content of social studies is left open to the felt needs and interests of teachers, students and the school community. The old, singular story line of Australian identity can no longer be imposed. With students as active investigators of their social world, it becomes obvious that there is no single, true answer to any problem, but rather that knowledge is a matter of one's perspective, particular circumstances, subjective starting-point and practical needs. At this point, the concept of relevance supersedes the old telling of universal historical and social narratives. Not that the old curriculum set out to be irrelevant. Relevance for progressivism, as distinct from the one old universal relevance, really means lots of different relevances, according to particular local community or cultural needs and circumstances, for example.

The move from traditional to progressivist pedagogy also implies a new underlying epistemology. For example, gone are the fixed rules of language. Language learning is not oriented towards a definable body of formal knowledge (such as 'standard' English, for example), but contingent and relative communicative competence. Gone are the 'facts' of the social sciences. In history, students study source documents representing conflicting perspectives on social events. Playing historian, they pose problems which can be resolved in a number of ways, in the last analysis explicable in terms of the individual student-historian's own point of view.

The important thing for this book about this radical change in pedagogy is the by no means coincidental confluence of the rise of multicultural education. In epistemological and pedagogical terms, the two are entirely compatible. For example, the emphasis on defining people by their formally equal cultural and linguistic differences, directly parallels a move to epistemological relativism across all realms of pedagogy. And the focus of many multicultural programmes on self-esteem is but one aspect of the move to a more child-centred pedagogy, in which the foundation of effective learning is perceived to be motivation and a positive sense of self.

The rise to dominance of both multiculturalism and progressivist pedagogy make Australia an unusually modern — some would say postmodern — place. They are both symbolic of adaptive, creative, indeed, culturally 'proactive', government. Historians argue that at the turn of the twentieth century Australia led the world in standards of living, the development of trade unionism, universal suffrage, the rise of a social-democratic Labor Party, and so on.[33] At the turn of the twenty-first century Australia may well be again leading the world, not in these now old-fashioned measures of modernity, but as a place where the nation is defined by its diversity, and where education is a site of open process rather a place where fixed knowledge is imparted.

To return to the question of pedagogy, the progressivists have pointed out that students might well be able to learn facts, social values and grammar by rote to be regurgitated in examinations, but this is hardly a potent form of pedagogy. The traditional emphasis on transmitting content by means of curriculum was at the expense of learning how to learn, or the process of learning. There is, moreover, an inarticulate and ill-thought out pedagogy at work in traditional curriculum: to teach students to be passive receptors of other people's knowledge, socially constructed in the form of facts and universal moral truths. This hidden curriculum works against autonomous, critical or creative thought, producing people unable to make their own knowledge, to innovate and to adapt to a society in rapid and constant change. Its obsession with formality works against a practical focus on the ends of schooling, such as communicative competence.

At the same time, traditional curriculum dictates a singular social narrative to students whose needs, cultures and interests are diverse. Being most frequently measured in the terms of the dominant culture, the old, centralized curriculum marginalized large numbers of students according to their class, gender or ethnicity through irrelevance or sheer boredom. Formal examinations of fixed social truths, standardized tests or IQ tests, moreover, do not measure learning the 'facts' or 'ability' so much as they measure a student's mastery of examination technique and understanding of school as a system of rewards and credentials. This is very much a class, language and culture-bound skill, and does not necessarily reflect learning in any lasting or effective sense.

In an age of constant change, all that schools can successfully impart to students who will still be working halfway into the twenty-first century, is an openness to change and an ongoing ability to learn and adapt. Rather than teach to content, the fundamental programme of progressivism is to teach epistemological openness. Moreover, its necessary institutional medium is liberal-democratic. From the whole school structure to lesson dynamics, consensus is a fundamental political principle. Schools are democratically run, with the principal as just one part of a complex decision-making web which includes, increasingly, committees representing teachers, parents and students. In contrast to the authoritarian, coercive politics of traditional curriculum, teachers now 'own' their own teaching, and students their own work and knowledge. Progressivism extensively recycles the metaphor of the market and the ethics of the individual as the epistemological centre. As in the real world of the market, the products (contents) come and go but the fundamental processes of individual ownership (and individual experience as an epistemic centre) remain constant.

Whilst progressivism might still appear to be a creative alternative in some other countries, Australia's large-scale educational experiment has some critical lessons which may well point one step further. By and large, the critical international literature on bilingual and multicultural education proposes measures which fit within the progressivist paradigm. Having lived with progressivism as a full-scale systemic approach, however, Australian educators also know its vices. The following is a summary of the main points that have come out in debate in Australia to date.[34]

First, rather ironically, diversification of curriculum in the name of individual needs, interests and relevance, has led to a new utilitarianism, a fixation on topical content rather than epistemological process. Special purpose courses often neglect the fundamental objectives of a traditional, general, liberal education. Studying Latin could never be justified as much more than an exercise in disciplined learning and memorization — an educational process, rather than an object of immediate utility.

Second, the progressivist claim that only diversified curriculum genuinely meets particular needs and interests is also seriously flawed. It certainly is a disarming truism that curriculum should be relevant. Authoritarian, centralized curriculum, in its profound irrelevance to the immediate needs of many students, was simply an institutionalized exercise in passing and failing particular social groups and rationalizing this, after the event, as evidence of individual 'ability'. But creating more and more diverse curriculum from school to school produces just as many inequities. Very often the curriculum is adjusted, in the name of relevance, to the particular community of students in a school in a very patronizing manner. Thus, some schools get into a multiculturalism of food and dance on the grounds that these are appropriate for the 'less able' or 'more disadvantaged' students, rather than harder options involving mastery of significant skills and developing the capacity to handle new information in testing ways. One justification sometimes offered is that the development of such 'relevant' programmes is to ensure that the students do not fail and that their self-esteem is not dented by placing unfamiliar and alienating demands upon them. The truth is that many such programmes offer no satisfactory introduction to the intellectual skills necessary for life and work in the late twentieth century, nor those necessary to get the marks for entry to high status tertiary education via the final school credential. But in other schools, usually those found in the more affluent communities, where parental pressure creates a demand for another kind of 'relevance', traditional pedagogy, perhaps moderated with some well tried innovation, is the order of the day. Despite the limitations of the programmes pursued, the students very typically emerge better skilled than those from poorer communities. Thus the school system often perpetuates inequality instead of overcoming it.

Third, progressivism is often naive about the relation of process to content. It is quite hard to imagine, for example, that you could become an historian (the process), unless you have a meaningful content to deal with. The obsession with process is at the expense of disciplined and systematic approaches to handling a defined body of content. Similarly, writing *ad nauseam*, no matter how powerfully motivated by communicative purpose, can only be frustrated by technical difficulties with language conventions. Accumulated knowledge and skills (contents) drive learning as much as the ego.

Fourth, naturalistic process curriculum serves middle-class English-speaking students from print-immersed home environments better than it does students from non-English speaking and poorer backgrounds. Some social groups, for example, end up seeing the logic of learning formal writing conventions more 'naturally' than others. They seem to respond more positively to the call to 'motivation'. For disadvantaged students, motivation simply cannot be assumed as the basis for any effective pedagogy.

Fifth, naturalism and 'discovery' learning are extremely inefficient pedagogical processes. For example, students under a process literacy regime learn by massive practical and contextualized repetition (as a baby learns oral language), developing rules of thumb more or less inductively. However, students who have gained the ability to generalize in oral language can learn much quicker if they are presented rules with which to verify language conventions deductively. Schools cannot strive to be natural microcosms of the 'real' world. In fact, they are rather artificial institutions with limited time and resources to do a very big job. Pedagogical efficiency is critical. The process of students each making their own knowledge is often a luxury. In other words, it is a distinctive feature of institutionalized schooling that curriculum knowledge is distilled from the infinity of possible knowledge, concentrated on the basis of its generative power, and represented as curriculum.

Sixth, progressivism assumes that effective knowledge is founded on individual senses of purpose and self. Language and knowledge, however, are social phenomena. Self-esteem in an unequal world comes as much from success in those things which mark social division (such as formal schooling) as it does from granting respect to one's particular cultural difference (which is often really, structurally, a mark of inequality). It is by no means the case that the social division is necessarily a result of lack of respect for one's difference.

Indeed, seventh, granting formal equality-in-difference is often no more than a facade, as if, for example, 'community' language programmes whose primary emphases are linguistic recognition, self-esteem and 'culture-through-language' are really as socially prestigious and as likely to provide 'the marks' for ultimate success at school, as the pedagogies of traditional 'foreign' language teaching.

Eighth, defining culture as difference can lead to a fragmentation of school and social life in which the differences are characterized stereotypically, culture is trivialized, issues of immigration are overly redefined away from the structures of the host society towards the dynamics of cultural dissonance, and the maintenance of cultures is more or less unproblematically advocated.

Ninth, progressivism and multiculturalism are only rhetorically open doctrines. Rather ironically, the liberal culture which is ostensibly so open to difference and change, finds itself at odds with those traditional immigrant cultures which are not open, those which believe that school is a place where fixed knowledge is imparted in an authoritarian structure, those which include long-cherished traditions of sexism and racism, and so on. Furthermore, the celebration of difference at the bottom of both multiculturalism and pedagogical progressivism, can just as easily create the environment for the reproduction of ethnocentrism and give voice to educational views that are contrary to its own principles. In fact, liberal, industrial society creates a definite culture of its own, despite its pretence to all-embracing neutrality. Immigrants who resist its 'decadence' find themselves, for better and for worse, up against the institutional and cultural weight of history.

Tenth, the ostensible openness of the situation means that, both at the levels of pedagogy and cultural identity, the scene is characterized by unrelenting flux. There seems to be no definite grounding for action, no definite guidelines for leadership.

Finally, and in addition to these problems of principle, the school-based curriculum necessary to sustain diversified, differentially relevant curriculum, becomes practically unworkable. Especially with cut-backs to the support structures, school-based curriculum really means curriculum on the cheap, and shifting curriculum responsibility onto teachers and students. There is no need now even for a significant textbook allowance. Teachers are curriculum developers as well as teachers. At the same time as the certitudes of the older curriculum were disappearing, the support to teachers working under the new progressivist regime has been reduced rather than increased.

Of course, this characterization of progressivism describes historical tendency, rather than the complexity of a situation in which residual elements of traditional curriculum are still in evidence and new pedagogies and curriculum structures are emerging as progressivism transcends itself in a new self-corrective phase. The Victorian curriculum 'Frameworks' documents and the current work of the Commonwealth's Curriculum Development Centre are evidence of this more recent development.

All these issues come out in the stories of the six schools that follow. As each unfolds, it becomes obvious that these schools have taken on both multiculturalism and pedagogical progressivism in a wholehearted and professionally committed way. There is much to learn form their experience. The concluding Chapter 9, by way of summary of the issues that arise in telling the schools' own stories, returns to the dilemmas of multiculturalism and progressivism mentioned here.

Notes

1 COPE, B., *Losing the Australian Way: The Rise of Multiculturalism and the Crisis of National Identity — A Study of Changing Popular Conceptions of Australian History and the Construction of New Cultural Identities through Schooling, from 1940s to 1980s*, Ph.D. Thesis, Macquarie University, 1987.
2 NSW DEPARTMENT OF EDUCATION, *The Education Gazette,* September, 1951, pp. 317–320.
3 NSW DEPARTMENT OF EDUCATION, *The Education Gazette*, April, 1955, p. 119.
4 *The Australian*, 26 July, 1969.
5 MCCAUGHEY, J., 'Migrants', in HENDERSON, R. *et al.*, *People in Poverty: A Melbourne Survey*, Institute of Applied Economic and Social Research, Melbourne, 1970; MARTIN, J. 'Migration and Social Pluralism?' in WILKES, J., *How Many Australians? Immigration and Growth*, Australian Institute of Political Science and Angus and Robertson, Sydney, 1971.
6 GRASSBY, A., *Australia's Decade of Decision*, Australian Government Publishing Service, Canberra, 1973, pp. 19–20.
7 CASTLES, S., COPE, B., KALANTZIS, M. and MORRISSEY, M., *Mistaken Identity: Multiculturalism and the Demise of Nationalism in Australia*, Pluto Press, Sydney,

chapter four, 1988; JAKUBOWICZ, A., MORRISSEY, M. and PALSER, J., 'Ethnicity, Class and Social Policy in Australia', Report No. 46, Social Welfare Research Centre, University of New South Wales, 1984.
8 GALBALLY, F., *Review of Post-Arrival Programs and Services to Migrants*, Australian Government Publishing Service, Canberra, 1978.
9 FRASER, M., Inaugural Address on Multiculturalism to the Institute of Multicultural Affairs, Canberra, 30 November, 1981.
10 MACPHEE, I., Australian Citizenship: Ministerial Statement, 6 May, 1982.
11 HANSARD, 27 September, 1979, p. 1678.
12 INTERIM COMMITTEE FOR THE AUSTRALIAN SCHOOLS COMMISSION, *Schools in Australia*, (Karmel Report), Australian Government Publishing Service, Canberra, 1973, 2.21, 3.23.
13 SCHOOLS COMMISSION, *Report for the Triennium 1982–84*, Australian Government Publishing Service Canberra, 1981, pp. 2.8; 1.32, 2.18.
14 AUSTRALIAN INSTITUTE OF MULTICULTURAL AFFAIRS, *Review of Multicultural and Migrant Education*, Melbourne, 1980, 5.1–5.23.
15 KRINGAS, P. and LEWINS, F., *Why Ethnic Schools? Selected case studies*, Australian National University Press, Canberra, 1981.
16 CAMPBELL, W.J. et. al., *A Review of the Commonwealth English as a Second language (ESL) Program*, Commonwealth Schools Commission, Canberra, 1984.
17 DEPARTMENT OF IMMIGRATION AND ETHNIC AFFAIRS, *Don't Settle for Less — Report of the Committee for Stage 1 of the Review of Migrant and Multicultural Programs and Services*, Australian Government Publishing Service, Canberra, 1986.
18 NATIONAL ADVISORY AND CONSULTATIVE COMMITTEE ON MULTICULTURAL EDUCATION (NACCME), *Education In and For a Multicultural Society*, Canberra, 1987.
19 COMMONWEALTH SCHOOLS COMMISSION, *Ministerial Guidelines*, Canberra, August, 1986.
20 *National Language Policy Conference Report*, 22nd–24th October, 1982. Conference convened by the Federation of Ethnic Communities Council of Australia, assisted by the Department of Immigration and Ethnic Affairs, and the Commonwealth Department of Education, Commonwealth Schools Commission, Canberra, 1982.
21 LO BIANCO, J., *National Policy on Languages*, Commonwealth Department of Education, Australian Government Publishing Service, Canberra, 1987.
22 COMMITTEE TO ADVISE ON AUSTRALIA'S IMMIGRATION POLICIES, *Immigration — A Commitment to Australia*, (The FitzGerald Report), Australian Government Publishing Service, Canberra, 1988.
23 OFFICE OF MULTICULTURAL AFFAIRS, *National Agenda for a Multicultural Australia: Sharing Our Future*, Australian Government Publishing Service, Canberra, 1989.
24 CHIPMAN, L., *Sydney Morning Herald*, 1 August, 1989.
25 COPE, 1987, *op. cit*.
26 VICTORIAN MINISTERIAL ADVISORY COMMITTEE ON MULTICULTURAL AND MIGRANT EDUCATION, *Education In and For a Multicultural Victoria: Policy Guidelines for School Communities*, Melbourne, 1986; LO BIANCO, J., *Languages Action Plan*, Victorian Ministry of Education, Melbourne, 1989.
27 ABDULCARDER, L., *Sydney Voices*, Catholic Education Office, Sydney, 1989.
28 CATHOLIC EDUCATION OFFICE, *Vision Statement*, Sydney, 1989.

29 KALANTZIS, M. and COPE, B., *Social Literacy: An Overview*, Common Ground, Sydney, 1989.
30 NEW SOUTH WALES DEPARTMENT OF EDUCATION, *New South Wales Multicultural Education Policy*, Department of Education, Sydney, 1983.
31 COPE, B., 'Traditional Versus Progressivist Pedagogy', *Social Literacy Monograph No. 11*, Common Ground, Sydney, 1988.
32 KALANTZIS, M. and COPE, B., 'Literacy in the Social Sciences', in CHRISTIE, F., (ed.), *Literacy for a Changing World*, Australian Council for Educational Research, Melbourne, 1990.
33 ROE, J., *Social Policy in Australia — Some Perspectives 1901–1975*, Cassell, Stanmore, 1976.
34 KALANTZIS, M. and COPE B., 'Pluralism and Equitability; Multicultural Curriculum Strategies for Schools', *Curriculum and Teaching*, Vol. 4, No. 1. 1989.

Chapter 3

A Mission of 'Empowerment': The Community Liaison Program at MacKillop Girls' High School

A Catholic girls' secondary school in the mid-western suburbs of Sydney, MacKillop Girls' High services the cultural and linguistic diversity of its community with a structured approach to basic sociocultural concepts in social science; a common curriculum, including compulsory study of the mother tongue (Arabic, French, Italian, Spanish, or Vietnamese) or, in the case of native English speakers, a second language; and a Community Liaison Program bringing parents into a closer relationship with the school. It is this last innovation which is the focus of this case study.

The Locality

MacKillop Girls' High School is a Catholic school within the Sydney Archdiocese. It is situated in the suburb of Lakemba, sixteen kilometres south-west of Sydney's city centre. 'Western Suburbs' in Sydney is synonymous with 'working class', and Lakemba is both of these. Here is the heartland of Sydney's suburban sprawl, where the carving up of the land into the traditional quarter-acre blocks has pushed the bulk of the population far from the harbour and the beaches and the amenities of the city. Cheaply constructed asbestos-cement 'fibro' houses of the 1950s are interspersed with the more solid, brick-veneer bungalows of the boom period proper, along with small-scale blocks of flats. There are few parks. The school is a few minutes' walk from the small, suburban shopping centre and railway station. Nearby suburbs have huge railway marshalling yards and workshops, and a lot of light to medium industry.

Since the influx of immigrants from war-torn Lebanon in the mid-70s, Lakemba has become a centre of the Lebanese background population in Sydney. Many are Muslims; the modern, concrete minaret of the mosque punctuates the streetscape. Many, however, are Maronite Christians, and the population of MacKillop Girls' High School reflects this fact.

The School

There were about 560 students at MacKillop in 1989; there had been 596 the previous year. In 1988, 86 per cent were of non-English speaking background (NESB). About half were Arabic speakers, mainly first generation Lebanese background immigrants. The next largest 'immigrant' group is of Italian background, comprising about 12 per cent of the school population. These are longer settled and mostly second generation 'immigrants'. The Vietnamese background group is steadily growing, currently around 7 per cent, nearly all recent arrivals in Australia; when they first arrived in the early 1980s they were largely refugees and most had been in refugee camps. Smaller groups include Spanish speakers, both from Spain and Latin America, and especially Chile; Polish speakers; some longer-established groups such as those who identify as Croatian; and some recent arrivals from the Philippines and Fiji. About 20 per cent of the students are from Anglo or Celtic ethnic background. In 1988 there were two Aboriginal students.

In 1985, when the school established the Community Liaison Program, which is the central innovation of concern in this chapter, an initial survey indicated thirty-six different ethnic backgrounds among the students, with 82 per cent being immigrants. The proportion of the students' parents identified as born in Australia was 18 per cent, compared to 44 per cent from the Middle East (mostly Lebanon); 17 per cent from Continental Europe (mostly Italy); 11 per cent from Asia (mostly Vietnam); 4 per cent from Latin America (mostly Chile); 3 per cent from Mauritius; 2 per cent from various Pacific Island countries and 2 per cent from Great Britain and Ireland.

Cultures of Schooling

The socioeconomic situation of the students' families was described by teachers as 'very working class', with most of those in employment working in factories. A survey taken by the school in late 1986 showed that 24 per cent were unemployed and 42 per cent were in unskilled or semi-skilled occupations. About 10 per cent of the children come from single-parent families. Only about 5 per cent come from single-child families, the median number of children in their families being four. Over 30 per cent come from families of five or more children. The original community liaison teacher, herself an Arabic speaker from Sudan, said that the nuclear family was the norm among her charges. Some had grandparents living with them, but not as an extended family proper. There were usually close ties with the rest of the family, but they would not necessarily live in the same household. The anglophone Australian teacher now responsible for the Community Liaison Program (who will henceforth be referred to as the community liaison *teacher*, to distinguish her from the non-teaching, part-time community liaison *officer* also currently employed) believed that there were a lot of extended families in the community, but that these were being broken up by the housing situation and by moving to place of work. The type of housing varied enormously, she said, but the situation was rapidly changing because of the current accommodation crisis in Sydney. Some five years ago, a lot of houses in the area were being rented by new arrivals from Vietnam or Lebanon, who would subsequently buy homes in the area. Now they were renting home units, then leaving for the outlying south-western suburbs (forty kilometres further removed), or moving interstate to Queensland or Western Australia; they simply could not afford to buy in this area now. The principal corroborated this, observing that enrolments had dropped through this process. She remarked that the school's population was a shifting one, responding to waves of migration. The neighbourhood used to be a 'nice' one, she commented, but now many residences were run-down, reflecting a period of transition in the area. The school's survey showed that only about 3 per cent lived in public housing. The liaison teacher noted the huge disparity in the standard of housing she would encounter on home visits.

> The poorest places . . . were some of the Vietnamese places: living behind sewing shops with very little furniture. At the other extreme would be some of the Italian people who have been here a lot longer and who have double-storey brick mansions.

The students' backgrounds were fairly representative of the neighbourhood, the principal suggested, except for the school's Arabic speakers being Maronite Christians in a predominantly Muslim area. The Lakemba mosque was a key influence in the community. The Vietnamese are also a very visible group, especially on weekends when, supported by those from other suburbs, the local churches are 'packed to the doors'.

The girls' leisure activities were described by one teacher as 'fairly limited'. She said that the physical education department encourages activities 'that the kids can pursue'. Some belong to clubs such as sports associations; some go ice-skating or ten-pin bowling. The 'Anglo minority' might be more interested in a Saturday netball team or the like. The principal explained that pastimes 'very from group to group'. Those of longer-established resident background, such as the 'Anglos' and Italians, played a lot of weekend sport such as tennis and basketball, while others were much more family-oriented. The Sudanese coordinator of the languages materials project, formerly the community liaison teacher, said that most leisure activities of her students are tied up with the family or the Church, but that there are some village associations. The present community liaison officer, also a Sudanese Arabic speaker and recruited through her friendship with the former, related how most of the Lebanese groups in the community would be comprised not only of relatives and friendship networks, but that sometimes whole villages had migrated, and socialized together through parties, dances and so forth. One teacher lamented, 'Our students are tremendously parochial; the majority of them are a sort of urban peasantry. Their idea of a tremendous voyage abroad is to go as far as the Harbour Bridge'. The girls' leisure revolved mainly around the family, going visiting and so on; there was little participation in sport. The Vietnamese girls, according to the Sydney Archdiocese Catholic Education Office liaison officer for Indo-Chinese students, engage in 'minimal' leisure activity. Their parents expect them to be with the family. They play with others living in the area, stay inside, or watch television. Parents, he said, expect their children mostly to study, and they do.

'Just about all' the students' parents would speak their first language at home; only a small minority had 'chosen not to', according to the community liaison teacher. A survey by the former languages coordinator, showed that, for those of Arabic-speaking background, 92 per cent of students reported that their parents spoke to each other in Arabic; 69 per cent of their parents said that they did so. Parents who said they spoke to their children in a mixture of Arabic and English represented 59 per cent; 78 per cent of their children believed that this was Arabic. Students responded that 78 per cent of them spoke to their siblings in English; 50 per cent of parents believed this to be so. Children answer their parents mostly in English, and speak mostly English with their peers, she noted. The observations of the community liaison officer substantiate this; there is a mixing of languages in most Arabic-background households, with children speaking mainly English among themselves, and parents communicating with them in a mixture — though many would say that this was Arabic, she remarked.

The school has forty-five teaching staff, of whom six speak Arabic, four Italian, two Russian, one Spanish and one Vietnamese; a number speak French. Most of the teachers do not live within the area of the school. The linguistic diversity was no accident, explained the principal. She had 'gone looking for it', actively recruiting the staff she believed the school needed. She described the school's management style as 'low key', saying that she worked well with the executive and delegated authority to encourage teachers to participate in the decision making in their areas. Most staff agreed on the principal's far-sightedness and supportiveness over issues of cultural and linguistic pluralism. One teacher identified a problem, however, with the school's deliberative processes, in that the staff 'have had not much input, except to solve short-term problems; and I don't think that we've got the administrative style that allows discussion, suggestions and "throwing the things around" '. Some in the hierarchy felt that there was perhaps too much responsibility devolved to the respective programme coordinators, who were not necessarily working in the same direction.

The principal described the school as 'well equipped'. She said that it supplemented the funds it received from the Catholic Education Office with an annual walkathon, which raised about $9,000 to $11,000; and the Parents' and Friends' Association contributed about $3,000 to $4,000 per year. Fees charged by Catholic systemic schools such as MacKillop were, for 1989: in year 7 and 8, $492 per annum for the first child, $369 for the second child, $246 for the third child; in Year 9 and 10, $561 for the first child, $420 for the second child, $282 for the third child. Of the 1989 budget of the Sydney Archdiocese of the Catholic Education Office, 83.2 per cent was comprised of federal and state government grants. The Catholic Education Office's estimates of government recurrent grants to Archdiocese of Sydney systemic secondary schools amount to $1665 per capita from the federal government and $725 from the New South Wales government. MacKillop would have attracted a greater than average proportion of this funding, however, because of its being classified as 'disadvantaged' under the Disadvantaged Schools Program, as we shall examine below in the context of the Disadvantaged Schools Program-funded community liaison initiative.

The principal said that the school received a lot of support from the Catholic Education Office, but that parents were a potential source of support not yet fully tapped. She added that 'If the Vietnamese could do anything they would', and so would the Italian-speaking parents. The problem was creating ways of keeping the support going. Some of the parent support had been organized in the form of the parents' committee with which she met regularly; she described this as the 'groundwork' for future development.

The school is small in physical size, occupying only 0.46 hectares, with a further 0.2 hectares shared with the neighbouring Catholic boys' school. The main building is a solid two-storey brick building of the uninspiring type which proliferated in many suburbs in the post-war decades to accommodate the progeny of the baby boom. A more recent wing has been added, and the entire block had been refurbished throughout last year: a process which, with its attendant relocation, led to certain 'problems and tensions' between subject departments, according to one teacher. There is also a canteen block and some portable buildings, one of which is used to house the languages materials development project. A pair of large steel transport containers next to these are apparently used to store furniture and equipment. The small playground is asphalted, with the standard lunch benches around the perimeter: physical education lessons take place here.

Virtually all the teachers interviewed considered their training less than adequate in preparing them for the linguistic and cultural diversity encountered at MacKillop. One said she 'learnt on the job'. Another said that she had to find out a lot after she started at the school. A number felt that their own background as migrants had made them sensitive to the needs of students from immigrant families. One, for example, told how, when she was applying for classification at the Catholic Education Office, she had been told that she would have problems because of her accent and poor English. This had particularly upset her, as she had been educated bilingually in English and another language since kindergarten, and had a university degree with honours in English and philosophy. Several staff believed that their postgraduate studies had proven useful in respect of cultural and linguistic diversity, in areas ranging from linguistics to the 'background' provided by a university 'Migration Studies' programme. Some parents thought that some of the teachers were 'not trained well enough', particularly in teaching languages.

Context of the Innovation

Language learning was at the centre of the school's range of initiatives in responding to cultural and linguistic diversity. The principal told how she had read widely about the importance of the acquisition of the 'community' language for NESB students. She believed that it was useful both in redressing the problems of those not 'academically able' and in helping students communicate better with their parents. She cited the example of one of her own students who had been discovered by an interpreter to be providing incorrect translations to her mother, quite unintentionally. Some of her students who were not good in either English or their first language were unable to develop their second language — in terms of conceptualization, for example — because of inadequate command of the first language. English language programmes were also crucial. Part of the reason for 'community' language learning was to have students become conscious of their own language and to improve their English. The school's English as a Second Language (ESL) programme, found across the curriculum, involves having an ESL teacher, at the request of a subject teacher, teach with the subject teacher in some lessons. There are some classes where students are withdrawn from the mainstream class, but in English most classes, according to need, have an ESL teacher providing support. The school teaches five languages other than English (LOTEs): Arabic, Italian, Spanish, French and Vietnamese. The study of one of these languages is compulsory in Years 7 and 8. There were also some sociocultural programmes designed to address cultural and linguistic diversity.

Cultures of Schooling

Year 7 began by utilizing units from the Social Literacy materials, an interdisciplinary social science programme aimed at assisting all students to understand the processes of their own enculturation. There were no 'Ethnic Studies' courses, however, because the study of ethnic cultures was covered in the language program, albeit only the cultures of the language groups being studied. The Community Liaison Program was designed eventually to reach all parents of students in the school, but targeted the Lebanese initially because they were the ones the school had found difficult to reach.

The principal pointed out that she hadn't thought of their programmes as innovations, simply as answering a need. She thought that, while each had its place, the Community Liaison Program had been most crucial, because the parent groups had come from this. The school had got to know people in the community, whom to ask for advice and involvement, and so on. The principal described the programme as arising out of a series of conversations with the present coordinator of the languages materials project, (who had been at the school some fourteen years), during the principal's second year at the school. There had previously been a liaison programme at the school, but it had ended. This current programme, according to the principal, arose from the problem of getting to know the Lebanese parents in particular. The school had been using interpreters, but realized that more was needed. The coordinator of the languages materials project (who became the first community liaison teacher, and had been coordinator of the languages department, a position she had formally relinquished but appears, *de facto*, to maintain in addition to her new, and paid, role; and who will, for brevity, henceforth be referred to as the languages coordinator) described the Community Liaison Program as being called for by the curriculum diversification in the school at that time. This was corroborated by both the current community liaison teacher and the Catholic Education Office's special projects officer. The latter was clearly supportive of the new progressivist approach, which entailed modifying the curriculum into a range of semester-length courses from which the students would choose, in an atttempt to make the school more 'relevant' to its clientele. From her perspective:

> the school was 'different' because of its 'interesting' enrolment of girls. There was the climate of the sort of thing that Michael Middleton was doing [see Middleton, 1982[1]]. The deputy there at the time was very influenced by Middleton. The principal shared this philosophy. There was a good staff; [one] history teacher was one of the best. The innovations were not forced on the staff. There were key people all over the school, people who clashed, but they got together and realized that they had to do something.

MacKillop was well suited, she judged, to the vertical semester system, because of the diverse 'range of ability'. It had not been sufficiently stretching the 'brighter' kids.

In an attempt to establish what the 'range of abilities' was, the school had commissioned an annual battery of tests of various 'abilities', including tests of 'IQ', 'Mathematics Reasoning', 'Mathematics Performance', reading comprehension, spelling and 'Reading Power Units', from R.P. Allwell, B.L. Cambourne and P.D. Rousch. Their *Profiles for Students of Year 10, 1985* states:

> When used in conjunction with the other tests of student achievement, IQ scores at this level are predictive and can indicate the fact that a student has little chance of academic success at Year 12, or is better suited to alternative courses of study. IQ ranges which fall below a high point of 95 (e.g., 84–93) would suggest that a student's talents would be better directed to avenues other than 'academic' senior secondary schooling.[2]

Nor was this battery of tests aimed solely at identifying the 'less academically inclined'. Earlier, the report outlines other uses:

> . . . comparison of the nature of a school's continuing enrolment may identify shifts or changes in the nature of students entering the school and may therefore identify the need for shifts of emphasis in the school's curriculum.[3]

Further:

> . . . in schools where facilities are provided for 'gifted' students, these students may be identified by consulting individual students' test profiles. Usually these students are those whose performance in all tests falls within the top 4 per cent or at Stanine 9.[4]

The school used the test results to 'help sort the incoming students into two broad groups — those who appear more able and those who appear less so'. Teachers had access to the results 'to examine the progress or lack of progress in a particular student', but they were normally kept on file with the principal and coordinators 'to avoid the possibility that girls will be labelled'.

In any case, the school introduced in 1981 the semester approach advocated by the New South Wales Legislative Assembly's McGowan Report in that year, with its similar concerns for 'relevant' curriculum for the 'non-academic' and extension of the 'gifted'.[5] According to the languages coordinator at MacKillop, with the introduction of the 'vertical semester' timetable there, a greater number of courses was offered to students. Each teacher would take 'one bit of a course'. Courses had to be advertised, and students would 'choose' between them. This placed a lot of demands on students and parents. The special projects officer surmised that there were ructions from the parents over this. The liaison teacher had gained the impression that the students had not been coping with the curriculum choice. According to the French teacher, 'the number of electives and courses offered was done in a salesmanship sort of way; you had to get the kids in, call it "let's be bopping" . . . and language teaching altogether, not just French, kind of slipped back there'.

The teaching of Arabic had continued, the French teacher believed, mainly because the parents made representations about it being dropped. The languages coordinator explained that new choices had to be made every term, resulting in 'lots of [diverse] courses'. Yet students had to meet certain requirements by the end of Year 10, so they had to discuss these choices with their parents. The languages coordinator thought that the school was deciding on the future of the student, based on the choices made, which she believed was unfair for both students and parents. The latter, particularly, often knew little about the system of education, and had difficulty understanding the information provided. The principal had found the system in place when she arrived at the school. She thought it good 'in principle' but, on closer inspection, it had proven inappropriate for 'the students' background', because of the need to assess English language development more reliably. The principal said that she therefore 'came down on the side of caution' and developed more of a core-based curriculum. This, she argued, made it easier to monitor students so that they did not 'fall through the net'. The French teacher's assessment of the 'McGowan scheme' was that, while at the time it had looked very attractive on paper, in hindsight it could be seen as a system that was pioneered in a very cohesive community, where the students had a predominant commonality of background. It had proven unsuitable for a school where there was such a wide variety of background in the students. It seemed that the McGowan-style semesterized curriculum, with its complicated system of prerequisites and co-requisites for optional courses, represented a form of unofficial streaming. The student 'choice' involved was therefore illusory.

These dynamics ultimately led to two innovations at MacKillop. The first was the incorporation of Languages Other Than English (LOTEs) into a common core curriculum in Years 7 and 8, instigated at the principal's determination. This involved the mandatory study of their first language in the first two years of secondary school by all NESB students from backgrounds of the languages offered: Arabic, Italian, Vietnamese, Spanish and French. Students from other language backgrounds must study either French or Spanish. This was keenly supported by Arabic - and Vietnamese-speaking parents; indeed it was called for by them through the parent-school liaison, which was the second innovation. Spanish-speaking parents also asked for their language to be included. The liaison teacher saw the language programme as an 'outcome' of the Community Liaison Program, which was the initiative of the languages coordinator.

The languages coordinator had proposed changes in the first year of the vertical semester timetabling system, 'to help the students and parents make choices', but nothing was done about this, she recalled. So she had raised the question again, suggesting that the school provide counselling periods in which teachers counselled students about 'options' — but this would have left out the parents. She developed the idea of the Community Liaison Program as an attempt to explain to parents the curriculum courses and options, to let them see what was happening and to help them make choices. She was laughed at, she recounted, when she first proposed this; only the then deputy saw the problem, but he said that he could not see how the parents could be reached. To achieve this, the languages coordinator wrote a submission to the relevant Disadvantaged Schools Program committee, seeking funds 'for a new initiative to bridge the gap between home and school in an attempt to ensure that the students will make informed choices in the selection of their courses'.

The school had been classified as a 'disadvantaged school' in 1982, giving it access to Disadvantaged Schools Program funding for such initiatives. The Commonwealth Schools Commission in 1985 allocated $36.6 million in supplementary funding to designated disadvantaged schools, of which $5.9 million was distributed to non-government, primarily Catholic systemic schools.[6] The 1985 Schools Commission Guidelines stated:

> The Commission regards parental involvement as essential to the programme's aim of encouraging declared schools to relate closely to the communities they serve. Committees at all three levels — State, regional and school — must include parents as members.
>
> A process of involving parents and the community at all levels is essential to this programme. Programme funds are intended to enable school committees, which include parent and community members, to: — ...
>
> - Develop curriculum more closely related to life experiences of students at the schools.
> - Bring about closer association between the school and its parents and community. . . . [7]

In this instance, it should be noted, the second of these objectives involved tension with the first. For the diversification of the curriculum into 'relevant', optional mini-courses aiming at the first objective, met with some resistance from the parents as the second objective was implemented. In the words of the Catholic Education Office special projects officer, 'Democracy was very hard to achieve; they were a very reactionary body of parents, who were not convinced that the curriculum was appropriate for their daughters'.

In the event, the funding was forthcoming. The allocation of Disadvantaged Schools Program money for Catholic schools in the Sydney Archdiocese was the responsibility of the Sydney Catholic Disadvantaged Schools Committee, chaired by the present special projects officer. The nine-member committee included two parent representatives and the then MacKillop deputy. The school's 1982 Disadvantaged Schools Program submission had been favourably received by the committee of that year, which had annotated it, 'First class submission. A school that is really getting to grips with its curriculum content and programming. Have introduced a semester approach for 1982. Priority 1 will monitor this closely.' The special projects officer stressed during her interview that it is important to note the types of programme funded in 1982–4, before the school applied, in 1985, for Disadvantaged Schools Program funding for the Community Liaison Program. The 1982 project was the key one, she emphasized; it was an 'evaluation and planning' project using funding for teacher release time, not to buy equipment, which was often the approach of the less successful Disadvantaged Schools Program submissions. Of the $38,105 applied for and $30,100 granted, $12,000 was allotted to the evaluation and planning initiative. In 1984, 0.4 of a full-time teacher's salary was granted, 'to undertake the assessment of courses being offered under the newly organised vertical semester grouping of the school'. In 1985, the Sydney Archdiocese funding guidelines booklet answered the question, 'What kinds of projects will be funded?', with five 'general categories', including:

- Curriculum innovation programmes designed to build on and broaden the life experiences of students and increase their self confidence. . . .
- School/community interaction programmes which assist home/school liaison and the participation of parents in the development and implementation of curriculum programmes.[8]

For 1985, the evaluation and planning project applying to the former category was granted one full-time teacher's salary, and the student-parent liaison project, falling into the latter category, received the same: approximately $20,000 each.

The Innovation in Practice

The languages coordinator suggested that, because she was not teaching face-to-face at that stage (as she was working on a NSW Multicultural Education Coordinating Committee-funded materials production project), she could see 'as an outsider' the problems with the curriculum changes. Eventually, she gained the support of the deputy and the new principal, who had arrived at the school in 1984 and had found the staff 'committed' to 'vertical semestering, in which students chose "bits" of courses'. This staff commitment was by no means unanimous, despite the perception of the special projects officer that its instigators were 'the whole school' — a key phrase in Disadvantaged Schools Program parlance: 'The Disadvantaged Schools Program advocates a WHOLE SCHOOL APPROACH . . .'[9] [original capitals]. This officer believed that 'the innovations were not forced on the staff'. Yet one teacher interviewed told how she and her colleagues found the system 'unworkable', though they could not say so publicly. It had been introduced with 'a great deal of push from the top':

> Obviously, before you can implement a scheme like that you've got to have all the teachers onside. We actually had a weekend away and had people talking to us about it, and discussed theory of education and so forth; and they gave us Brandy Alexanders and got us onside.

At that stage, Arabic was 'the only language consistently taught', the principal observed. We have already noted that languages had been losing out in the competition for popularity since the market mechanism of choice between many optional course modules was introduced.

In this context, the languages coordinator was authorized to conduct an evaluation, with the parents, of the problems. She began by inviting parents to the school, showing individuals the 'different aspects of what was happening in the school'. Finding that personal contact worked best, she discovered that talking to parents at home was more successful, as they often would not come to the school, or, if they did, they were uncomfortable. She visited five to six families a day, and concentrated on Year 8 students. Her successor explained that Year 8 was chosen because by this stage the students had settled down into the school. Interviews were conducted in the family's first language. It should be borne in mind that this teacher was a native speaker of Arabic, and was dealing in the first instance, as the principal had explained, with Arabic-speaking parents. The principal described the programme as 'a developmental thing'. Thus it began, in the liaison teacher's words, as a period of assessment when the languages coordinator had 'gone around and talked to parents' about the school and its curriculum. She told how interview topics ranged over teachers, curriculum, social chit-chat. Sometimes she just listened. She was able to find out about the students' backgrounds, and was alerted to their problems. Some parents were unhappy at first, because they thought the school was trying to find out why they were not paying fees, so the coordinator made it clear that she was not there to discuss finances. As the school's project application had observed:

> Parent-school meetings generally take place on school territory, at school set times, with the school setting the rules; the parent will meet with the teacher or principal as someone being interviewed from behind a desk, the petitioner. . . . Quite unaccustomed to playing any part in the life of the school, they are ill at ease on any occasion when they must come to the school. Many avoid coming at all. Others come out of sheer necessity. . . . They are summoned to the school because of problems which teachers are having with their daughters, or they must come to the school as suppliants to beg for a reduction in school fees because of difficult economic circumstances.

She thought that the interviews were 'excellent' and that the home visits remained the most important feature of the programme. Other participants would not agree on this point, as will be detailed below.

Cultures of Schooling

The coordinator related that, as she did not have as much time to spend on the Community Liaison Program in its second year, they began group meetings of parents to conduct the liaison collectively. The 1986 Disadvantaged Schools Program submission was for $9,600, or 0.4 of a full-time teacher's salary, plus $500 for materials for the Community Liaison Program, out of a total Disadvantaged Schools Program grant to the school of $41,100. An ESL teacher was also employed part-time in that year, initially conducting withdrawal classes for Vietnamese students. Her work had extended into 'classroom' teaching, and she had been asked to undertake part-time Community Liaison work as well. (This is the staff member referred to as the liaison *teacher*.) She found that her ESL work with the Vietnamese students had been good preparation for the programme, because of the many 'cultural factors' involved. This teacher saw the opportunity to work with immigrant parent groups as a means of 'empowering' them, and of constructing an alternative to the 'Anglo'-dominated Parents' and Friends' Association. In her understanding, the initial goal of the Community Liaison project had been to enable the parents to understand the values and aspirations of the school, and vice versa. This goal was then extended to encompass the actual participation of parents in the decision making of the school. The special projects officer drew a distinction between the new liaison teacher's aim of 'empowering' *vis-a-vis* the 'informing' approach of the original coordinator. She thought that the fact that the former was monolingual and not an Arabic speaker was significant in this respect in terms of her relationship with the community.

The liaison teacher said that, while 'we don't yet have parents in the position of making decisions . . . the school has been responsive to what they want'. The first thing that the parents had asked for had been a language programme, and the principal responded positively to this request. 'That was a fairly big coup in terms of funding'. It was a direct response to the parent meetings. The parents saw it this way as well; one parent, a Spanish-speaking Uruguayan tradesman, said:

> Our group is lucky. At the first meeting there were questions about what the parents prefer to have at the school; they said Spanish and got it. They felt more confident, more free to talk and discuss subjects. They get no other opportunity.

The Vietnamese teacher confirmed that the Vietnamese language programme was instituted in response to the requests of the Vietnamese community. 'There were many approaches through the parent liaison programme'. An apparent contradiction over this points to a need for such a programme to 'voice' parental wishes, as well, perhaps, as indicating cultural differences in the nuances of the concept of 'pressure'. Asked whether there had been 'community pressure' for the project, the Indo-Chinese student liaison officer replied that the Vietnamese community were not wont to apply such pressure:

'It's not on with our people.' They would not stand up and speak out. They were, however, very happy with this initative of the principal.

The language-based parent groups were formed in 1987. In this year, the project was funded for 1.4 full-time equivalent teacher salaries, at a cost of $33,600. The responsibility was shared between the languages coordinator and the liaison teacher, who relied on translators and bilingual teaching staff where necessary. At first, they had gathered the parents together in one group for a general introduction, and then asked them to divide into various sub-groups, depending on language: Arabic speakers in this room, Spanish speakers in that room, and so on. To the organizers' surprise, all remained where they were, refusing to leave the 'English-speaking' group. They learned from the experience; for the next meeting they worked out language groups from the roll and gave parents slips of paper with room numbers on them, separating them into language groups. No-one objected. The principal thought it important to have the 'symbolic unity of the general meeting' before breaking up into language groups.

One parent, an Italian-speaking housewife, said, 'We have lots of little groups and I'm not sure whether this benefits the whole of Australia having all these groups. I'm not saying it's a problem; I'm just saying it would be interesting to know'. Another mother, an Italian-speaking labourer, agreed, saying 'We don't get together enough, or at all'. (Six parents, three Italian-speaking women, and three men: one each of Uruguayan, Filipino and Lebanese background, were interviewed together.) The third speaker of Italian, an unemployed mother, suggested that not many would come to a combined meeting: 'because in our groups we can speak Italian; in the larger one we can't'. The Spanish-speaking tradesman concurred, saying that if parents could not speak together, that would be a problem. The second mother conceded that they 'wouldn't accomplish much at a big meeting, anyway'. The Arabic-speaking father, a journalist who had been a teacher in Lebanon, confirmed this: 'They had one. It was terrible. People need to speak in their own languages'. The other parent, who had been a business manager in the Philippines, but a labourer here, maintained that they should meet together. 'If we continue to meet as little groups, then we only see the little things; if you get together, you see the big things'. One parent thought it would take too long to translate; several thought it should be tried. Perhaps this little interchange illustrates the view of the liaison teacher:

> The main point is that [things] are raised and that they are discussed. I think it is the discussion that is the important thing, because you don't necessarily change people, but if they understand why we're doing something and we understand why they say something — that makes the difference. It's the discussion that's important, not the resolution. But I think a discussion *is* a resolution in a way.

This was an example writ small of the contradiction, which was raised in interviews, between incorporation into the mainstream, on the one hand, and

Cultures of Schooling

giving recognition to cultural differences, on the other. There were 'always' incidents of such tension, according to the liaison teacher. She related an instance of this in the linguistic area: a Vietnamese-refugee background father, with whom they had spent a whole session discussing the value of bilingualism and first language maintenance. In the next parent liaison group meeting, he had stood up and said, 'OK. Well, we've been maintaining Vietnamese. [Mimics his thumping the table.] *How's our daughter's English going?*'

The home visits continued, as well as the group meetings. The liaison teacher described these as an 'extremely valuable' aspect of the programme. Indeed, she maintained that it was only after initial contact had been established through the home visits, that parents could be motivated to attend the group meetings. The liaison staff visited the home of every girl in Year 8, of NESB and English-Speaking Backgrounds (ESB) alike, taking with them interpreters or teachers from the appropriate language background as required. The visits yielded invaluable information about individual students and their particular problems and needs, as well as familiarizing parents with the school, and providing practical assistance in a variety of areas, from careers advice to applications for Austudy (government financial assistance for students). A key element of the programme, which had made it peculiarly successful from the point of view of teachers, was that they could find out the *reasons* for problems with individual children, and could therefore deal with them appropriately. The liaison teacher cited the example of a girl who had been withdrawn from classes because of her extremely erratic behaviour. It had transpired that she was a diabetic, whose mood changes were resulting from a difficulty in controlling the diabetes. This had been compounded by the fact that the mother would cry with shame every time the girl injected herself with insulin. To add to the child's problems, she had been required to wear a black robe to school for six months, as part of a religious custom involving her dedication to a saint: this had proven traumatic for the girl. When the class teacher was made aware of this student's background, there was a complete reversal of behaviour, because her special needs were then catered for.

As well as conducting home visits and convening parent groups, the two liaison staff were deployed in 1987 (according to their Disadvantaged Schools Program project evaluation report) for, *inter alia*:

- Regular discussion with Principal regarding progress, evaluation and assistance required.
- Regular contact with teachers, Pastoral Care Coordinators and Form Mistresses, subject coordinators and Curriculum Coordinator.
- Informing parents about school events, regular fortnightly newsletters, translating school notices, bilingual handbooks, translation of new school report forms (Ethnic Affairs).
- Communicating with other liaison officers in the area; regular regional cluster group meetings to share experience and ideas.
- Work with Diocesan Liaison Staff. . . .

- Work with Referral Network hearing/reading tests, Sp.[ecial] Ed.[ucation] assessment, psychiatrists, legal aid, bilingual doctors, social workers, speech pathology. Also through newsletter — referral agencies information. . . .
- Discussion with parents of careers/job opportunities and implications of subject choices.
- Liaise with incoming students/parents from Intensive Lang[uage] Centre. . . .
- Liaise with Primary Principals.

The 'cluster group' referred to in this list of duties was regarded by the liaison teacher as central to the liaison initiative. MacKillop, though it was the initial innovator, was but one of a number of schools in the area comprising a cluster group, collectively developing the parent liaison initiative. As one of the major challenges was to stimulate change at the system level, it was important to keep this wider perspective in view. In fact, this teacher stressed that it was not possible to understand the nature and context of the innovation by focusing on one school. The special projects officer pointed out that many of the (Catholic systemic) primary schools in the Inner West are Disadvantaged Schools Program classified. Staff from all these schools met with MacKillop in a community liaison network, set up by the Catholic Education Office adviser in the region. They now run their own network, which was the original aim. They provide annual Disadvantaged Schools Program evaluations to the system as a condition of their funding.

Within the school, there were close links with the careers programme. The liaison staff worked together closely with the careers adviser — there was a careers content in the home visit interviews. Part of the 1986 Disadvantaged Schools Program submission provided for the employment of a full-time careers adviser, at a cost of $24,000, plus $1,500 for fifteen staff release days and $500 for materials, for a tertiary awareness and careers project.

The close cooperation with the ESL programme was fortuitous; the liaison teacher, originally employed to teach ESL part-time, worked fourteen teaching periods per week on community liaison and twenty-two periods per fortnight of ESL at MacKillop, as well as one day per week at the intensive language centre. She commented that, although it had happened accidentally, it had proven very useful to have the one teacher doing both ESL teaching and community liaison:

> Educationally, they are very related. The fact that [NESB] children don't do very well at school is not always just an ESL problem; half the time it isn't at all. You can't remove language problems from their social context. So being able to see their problems from the two sides is very useful: it's useful to me, it's useful to the teachers because you can contribute both aspects, and it's useful to the parents because you

can explain the linguistic problems as well as looking at cultural problems. The other advantage is that working in the school as a teacher gives the community liaison person another perspective; other community liaison people miss out on that.

The liaison teacher saw the ESL programme, which was taught across the curriculum rather than exclusively by withdrawal, as part of the languages programme. She felt that, apart from the connection with the languages programme which was engendered by the community liaison project, as we have seen, the community liaison initiative had had little effect in penetrating the mainstream subjects: 'it's peripheral to them'.

The principal described the Community Liaison Program as linked with a number of other aspects of the school, particularly in curriculum and the school's pastoral care policy. While the pastoral care coordinator did a different job, and the liaison personnel were a separate staff, they talked with the pastoral care coordinator whenever necessary.

In 1988, the school received $23,000 from the Disadvantaged Schools Program for 0.8 of a full-time teacher equivalent as community liaison teacher, as well as a half-time equivalent ($11,500) tertiary awareness teacher, $500 for travel and $500 for resources, 'to work with staff in the development of structures to facilitate home/school communication in relation to curriculum choices and options for their future choices in education and employment'. The grant details form for this year bears the note, 'This whole project needs to be monitored and evaluated closely in 1988 as it is expected that funding will cease at the end of 1988 for this particular project'. The special projects officer explained that there is an informal rule that Disadvantaged Schools Program funding is only granted to any one project for a maximum of three years. The rationale for this is that the supplementary finance is supposed to cover the cost of producing 'whole school change', after which the changed school is expected to undertake the ongoing costs of maintaining its new arrangements. In this case, an exception was made, and MacKillop was extended Disadvantaged Schools Programme funding for the Community Liaison project for 1989: $14,000 for 0.5 teacher salary, $200 travel, $500 stationery, plus the costs of interpreters and translators. It was made clear, however, that 'This will be the last year of funding for this project'.

In 1988, the other Sudanese Arabic-speaking community liaison officer was engaged to take over the work on the Community Liaison Programme of the languages coordinator, who was busy with the Arabic materials development project. She and the community liaison teacher have been working jointly on the programme in 1989. This community liaison officer is not a teacher; she had previously worked in a bank. Having herself immigrated in 1971 with her husband and family, she felt that the Arabic-speaking parents could 'relate' to her; they had something in common. Educated in a francophone boarding school in Lebanon, she could speak the Lebanese dialect which was spoken by most of the Arabic-speaking parents. It was pointed out that it had been a deliberate strategy to employ a person for the job who was not a member of the Lebanese-speaking community, and was therefore distanced from the sometimes problematic communal politics. She was certainly distanced from her clients in socioeconomic terms; she observed that most of them were 'not educated' and came 'from the mountains'. Asked if she had become a special person in the community because of the programme, she replied, 'No. I don't move in their circles socially. I don't mix with them'. Her role was thus one of an intermediary rather than a spokesperson.

The community liaison officer reported that, with the funding halved, it was no longer possible to visit the whole group of Arabic-speaking families in the year; it was necessary to deal first only with those experiencing problems. She made home visits with a special questionnaire to be followed, and communicated to the school any problems which the parents raised. More of the time, however, she was 'used' at the school; relatively little of the liaison was initiated by the parents. One example of a problem which the school asked her to address was the case of a girl whom the school wanted to undertake a special work preparation course and whose parents were opposed to her travelling to Marrickville (an inner western suburb, seven kilometres away) by train. She believed that it was not her job to attempt to resolve such problems, merely to communicate them. There was one instance where parents had aired a problem: they felt that their daughter was 'going nowhere'. They had been told in primary school that her results would improve, but they had not. She had passed on their concerns. Asked if parents complained of racism at the school, she replied, 'Yes, I get a lot of that'. It was a very sensitive issue, she said. If parents were unhappy, she 'did her best to comfort them'.

Evaluation

The liaison officer believed that there were not enough links between the Community Liaison Program and the other structures of the school. There was no opportunity, for instance, for her and the liaison teacher to talk to the whole staff. They would like to have a staff seminar, to explain the problems of labelling and stereotyping at the school.

The community liaison teacher also spoke of the need to familiarize the whole staff with the goals and the process of the liaison project; she intended to attempt that in 1989. It was up to the staff, she believed, to be very sensitive about the values that they were passing on. 'I don't think they are sensitive enough', she remarked, 'but that might be my fault'. There was a need for much more discussion of value differences: this was at the crux of the shortcomings of the programme. In part, this was a function of management style, she thought. Examples of key value differences between the school and the 'community' were attitudes towards the role of women:

> You can push kids to do maths and science, but if you continue to expect girls to do certain things with their lives, there's going to be a contradiction set up. *Academically* they're pushed, but whether there's enough questioning of stereotypes is another matter.

The community liaison staff did have links with the subject coordinators, as well as with the careers teacher and ESL staff. They worked with the 'special education' person. They also worked extensively with the form coordinators, who were 'responsible for behavioural problems, dealing with kids' crises and so on'. It was because of the efforts of the ESL and 'special education' staff, arising from the Community Liaison Program, that it had become apparent that there was a need to 'target' particular teaching staff, according to the community liaison teacher. Yet there was a difference, she pointed out, between individual links between members of staff, and everybody knowing what was going on. Although the liaison staff personally made the above links, and the programme worked well because of that, these links were not 'built in'. This meant that the programme was dependent on these individuals' personal networks, rather than being structurally interlinked.

At the systems level, the liaison staff had made representations to the new director of the Catholic Education Office, Inner West Region, who had in fact been quite responsive. There were problems arising from the fact that this particular programme was funded by the government under the Disadvantaged Schools Program. This was not the case for all community liaison work within the system: some was funded by the schools themselves, some was allocated by the Catholic education system. The argument from MacKillop was that, although there were lots of schools doing this sort of work, there was no necessary coordination of this at the system level. A Disadvantaged Schools Program person who worked for the Catholic system on the community liaison initiatives was available, but 'her basic job was to administer government money, not to push parent participation within the Catholic school system'. The liaison teacher felt strongly that there was not enough systemic commitment to parent participation. There had been, quite recently, a development of *policy* in favour of parent participation, in the Sydney Archdiocese, but it remained to be seen what this amounted to in terms of material support. Historically, there had been within the Catholic Education Office a 'Parent Participation Unit' with part-time funding, but this had been entirely limited to dealing with sexuality lectures in primary schools. In this teacher's view, the higher echelons of the system did not fully understand the community liaison innovation; they were not sympathetic to its implications. It was fundamentally a hierarchical system, she observed, whereas the effect of parent participation would be to 'break down' hierarchical relations.

A major critical lesson at the school level, the community liaison teacher found, was that 'you need to have staff committed first. If you don't work through the process with them, you've got one hand tied behind your back'.

The whole staff should have been involved from the outset. There was a need for staff development: collectively to 'talk about the issue, examine it, and look at the implications'. The special projects officer agreed that the school needed 'to regularize ongoing inservicing'. There had been some surprises caused through the lack of this. For example, the community liaison teacher told that:

> we were doing some inservice work with the social science staff, whom I expected to be fairly in tune. . . . but the kind of things that came out were still that kind of perception of something being wrong with the kids. That's bad, I think, because [you need to] look . . . for causes [of] why this child isn't doing what you expect. . . .

The 'fault belongs to the child' perspective had been expressed by some teachers on parent-teacher nights. It was sometimes adopted by bilingual staff of non-English speaking background (NESB), who could think, 'Well, I made it; why can't you?' The liaison teacher agreed with the proposition that the staff tended to see her as given the job of going out and fixing the problems 'out there' so that the school could continue to function 'happily'. 'If you look at the implications,' she asserted on the other hand, 'they have to personally change'.

A crucial problem was funding. 'Money affects it directly. This year, with half our funding cut, it's so slow to do things'. Disadvantaged Schools Program funding was always on a temporary basis, to set up new projects. This left the difficulty of how the innovation was to be financed on an ongoing basis, once its three years of funding had expired. The opinion of the special projects officer was that 'a school should not rely on one person' such as the liaison teacher. 'The *whole school* should undertake the liaison process.' Asked whether this would make demands on teachers' time which would mean less hours to spend on, say, English or languages teaching, this officer replied that the school should cut back in these areas if necessary, as the pastoral role is just as important as the curriculum role.

The principal believed that the school would not have been able to mount the Community Liaison Program without the Disadvantaged Schools Program funding it received. With the cut to the funding, they were having to change the approach to one of referral, because they could not afford to visit every family in the school. The community liaison teacher thought the lack of exhaustive home visiting had weakened the programme, while the Catholic Education Office special projects officer perceived a 'need to de-emphasize home visits'. The staff were now targeting specific groups: 'special education', 'new arrivals', 'problem kids'. They had previously tried to avoid focusing on 'problem' students, fearing that this would stigmatize the programme.

The special projects officer asserted that 'many use the fact that funding is being reduced as an excuse not to go on to parental involvement'. She said that community involvement was seen as a threat by teachers. 'There is a need to do more work on this with teachers, but this is demanding on their *time*, which is then reflected in their classroom practice.' The principal thought it necessary to be careful that staff were not overstressed, so expectations of teachers were kept at a reasonable level. The staff 'didn't grumble', she believed, because she did not ask more than was fair. Staff were invited, not required, to attend certain meetings, and she found that staff would willingly come to those which concerned them most, or where they were most needed.

The liaison teacher saw the objective of parent influence actually being met. She added the rider, however, that it would be another question whether this would be extended to parent *power*; the existing hierarchy did not lend itself to this, and there was a management style which sought to avoid 'rocking the boat'. She remarked that the more 'like the school' that parents were, the more influence they had. The numerically smaller ethnic groups, such as those of Korean background, had less influence. The more educated and articulate parents, who occurred particularly among the Arabic-speaking groups, were more influential. The special projects officer also noted the question of who are the 'representative' parents, and commented on over-representation by tertiary-educated parents.

There were indeed two university graduates, both men, among the six leading members of the parent groups who were interviewed. One of these, a former manager in the Philippines, was working as a labourer in Australia; the other had been a teacher for twenty years in Lebanon, but was working here as a journalist. Yet their views on parent participation and on the curriculum were remarkably congruent with those of the Uruguayan background tradesman and the Italian-speaking women who described themselves respectively as a 'labourer' and a 'tradesperson' in the homeland and 'unemployed' here. The Filipino background father expected that they 'will get a lot out of it. Parent groups should have an influence on the policies of the school'. One Italian-speaking mother said that she was trying to get knowledge about how the system worked, and to 'have a say'. She thought that there was a lot to get out of it; they had only held two meetings so far. She had reached the stage where she was ready to make suggestions. She said that they had asked for Italian classes, but had not yet obtained them for all years, because of the numbers.

Parents agreed that there was more learning about culture, particularly history, in their own education, and felt that this was lacking in their daughters' curriculum. There was a need for a more ordered approach to teaching the basic concepts in these areas. Curriculum here was more directly vocational, which was not necessarily a better education:

> Things have changed, even in my country. Things are prepared differently, with more emphasis on what to do as a career. Twenty years ago in South America, I learnt more about literature and history and philosophy, not practical work. When I finished Year 10, I was well educated, but . . . I couldn't use a screwdriver. There is more time for practical work here, but things are different. . . . They need to be told things differently. . . . [Here] it seems to be a bit loose; it doesn't seem

to be a straight line. Friends in South America say it's a more common curriculum there.

Another parent said that his education had provided theory, culture and 'knowledge'; here it was more 'for life', more material. One mother said that there was not a strong 'today we listen, tomorrow we think' approach.

Asked whether the school should concentrate on teaching them more about Australian culture or their 'own' culture, there was general agreement that the focus should be on 'Australian culture, background, geography, history, *et cetera*, because they came here to be part of it. If you mix it up, they can't do it'. It was made clear, however, that this should be studied in its international context: 'It needs to be more general, for the world culture when they grow up'. It was, moreover, not just 'Anglo-Australian' culture that was intended: 'Obviously they have to know about the English, but they should also know about things like the Chinese, who came here in the last century, and the Italians, too.' 'We need true history, not just English, but one that has Aborigines and migrants.' Pressed about whether students should learn about their homelands, parents mentioned 'the problem that students feel embarrassed about their own culture. The parents are the culprits':

> A girl doesn't go to school until she is five, so that bit should be started by the family, to know your own background. But it should be shared by the school and the family. Knowing geography, for example, can be done by the school. I did Australia here, but here they think that England is the only other place that exists.

Others agreed: 'It needs to be general, to be more aware about other countries.'

There was evidence that the school had responded to some extent to all of these concerns. We have already seen how the core curriculum was reintroduced after a period of experimentation with a fragmented range of options. LOTEs were part of this common core, as requested by parents, and were being extended year by year, currently going to Year 8. The community liaison officer said that parents were very happy with the Arabic teaching. The Catholic Education Office liaison officer for Indo-Chinese students reported similarly for the Vietnamese programme. The Spanish- and Italian-speaking parents were less pleased with their language programme. One commented that the language they taught at school was not as good as the language they taught at Saturday school, and thought that perhaps this was because the teachers were often not trained, and that therefore perhaps they should only do conversational language. Another believed that teachers were not trained well enough as language teachers, and sometimes could not speak the language well. All parents interviewed thought that the children did not learn much from the language classes.

Cultures of Schooling

This could well be a function of pedagogy. It was clear both from interviews and lesson observations, that the progressivist approach currently pervading Australian schools was proving problematic for NESB students. The task of studying their first language, for students many of whom and many of whose parents are illiterate in that language, and who habitually use 'mixed' forms of the language often without realizing it, rendered a loosely implemented immersion model unsuitable given the time allowed in period allocations. This was realized by the former languages coordinator, who has spent a number of years producing structured teaching materials with content appropriate to the Australian context, with federal funding first from the NSW Multicultural Education Coordinating Committee and then from the Australian Second Language Learning Program of the National Policy on Languages, both federal initiatives to support multicultural education. Yet she believed there was an unwillingness to promote or distribute these materials at a regional systems level, given the preference for school-based curriculum development.

In classroom practice, moreover, structured and rigorous materials can be undercut by the less structured teaching style and less disciplined learning style characteristic of progressivism. The Arabic teacher, observed teaching Year 7 students for a double period of the language, had the difficulty of coping with one speaker of the Syrian and one of the Egyptian dialect in a rather large class of girls, otherwise of Lebanese background, with widely varying levels of oral proficiency. Few were competent with the Arabic script. The teacher was trained in Lebanon to teach Arabic and French, and had taught these there for about four years, but as first languages. She experienced similar difficulties to those found by English teachers in Australia, who were trained with a literary approach, and find themselves confronted with secondary students who are not fluent in speaking and are incapable of basic reading and writing in the language. (The special projects officer related her experience of this as an English teacher at a state secondary school with high NESB enrolment.) This Arabic teacher's English was not always correct in formal grammatical terms or idiomatic: often less so than that of her students. 'What means the fridge?', she asked at one stage. 'What's mean potatoes?' [pronounced to rhyme with tomatoes]. 'What's mean eggs?' The Vietnamese teacher who was observed, by contrast, used no English whatever in his lesson, although he accepted it from students in the first instance when they were incapable of certain expressions in Vietnamese (and he appeared then to provide the terms in that language). The Arabic teacher gave simple greetings and courteous phrases, instructions and managerial directions in English, though the students would have understood them in Arabic. 'Good morning. God bless you'; 'Quiet!'; 'Thank you'; 'Good'; 'Look at me'; 'Turn to the back'; 'Girls, you're gonna lose your break'; 'Yeah' and 'We stop now' were some examples. The French teacher, on the other hand, often delivered such utterances in French, or both languages consecutively, to students who were mostly not native speakers, to familiarize them with the language; they appeared to understand quite well. The Arabic teacher seemed unaware of the extent to which she mixed the languages, frequently in the one sentence. 'That's a [Arabic word/s]. You close it at the end.' 'Yes, Paula, [Arabic words].' '[Arabic words] alphabet [Arabic words].'

Students would address her in like manner, substituting English words in their case through lack of vocabulary or possibly lack of application, concentration, or even awareness of the process. '[Arabic words] on holidays, [Arabic].' 'Miss, [Arabic] cousin's place [Arabic].' Whereas the missing phrases were apparently supplied in the Vietnamese lesson, the lapses appeared to be overlooked in this one. This approach is consistent with the goal for the languages programme of enhancing self-esteem, as outlined by the liaison teacher. Part of the school's approach to 'values', she had explained, had involved the question of granting esteem to cultural differences. It had been felt that some of the students, particularly the Arabic-speaking ones, 'didn't really "value" their Arabic background'. The school's response was to 'make public' this culture and to encourage appreciation of it. So the language programme was introduced with Arabic as a subject; the Arabic language was used in newsletters; the Arabic parents' groups were initiated, and so on. In the Arabic class, girls who had been initially embarrassed or unwilling to speak in their first language, claiming that they could not do so, appeared to be fairly fluent once they began. There could well be a clash of objectives between the boosting of self-image, on the one hand and, on the other, the attainment of linguistic competence in both languages as desired by the principal and the languages coordinator, when the main rationale for language teaching drifts away from mastery of the language.

The French teacher belonged to an earlier generation and had long taught in a more traditional pedagogy. She had not trained as a French teacher, but was bilingual in English and French, having completed her secondary education in French in New Caledonia, and trained as an English teacher in Adelaide in the 1950s. She had been at MacKillop for fifteen years, over which period progressivist pedagogy had become *de rigueur* at the school. She gave every appearance of attempting to accommodate the new approach now expected by her colleagues and virtually demanded by the students, but she never seemed 'at home' with it. Progressivism, at its rare best, gives the *appearance* of spontaneity while in fact being carefully *structured* such that 'discovery learning' and so on can result. The common course, followed virtually in tandem by all of the LOTEs at MacKillop, was not structured in this way, nor was the timetable amenable to such structuring. What remained was the most commonly found aspects of progressivism: the free-ranging style and the 'relevance' approach:

> Here the programme seems to be trying to put the personal relations: making friends, getting to know people, how do I talk to you, how do I ask directions — not quite tourist French, but getting on that way — and only as much grammar as is needed for comprehension. With two

lessons a week for the Year 8s, one lesson on Monday and one lesson on Friday, the amount of grammar that you can do effectively is quite small. And of course with the Year 7s with the double period, you have to arrange your material in such a way that they can take it comfortably. And so I look for connections with their ordinary daily life, their experience, what's on the shelves at the supermarket, what sort of car Dad's friend's got — that sort of easy... the impact of France and French culture on Australia: *'Les Mis'* and anything that's on television... that sort of thing.

This contrasted starkly with the pre-progressivist era:

When I was teaching here first, at the end of Year 9, because of the system we had and the number of classes — it was treated as a full subject equivalent to history or geography — we had four or five lessons a week at sensibly spaced intervals, like one every day. At the end of Year 9, apart from the subjunctive, they knew everything they had to know, grammatically. They worked through a textbook. The emphasis wasn't nearly so heavy on 'culture': it was on grammar and spelling. They could not only speak French, quite adequately and reasonably comprehensibly; they could also write it adequately and comprehensibly, and they could read material of a very decent level of difficulty. So they were quite prepared to do more of the reading in Year 10. The emphasis was there on reading and vocabulary, and they were well equipped to go on to Year 11 and 12, with French as a subject, because the cultural area was stressed then... as they did more reading and watched films and that sort of thing.

This teacher explained that she used to teach in a more traditional manner — 'I'm more a grammar person' — but had adapted her style over the years. She was quite happy about this, although:

I feel a bit guilty sometimes. You think, 'Oh, I ought to be teaching them the preterite tense or something like that.' But it's the same accommodation that's taking place in English exactly. There was a stage when grammar became a dirty word. We *are* allowed to teach it again, now, thank God!

Ironically, it is probably the more rigorous pedagogy to which two parents were referring when they said that they wanted their daughter's education to be more 'academic'. Conversely, the two others who thought the current offerings were too 'loose', were doubtless objecting to aspects of the progressivist approach. Perhaps this is what the special projects officer meant, when she adjudged that 'they were a very reactionary body of parents, who were not convinced that the curriculum was appropriate for their daughters'. She held that the school had been 'able to introduce a more "meaningful" curriculum because of the lack of power and influence in the families. Where people are powerless, changes sometimes seem to come more easily than where people are influential.' This would appear to contradict the espoused aim of 'empowerment'.

The other area of need identified by the parents, it will be recalled, was the call for a rigorous, general, sociocultural curriculum. It was to this end, according to the principal, that the Social Literacy materials were introduced to the school four years ago. The Social Literacy materials are the product of an action research/curriculum development project which was funded by the NSW Multicultural Education Coordinating Committee, the Catholic Education Office, Sydney, and the Centre for Multicultural Studies at the University of Wollongong. The materials form a comprehensive social studies/science programme for Years 4–12. They follow an interdisciplinary approach, which incorporates the academic skills of history, geography, sociology and commerce, with a strong language across the curriculum emphasis. The aim of the Social Literacy approach is to teach about social concepts as essential tools for the understanding of society and culture rather than the commonly encountered approach in sociocultural curriculum of merely celebrating cultural diversity at a superficial level.[10]

The teacher who introduced the Social Literacy materials to the school, with the 'very keen' support of the principal, was interviewed about this innovation. She had heard that the draft materials of the project were being updated, and involved the school in trialling them. When the new books were introduced, she attended an inservice on them with the new curriculum coordinator. The school uses four of the Year 7 series of texts: *Social Values, Social Structures, Socialisation* and *Groups in Society* in its compulsory core of Studies in Society work. Classes spend four periods per week for one year on the programme. There are four teachers of the Social Literacy courses, only the teacher interviewed has a full teaching load on the programme; two have half a load each and one has one-fifth of a load.

The Social Literacy teacher described the goals of this innovation as:

> For girls to be more confident; for students to be equipped to make decisions and judgments; to provide the 'tools' necessary for further study and their own decision making; and also the 'academic', 'English teacher-based' goal of carrying the standards of writing through the curriculum: to make the students more literate.

This teacher believed that the programme met its objectives in practice. it prepared students for other social science subjects, and also worked on their 'self', building confidence and so on. 'One can see the changes in the girls. They like what they do in Social Literacy. They are eager to work at home; they share work with their parents and they are encouraged to do so'. She felt that one of the reasons that the programme was instituted was that the school was

Cultures of Schooling

very aware of its cultural context. They perceived the need to 'remove the students from their own personal experiences and look at something from afar'. The nature and structure of the materials, she found, with their definitions, repetition, and so on, made them very accessible to NESB students. All the parent feedback about the materials had been positive, she reported.

Sometimes the parents think the material is 'funny'. They ask, 'Why are the children doing this?', but they ask out of interest, not opposition. There had been some resentment from other teachers, believing that Social Literacy teachers had an easy workload because their lesson materials were provided for them. Unfortunately, the Social Literacy teacher believed, the subject was often treated like 'leftovers'. Teachers would be given Social Literacy classes just to fit in with the timetable. Of the four teachers currently teaching on the programme, two have not taught it before; one is trained as a physical education teacher. None is trained as a social science teacher. The deputy principal had not seen Social Literacy as important. There had been problems in getting through the material in the time available, and in fitting it in with other social science subjects, so the Social Literacy component had been cut down from two semesters to one.

In three key areas, then, the school has moved towards accommodating to the educational aspirations of the parents: a structured approach to basic concepts in sociocultural studies; a common curriculum, including compulsory study of the mother tongue; and the enhancement of self-esteem in (especially second generation) NESB girls.

The several strategies being implemented at the school to adapt to serve the interests of a culturally and linguistically diverse local community appear to be having a significant effect — at least on public examination results. For a school with the socioeconomic and ethnic composition of MacKillop, the fact that its School Certificate English Reference Test results have come slightly above the state mean is remarkable. [They were 1986: MacKillop 46.2 (standard deviation 11.63), state mean 46.6 (s.d. 13.78); 1987: MacKillop 45.7 (s.d. 11.06), state mean 44.5 (s.d. 13.50); and 1988: MacKillop 48.4 (s.d. 10.78), state mean 48.2 (s.d. 12.78), out of a possible 90.] The liaison teacher said that this meant that 'in terms of academic effects as measured by the School Certificate, the bulk of the students are now in the middle instead of at the bottom.' The students were already a lot better at communicating than they had been before the innovations, particularly the language programme. She believed that the school was operating more efficiently because of the liaison programme, in that 'the parents know what we're doing and we know what they want'.

The community liaison teacher judged that the liaison programme could be easily transferred to other schools if the human resources were available and if staff were prepared to undertake the considerable effort involved. Home visits, for example, required evening work. The languages coordinator noted that some liaison staff had complained about having to work at night, which was necessary.

There had been no active opposition to the Community Liaison Program at the school. In response to an anonymous questionnaire early on in the project, some staff in a less language-based discipline had written that 'teachers should be in the classroom'. This resistance had been no real barrier, but the liaison teacher's opinion was that inservicing was the way to deal with such attitudes. There were some problems involving resistance on the part of the students. Bilingual children would often play the game of telling their parents only what they wanted them to hear about the school, and this was broken down, of course, by the liaison programme. Sometimes the parents were greatly shocked to hear that their child was not doing as well at school as they had believed, or was in fact behaving problematically. The languages coordinator recalled that only two parents had objected in all the time the Community Liaison Program had existed; one was an 'Australian' father who said it was intruding on their privacy. The principal said that some parents had said 'No, thank you' to the Community Liaison Program, but that was all the opposition. No-one had objected to the LOTEs programme. She thought that parent liaison would work well anywhere, and that compulsory LOTEs courses would, too, depending on the personnel and how they were run.

The principal predicted, as did other teachers, that the future of the Community Liaison Program depended 'very much on finance'. The school will apply to the regional office of the Catholic Education Office for funding to staff the programme once the Disadvantaged Schools Program financing has terminated. Since the school is committed to the programme, she said, it will continue 'in some form'.

Notes

1. MIDDLETON, M., *Marking Time: Alternatives in Australian Schooling*, Methuen, Sydney, 1982.
2. ALLWELL, R.P., CAMBOURNE, B.L. and ROUSCH, P.D., Profiles for Students of Year 10, MacKillop Girls' High, Sydney, 1985, p. 6.
3. *Ibid.*, p. 4.
4. *Ibid.*
5. MCGOWAN, B., *et al.*, *Report from the Select Committee of Legislative Assembly upon the School Certificate*, Government Printer, Sydney, 1981.
6. CATHOLIC EDUCATION OFFICE, Commonwealth Schools Commission Disadvantaged Schools Program, *Funding Guidelines*, Canberra, 1985, p. 193.
7. CATHOLIC EDUCATION OFFICE, Commonwealth Schools Commission Disadvantaged Schools Program, *Sydney Archdiocese funding guidelines*, Catholic Education Office, Sydney, 1985.
8. *Ibid.*, p. 3.
8. *Ibid.*
10. KALANTZIS, M. and COPE, B., *Social Literacy: An Overview*, Common Ground, Sydney, 1989.

Chapter 4

'Australian is a Wide Word':
The Bilingual 'ESSPRO' and Languages Other Than English Programmes at Brunswick East High School

> Eighty-three per cent of students at Brunswick East High School, in inner suburban Melbourne, are of non-English speaking background. Over thirty language groups are represented in the school. Four languages other than English are offered: Italian, Greek, Arabic and Turkish. One of these is compulsory for each student in Years 7 to 10. They are then offered as optional subjects through to Year 12. In addition, there is a two period per week bilingual component in the English and Social Science Program (ESSPRO) in Year 7.

The Locality

Brunswick is an inner northern suburb of Melbourne. Traditionally an area of lower socioeconomic status, streets of late nineteenth-century working-class terraces and cottages are dotted with light manufacturing industry — a hosiery factory, small rag trade businesses and a stove manufacturing factory, for example. In the decades of mass immigration since the Second World War, the population in the Brunswick neighbourhood has been markedly transient, as new waves of immigrants arrive and some of the older waves move on. In the past, some of the moving on was the result of upward mobility — buying a house in a 'better' suburb as the reward for exceedingly hard work.

In recent years, rapidly rising real estate values in inner city areas have changed the dynamic behind the relative transience of Brunswick's population. There has been a minor trend to gentrification as some well established Anglo-Saxon Australian professionals move in. At the same time, immigrants have tended to move to the newer working-class suburbs on the distant outskirts of Greater Melbourne. These outer suburbs are either a new first stop or a relatively more affordable place to move to if one wants to buy a home. This process of gentrification is obviously a long term one, and is only just beginning.

The School

Already this demographic change in Brunswick is evident in a handful of enrolments at Brunswick East High School. The 'Anglo' population has stayed about the same size, but changed its socioeconomic complexion. Nevertheless, most of the students are still from non-English speaking families and mostly working class. One third of the students are from families receiving welfare benefits, unemployment benefits in most cases. Often students call this a 'pension' to avoid the stigma of unemployment. A good deal of this representation is undoubtedly genuine. Workers' compensation and sickness benefits are a common phenomenon in the sort of employment available locally. Students' leisure activities outside school time are limited mostly to the family arena or community-based sports, particularly soccer.

There are 425 students at Brunswick East. Despite dramatically declining numbers in some adjacent high schools, Brunswick East has managed to keep its numbers steady: a fact attributable, according to its senior staff and the parents interviewed, to the strength and reputation of its languages programme. Over thirty language backgrounds are represented in the school, the largest being Greek (21 per cent), Arabic (17 per cent), English (17 per cent), Italian (15 per cent), Turkish (13 per cent) and Vietnamese (9 per cent) and Portuguese (4 per cent). Eighty-three per cent of students are of non-English speaking background.

The number of students of Italian background in the school has dropped since a point in the 1960s and 1970s when they were the majority. This is reflected in the decline of the large and dynamic Italian parent evenings at the school during the 1970s. In socioeconomic terms, the Italian background group is now significantly divided, with some families living below the poverty line and others, by now, in the words of one of the teachers, 'probably more wealthy than they say'. The Greek-speaking community has also declined in numbers, reaching its high point at Brunswick just after the Italian speakers. Many of the Greek-speaking families remaining today are relatively poor, as the wealthier ones have moved out to the 'better' eastern suburbs. From the early 80s, significant numbers of Turkish- and Arabic-speaking background students entered the school. Most Turkish parents, the Turkish teacher reported, work in local factories, many on night shift. Eighty or 90 per cent have bought their own homes, often because both parents work very long hours. Twenty to 25 per cent of Turkish background students themselves work after school. In recent years there has been a trend on the part of the Turkish parents to move to outer suburbs where the real estate prices are cheaper. Some of these students still attend Brunswick East High School in order to continue their Turkish study, sometimes travelling for up to an hour each way, to and from school. The number of Turkish background students at Brunswick East has subsequently fallen. Indo-Chinese groups have been strongly represented in the most recent waves of migration.

The first language abilities of non-English speaking background students vary according to recency of arrival, although the mother tongue is spoken as the main domestic language even in many longer-established families. Second generation Greek, students move freely from one language to another, speaking English amongst themselves at school but moving into Greek, for example, to 'tell a secret'. Greek, according to the Greek teacher, is spoken to parents at home, but there they mostly go back to English whilst operating in peer culture with siblings. Dialect is often spoken at home, amongst the Italian students, for example, although the school teaches the 'standard' forms of the language.

Context of the Innovations

Over a twenty year period, everything about Brunswick East High School has changed. In the area of curriculum, this case study documents the school's response to cultural and linguistic diversity, focusing on the bilingual programme in Year 7 and the Languages Other Than English (LOTEs) programme. Curriculum change, however, needs to be set in the context of two dramatic institutional changes. The first was the public campaign to improve the physical amenities at the school, which were appallingly overcrowded and substandard two decades ago, reflecting Brunswick East's origins as a working-class girls' school. Now they are as good as at any public school in Victoria, with a gymnasium, drama and music centres, computer facilities, and so on. Old buildings were restored and extensive new buildings constructed.

Brunswick East High School

The second is the fact that Brunswick East was at the forefront of the community schools movement, as a member of the Brunswick Secondary Education Council (BRUSEC) cluster of schools which began meeting formally in 1977, in which a premium was put on establishing community connections, involving parents as much as possible in the school, providing curriculum relevant to community needs and introducing innovatory programmes in the areas of equal opportunity, 'migrant education' and peer tutoring, and a creche. The current principal was also involved in the establishment of the Sydney Road Community School, another member of BRUSEC. The multilingual newsletter *Ascolta*, published by several schools in the area, is an example of the attempt to inform and establish greater links with the community. It has received many awards acknowledging its important role as a school-community paper.

La Trobe University academic and an early, influential proponent of multicultural education and the 'community' languages movement, Marta Rado, referred to the school as an exemplary case study, in the 1977 book (with Claydon and Knight) *Curriculum and Culture: Schooling in a Pluralist Society*.[1] Rado had been involved in an earlier attempt at bilingual education in the school. With its wistful title, *A Mediterranean View of School*, Bill Hannan and Gianfranco Spinoso's 1982 book evoked a sense of the importance of linking school to the cultural aspirations of parents, by surveying attitudes of parents with children in BRUSEC schools.[2] Bill Hannan has since gone on to become Chairman of the Victorian State Board of Education. The now defunct Ministerial Advisory Committee on Multicultural and Migrant Education, which administered the federal allocations to Victoria under the Multicultural Education Program, funded various innovatory projects, including the 1983 booklet, *A New Life*. Chaired by Joe Lo Bianco, this committee saw the innovations at Brunswick East as one of the jewels in its crown, an exemplary school which it was very willing to publicize. Joe Lo Bianco has since gone on to write Australia's *National Policy on Languages* and administer the $28 million allocated annually to implement this policy from 1988 to 1990. A succession of dynamic principals with a keen eye to publicity as a means of assisting educational change, particularly June Engish and Gil Freeman, got the school involved in publications about its history and innovations (such as the book by Jim Lucas, *Languages Other Than English: Developments at Brunswick East High School*),[3] video productions (*Parent Participation in a Multicultural School; Australian is a Wide Word; Building Bridges, Alternatives: English as a Second Language; Cos School Sucks, Miss*), and the news media. These principals successfully plied connections with the Victorian Ministry of Education to draw special attention to the school. The school's innovations were the result of attracting supplementary funding available from the early 1970s: under the Disadvantaged Schools Program, the Multicultural Education Program and the Participation and Equity Program, all programmes very much reflecting the prevailing mood for specialist, 'compensatory' education. Brunswick East, in other words, has been at the centre of educational innovation in

Cultures of Schooling

Victoria for the past two decades, and some of the leading lights of educational reform in Australia have been closely associated with the school during this period. Its annual educational conferences, and their resulting publications, exemplify this input. In historical terms, it is a very significant place.

The school has a multicultural education policy to be found in the staff handbook which, as its point of departure, links the school to its constituent community. 'We are part of the Brunswick community which is also very ethnically diverse and affirm our intention to be a school which is truly part of its neighbourhood.' Building actively upon this context, and moving beyond the paradigm of disadvantage at the heart of compensatory education, the policy goes on to 'recognise this diversity as a source of strength and advantage which our school curriculum policies and practices needs to build on for the benefit of all our students'. Consequently, as a result of their experience at the school, 'all students should be able to communicate competently in a language or languages other than English, particularly those used in Brunswick and the students' own homes', and 'all students should understand the cultural origins of the other members of the school community, the role and effect of immigration in the development of our society and cultures which contribute to our common Australian heritage'. Linking students' life histories to the purpose of their schooling, 'all students should see their life experience and skills as being of value and of natural advantage as they grow as educated citizens in our school and wider community'.

Four languages other than English are offered in the LOTEs programme: Italian, Greek, Arabic and Turkish. These are compulsory in Years 7 to 10 and then offered as optional subjects through to Year 12. Students take the language of their family's background. Those without a background in one of the four languages must take Italian. In addition, there is a bilingual component in the English and Social Science programme (ESSPRO) in Year 7. In all, about 350 of the 425 students in the school are currently studying a LOTE. Of the sixty to sixty-five students who stay on to Year 12, thirty-five to forty continue with their LOTE. There are forty-four teachers in the school (including those in part-time positions), seven of whom teach languages other than English: three Italian, two Greek, one Arabic and one Turkish.

There are four English as a Second Language (ESL) teachers at Brunswick East. The ESL programme has changed from one wholly based on withdrawal classes to one where team and support teaching are the norm. There are four ESL teachers. This change, according to the school's ESL policy document, was made for a number of reasons. Many students saw withdrawal as a stigma, and were reluctant to miss their mainstream classes. On the other hand, mainstream subject teachers sometimes tended, mistakenly according to the preamble to the current ESL programme, to see the ESL class as a place to dispatch students with learning difficulties. At the same time, in a school with students largely of non-English speaking background, withdrawal meant inefficient and selective use of the ESL teachers' expertise. For example, students in the senior school often exhibit patterns of English usage that require attention for success at school, but these students would not have been eligible under the withdrawal system. The number of newer arrivals has also declined in recent years. First phase learners (new arrivals with little or no proficiency in English) all now undertake a special twenty week course at the Brunswick Language Centre before they enter Brunswick East High. The most pressing need has thus been perceived to be to assist students in dealing with English as a medium of instruction across the curriculum. As support/team teachers, the ESL staff now works with subject teachers adding language-based activities to mainstream curriculum areas, to make classwork more accessible. ESL teachers now work jointly with classroom teachers to modify texts, share the planning of assessment and, indeed, share overall responsibility for the classes that they jointly teach. The greatest difficulty in the new programme, it was reported, has been to find time to plan the team teaching. Perhaps the most significant positive side-effect has been to make mainstream teachers more aware of language issues. In addition, ESL is a full, independent subject in Years 11 and 12.

The school has never had an explicit sociocultural programme. Ethnic studies courses, for instance, the principal thought were an example of multi-cultural programmes which 'wander through different cultures', tending 'not to come to grips with the real cultural context of the students'. The belief that this alone could help different groups to understand each other, he felt was probably ill-founded. Understanding is something that 'happens in the class and in the playground', in handling the inescapable reality of cultural diversity. On the other hand, teachers testified to the importance of all aspects of curriculum reflecting the ethos of multiculturalism, especially subjects such as history and social science. This general sense of 'awareness' meant, for example, that a Year 9 history class looked at the Crusades from a Muslim as well as a Christian point of view. Year 8 social science, to give another example, includes work on Aborigines and immigration. This has entailed, as much as anything, 'a commitment on the part of the staff to educate ourselves' to the issues. The bilingual component of the Year 7 ESSPRO programme contains a section on 'survival' which looks at basic needs and includes a multicultural food day. One teacher said that although the emphasis on languages at the school was strong, on the sociocultural front 'I have a feeling we should be doing more'. Nevertheless, given the diversity of its student population, all teachers, students and parents attested to the fact that the school is a relatively harmonious place. When, as one teacher reported, there was a problem of racism last year — a gang of Lebanese boys picking on Chinese boys — it shocked everyone because, she maintained 'it just doesn't happen here'. She went on to explain:

> Everyone is in the same boat; it's all wogs versus the world here. Respect for the differences in people's cultures is not just a platitude here. It's something we live because of the language programme and because of the attitudes of the people who teach in the school.

In wider structural terms the school 'enjoys a tremendous sense of community' attributable to the 'little things' such as a school bus which the community health service also uses, bringing community members in regularly to talk to the students, the creche on the site and school involvement in local council issues (they are currently involved with residents in lobbying to have a local street closed to traffic). There are four ethnic aides, speaking Turkish, Arabic, Greek and Vietnamese, whose job it is to assist in the classroom and liaise between students, parents and the school: as interpreters at parent information nights, by being part of the parent associations, and so on.

The principal described the style of management in the school as 'consultative', relying heavily on committees. There is an administrative committee and a curriculum committee to develop school-based policies. These feed into the school council — a body of review, rather than one that initiates policies. This is not to say the principal has, in his view, a diminished directive leadership role. 'Where there's something important, I go for it.' Negotiating within democratic structures as a leader is 'a subtle, time-consuming business'. In any event, 'very few schools are able to have school councils take an active role, unless they are middle-class'.

The school prides itself on having a good relationship with parents, and all the parent positions on the school council are filled, representing a range of the ethnic groups in the community. The most important role of the school council, the principal felt, was as a source of information and for providing comment on school plans. The committees come into their own when there are problems requiring resolution. From the point of view of one of the teachers, democratic modes of decision making gave them more control of curriculum, but they were also time consuming and sometimes meant delays in decision making.

Evaluating his own leadership role, the principal admitted that 'it could have been different without me'. He said he publicly and clearly stated an educational philosophy on cultural and linguistic pluralism, and that was probably very important. 'People need to know that there is a continuity of purpose; language teachers and parents can sometimes feel besieged.'

In the selection of staff the principal explained that he had some 'recruiting powers' albeit limited to suggesting to certain people that they should apply when a vacancy came up. If a staff member was unsympathetic to the needs of parents and students, people would register dissatisfaction immediately.

All of the more senior English-speaking background teachers interviewed said that their ability to deal with cultural and linguistic pluralism had been learnt 'totally on the job'. Several of the younger teachers and non-English speaking background teachers had had specialist training, including linguistics, ESL method and multicultural studies. Teachers who had themselves migrated or who were from minority language backgrounds found that their own personal experience and community contacts were invaluable resources. 'As a migrant', said one, 'you realize all the difficulties of migrants.' Most teachers felt that there was no substitute to 'constant immersion' in a school such as this as a way of coming to grips with the issues. Even a social science teacher who had herself gone to a school quite similar to Brunswick East declared that 'nothing can compare to this school'. Nothing in her teaching experience before coming to Brunswick East had prepared her for 'the shell-shock of getting back into a school like this'.

Teachers testified to the school changing their lives in a profound sense. The principal, for example, said that his work had consumed and challenged him. He now knew much more about value structures and spent a good deal of time thinking about different world views. He had never been xenophobic or unaware, but he was 'a richer person' for having worked at the school. Another English-speaking background teacher spoke lyrically about her life in the school:

> The reality is that we live in a melting pot. It's a really exciting and important place and we should be revelling in it. We have this wonderful opportunity. It's like New York at the turn of the century. It's vibrant and exciting, and rather than putting a brake on this, schools should be making the most of it.

Others testified to the difficulties of working at a school like Brunswick East. The practical demands of diversity 'can be pretty overwhelming at times'. 'Many kids have enormous language difficulties, and for the first time this year I've encountered kids who do not want to learn English; some of our kids need such intensive teaching that it really gets you down.'

The Innovations in Practice: The Bilingual Social Science Programme

The most distinctive and sustained innovations at Brunswick East High are the two programmes in languages other than English. One is the bilingual component of ESSPRO which has a block of ten fifty-minute periods in Year 7, six periods for English and four for social science. Two periods of the social science are taught bilingually. The other is the offering of four languages other than English for compulsory study until Year 10. In Years 7 and 8 language is taught for three periods per week, in Years 9 and 10 for four periods and in Years 11 and 12 five periods. Those whose mother tongue is not one of the four on offer, must join the Italian programme in Years 7 to 10, and each student's bilingual ESSPRO must be the same as the language they are studying.

Bilingual teaching was introduced into the ESSPRO programme (which had been running for some years) in 1986. The teaching of community languages other than English, however, has a much longer history at Brunswick East. Italian was introduced in 1968, Greek in 1973, Turkish in 1975 and Arabic in 1981. Whilst bilingual ESSPRO was innovatory as a programme and

Cultures of Schooling

pedagogy, languages teaching has by and large been traditional in its pedagogy. The unique thing about Brunswick East in the Australian context was that it is compulsory in Years 7 to 10 and supported by bilingual ESSPRO in Year 7.

There had been an experimental bilingual programme earlier at Brunswick East. Marta Rado from La Trobe University began a research project at the school in 1972 in which she organized a Year 10 group of two Greek, two 'Australian', two Italian background and two Turkish background students into a bilingual class held during lunchtime. There would be a discussion topic, and a sentence in English would be translated into Greek, Italian and so on. This was tape-recorded and books in the various languages were produced. From this, eventually, Marta Rado's books *Animals, Transportation, My City* and *Aborigines* were produced. In the following year, however, there were problems because of lack of resources. The teachers, it was reported, had to produce their own materials in a hurry and were not supported with release time or subsidies to do this. The school's one language teacher taught Italian. The students were at very different language levels. But the programme ended basically because there was no money provided for it.

The two teachers who implemented the bilingual component of ESSPRO in 1986 — one a social science teacher and then ESSPRO coordinator and one an Italian teacher and the original and current bilingual programme coordinator — testified to the way innovations such as this are frequently sparked by available supplementary funding. The former said 'It started with the two of us being called into the office on almost the last day of school several years ago, and the principal saying that there was this funding available for bilingual ... would we be interested? He said he had thought of targeting social science.'

This seemed an interesting thing to be doing, so they agreed. The principal certainly played an initiating role, but, said the coordinator, 'I don't know what would have happened if I'd said I wasn't interested'. 'Somewhere along the line the principal applied for funding, and probably raised it with the curriculum committee; there was never any real discussion.' In fact, the proposal was part of a joint Post Primary Bilingual Education Project, representing three schools — Preston Girls', Collingwood Education Centre and Brunswick East — and the principal and the steering committee for the project had to lobby hard to get the funds, including getting people to write to their local Members of Parliament, the Minister for Education and the Victorian Premier.

The current Manager of the State Multicultural Education Coordinating Unit, who was referred to by one teacher as central in initiating the project, pointed out:

> the network made it, whether it be at Richmond Community Centre or the MES [Multicultural Education Service]. They were concerned

that there was some initiatives at primary level, but nothing in transition. And there's still nothing much happening — there's next to no emphasis on post-primary.

I knew a teacher at Preston Girls' who was battling on. I knew Collingwood and Brunswick East. I wasn't tied to a classroom so I got them together.

There had been programmes in transitional bilingual education in a few primary schools for several years, including the Collingwood Education Centre, which had primary programmes since 1981, and this had interested people in doing something at the post-primary level. There was a belief of LOTE teachers that English could only be taught if students were literate in their first language.

They got support from the union because at the time they were negotiating their special needs funding, and so they got some 'siphoned off' and got additional funding from the state. 'Special needs was always an area where the union could decide the priorities. It was enough to get each school under way.'

The submission set out in some detail the objectives and rationale of the broader project. It frames itself within the state government's commitments given in policy and election platforms — or lack of commitment, because 'the rhetoric is not being supported by resources'. It claimed that the 'lack of support by the government for community languages and bilingual education in state schools has future implications for the ability of schools to respond to their communities'. The committee saw itself as implementing Ministerial Paper No. 6, *Curriculum Development and Planning in Victoria*, and building on bilingual and LOTEs programmes in primary schools, and LOTEs programmes in post-primary schools.

The submission, which was prepared by a committee made of school, regional and departmental representatives who met regularly during 1985, was accompanied by letters of support from community and parent organizations, staff, unions and individuals. It also referred to ministerial documents and Commonwealth reports, evaluations of existing programmes, feasibility studies and academic research, stressing the importance and value of language maintenance and second language learning programmes. The aims of the bilingual project included: to further the development of English and the targeted home language to enhance educational life chances; to offer more languages in the schools to promote multiculturalism; to enhance individuals' cognitive development by continuing it in the first language; to overcome the blockages to learning for NESB students; to respond to community needs and encourage community involvement; to provide integrated programmes, models and materials in bilingual education; and to establish a cluster network which facilitated consultation and development.

The plan was to ask for additional staffing on top of the commitment already made in the school to provide most of the staff and inservicing, and to develop materials and evaluation procedures from existing resources. Apart from the individual school's requirements, the submission requested a teacher coordinator to work in all three schools to facilitate the project.

The lobbying bore fruit. Brunswick East, along with Preston Girls' and Collingwood Education Centre, as the result of a detailed and planned submission, embarked on bilingual programmes initiated together on the basis of a special supernumerary staffing arrangement. (The other two schools have since abandoned their programmes, and Brunswick East's plans to extend the programme into Year 8 or other subjects were postponed indefinitely when projected additional teacher allocations were not forthcoming.) With the extra funding, the coordinator was initially given thirty periods to work out a programme. She reported that other coordinators, such as those who filled in while she was on maternity leave, have suffered in subsequent years for not having had that opportunity. There would also need to be an extra two staff allocations to teach the programme, she added.

The coordinator visited Preston Girls', but found the model they were beginning to use there — bilingual support within the general classroom across a range of curriculum areas — did not necessarily suit Brunswick East which had fewer, larger language groupings. In addition, at Brunswick East they wanted to reach all the students.

It was decided that no more than two periods could be allocated to the bilingual element of ESSPRO at Brunswick East because there was only one teacher each for Arabic and Turkish in the whole school, and their timetable would not stretch beyond this. A number of people reported that timetabling, in fact, was the biggest hurdle in getting the programme started, with some of the social science teachers regarding bilingual as an extra, outside the normal parameters of their job. The coordinator, in fact, had to demand that timetabling changes be made in order for the programme to go ahead. The school agreed to this.

The stated rationale for ESSPRO has cognitive, social and developmental aspects. 'Building on the conventional modes of bilingual discourse many of our students are involved in through their home and community life', bilingual teaching is aimed at 'enhancing the vocabulary power available to all students when dealing with a social studies concept'. This will also 'strengthen the English language through focusing on language meanings from a range of viewpoints'. Socially, the privileging of 'mother-tongue languages will lead to an increase in the individual and community's self-esteem'. It is evidence of 'the respect the school shows for the culture and language of the home and community groups'. Developmentally, language learning in the mainstream subject context of social science 'will facilitate communication skills and the ability of the individual to describe experiences'.

As a background, a number of official documents were recognized to have influenced the development of this rationale, including the 1984 *National Language Policy* of the Senate Standing Committee on Education and the Arts (1984)[4], the 1985 Karmel Report[5], the 1985 Blackburn Report[6], the 1985 departmental document *The Teaching of Languages Other Than English in Victorian Schools*[7], and the 1985 Ministerial Paper No. 6: *Curriculum Development and Planning in Victoria*[8]. The last of these, in particular, stated that:

> while the main medium of instruction for students will be English, whenever possible the Education Department will assist schools in developing resources for bilingual programmes to enable students who speak another language to continue using that language for some learning in other subjects.

The task of implementing the programme at Brunswick East, according to its initiators, began with comparing the language of the social science inputs with the languages programmes and working out viable language levels. This was particularly important for the Italian class with so many who couldn't speak Italian. 'We had to stop and coordinate the syllabuses.' The social science content was determined by what they had happened to be doing in social science in previous years. 'We really didn't have time to do a complete revision.'

The topics studied in ESSPRO are, in order, 'Me', 'Animals', 'Food' and 'Survival'. The 'Me' unit asks 'Who am I?', 'Where do I come from?' and gets students to research and present their family tree. The 'Animals' unit covers classification, animals in literature and art, the zoo, endangered species, conservation, pets and evolution. The 'Survival' unit begins by examining basic needs, including health and nutrition, a geographical component on climate, soil and habitat, and a multicultural food day. This is followed by components on the survival of Early Man and then a study of an historical theme relevant to each language group, such as the Roman Empire for the Italian group.

LOTE and social science teachers are allocated one period per week to plan and prepare materials for the programme. There had been a big fight to get the planning time. 'Certain sections of the administration didn't acknowledge that last year', according to one teacher, but 'it's essential', she maintained. There were also regular voluntary bilingual steering committee meetings, after school and in the staff's own time, including people from right across the school.

The guidelines for curriculum preparation developed by those involved in the bilingual programme at the school emphatically state that in bilingual ESSPRO 'we are not teaching language; we are teaching concepts'. Language teaching proper is the domain of the subject languages. For the two periods per week of bilingual ESSPRO, classes are team-taught by a social science and a language-trained teacher, the intention being to extend the work done in the other two social science periods. Teacher talk and all written materials are presented in two languages — in English by the social science teacher and the other language by the language teacher. In the programme's guidelines for the preparation of materials, it is recommended that teachers locate resources in

Cultures of Schooling

English and clarify the concepts in these; select the concepts according to the availability of resources, student interest and suitability; identify the language skills they wish to develop, such as reading, speaking, listening or writing; and then devise specific teaching activities to achieve these ends, such as discussion, cloze technique, numbered sentences or researching.

All ESSPRO curriculum development, in other words, is school-based. This, it was reported, is not without its drawbacks. 'It's one big, time-consuming, energy-draining scramble to produce materials.' The pressure has eased off a bit now 'because there's a reasonable bank of materials built up'. The method of development was said to depend very much on circumstances. 'The materials I use in the Arabic programme are basically my own, translated by the Arabic teacher or an aide', explained a social science teacher, 'but the Turkish teacher has a vast bank of already translated stuff — but translation also changes the material to make it more appropriate for the students and has the added benefit that the language teachers become more aware of the possibilities and directions of the programme'.

An example of the relationship between bilingual ESSPRO and the remaining ESSPRO taught by the social science teacher alone was given by one of the teachers:

> Billingual ESSPRO supports rather than duplicates the work. For example, in social science you look at wild animals and endangered species. In bilingual you look at the terms 'wild' and 'domestic', and then go on to do work on pets, which is a thing very close to kids' hearts. It allows a spread of things which are related.

On the other hand, a LOTE teacher explained how she would take language issues that arose in bilingual ESSPRO back to her language class for additional work.

In practice, however, there could be some contrast in what happened in each of the lessons. In a class where there were fewer students than the norm, each of whom had fairly good command of both English and the other language (being all native speakers), the teachers were able to develop both through activities involving classificatory skills as well as covering content. In another, very large, class where there was only one native speaker amongst a wide variety of language backgrounds, students did little more than vocabulary exercises with little emphasis on cognitive development or subject content.

Preparation and coordination between pairs of teachers, it was agreed, is essential. 'You have to sit down with the person you're working with', particularly in the early stages, and:

> work through who's going to do precisely what in the classroom, which bits will be in this language and which bits will be in that language; it's painstaking, it's annoying, but once you've got that going, you're on the way to the development of natural interchange.

Otherwise, in the classroom 'one of you is nervous and watching the other'. A social science teacher explained that this was a particular problem because she didn't know what was being said when it was not in English, and if there's a pause, she always wonders if it's because she should be saying something. Sometimes the other teacher would be telling the kids one thing and she'd be telling them something else, which only confused them. The key, it was reported, is detailed planning and putting a lot of energy into the working relationship. Movement of staff was viewed as particularly frustrating and wasteful of resources in these circumstances.

Ultimately, the success of the team-teaching arrangement was said to depend very much on the shared understandings of the teachers involved. When the Arabic teacher left, according to a social science teacher, they had a series of Arabic teachers and it took them until the end of the year 'to find the perfect teacher', who himself eventually chose to go and work at a primary school instead. The problem is that:

> it's more than your expertise in your particular subject — it's more a philosophy of education in general. This guy had an outlook that was very compatible with that of many of the teachers here. It takes time to establish the relationship with your co-teacher and until you do the lessons may function well in that they are fastidiously prepared but they don't work until the two of you reach that personal point.

It seemed that language teachers, familiar with a more traditional pedagogy, often effectively underwent 'retraining on an individual basis' through the inevitable process of 'discussion and demonstration' in the team-teaching context of the classroom. One language teacher, for example, was more used to providing knowledge to students than getting them talking or learning actively. As a result of becoming involved in bilingual ESSPRO, however, his own cultural assumptions about teaching were thrown into question. 'After one lesson where I asked them to get talking', said a social science team-teacher,

> he commented he'd found it very interesting because he never knew the kids thought that way.... Some community language teachers have gone through a very different education system and have extremely different values; making ESSPRO work often comes down to personal adaptability and a willingness to assess what you're doing and why you're doing it.

It was reported, however, that sometimes these cultural gaps are left as personal differences. The social science teacher lamented that 'You'd say "do this", but when you got into the classroom, something else would happen.'

This appeared to lead to less than fruitful situations where, for example, one of the team might view the exercise as a competition in which 'they tried to get in as much language as they could rather than seeing bilingual as a synthesis of the two'. Or, if they were unsympathetic, they viewed it as something they had to do 'so they just showed up and did it'.

Parents, it was reported, are minimally involved in the bilingual programme. 'Usually they respond with blank amazement when you mention it.' The 'Anglo' parents 'are usually very excited about it; the non-English speaking background parents are usually very keen once you've explained it'.

Assessment of bilingual ESSPRO is through project-based work, which is checked and re-checked until it is acceptable. According to one teacher, no tests are used. Reporting to parents is descriptive, in two languages. Apart from being on agreed topics, what goes on after this is essentially between the two classroom teachers because there are great differences between the classes. 'If bilingual is going to be successful it has to be seen by the kids as an area of opportunity, in other words, something that they don't think they can fail at.' There has been an attitude sometimes that 'bilingual is a bludge'. But 'time is so precious and there is pressure on the kids, not a pressure to avoid failing, but whether they want everyone to think this is the best they can do'. The biggest mistake you can make, it was asserted, is 'to think that if a kid scratches a pencil across the page then that's good enough, because this makes the kid think of it as a bludge'. Other ESSPRO teacher said they used 'topic tests'.

The Innovations in Practice:
Teaching Languages Other Than English (LOTEs)

Taking the LOTE programme at Brunswick East as a whole, a number of overarching intentions were expressed. The most mentioned were language maintenance and self-esteem. When she first arrived at the school, one of the teachers said, 'a lot of kids refused to speak their own language because they were ashamed of it'. The presence of their languages in the school, she believed, 'maintains the prestige of the language; the kids learn a value within themselves, but they also get an appreciation of their parents'. The principal linked the LOTE programme to his conception of the ideal school-community relationship. 'People learn when they're involved, when they feel respected, when they have integrity.' Ultimately, if the school succeeds, it will manifest itself in 'the feeling that the community is healthy', the 'multicultural vision of people living in communities that all contribute to the broader community, giving it strength and confidence'.

The coordinator stressed, on the other hand, the relation of developing first language and English language skills, but this was less prominent amongst staff responses to the overall role of the LOTE programme. And when it came to broad learning objectives, one of the previous social science members of the ESSPRO team said that these goals were never spelt out really clearly but she 'gathered that it was just a matter of facilitating learning because, supposedly, learning is best done in their first language'. And for another, bilingual ESSPRO:

> helps extend the concepts that are being learnt in social science, but equally it dignifies both languages it is taught in. You get some kids who think their home language is blah. Others, because they can function in their home language, don't think they need to learn English. This shows you need both.

The LOTE programme, according to the principal, however, did not imply any imperative to maintain culture. 'Culture is always being formed and reformed; there's no such thing as pure Greek culture.' He believed that culture was always being modified in relation to the mainstream and never static. When it came to culture, he insisted, schools could not 'make it happen'. As a principal, he felt he was not in a position to make decisions about the maintenance or not of other people's cultures. 'Kids are volatile and can't be treated in an authoritarian way, particularly at this school; we have to think with them, alongside them.'

In contrast, the Turkish teacher thought language maintenance was inherently desirable because it was a means of promoting cultural maintenance and family unity. Children could thereby communicate effectively with older family members, thus reducing the risk of serious intergenerational conflict. He cited the case of a friend who had said he didn't mind if his child did not learn Turkish but who is 'now regretting it'. Children, he added, need to be aware of traditional Turkish family and cultural values if they are to return to Turkey, often to villages, to live. A female student interviewed, soon to return to Turkey herself, also made this point on the value of learning Turkish at school. The Greek language teacher, in spirit, concurred with this view of cultural maintenance:

> I strongly believe in it. When I came to Australia, the first thing the teacher told us was 'Now you are in Australia, you have to forget where you come from if you want to learn English.' That's all bullshit to me. It's absolute rubbish, because I've managed to learn English and not forget my background. Australian culture is not as rich. A lot of people believe you can choose from different cultures: what is good and what is bad. But Greek culture is more than souvlaki. I'm not a religious person, but religion is part of our culture. Others who do not have this are jealous, for example at Greek Easter time when we have special food at school.

An English-speaking background ESSPRO teacher also argued that cultural maintenance was essential but only justifiable in a context of cultural pluralism:

Cultural maintenance is incredibly important because it is tied up with a person's dignity. But cultural maintenance can only be effective when you are maintaining more than one culture at a time, not just the Anglo-Saxon culture or one other language or group. It's got to be more than that, otherwise you get a kind of arrogance. What's good here is that obviously we think it's valuable to be Greek *and* Lebanese *and* Turkish *and* Chinese.

Divergences in pedagogical approach were also in evidence at Brunswick East. Generalizing broadly, several staff said that the LOTE programme at the school employs a more traditional pedagogy than other subject areas such as English and social science. For example, there is greater use of textbooks and disciplined, formal learning, such as of grammar and other language conventions. In one case, for example, textbooks from the homeland were used. One teacher saw this encapsulated in the difference between the inquiry-based philosophy of modern social science teaching and the more teacher-centred approaches of traditional foreign language teaching. Several of the language teachers complained that it was hard to get on with the language when the kids were not taught grammar in English.

According to the deputy, however, there is tolerance amongst the staff of these sorts of differences. (During the course of this study the deputy became the acting principal while the principal was seconded to the Ministry, but for convenience we will continue to refer to them in their former positions.) The reason for the more conservative approach seemed to have a lot to do with a teacher's own educational and cultural background. But it was also said that 'the parents often appreciate the traditional style', and it's 'probably good for the kids, such as the Arabic and Turkish kids'. One teacher commented, on the other hand, that some of the students found the traditional teaching style in language difficult to handle. Yet one of the students suggested that, compared to the Department's Saturday morning language schools or community-run schools, both of which she had experienced, language was 'taught easier' at Brunswick East. An Italian language teacher saw her pedagogy as a necessary compromise:

Grammar. Oh yes! Once upon a time we would have a lesson on 'The Definite Article'. That was boring. Now I try to teach grammar in context. Even in Year 7 you have to teach grammar. Italian is a very inflected language. It is more difficult with less grammar taught in English these days, but they respond well.

A senior lesson in Italian involved constant reference to aspects of grammar by this teacher, to which the students did respond well, and she kept an old grammar text by her side.

When it came to assessment, there were also differences. One of the language teachers reported that he has two main exams in every year, extending their length over Years 7 to 10 and oriented to the Victorian Certificate of Education (VCE) in Year 12. In the ESSPRO classes, some of the teachers do not give exams, but it was generally accepted that the parents were worried that if there were no exam, students did not study.

The learning styles of students, according to the deputy, are adaptable, although he believed that students of non-English speaking backgrounds often prefer 'a more conservative style'. He gave as an example, the new Victorian Certificate of Education maths syllabus which focuses on problem-solving and requires students to approach maths as active investigators. The Vietnamese students would, he suggested, 'prefer to be taught with the rules on the board, and in highly organized classes'. As someone closely involved with the development of the new syllabus, he viewed this as a challenge because 'we should be teaching in a way that does not produce rote responses; they should fit maths into their life, think about real problems and put all the bits together'. There were always exceptions, one teacher pointed out, such as one outspoken, independent Vietnamese kid. But 'he was rare; most have a narrow view of education'. Another teacher had reservations about imposing the cultural presuppositions of her preferred teaching style:

> I think I failed one class because I tried to teach them using lots of student participation. They didn't like it. Perhaps it would have been better for them if I taught them the way they wanted, although they did start to shift by the end. They think they do more work when it is teacher-centred. This is culturally related. But, as the new VCE is much more student-centred, they are going to have to be pushed more toward that style if they are going to succeed.

Parents attending a Vietnamese parent information night, although obviously happy with Brunswick East High, said that the most disturbing things about Australian education generally were a lack of emphasis on instilling solid moral values such as respect for elders and teachers, and too weak an emphasis on 'hard' academic disciplines, particularly maths. 'They put maths on a pedestal', said the deputy, 'because they see it as a path to lucrative careers'. And at this information night, certainly the area that concerned most of these parents was the new maths syllabus. On the school council, non-English speaking background parents also express a traditional view of education. The Turkish parents on the council, for example, are most interested in stricter discipline and the re-introduction of compulsory uniforms. Parents have also been instrumental in insisting that grades be given, rather than alternatives such as goal-based, descriptive assessment.

One of the most distinctive features of the whole languages offered at Brunswick East is that they are compulsory in Years 7 to 10. Indeed, according to the principal, the very fact of making it compulsory had helped make it successful. It 'was just accepted as part of the routine; if there was choice then they'd desert in droves'. The variety of languages on offer, according to the deputy, was a 'nice contrast' to making them compulsory; 'the kids are generally happy to be cajoled'. The most murmurings are from non-Italian language background students in the Italian class, but the school's stated policy on this will remain, he said, although the school was looking to introduce Vietnamese if it could find a teacher and the resources and fit it into the curriculum. The principal's attempts to have the school classified as a specialist language school would allow them to address these issues more appropriately, he believed, but as yet the Ministry had not approved this move, particularly as declining numbers in the region and school amalgamations were of a greater concern.

Evaluation

As for evaluation of the school's performance, the principal said he was 'not good at ongoing evaluation; evaluation works better through informal discussion'. There are no formal procedures except the curriculum committee which discusses problems. 'We talk to students after they leave the school, and most seem to settle into their first or second choice.' He added that of the fifty who left in 1988 only four or five are still 'footloose' a third of the way into the following year, while the others are, by and large, 'settled and happy'. According to one of the teachers, however, a general problem in a school like this is to 'lower one's expectations', to do 'what is reasonable'.

Very little racism, it was repeatedly reported, is to be found at the school. In the words of the principal, 'there's the occasional Anglo-Australian who rails against the wogs', but generally 'they don't identify as a besieged minority group'. As one teacher said, even when racism does appear in word only, 'it's not even really racism because while the kid's going on about "wog bastards", he'll be sitting next to his Greek or Syrian mates'. One of the teachers commented that 'despite the representation of so many cultures, they integrate very well'. Another person who had been at the school for most of her teaching career said there had been significant friction twenty years ago, but not now; 'they all blend in very well'.

Commenting that there was some conflict about the bilingual ESSPRO programme, which was 'underneath but never really surfaced', some people, according to one of the team members, called for some sort of evaluation in its second year of operation. But they said they were unsure of how to do it. In the words of one person, 'it is hard to know what the possibilities of the programme are'. Perhaps the programme could have been implemented better but she wasn't sure how. 'There's been no systematic attempt to evaluate whether the programme really helps kids, nor to modify its operation if we felt we could do it better; we have relied on other people's research and justifications.' It was explained that this is in part because it is hard to get beyond the day-to-day demands of teaching to consider these sorts of questions. In any event, 'with teaching, you can't see the results of what you do straight away — they take years to have the full effect'. But 'because it starts and stops in Year 7, its achievements have to be limited'. Another person put this more strongly. 'It's a good foundation for something that goes nowhere; until you get the staffing situation sorted out. . . .'

Teachers' own professional appraisals of the bilingual component of ESSPRO pointed to a degree of hesitation about its success in meeting its concept objectives:

> The bilingual content is meant to be an extension of the rest of the ESSPRO course. But as it turns out I'm not so happy with the content. I would have liked it to have a much clearer social science method, using concepts, and so on. From the beginning, the programme was seen more as an extension of the language programme, which is fine, but I thought it would be more concerned with helping kids' understanding of the social science content.

Too often, another teacher reported, there is a gap between the type of material offered — which can be too easily seen as 'doing animals', for example — and proper social science skills such as classification. 'I feel frustrated at times because it is meant to be social science taught bilingually; for people who are social science trained, the method is really quite important, and it is upsetting to see things like posters with just the animals named in two languages.' With a language emphasis, 'the work tends to be a bit too simple', partly because the teachers still need to be taught what the programme is about. One student reflected on the level of the content: 'I thought it was good but I got bored with animals'. This was further reinforced by another teacher:

> Over the last few years, the bilingual programme has come to be seen as part of the language programme, which is wrong, because what goes on in language compares with what goes on in English whereas the bilingual programme is trying to teach kids something else in that language. There was a lot of trouble with the timetable at the end of last year because we couldn't get the administration to see that bilingual was not a separate area but two periods out of ESSPRO. If you lose sight of that — social science taught bilingually — then these two periods may as well be absorbed into language.

On the other hand, one teacher felt the programme worked because 'the students have a strong grasp of the concepts taught in ESSPRO' when she teaches them in social science and English in Year 8. As indicated above, in practice the lessons vary between having a conceptual or cognitive basis and being at times little more than vocabulary exercises.

One of the language teachers saw the language outcomes of ESSPRO as paramount, and if it came to a choice between bilingual and normal language teaching, he considered the latter to be more important. Another language teacher likewise stated that the main benefit of bilingual ESSPRO was that it lifted language abilities in her language class. Another still, maintained that 'at least it gives kids access to their own language for another two more periods'. Improvement in English as a result of the programme, however, was 'difficult to measure'. But most teachers believed that even in the class where students from a variety of languages were learning in a third language there were appreciable benefits, even though they were not able to offer any clear evidence of this.

The least equivocal assessment of the ESSPRO and languages programmes were of their social outcomes. It can become 'an opening up'. 'You see the kids in entirely different lights and discover talents you may not see elsewhere.' In Arabic, commented one teacher, the unit on the family had involved little more than translating. But in Turkish, they told her all about why certain relations are called certain things. 'The kids brought their own experiences to bear in social science, and that was tremendous.' More generally it was believed that, 'when these kids come around to educating their own kids, they'll have a different set of values because of experiences like this'. The principal felt that, in the long term, the whole cluster of innovations around language at the school have had 'a centring effect; the school has a clear identity and the students know this'. Parents and students also attested to this.

There were repeated calls from the staff interviewed for bilingual teaching in a wider range of subjects and more than for just two periods a week in one year. Maths and science were most frequently mentioned as crucial areas of need. In particular, Year 8 bilingual science was considered necessary. They realized, however, that even though 'the will is there, there's not the means'. All teachers interviewed believed that if this expansion could take place — if, for example, the school became a specialist language school — then many of the shortcomings of their offerings could be resolved.

In evaluating the success of his language teaching, the Turkish teacher thought the final school examination results were the ultimate arbiter. Eighty to 90 per cent of Turkish students go on to study Turkish to the end of school (this year only three have not) and in his fourteen years at Brunswick East only two students have failed Turkish at Victorian Certificate of Education (or, its predecessor, the Higher School Certificate) level. Indeed, he argued, one of the main values of learning Turkish was the marks students got that contributed to their final school credential. He insisted that it was very important that Turkish was a Group 1 subject because this means Turkish can be a really useful subject in helping Turkish students get the marks to go to university. (The Victorian Certificate of Education is currently divided into Group 1 and Group 2 subjects, with the former considered more 'academic' and prestigious, and carrying more weight in qualifying for tertiary education. This distinction is being eliminated, partly because of arbitrary divisions: Macedonian, for example, is a Group 2 subject.) Turkish became a Group 1 subject, he said, because he and another teacher made a submission before applications closed in 1976. There are currently 150 students doing Turkish in Year 12 across Victoria, and he believed 90 per cent of these made it into university, in part the result of the high marks they got in Turkish.

There is no other mainstream school in Victoria teaching Turkish at Year 12 level, according to the Turkish teacher, so all the remaining students are studying at the Saturday schools. This teacher felt the Saturday schools were less satisfactory because there was less time available (only three hours); they also frequently involved students travelling long distances; they disrupted weekend family life; and only 25 per cent of Turkish teachers at these schools were registered as teachers.

A Greek teacher thought an important outcome of his programme was to have taught the students grammar, which helped them in English, and to get them to write essays, even at Year 7 level, which they are not asked to do in other subjects.

Most of the opposition to the innovative responses of Brunswick East High to cultural and linguistic pluralism has centred around timetabling and workload. There was opposition when Arabic was introduced, the principal noted, because it meant stretching staff. He had to argue strongly for it on cultural and educational grounds. Also, members of other faculties sometimes grumble that languages get a special deal, as some class sizes are very small. This was used in an argument last year that other class sizes should also be smaller. As one teacher said, 'they have twenty-five kids in an English B class in Year 12, so how can we justify having two teachers for four kids in the Year 7 Turkish bilingual class?' But generally, the staff, in the words of the deputy, 'recognize that we trade on our languages; this keeps our numbers up'. There was also pressure from systems administrators to rationalize inefficient teaching situations. Said one teacher:

> the systems people are prepared to take the credit, but every year we have to go through the same process of fighting for your staff. It devalues in your own mind what you've been doing. I know that some people are very, very bitter about it, and that can make for divisiveness in many areas around the school. How often do you have to prove that you've got a good thing going?

Forced amalgamation with other local secondary schools with dramatically declining numbers, it was feared, could adversely affect the teaching of languages at the school (a situation which will be exacerbated, the principal said, by the decision to allow the establishment of private Greek community schools in the area). Nevertheless it was thought likely by a number of key staff that both bilingual ESSPRO and the languages programme had an assured future. The programmes had been established as an important part of the school's structure, not as a marginal experiment, and a degree of planning had gone into this to ensure their centrality. There was a temptation, however, according to the principal, to set up a specialist ESL class against languages to cater for the influx of Vietnamese students, instead of them doing Italian, which would end the compulsory language other than English element in Years 7 to 10.

The 1989 Year 12 cohort at Brunswick East is 92 per cent of the size of the 1987 Year 10 cohort. This represents an above average retention rate in the post-compulsory years, although the figure is distorted somewhat by new students joining the school in the senior years, some for its language offerings. Of the fifty-two students who completed Year 12 at Brunswick East in 1988, sixteen, or 30.1 per cent, were deemed by the Victorian Curriculum and Assessment Board to have 'satisfactorily completed the Year 12 course of study'.

Eleven of the fifty-two students completing Year 12 in 1988 attempted and passed the mainstream English course: two in the 60 to 69 marks bracket and nine in the 50 to 59 marks bracket. Fourteen students failed, with eleven getting below 39 marks. Eighteen students undertook and completed the descriptively assessed English B, which cannot count in a score for tertiary entrance. Nine students attempted Alternative English-ESL. One failed, six scored in the 60 to 69 marks range and two above 70.

All ten students attempting Australian history failed. All eight students attempting accounting failed. Two out of eleven students passed legal studies; eight students were in the 0 to 34 range. Three out of the five politics students attained less than 39 per cent. Nine of the eighteen students attempting art, passed; of these, seven were in the 50 to 59 range and two in the 60 to 69 range. In graphic communication, five out of eleven passed, all five of whom were in the 50 to 59 range. Five out of eighteen passed textiles, four in the 50 to 59 range and one in the 60 to 69 range.

Of the fifty-two students, eighteen attempted mathematics; eight passed. Five out of eight students attempting the more advanced additional mathematics B passed, all in the 50 to 69 range. One out of sixteen students passed biology; nine out of sixteen passed chemistry, six of whom were in the 50 to 59 band; three out of six passed physics, two in the 50 to 59 range and one in the 60 to 69 range.

With the exception of one student's chemistry mark which was in the 70 to 79 range, the only results above 70 marks were in Alternative English-ESL (two out of nine students), Turkish (six out of nine), Greek (one out of eight) and Arabic (two out of eight). In the case of Turkish, the contrast in the span of results for individual students, from Turkish to their other subjects, is quite remarkable. This can in part be explained by the special advantage Brunswick East students have, competing only against students attending the Saturday morning classes. No student failed Turkish; three out of eight failed Arabic; three out of six failed Italian and three out of eight failed Greek.

Notes

1   CLAYDON, L., KNIGHT, T. and RADO, M., *Curriculum and Culture: Schooling in a Pluralist Society*, George Allen and Unwin, Sydney, 1977.
2   HANNAN, B. and SPINOSO, G., *A Mediterranean View of School*, BRUSEC/Hodja, Richmond, Victoria, 1982.
3   LUCAS, J., *Languages Other than English: Developments at Brunswick East High School.*
4   SENATE STANDING COMMITTEE ON EDUCATION AND THE ARTS, *A National Languages Policy*, Canberra, 1984.
5   QUALITY OF EDUCATION REVIEW COMMITTEE (Karmel, P., Chairman), *Quality of Education in Australia*, Australian Government Publishing Service, Canberra, 1985.
6   BLACKBURN, J., Discussion Paper, *Ministerial Review of Post Compulsory Schooling*, Melbourne, 1985.
7   VICTORIAN DEPARTMENT OF EDUCATION, *The Teaching of Languages Other Than English in Victorian Schools*, Department of Education, Melbourne, 1985.
8   VICTORIAN DEPARTMENT OF EDUCATION, Ministerial Paper Number 6: *Curriculum Development and Planning in Victoria*, Department of Education, Melbourne, 1985.

Chapter 5

'Different Paths We'll Tread': The Translators' and Interpreters' Course at Burwood Girls' High School

> An Interpreting, Translating and Multicultural Studies Course was conducted at Burwood Girls' High School, in Sydney's inner western suburbs from 1986 to 1988. Available in Cantonese, Greek, Italian, Turkish and Vietnamese, the course covered the final two years of secondary school. As an alternative, school-based 'Other Approved Studies' subject which could not count in the calculation of a tertiary entrance score (unlike the traditional language programmes also run at the school), the course was aimed at less 'academically inclined' students.

The Locality

Burwood is an older, established suburb, some twelve kilometres west of Sydney's business district, just past the penumbra where narrow streets and terrace houses have given way to leafy avenues, spacious gardens and the seventy-odd year-old 'Federation' style brick bungalows now achieving 'sought-after' status. There are several more or less exclusive private schools in the vicinity. By contrast, there is a significant number of multi-storey blocks of rented flats and home units, a large shopping centre, and a considerable commercial zone.

The locality from which the school draws its students, however, takes in the suburbs of Ashfield, Summer Hill, Haberfield, Croydon, Croydon Park and only part of Burwood. The first two of these are closer to the inner city and are situated on the railway line and the main highways west from Sydney. There is a predominance of flats, home units and smaller semi-detached and terrace houses; with a good sprinkling of light industry: a biscuit factory, for example, towers over the main road. The former principal of Burwood Girls' High School observed that it is from these first two suburbs that the school's population is drawn most. The other suburbs are more like the immediate Burwood vicinity in composition. An endemic housing shortage in Sydney has boosted property prices and rent, especially in these inner suburbs; this is compounded by rising home-loan interest rates. As families move out to settle in less expensive areas, this has produced a degree of what the school's former deputy principal referred to as 'transient, fluctuating population'.

According to the Australian Bureau of Statistics, 30.7 per cent of the population of Burwood was born in non-English speaking countries. Adding to this, of course, those born in Australia of non-English speaking background (NESB) migrant parents, would produce a much higher NESB percentage. The Commonwealth Employment Service has noted that South-East Asian and Arabic-speaking people are proportionately overrepresented among those registered as unemployed in Burwood. There is consequently, in the words of one teacher, 'a lot of movement related to jobs'.

The School

Opinion among the staff differed over the extent to which the demography of the school was representative of the local neighbourhood. The former principal maintained simply, 'This *is* Burwood to a large extent'. Another teacher, who concurred that the school was 'quite representative of the local area', remarked, however, that some of the students, especially Muslim girls, travel quite large distances, even from west of Parramatta (twelve kilometres further west), to attend this all-girls' school. One headteacher, who corroborated this, noted that the school was, in fact, in Croydon, where property was expensive, whereas students would come from 'the bottom end of Croydon', Fivedock, and the like. Also, as the age of local residents was older than the average, there were not so many with children of school age. One language teacher, who lives in the neighbourhood, observed that the wealthier people in the area tended to send their daughters to the private schools, of which there are a number nearby. Further, 'Because Strathfield [Girls' High School, several kilometres away] has an "academic" reputation, middle-class parents send their kids there. We get kids more from the Ashfield end.'

All of these processes; the shift of younger, working-class families to the outer western suburbs, the ageing of the population with the end of the post-war 'baby boom', and the funding-induced drift from state to private schools, have contributed to the falling rolls at Burwood Girls' High School, as at other state schools in the region. Enrolments have dropped from 927 in 1984, to 708 in 1989. The vast majority of students, some 78 per cent, are of non-English speaking background. These are spread across about thirty different language groups.

In 1985, when the interpreters' course, which is the focus of this examination of educational innovation at Burwood Girls', was initiated, the largest language group was Greek, with about 27 per cent of the school's population. The next was Italian, with 20 per cent — about the same as the proportion of students from English-speaking backgrounds (ESB). The various Chinese language groups, mainly Cantonese, comprised 9 per cent, and the Vietnamese speakers comprised 5 per cent. Since that time, there has been an increasing number of Arabic speakers, mainly Lebanese, and Spanish speakers, largely Latin Americans. There is also a growing group of 'Pacific Islanders' (now 8 to 10 per cent) from various language backgrounds, including Fijian Indians. There is a significant Turkish language group. Amongst the other language groups there are Yugoslavs, mainly Croatian, some Polish and Hungarian, a few Portuguese, a small number of Cambodian and Laotian girls, and several Koreans. The school is now beginning to receive students from Iran and Pakistan. There are also a few Aboriginal students at the school. 'Burwood girls from many lands' is the first line of the school song.

Most of the girls of Greek or Italian language backgrounds are 'second generation migrants': Australian-born children of immigrants. Some are third generation. These are the longer-standing immigrant groups, and have well-established communities in the area. The students of South-East Asian, Chinese, Arabic and Turkish backgrounds are mainly first generation. Virtually all the children from immigrant families speak their mother tongue at home. The former deputy, a language specialist, claimed that the second and even the third generation NESB students faced problems with English, and that many spoke their first language 'in a broken way'.

The parents of the Burwood pupils are predominantly working class; most families have both parents in the workforce. There is a significant proportion who are self-employed in occupations such as shopkeeping. They evince the hard toil and the fervent desire for a better life common to immigrants. For many in the more established groups, this has paid off. The former principal commented, 'Many of the families are classic "made good in a new country people" '. This can give an exaggerated appearance of social mobility. The previous deputy characterized the school population as 'middle class'. When asked the parents' occupations, she replied that they were largely in 'factory work' and 'sometimes shops'. Whereas the principal had expressed the viewpoint that 'There's not a lot of real poverty in this area and there's some people that are quite well off', one headteacher reflected, 'This is not a rich school — parents are manual workers or unemployed.'

Their type of accommodation would also in many cases reflect the recency of immigration. One teacher, commenting on this, noted that those of Greek background tend to live in bigger houses, and those of Asian background in rented accommodation. Another remarked that the Italian-speaking community were 'very proud of owning their own houses'. Many of the school's families live in 'rented high-rise dwellings', a number have Housing Commission accommodation.

The types of household depend upon many factors, including ethnic group. Those of Lebanese background are often in 'large nuclear families with married siblings'; the Islanders in 'extended groups'. According to the principal, 'There are rather more extended family units than in some other parts of Sydney: quite a lot of grandmas and aunties. . . .' One teacher, who stipulated that she has more to do with the 'welfare cases', noted that a lot live with brothers and sisters. In short, their forms of household cover, as one teacher put it, 'the whole range of society, including "disasters" '. The deputy referred to a lot of 'broken homes'. The principal pointed to a proportion of single mothers, distributed evenly across ethnic groups. She also acknowledged 'a large percentage of kids who come from pretty "stable" families'.

The leisure activities of the girls are heavily circumscribed by ethnic custom. The Muslim girls are usually closely supervised and discouraged from going out: their activities tend to revolve around the home and the family. They watch television and videos. The Chinese background girls study more at home. Few of the Muslim or Chinese background girls, for example, are to be found at the otherwise popular school discos; the 'Anglos' frequent these. The Islanders like 'hanging out at milk bars'. While nearly all of the girls *like* going to the pictures, parties, concerts and discos, many are limited to family group activities.

There are fifty-one teaching staff at Burwood Girls': thirty-seven women and fourteen men. Staff numbers are being reduced in line with falling enrolments and further state government cutbacks. Six men and three women are headteachers. The principal and deputy are both women. It was the popular wisdom among the school administration that staff were extraordinarily ethnically diverse. The former principal described this as 'a great advantage' and 'a fortunate accident'. A check through the current staff, however, showed only about 10 per cent of them to be of NESB.

Staff described the school as reasonably well equipped. The main building is of about World War I vintage and is currently being repainted and carpeted; it looks overdue for it. The new principal was welcomed in a staff common room housed in a demountable 'temporary' building which has apparently been there several decades. The grounds appear adequate, if not extensive, with their asphalt surface and wooden benches shaded by plenty of trees; but in common with many girls' schools there are no playing fields. The large and spacious library, a legacy of the 1970s expansion in funding, is, in the former principal's assessment, 'obviously above the minimum requirement, but not miles above it'. The librarian lamented the datedness and worn condition of many of the books; the increasing budget stringencies would exacerbate this. There is a newly set up computer room. Unique to the school is the language laboratory with twenty-five booths and cassette decks for each student, acquired for the interpreters' course. Worth about $50,000, it was purchased second-hand for $8,000 from Macquarie University through the contacts of the former deputy, who lectured there, with funding from the federal government's Participation and Equity Program (PEP).

All of the staff interviewed regarded their teacher training as inadequate preparation for the cultural and linguistic diversity with which they had to engage at Burwood. Most commented that they had learnt 'on the job' in this regard. One mentioned the inadequacy of the Department's six-week English as a Second Language (ESL) 'conversion' course. She also commended the usefulness of her university (in this case Macquarie) MA programme in Migration Studies.

The school's links with the wider community tended to be associated with particular individuals and specific purposes, rather than organic and ongoing. For example, when a group of Muslim girls began attending the active and sociable Inter-School Christian Fellowship club at lunch times, one of the girls in contact with the youth worker at the nearby Lakemba mosque initiated a students' Islamic club at the school, with luncheon speakers from the mosque, and so on. A further link was forged with the Homebush West Community Centre, associated with the Uniting Church, through a programme supporting community liaison officers shared between four local schools. Yet, explained the principal, '[i]t was one of those one-off things. We do those very well in Australia; we get a wonderful programme and then the funding disappears'. A number of contacts with the community were utilized by the deputy in seeking support to instigate the interpreters' course, and further associations were developed in the process of running this programme, as will be outlined below. With the transfer of the deputy and the discontinuation of the course, these links are no longer active.

The management style at the school was 'a team effort', 'supportive of student and staff initiative', according to the former deputy. The principal expanded on this:

> What's the adjective we use? 'Participatory', I suppose. No principal in New South Wales has much control in a direct sense. It means that staff development and promotion of understanding of what school

policies are, becomes particularly important. For example, the process of developing the 'Aims and Objectives' last year and involving the staff in that; the important part of that process was that you collectively talk through all of these things, . . . especially with a big changeover of staff.

There were limits, however, to this participatory democracy. As some opposition developed to the 'staff-expensive' nature of the interpreters' and translators' course in the process of timetabling with declining staff numbers, the principal's commitment to the course was such that she responded, 'It is important. Go and do it!'

Context of the Innovation

For a number of years, Burwood Girls' has been attempting to develop appropriate educational responses to the changing ethnic composition of the school. One head of department related that 'people had been trying to come to grips with this' when he had arrived at the school seven years ago. Concomitant with this was the surge in youth unemployment and the consequent rise in secondary school retention rates, with the subsequent attempts to restructure the post-compulsory curriculum. The federal government's Participation and Equity Programme was targeted at just these types of need. It sought:

> to develop education systems under which the less advantaged groups in the community can receive a fair share of the range of benefits education brings. The position of women and girls and other underrepresented groups such as Aboriginals and some ethnic groups will be given particular attention under PEP.[1]

Under the Participation and Equity Program guidelines, Commonwealth funds were made available:

> to stimulate broadly based changes in secondary education including:
> - catering at all stages more adequately for the needs of the full range of students;
> - making changes to secondary schools' organisation to accommodate more adequately the social, economic and cultural diversity of students, and to promote self-confidence, independence and a sense of autonomy in all students;
> - reforming and diversifying the curriculum;
> - reviewing credentialling and assessment arrangements, including provision for accreditation of work experience. . . .[2]

Although not a targeted school under the Participation and Equity Program and not classified as a 'disadvantaged school', Burwood Girls' was successful in

Cultures of Schooling

obtaining Participation and Equity Program funds in three out of the four possible funding categories: initiatives for school change, projects for girls, and initiatives for students from NESB (the remaining category being initiatives for Aboriginal students). In 1985, the school used Participation and Equity Program funding to diversify the Years 11 and 12 curriculum, introducing a series of 'relevant', non-matriculation courses: Ceramics, Drama and Theatre Arts, Food for Living, Legal Studies (taught by social science staff), Micro-Computing in Studying Social Issues (taught by history teachers), Psychology (offered by the maths department), and so forth.

It was in the context of these curriculum changes that the Interpreting, Translating and Multicultural Studies course was produced. There were two other aspects of the 'whole school change', seeded by Participation and Equity Program funding, which formed part of the matrix in which this particular innovation was developed. The first was regarded by the principal as 'probably just as important as the language work'. This was the process through which 'multicultural perspectives have been written into all the subject programmes: in history and science and social science and art and music and everything', in line with the 1983 state Department of Education's *Multicultural Education Policy*.[3] The second was a language across the curriculum approach, fostered by the school's Language in Learning Committee. This favoured a progressivist, 'student-centred' pedagogy, with less emphasis on formality and content, and more attention to creativity and 'process', very much in accord with the 1988 NSW Department of Education's *Writing K-12* policy.[4] The school's Language Learning Policy, produced by the committee over a two-year period, advocated the 'process writing' approach, which it outlined as follows:

1 *Ownership* — a student has the choice of topic, form and full control of the writing without the restraint of formal grammar and spelling in the initial stages.
2 *The Process* of writing — including drafting and revising to make her meaning clear to her audience. This involves opportunities for editing and conferencing with both peers and teachers.
3 *Writing time* — the provision of time in the classroom is important for practising writing.
4 *Publication* — a writing task is reqarding [sic] and a source of gratification if a student has her work valued by others besides the teacher. The teacher should refrain from marking out 'errors' in the published text.
5 *Assessment* should be an evaluation of the *development* of the writing skills of the young writer *NOT* a ranking mark of the final published works.

Stage 2 of the Language Learning Policy incorporated specific strategies for teaching writing in each of the subject areas. The language department's policy states:

Student-centred learning activity will take a major place in writing activities ... As cultural context has always been an integral and important part of language learning, writing activities are seen as stimulating interest in this part of courses and as an excellent means of cultivating students' English writing skills in the foreign language classroom. ...

Linguistic conventions (grammar, syntax, vocabulary) must be taught in the context of the communicative tasks at hand. ...

The interlinking of all these areas of curriculum innovation is demonstrated in the school's submission for further Participation and Equity Program funding for 1986:

In 1985 various faculties reviewed their programmes as part of the School's multicultural PEP initiative. Such reviews necessarily draw attention to the language needs of our students and produced a common concern among the School staff that the matter should be addressed at school level. Three committees were formed which looked at a) Language Development b) Subject specific areas c) the total senior school curriculum.

The Subject Specific Committee examined nine faculty areas with regard to multicultural non-sexist and aboriginal perspectives. All faculties have been reviewing and rewriting their programmes in Years 7 and 8 with this in mind. A continuation of this programme is required in the heavily content-based subjects of History, Social Sciences and Science to review their programmes in Years 9 and 10. The senior curriculum committee looked at the introduction of an Interpreters/Translators course in Arabic, Contonese [sic], Greek, Italian, Spanish, Turkish and Vietnamese, in an attempt to draw and build upon the bilingual skills of the ethnic community.

The initial idea for the Interpreting, Translating and Multicultural Studies course sprang from an innovation at Casuarina High School in Darwin, which the principal and deputy from Burwood had seen in a video shown by one of the Department's regional consultants in multicultural education. The language teacher there was using Darwin's tourist industry and her own experience as a trained interpreter to construct an orally-based interpreting course in the junior classes as a means of teaching French and German. The deputy, herself a qualified linguist, had expressed enthusiasm for such a course at Burwood Girls'. The principal had supported this proposal, with the suggestion that it would be more appropriate at their school to target the programme towards NESB students, capitalizing on their existing non-English language skills and practice as *de facto* interpreters for their families, while at the same time improving their English. The obvious way to introduce such a syllabus seemed to be as one of the new 'Other Approved Studies' courses being designed at the school level to cater for the 'non-academically inclined' students now staying on to Years 11 and 12 in unprecedented proportions. Participation and Equity Program funding was available to initiate this: $12,000 was sought for 1986, to be used in conjunction with language across the curriculum initiatives and the reviewing of the junior curriculum. The lion's share of this was to go towards staffing the interpreters' course.

The rationale for the course, as expressed by the deputy principal, was to make provision for the 'large body of students who were disadvantaged, because they had a wealth of knowledge in their own language, but couldn't show it'. Such a course would give them confidence and pride, and the ability to use their first language to best advantage. All of them were called upon to interpret 'at home', but they did not have the necessary skills or vocabulary to do this properly. The course could offer both a Higher School Certificate subject with which they could cope more easily, and also a qualification which would be useful for employment.

To secure the credential status of the programme proved no easy task: the process took about eighteen months of negotiation. The deputy applied to the National Accreditation Authority for Translators and Interpreters (NAATI) for accreditation. The plan was to have the students follow the NAATI Level 1 Language Aide guidelines in Year 11 and sit a NAATI Level 1 Examination at the end of the year. Year 12 would follow the NAATI Level 2 guidelines, and sit a school-based examination for Higher School Certificate purposes, the NAATI requirements being deemed too demanding at that level. This was virtually unprecedented: Casuarina had been accredited as a NAATI school, but its students had not as a matter of course applied for the NAATI credential. The deputy 'actively sought community support'. The Turkish Teachers' Association, for example, backed the proposal. The submission to NAATI lists meetings with Vietnamese-, Cantonese-, Mandarin-, Spanish-, Greek-, Turkish-, and Italian-speaking parent groups, with the support of the Parents' and Citizens' Association. It claims 'ongoing communication' with Canberra and NSW Divisions of NAATI, the Directorates of Studies and of Special Program in the NSW Department of Education, academics from the university and college of advanced education sectors, practitioners in technical and further education colleges and high schools, a NAATI Level 3 Vietnamese interpreter and a representative of the Australian Chinese Association. Approval was forthcoming in July 1986 for courses in Cantonese, Greek, Italian, Spanish, Turkish and Vietnamese.

The NAATI endorsement and the community support proved useful in the 'endless communication and negotiation with the Department' undertaken by the deputy with the imprimatur of the principal. Certainly, the NAATI credential figured prominently in the ensuing applications for approval as an Other Approved Studies course and for Participation and Equity Program finance. Both of these were granted. New South Wales Multicultural Education Coordinating Committee funds were also forthcoming, and were used to pay for the part-time Turkish and Vietnamese teachers in the first year. Burwood Evening College contributed $200.

The Innovation in Practice

The voluntary contributions of the teaching staff, in terms of labour extending far into their own time, were very significant. The fact that such considerations are taken into account during assessment for promotions listings does not discount the essentially unpaid nature of this very significant amount of work. All staff involved with the course, irrespective of how favourable was their judgment of the innovation, attested to the long hours and arduous nature of the preparation entailed. The units of work had been prepared in 1985, the year before the course began, largely by the deputy principal and the English as a Second Language (ESL) coordinator, who became joint conveners of the course in its first year. No teaching time was allocated for this, except for a small amount of Participation and Equity Program relief. As with the team teaching in the school's ESL programme, the preparation was detailed and exhaustive. (The ESL coordinator joked about the local cafes doing a roaring trade with teachers involved in after-hours preparation and meetings.) When the course was running, the 'language' teachers received all their material in English; it had to be translated and rendered conceptually appropriate in the language and culture involved, with cassette tapes and other specialized materials prepared — all beyond *normal* lesson planning — all in the teachers' own time. For the Cantonese teacher, actually trained as a science teacher and originally employed as a 'Chinese'-speaking maths/science person for the Transition Education programme, lesson preparation took about three times as long for the interpreters' course as for science lessons, with no allowance. The ESL coordinator found it necessary to relinquish her role as joint convenor of the programme after the first year. 'It was taking too much time' and she felt unable to devote enough energy to her ESL work. Nevertheless, she thought the course was worthwhile, because it was 'doing something for minority language maintenance in the school'.

Language maintenance was indeed one of the explicit objectives of the course. Another, as expressed by the *Teacher's Handbook*, was 'to increase competency in English'. The aim, 'to examine the cultures and historical traditions of Australia and her peoples [sic] psychological make-up as reflected in language usage and behaviour', though somewhat confusedly expressed, appears to incorporate both cultural maintenance for ethnic minorities and the requisite knowledge of mainstream culture. For the ESL teacher, facility in the mainstream language and the mainstream culture were part of the same task: 'From the ESL position, teaching parallel was more difficult because of the need to work in specialist subject areas. So it seemed important to have another three periods of "English/living skill" work to provide a "life skill vocabulary".' The principal expressed the view '[t]hat schools have an opportunity and a responsibility for children in *our* particular society. . . . So that for an Italian-Australian or a Turkish-Australian lass coming here to Burwood Girls', our job is to prepare them to fit into Australia and to be confident'. She saw this self-confidence or self-esteem (a Participation and Equity Program goal) as related both to the maintenance of their own language and culture, and to functionality in the mainstream language and culture. Two other objectives, already discussed above, were expressed in the handbook. The first, 'to provide a curriculum alternative . . . giving realistic goals and incentives' (another Participation and Equity Program goal), may have been in tension with the second aim of providing a substantive credential: 'to prepare students to act as interpreters and translators [sic]'. Holders of NAATI Level 1 are only qualified as language *aides*, not as fully-fledged translators or interpreters.

The ESL teacher expressed an unofficial objective. 'We had hoped that for kids whose first language [level] wasn't good, that we could encourage them to study it further; but also to make the kids aware of their *limitations* and that they are not qualified to interpret in serious situations such as hospitals.' There was a potential contradiction here between aiming at the consciousness of shortcomings, on the one hand, and the express goal of self-esteem, on the other. In practice, there was a further conflict played out between the pedagogy aimed at self-esteem and the objective demands of the tasks of interpreting and translating. Thus the application for Other Approved Studies approval stated, 'The course will create a learning environment that contributes to the self-esteem of all persons and positive interpersonal relationships' (p. 2). Therefore, 'in Year 11 rigid attention to "correctness" will be avoided until the student becomes confident in the language. Linguistic competence will be developed through social awareness and self-esteem building strategies' (p. 5). Yet, according to the submission for NAATI accreditation, 'Students will be expected to — . . . Understand vocabulary, simple idioms, grammar and syntax in English and another language in areas of specific relevance to the practice of interpreting and translating in Australia' (p. 2). Similarly, the handbook demands,

> Students are required to translate official forms into either language. This will show their familiarity with:
>
> > exact terminology
> > grammatical structure
> > different styles. (p. 6)

Further, under 'Translation Techniques', the handbook lists:

1 split sentence into sections that can be analyzed separately.
2 watch out for commas, colons, semicolons, and words like 'that' or 'which' etc.
3 note ending of verbs and the different lenses [sic].
4 be aware of different case in languages with declension . . . . (p. 10)

The course was comprised of three major components. The first consisted of three forty-minute periods per week with English as the language of instruction, dealing with the ethics of interpreting (for example, accuracy, confidentiality, impartiality); 'interpreting skills' such as 'personal presentation, resistance to nervousness, verbal-non verbal communication, developing sensitivity to situations'; language in such fields as health and welfare, immigration, travel, law, social services; and role-plays practising the skills concerned. Along with this segment, which constituted 25 per cent of the course in Year 11 and 40 per cent in Year 12, was a 'Cultural and Social Studies' strand involving the history of immigration to Australia and 'the culture of the language groups selected by the student', being 15 per cent of the Year 11 course and 20 per cent in Year 12. The former was taught by the deputy principal, who speaks five languages and qualified for NAATI Level 2 for the purpose. The latter segment was taught by the ESL teacher, who had gained postgraduate qualifications in this area. All the language groups were together for this part of the course. The second component, also of three periods a week, was conducted in the various languages' respective groups:

> This part of the programme is constructed around a framework of components comprising of topics, key functions, speech acts, cultural aspects of language, syntax, registar [sic] and very simple grammar. The speech acts indicate ways of performing those key functions most likely to be needed in the specific topic areas. The extension of vocabulary and idiom will be conducted in English and the other community languages in pertinent interpreter/translator area.

Italian and Greek interpreters' classes were taken by the school's full-time language teachers of those subjects, both of whom sat for the NAATI Level 2 examination for this purpose. Cantonese was taught by the Indonesian-born ethnic Chinese science teacher, whose first language was actually Hokkien, but whose husband was a Cantonese-speaker from Hong Kong. She had lived in Hong Kong for about ten months, and had taught there for one teaching year. She attended an interpreters' course at the local Technical and Further Education College in order better to teach in this innovation, and also passed NAATI Level 2. Another language teacher involved said of her colleagues: 'The Chinese teacher worked very hard, was very keen and got virtually no recognition. The Italian teacher did feel especially burdened, because of the tremendous amount of preparation. The kudos all went to [another party] who did not meet the problems in the same way.' The Italian teacher transferred to another school and so was lost to the programme. The Vietnamese teacher was externally funded to teach part-time on the course, but then was employed full-time at Cabramatta High School. Turkish was also taught part-time with special federal funding. This second component of the course represented 60 per cent for Year 11 and 40 per cent for Year 12.

Cultures of Schooling

The third component embodied the fieldwork required by NAATI and was incorporated into the school's work experience programme. It began in the third term of Year 11, and amounted to not less than forty hours practicum over the duration of the course. It involved, for example, observation sessions with experienced interpreters at work in such places as hospitals. Students were also called upon to practise interpreting for NESB parents on parent-teacher nights.

A prerequisite for the course was that the student be a native speaker of the language concerned. Students 'requiring ESL' had to take one unit 'Supplementary English' in Year 11. The course was worth two units out of the minimum of twelve units in Year 11 and eleven units in Year 12 required for the Higher School Certificate. As an Other Approved Studies course, however, the marks from Interpreting, Translation and Multicultural Studies would not count towards the aggregate score calculated for university or College of Advanced Education entrance. This was a strong disincentive for intending matriculants who would tend to opt for universal, centrally devised 'Board' [of Senior School Studies] courses instead. Other Approved Studies courses were promoted on a seminar day in Year 10, when students chose courses after perusal of a fifty-page 'Prospectus' and discussion with their teachers and parents. The ESL coordinator spoke of 'a problem here with kids' high expectations — they want to be doctors and lawyers, but 10 per cent or less actually matriculate; 80 per cent or 90 per cent pick subjects thinking that they're going to matriculate — courses that are too difficult for them'. Another teacher explained that at the seminar, 'Girls who don't know what to do, depending on their background, if they are not "academic" they are encouraged to take Other Approved Studies courses'. She said that 'academic' girls would choose the Chinese language course. Three Year 11 girls had done both the interpreters' and Board courses in Chinese in 1987, but had dropped the Other Approved Studies course in Year 12. The former deputy also referred to the Board course as the 'academic' course, and related that it was noticed by the staff of Italian and Greek that those (few) students who did both types of course were more advanced.

The principal observed:

> You tended to find that the kids doing the interpreting course were the 'less academic girls', who probably could not have coped with the highly academic nature of HSC Italian or Modern Greek. I'm not too familiar with the HSC courses in the other languages, but I know that both of those are very literary, very academic courses, and you've got to be pretty bright and good [at the language] to start with. So we did have a *couple* of students who did both courses.

The deputy spoke of a group of girls of Greek language background who took the course who 'did not come out as academics, because they were not academically equipped to do so — they probably *never* would do that'. The second verse of the school song perhaps underlines this assumption: 'Who knows what lies ahead? Different paths we'll tread.' So there was a certain amount of self-selection and a certain amount of guidance with regard to 'academic' inclination or capacity. It is clear that the course was targeted to the 'non-academic', and most of the staff involved agree that, in one way or another, this fact is related to its eventual demise, as will be detailed below.

On the other hand, four of the seven girls in the first Italian class went on to study three-unit Italian. This 'success' in their mother tongue, however, was not replicated in other subjects. Of the seven students in this class, all of whom had applied for entry into the interpreters' course at Macarthur Institute of Higher Education, only one student achieved a high enough aggregate to be accepted.

Some twenty-five students opted to do the course in each of the three years that it ran, 1986-88. Four languages were offered at the outset: Italian, Cantonese, Turkish and Vietnamese. Greek was introduced in the second year. The Italian classes were the largest in each year, with around seven students. The school was unable to procure a part-time Spanish teacher, as was originally planned. The Vietnamese and Turkish teachers could no longer be afforded after the funding ran out and, in any case, only five girls from three different language groups wanted to take the course in 1989, so it could not be viably mounted. As the principal pointed out, it was always:

> a very staff-intensive course, which is one of its problems in terms of innovation. The first group was only twenty to twenty-five pupils, quite a decent-sized senior class for the three periods a week when you had them together. But broken up they were four groups of five or six, with one member of staff for the five or six. Now there *are* senior classes with one member of staff for five or six, but you can't afford too many of them.

Not only was it a staff-intensive course, but it was a very intensive workload for the staff involved, as has already been pointed out. This is the nature of school-based curriculum development. 'Everything had to be *written*, everything was done by *us*', explained the deputy. NAATI did not supply resources; the school had to buy them if they wanted them. Some materials were obtained from Macarthur Institute of Higher Education, which has an interpreters' course. Not only cost, but *availability* of curriculum resources was a problem; with Chinese, for instance, there was plenty to be found in Mandarin, but very little in Cantonese. The 'relevant' curriculum approach, moreover, demanded that actual pamphlets, forms and the like, be obtained in the areas of health, retail, travel, banking, insurance, immigration, law. The Health Department was very helpful, but some areas, such as insurance, proved quite difficult. All of this material had to be translated and formulated into dialogues. Some terms and concepts were not easily translatable. The dialogue material was devised collectively in English and then translated into the individual languages — a labour-intensive process. 'There was a plethora of meetings. We were forever having consultation', said one teacher, who stressed the time-consuming nature of the preparation. 'I felt as if I was writing a textbook half the time.' She was. The NAATI submission cited the 'Basic Text' as 'Materials supplied by the coordinators of the course, based on the syllabus set down for the HSC in interpreting and translating within the Australian context, *to be developed into a text for publication*' [emphasis added]. The former deputy, lamenting that all the resources prepared would probably no longer be used, said that she still had the material and would like to publish it some day.

It was differences over pedagogy, however, as much as tensions produced by the workload, which limited the long-term viability of the course in terms of commitment from staff and students alike. If the course was implicitly aimed at the 'non-academic', then an appropriately non-academic teaching style was called for. The deputy explained:

> You couldn't be the old-fashioned, traditional language teacher. You had to have a modern approach to teaching. You had to forget you were teaching a language syllabus as required by the HSC and remember that it was an *interpreting* course.

This demanded a 'student-centred' and 'needs-based' approach. You could not spend time teaching things like the accusative case or the subjunctive mood, she explained.

Some other language teachers, while recognizing the need for interpreting in the girls' ethnic communities, stressed the 'needs' — the prerequisites — of the interpreting process itself:

> The goals were misguided. It was a very good programme on paper, because it could have provided language specific to their needs in the community. The basic problem was the girls' background in the language. The kids didn't have the linguistic background to do the interpreting work.

The language concerned here was a highly inflected one, and interpreting in it required a sound grasp of grammar. It was all the more necessary to teach grammar in LOTE work, said this teacher, because of its relative neglect in current English teaching. 'The attitude seems to be that if they get the idea across, that's enough, but when you're born here, that's *not* enough.' When she had been drafted to teach some English, because of her ESL experience, she had been 'scandalized' by the lack of care given to grammar. She had tried to adapt her teaching to extend the girls' limited English vocabularies and to teach them more grammar. In LOTEs teaching, then, 'You have to assume they don't know grammatical terms. You have to teach it to them. The English staff see it as a "languages" responsibility'. The head of the languages department agreed with this. He felt that every child should be taught reasonably formal English. People might think him a 'hideous reactionary', he conceded, but students needed to know the 'ins and outs' of grammar, rules and so on. As language teacher, he maintained that it was very difficult to teach a 'foreign language' at a higher level because the students do not have the requisite knowledge of grammar and other basics. By contrast, the educational approach of the deputy and the person who briefly succeeded her as coordinator of the interpreters' course was closely aligned to that of the ESL coordinator and the currently predominant approach to teaching English. This stresses communicative competence as against structure and accuracy, and underlies the 'process writing' method clearly encapsulated in the *Writing K-12* document cited earlier. This pedagogy of 'relevance' is also related to the promotion of curricular instrumentalism found in the quest for 'alternative' courses. 'That's the problem now with languages at school. "Relevance" has got to be the big buzz-word, and everybody tells [the students] that you can't use [languages].' 'The girls saw [the interpreters' course] as different', observed another teacher, 'and it was pushed as something useful to them'.

One student commented that there was little grammar in the course because 'it wasn't really necessary'. 'It was mostly just terminology, not language as such.' She added, however, that they didn't get much grammar in their language classes either, because they 'did mostly literature'.

Evaluation

Virtually all who were involved with the programme agreed that it *was* a useful course for those who succeeded with it. Most participating staff concurred that its discontinuation was in large part attendant on the loss of its primary instigator to 'push' the course. The deputy principal, who even one student described as 'the driving force', received a transfer and promotion at the end of 1987 to become principal of another — quite prestigious — state girls' school. We have already noted the return of the founding joint coordinator of the course to full-time deployment on her ESL duties. The deputy, her promotion imminent, tried to 'train' one of the other enthusiastic language teachers to take over the coordination of the interpreters' course, but this teacher was shortly to take maternity leave, followed by a position in a private girls' school.

Thus the main protagonists of the programme, those who warmly advocated the pedagogy involved, were all 'lost' to the course by 1988. The principal pointed to the loss of key personnel and their enthusiasm as a reason for its cessation. 'If you then move the coordinator who is the driving force behind it, that's a major factor.' It is perhaps worth observing that, where there is a market-like mechanism for course selection such as with Other Approved Studies courses, involving considerable advertising of and competition between particular programmes, the loss of a 'sponsor', in this sense, can be devastating. Other Approved Studies courses, as a whole, moreover, had been devalued in the 'market place' at just the same time as this 'driving force' was lost:

> It would also have got the backwash as a number of our Other Approved Studies courses did this year. They came in with PEP [which was recently wound down]. The interpreting was part of our whole innovation of developing independent curriculum. There has been a real falling off in the Other Approved Studies this year.... I've got far more kids saying to me, 'That's not a Board course, Miss, and maybe I'll be marked down.' The whole government approach changes the H[igher] S[chool] C[ertificate], with an implied denigration of O[ther] A[pproved] S[tudies] courses.

This downturn in the popularity of Other Approved Studies courses, following the New South Wales government's introduction of a Higher Education Assessment Score from which they are excluded, to be shown on the Higher School Certificate, was remarked upon by several staff.

The principal added another reason for the drop in student commitment to the course. 'One of the things it appealed to most were the kids from what I call the "fringe" language groups. Turkish and Vietnamese now have Saturday schools and now kids can do Vietnamese for the Higher School Certificate.'

It is possible that the students were 'voting with their feet' at the Saturday schools for the sort of preferences which one of the teachers (seen as a keen worker on the interpreters' course) expressed:

> I prefer to teach the academic course myself. I would want my kids to do the 'HSC' course. It is more intellectually demanding, more stimulating.

This teacher also favoured the introductory 'Z' courses over Other Approved Studies courses in languages. These are two-unit Higher School Certificate language courses for 'beginners', who have not studied the subject from Years 7 to 10, available in a range of languages, including Chinese. As the school's 'Options'87' prospectus explained, these courses have the advantage that they *are accepted for matriculation purposes by the universities and count fully towards your aggregate*' [original emphasis]. There was some agreement that the Other Approved Studies status of the interpreting course was problematic. One teacher suggested that it could be strengthened only if it were a 'recognized' course. The principal thought likewise:

> You would need some kind of recognition of the value of such a course. I know [the deputy] talked about this at one stage with [the

former regional consultant]. It needs to be designed in a way that is going to give it more prestige. . . . ..Really, a Board course would be the long-term answer. That would give it some status and it would also mean that its teaching methods would become more widely accepted.

While these views coincide in seeing as an obstacle the 'alternative' standing of the course, they are diametrically opposed over the issue of appropriate teaching style. The second viewpoint sees a need for a less 'traditional', more 'confidence-building' pedagogy, geared to 'life situations', as being particularly called for with the 'less academic' clientele now to be found in the senior years of secondary school. The quite unproblematized incidence of particular ethnic groupings in this category appeared to be the reason that an Interpreting, Translating and Multicultural Studies course for NESB students was conceived as ideal for this purpose. The former viewpoint, on the other hand, sees a certain linguistic foundation as prerequisite to the possibility of interpreting. Yet the selection mechanisms of the course tended to pick up precisely those without such a foundation: the 'wrong clientele'. 'The interpreters' course assumed proficiency in language. Yet the best "academic" students wouldn't touch non-Board courses.' According to this teacher, such a course would have been most appropriate after a standard Higher School Certificate language course, not as an alternative to one: 'It was an endpoint course, not a beginning course; that needs to be understood.' It is noteworthy that both of these positions operate relatively unproblematically with the notion of 'non-academic'.

What this meant in practice can be gleaned from the teachers' accounts. 'If you get the kids who don't really want to do anything, it's very disheartening', explained one. Another volunteered the advice, 'You need to be very clear about the assumed level of [the language concerned]. You need an entrance test. If a student cannot do basic written [language], she should not be allowed in, because it frustrates the students as well as the teacher.' Again, 'I minded because *I* was doing the work. The girls gave up, I realized, but the teacher couldn't.' Most of these students did not drop out; they just lowered their standard. Only one or two 'were capable or worked hard'. The others 'sat it out to qualify for the Higher School Certificate'. 'Capability', in this sense, is not a reflection of some innate level of intelligence or intellectual inclination. It is a facility gained through learning the linguistic prerequisites. Thus, from the point of view of a LOTE teacher on the course, '[t]he course would have been good for new arrivals, those who were studying the language at afternoon school, or those who had studied the language and worked hard since Year 8'. The students did not regard the course as a soft option, but they did think that they could do it without the necessary background. In her opinion, they were poorly advised in being encouraged to do the course, perhaps by a well-meaning 'year patron who may be a geographer or a maths teacher or whatever, who doesn't have language training', seeking what they believed to be the 'realistic' alternative supposedly found in Other Approved Studies courses.

Cultures of Schooling

The ex-deputy principal cited the 'mixed abilities' of the students as one of the difficulties encountered by the interpreters' course. One would expect the newer arrivals, of course, to have more fluency and a wider vocabulary in their first language than the second generation migrant groups. Yet they would have different problems with the course, and may not be as well suited for it as the LOTE teacher, who was concentrating on the first language, suggested. For many newer arrivals, their English would not be up to scratch. They may also be quite illiterate in their mother tongue, as was the case with one student in the Chinese group. It is probable that the 'Admission Requirements and Assumed Knowledge' — that '. . . [s]tudents must be bilingual with a basic level of competency in two languages' — and '. . . Students must have completed a satisfactory admission test in English and the other language', which the school submitted to NAATI, proved incompatible with the envisaged role of the course as an Other Approved Studies subject for students who were 'not achieving' in 'traditional' curricula. It is also reasonable to conjecture that one weighty factor in that very lack of 'academic' achievement would be the want of precisely the linguistic foundation (in either language) which was one of the *raisons d'etre* for the course cited by its instigators. One student, as we have seen, commented that the course didn't teach language 'as such'. Yet she also said that interpreters' course used 'harder language' than the LOTEs course, largely because it was a technical terminology.

Staff involved differed over whether the course had met its objectives in practice. One judged that it did not, 'because the students at the end wouldn't have been able to go out and do what we were trying to teach them to do'. Another observed that the girls had been interpreting for their relatives anyway, and that now they were more confident. This disparity may reflect differences between the longer-established migrant groups and the newer arrivals. The principal underlined the point about confidence and self-esteem:

> [The students] had a lot of confidence and pride in what they were doing. It was noticeable that their English skills had improved and so on. Certainly, the people teaching the course saw that the girls' English skills improved greatly over the two years of the course.

The deputy said, 'I know they *enjoyed* it; they thoroughly loved the course'. She cited the instances of one girl in the Vietnamese group who had found the course useful for her job in the bank and was now called upon to interpret for customers, and another former student of Italian language background who now works for the Department of Immigration. Two of the Italian-speaking students had been accepted with advanced standing to the interpreters' course at Macarthur Institute of Higher Education, to pursue NAATI level 2 there. Three students 'went on to do interpreting professionally', according to the languages head of department, and 'others stuck it out for two years and got satisfactory results'. In the first year of the Interpreting, Translating and Multicultural Studies course, fifteen out of twenty-five qualified for the NAATI

Level 1 certificate: one in Cantonese, three in Turkish, five in Italian and six in Vietnamese. In the final year which the programme ran, two out of seven of the Chinese students, for example, received the certificate according to the Cantonese teacher. It should be pointed out that the students had to pay NAATI for this certification, although the school set and marked the exams, with NAATI approval. In the first year, the total charge was $25 each, of which the students paid $6 with the school subsidizing the rest. In the final year the cost was $30 each, and there was no school subsidy.

Of course, a slightly greater number of students completed the Other Approved Studies requirements satisfactorily for the Higher School Certificate. All who completed the Other Approved Studies course satisfactorily, irrespective of whether they qualified for the NAATI accreditation, were given a certificate from the school stating their achievements.

Even the teacher who regarded the course as 'misguided' and having fallen short of its objectives identified successful elements of the innovation. The 'unacademic' girls who undertook the programme were 'put in touch' with their own families in new ways. It enhanced their self-esteem, particularly for those who had not previously regarded themselves as speakers of the language concerned. One student commented that one of the most important things for her was that she 'found out about my own background. There were so many things I didn't know.'

It seems clear from the interviews, but also from the documentation, that the affective aims of fostering 'feelings of self-worth', 'building self-esteem' and 'encourag[ing] students to recognize and value the wealth of their cultural and linguistic backgrounds' are at least comparable in importance, in the estimate of the course's proponents, with the provision of an interpreting and translating credential and the cognitive aims associated with this. Yet there is no rationale to be found, in either written or verbal objectives, for the identification of particular migrant groups as requiring enhancement of their self-esteem. Ironically, it was pointed out by one teacher, their estimate of their own value (as well as their productive capacity in the wider community) might best be advanced by the more difficult task of imparting those linguistic and conceptual abilities of which it has been judged they are 'less capable'. Certainly, one girl said the course made her 'a more confident person' and taught her to relate better to people of different ages and nationalities. It made her 'feel more intelligent' and gave her a better 'outlook' on life. Other 'social' goals were mentioned. A former student said the course 'taught me about morality . . . , by seeing other ways of living and doing things. I've grown to respect the ways of other people'. She added that she could interpret better as well, but she had had to do that 'for her parents anyway'. 'That's the way of things in Australia.' She did use her skills, however, in her job in a social security office, interpreting for clients of her language background. More pragmatically, the 'credential' also got her 'extra pay'. Another benefit of the course was the 'attention' the students received, both in being in small classes and in being in a special programme. This allowed students 'a closer relation-

111

Cultures of Schooling

ship with teachers'. Students and teachers would, for example, have lunches together. The 'publicity', similarly, was a major benefit for the school, commented one student.

While several teachers mentioned the significance of these students having been taught about social welfare agencies, insurance, banks and so on, it was also pointed out that a generalized 'Society Studies' course could have done this more efficiently.

One impact of the course may have been to increase contact between the school and NESB parents. This was articulated clearly by an ex-student, who said events such as the 'international food night' produced 'more interaction between school and family'. As part of the students' practical experience in interpreting and as an obligatory assessment task, a 'multi-lingual Parent-Teacher-Student evening' was arranged. The note to parents read, 'The students in the Multicultural Course will interpret for members of staff so that parents have an opportunity to discuss any problems connected with the issues in *their language*' [original emphasis]. In the event, one teacher recalls, her students were not able to interpret and could merely act as 'guides'. The principal recollected, 'we had a multicultural evening, when the girls got up at the end of their second year; they got up and discussed the course, and the girls from the course interpreted in four languages. The hall was full'. The Chinese teacher recounted that they 'made' the girls' parents come to the parent night and got the girls to interpret, but that only about ten parents had turned up. She explained that the Chinese don't like to ask too many questions in public, and had only come because they knew the interpreters would be there. All were happy with that evening, however, and were pleased to see their mother tongue being used by the school in a course. The principal said:

> One of the things that we learned was that such an innovation gave a lot of parental and community support to the school. The parents of the communities concerned, for example, were quite delighted with the whole thing.

A number of contacts with the wider community were established in conjunction with the fieldwork/work experience aspects of the programme. This component of the course was not without difficulties, however. The course coordinator was unable to obtain parental approval for several of the girls of Italian background to pursue their practical experience in a hospital, because of the fact that a young male interpreter was involved. Overall, however, parents interacted little with the school over the programme, thought the head of the languages department, but this was quite usual at Burwood Girls', he added. The local community interacted quite a lot, because the school needed access to solicitors and other specialist help: medical, Commonwealth Employment Service, shopkeepers and so on.

Communication with other schools was enhanced by the course. According to the deputy, some of the students were called upon to assist in parent-teacher interpreting at local primary schools. This was part of their work experience, and 'they got a lot of status' through it. The deputy herself 'talked at regional conferences and inservices'. 'We constantly gave inservices to staff from other schools.' A former student, however, believed that such a course could be improved if there were greater 'liaison between schools — we were the only one, which was hard for teachers. They had to rely on just what they did'.

How much these links will survive with the discontinuation of the course is questionable. The prospects for the programme's revival appear slim. Staffing of the Turkish and Vietnamese courses, which 'gave the course a special and different flavour', was dependent upon a combination of Participation and Equity Program and Multicultural Education Program (MEP) funding. The MEP was ended in 1986 by the federal government, with no funding for 1987. The Participation and Equity Program was also abolished in 1987. It had been commented how the former deputy had 'got funds amazingly', but that was 'at a time when there were more funds around'. The former principal explained the effects of the cutbacks:

> If I were here at the end of the year, I would certainly put it down on the curriculum for Year 11 again, and see if we could get it going. We would not, obviously, have the funding, and this is one of its limitations. . . . The only [uncommon] thing we could offer would be Chinese, probably Cantonese. We now have a [federally funded] Mandarin teacher at the school, but for our Cantonese speakers it is exactly the same problem as with our Greek girls finding the modern Greek course quite hard. . . . [W]e could start Greek, Italian and Chinese. . . . But, quite frankly, . . . I don't see it going again here.

Most of the staff agreed with this prognosis, the main problems being, as well as funding, loss of the course's instigator without staff prepared to 'step into her shoes', logistics of staffing the course, and the vastly reduced number of students choosing to do the course. There was some staff disillusionment. One teacher said, 'I wouldn't feel motivated unless I could be assured that the clients would be appropriate'. Another, for whom 'moral support is important', would 'think twice before [she] got involved again'.

The majority of teachers involved thought that the interpreters' course could, in principle, be replicated at other schools with appropriate NESB populations. One had reservations: 'Whether there is time is questionable. It is the sort of course you begin at the end of Year 12 rather than the beginning [of Year 11].' She thought that it would be more feasible at a 'front line' school such as she had previously taught in, with more newly arrived NESB migrants who attend afternoon schools in the language and 'come in at Year 8 with a higher competence' in the mother tongue.

Staffing would always be crucial factor. The head of the languages department observed that few language teachers would be prepared to work part-time for just three periods a week, which is why the school was unable to staff a Spanish interpreters' group. Also, 'you need to have specialist staff with nothing else on their plates. It's hard for, say a Greek teacher with twenty periods a week teaching Greek, if she has six periods a week which take up half her time.' Some of the difficulties associated with staffing the course could be alleviated by supplementary funding.

An associated and equally important factor in the viability of such an innovation in any school is that it needs to have 'normal' subject status in the timetable, rather than being marginalized or seen as a special case. Various teachers on the interpreters' course referred to the difficulties caused by running lessons in lunch hours, or working on the programme on Tuesday afternoons instead of sport. Similarly, an ex-student said the only thing she didn't like about the course was 'the times when you had to do some classes' — at lunchtime, for example, or missing out on sport.

A number of informants, including the former deputy, highlighted the programme's staff-intensive nature as a difficulty to be overcome: 'It uses a lot of staff; that's a consideration that has to be given.' Nevertheless, she was considering introducing such a course at the school where she is now principal. Continuity of staff, especially course coordinators, was preferable, but could not be provided for within the system. 'It's an idealistic thing to think you can have some sort of stability.' This being the case, inservicing becomes particularly important. This was mentioned by several participants.

The call for inservice courses is also related to the vital issue of pedagogy, and was raised by the course's proponents in this context. It is obvious that an innovation such as the interpreters' course depends upon teachers committed to a progressivist, student-centred, 'relevant' pedagogy. The former principal commented:

> ... pedagogy is probably an issue in foreign language teaching in NSW anyway. We've still got a number of people who are still very traditional; and then you've got a lot of other people who are saying you can teach language better in realistic life situations. Oral skills and getting confidence in speaking is a very important thing. Now the kind of teacher who's been brought up the second way, such as the member of staff whom we had last year, who unfortunately had to transfer, was an example of the most modern ... language learning process. The kids adored language learning with [her]. This has a great deal to do with the kind of confidence-building that the interpreting course was developing as well.

'Traditional' teachers, on the other hand, argued that 'realistic life situations' by themselves can reproduce unwitting use of dialect and 'Australianized' forms of language which in their opinion was inadequate for interpreting. Their case in the debate over pedagogy extended beyond language teaching. Several language teachers suggested that NESB students could acquire more warranted confidence, and in the longer term, more social empowerment, through a more formal and structured learning of the standard, literary form of their language and the conceptual tools which this approach entails.

Notes

1 RYAN, S. Commonwealth Minister for Education and Youth Affairs, quoted in COMMONWEALTH SCHOOLS COMMISSION, *Participation and Equity Guide for Schools*, (PEP), Victoria, 1984, p. 3.
2 COMMONWEALTH SCHOOLS COMMISSION, *Guidelines*, Canberra, 1984, p. 1.
3 NEW SOUTH WALES DEPARTMENT OF EDUCATION, *Multicultural Education Policy*, NSW Department of Education, Sydney, 1983.
4 DIRECTORATE OF STUDIES, *Writing K-12*, NSW Department of Education, Sydney, 1988.

Chapter 6

'Two Steps Forward, One Step Back': The Bilingual and Languages Other Than English Programmes at Collingwood Education Centre

Designed as a community school which involves students from the first years of primary school to Year 12, Collingwood Education Centre has responded to the needs of its students of Vietnamese and Turkish background by introducing bilingual programmes at both primary and secondary levels. While the secondary programme is no longer in operation, the school continues to offer language maintenance classes in Vietnamese, Turkish and Greek, compulsory to Year 10; and second language and maintenance classes in Spanish, Greek and French.

The Locality

Sitting at the foot of a large high-rise, Collingwood Education Centre is located in a Ministry of Housing estate in the Abbotsford/Collingwood area, in the inner north-eastern suburbs of Melbourne. It is an old, established area of low socioeconomic status, reflected in the school's position as one of the most disadvantaged schools in Victoria. One teacher described the area as 'lower working class'. Apart from the two high-rise apartment towers that dominate the immediate environment, there are more nearby, as well as walk-up flats that are sprinkled throughout the area. The are also a few terrace houses being 'gentrified'. The lower socioeconomic character of the area is likely to remain for some time, thanks mainly to the presence of the public housing — modernist monoliths from the 1960s which once embodied the promise of the welfare state, but that have now lost their short-lived shine to become the decidedly down-market end of the housing spectrum in the Melbourne of the late twentieth century.

The area has a high and relatively transient migrant population, that corresponds to the waves of migration in the post-war period. Where people of Greek and Yugoslav background were the major groups in the 1970s, during the 1980s families from Indo-China have become predominant. Turks have also entered the area from the early mid-70s on. The secondary principal of Collingwood Education Centre said that the first Vietnamese migrants were ethnic Chinese and middle class — shopkeepers and army officers — but as 'migration bit deeper' there were more ethnic Vietnamese from village and peasant backgrounds.

The School

The Collingwood Education Centre was designed in the 1970s as a public, co-educational preparatory school to Year 12 centre, and has both a primary and post-primary section. There are about 490 students in the secondary school, with more than thirty language groups represented. Students of Vietnamese background are the largest language group with 23 per cent of the secondary student population; followed by 'Chinese', predominantly Cantonese speakers, with 14 per cent; Greek speakers (13 per cent); Turkish speakers (10 per cent); and so on. Twenty-six per cent are of English-speaking or third-generation non-English speaking background (NESB), and there are fourteen language backgrounds with less then 1 per cent of the secondary population each. About 17 per cent had arrived in Australia in the previous three years, and 5 per cent in the last year. Twelve new students arrived in just two days during the course of the project, many coming straight to the school because the nearest Intensive Language Centre could not take them.

The student composition has changed dramatically over the years. As in other schools in the inner suburbs of Melbourne, the school has seen falling enrolments over the years. The primary school has less than half of the number of students it had in the mid-1970s, while the secondary school has also had decreasing numbers over the decade, although there has been a slight rise in the last two years. Where those of Greek background were the largest group in the 1970s, with large numbers of students from Turkish and Yugoslav background, these have been surpassed by students of Indo-Chinese background. Where the latter made up 4 per cent of Year 7 enrolments in 1979, they currently are about 34 per cent of Year 7. Almost half of secondary students were born overseas, with another 30 per cent having overseas-born parents. A lot of families of Greek background have moved out of the area as they have become more established. The number of Turkish-speaking students has fluctuated dramatically over the years, but is currently fairly stable and, given increased numbers in the primary school, will rise slightly in the next few years.

Process and factory work are common sources of employment for parents, while some also work in restaurants and shops, but many are unemployed or on welfare of some sort. There is a large number of one-parent families in groups of English-speaking or Vietnamese background, and many Vietnamese-speaking students live with older siblings or other relatives. Families of Greek ancestry are more established and stable, and are much more likely to be two-parent families.

There is some diversity in students' leisure activities; there are some clubs and gyms in the area, including one in a nearby apartment block, and a community centre, but some students of particular ethnic groups are frequently not allowed by their parents to use these, and they are mostly for 'Anglo' youth. This has concerned some staff. Some students, especially those of Vietnamese background, work after school. Many students, particularly those who live in the apartment blocks, 'hang around' the school after closing time and during holidays, or play in the grounds or the park next door. Boys of Vietnamese background often play sports, play billiards or watch TV and Kung Fu movies, while the girls stay inside the house helping the family.

The Greek-speaking community had been very involved in the school during the 1970s and helped start the Greek bilingual programme in the primary school, but were not active any more. Although those of Vietnamese origin are now the largest group, and there is a Vietnamese Association nearby, they have not become as involved as the Greek speakers had been.

There are fifty-eight teaching staff in the post-primary section of the school, and twenty-seven in the primary section — there is some overlap because not only is the Collingwood Education Centre a preparatory to Year 12 school, but it is also divided into five administrative units, around grade divisions, which have some control over curriculum. One of these is the 'transition unit' or unit three, for Years 6–8, which oversees the transition from primary to secondary school. There are two others in the secondary school:

one for Years 9 and 10, and one for Years 11 and 12. In the recent past this structure has been more complicated. In 1986, when the bilingual programme, which is the key focus of this study of innovatory multicultural programmes at the Collingwood Education Centre, was implemented, there were units for Years 6 and 7; 8 and 9; and 10, 11 and 12. There were also two units across Years 8 and 9 which had slightly different curriculum offerings.

There are three ethnic teacher aides — Vietnamese, Greek and Turkish. These perform the function of home-school liaison. The principal described the staff as 'highly multicultural', with teachers from backgrounds as diverse as Greek, Polish, Yugoslav, Dutch, Turkish, Malaysian, Arabic, Vietnamese, Italian, Mexican and South African. All the language teachers, for example, were of the language background they taught, except for the French teacher.

The principal described the school as 'well-resourced' in comparison with nearby schools, but not in terms of its real needs. The Centre has a theatre and other audio-visual facilities, a dance studio/drama room, two libraries, two buses, music rooms, computer facilities, a publishing centre and gymnasia, but the school facilities generally are shared by the primary and post-primary sections, an Adult Migrant Education Centre and a centre of the Victorian School of Languages.

The school's budget is in excess of $300,000, over and above staff salaries, and extra funding reflects educational fashions. The principal said that the Disadvantaged Schools Program (a programme which aims to improve the quality of education for disadvantaged groups by funding specialist programmes) was a key source once, but no more, because it was too 'fickle' and 'unreliable' as a result of quasi-democratic committees who follow 'the flavour of the month'. He cited several programmes which had come and gone because of short-term funding for individual programmes — in maths, music and theatre, and for a camps programme, each of which was dropped without warning, after being a top priority the year before. He also said that one proposal for a 'club' at the school to promote parental involvement was knocked back because there was no parental input into the submission! The Participation and Equity Program (a programme designed to promote increased participation and equality of outcomes for disadvantaged students) was 'dead', which the principal regretted because it had been powerful. They had recently received funding for a joint project in vocational education with a Technical and Further Education college.

The school's committee structure is complicated by the fact that it is a preparatory school to Year 12 centre. Apart from the school council and the principals (which are the main sources of decision making), there are advisory bodies: monthly sub-committee meetings for finance, Centre curriculum, and buildings and grounds; and fortnightly meetings for secondary and primary staff, faculties, the two local administration committees (one each for primary and secondary), the sectional curriculum committees, and unit leaders. There are also student welfare committees, programme teams, special task forces, coordinators' meetings, unit meetings, meetings for the primary and

Cultures of Schooling

secondary unions, and so on. Parents may also have meetings for their languagebased clubs or special purpose committees. The Staff Information Manual outlines the decision-making structures and processes at the Collingwood Education Centre over ten pages. While both the primary and post-primary sections have their own administrative structure headed by their own principals and deputies, the whole Centre is overseen by a superintendent (it should be pointed out here that several of these positions are filled by people working in an 'acting' capacity, but will be referred to as the positions they are filling. Also, the current superintendent, on leave during Terms 1 and 2 of 1989, was the secondary principal when the bilingual programme was initiated).

Of the nine staff interviewed, two who had recently arrived in Australia had completed, or were completing, further studies here. There was some further specialist training — one with Special Education training, one with English as a Second Language (ESL) method — and four were trained as language teachers. Only one teacher claimed her training was adequate for meeting the demands of the school's cultural diversity, but that was in terms of teaching a language, not in terms of the problems in implementing programmes. The former bilingual coordinator felt her training was not adequate. Even in terms of her language training, she said that the system had not been ready for the 'community language' trainee teachers. Some of the staff interviewed had travelled but not worked overseas. The three members of staff of Turkish or Vietnamese background had been trained as scientists in their homeland. Most of the staff indicated that their teaching experience was more valuable than their training in preparing them for a diverse student population. One argued that her own NESB background, understanding the problems of her community, was most helpful.

Several claimed that a culturally diverse student population did make teaching harder, but, as the language coordinator put it, it was also more 'interesting' and would be more so if the school were multilingual. Others saw it even more positively. The principal said explicitly that it wasn't a problem but an asset because 'everyone got along well and it made it easier'; 'when you have dozens of ethnic groups, other things become the most significant qualities: honesty, friendliness, reliability . . . ; we make a joke about being a "wog" school and proud of it'.

The former bilingual coordinator commented that the thing she liked about Collingwood was that the students mixed well and there was no serious racial tension. When she was doing her teaching rounds prior to getting a job, she came to Collingwood and was impressed, so she put it first on her list. The 'Anglo' students, she proposed, come from such diverse social backgrounds themselves that they end up mixing well with the NESB students. The ex-principal suggested moreover, that the was a tendency to place too much attention on the needs of NESB students at the expense of ESB students, who were economically deprived. The current principal pointed out that they were the ones who felt the greatest amount of socioeconomic depression and therefore often brought unsettled attitudes to school. Even so, he maintained that there 'is remarkably little resistance; a little nasty name-calling, lots of good-natured banter. The parents, he alleged, are more likely to come in and say, "They're all taking our jobs" . . . but very few'. The Vietnamese teacher likewise spoke of harmony between groups, claiming that the language programmes contributed to a mutual understanding of cultures: 'we always try to explain about the diversity of different cultures in our society'. Students echoed this sense of 'a pretty good feeling in the school', with one saying that while there was 'racism in the streets' there was much less in the school and this was usually 'just name-calling, or teasing the Asian students'.

Those staff interviewed generally saw the cultural diversity of the school as an enriching experience for their personal lives. The former bilingual coordinator commented that she was often shocked by the outside world, because she had got used to thinking that the world was like 'multicultural Collingwood', but the outer suburbs, for example, don't share the school's views and values.

The secondary school has a range of programmes and features designed to service linguistic and cultural diversity, framed by documented policies. ESL instruction is provided right through to Year 12 — there are beginners' classes for new arrivals, parallel and withdrawal classes in English and the various social science/humanities courses, and in senior years there is Alternative English. Support is also provided in the sciences, through the presence of the ethnic aides, an ESL teacher or a languages teacher in the class, or sometimes through team-teaching, where the second teacher is more actively involved in the structure and teaching of the lesson. There is also a remediation programme at the school, but that serves students regardless of ethnicity.

A Greek bilingual programme was introduced into the primary school in 1981, followed by programmes in Turkish and Vietnamese, and bilingual programmes in Vietnamese and Turkish were implemented in the secondary school in 1986. These involved the teaching of a mainstream subject in the mother tongue as well as, or instead of, in English. The bilingual programmes no longer exist in a systematic way in the post-primary section, but there continues to be Greek (as a language maintenance programme), Turkish and Vietnamese bilingual classes in the primary school to the end of Year 2. Ethnic aides provide support for teachers in mainstream classes in the secondary school by being present, when requested, to interpret or answer specific questions as they occur. The Vietnamese teacher runs a science class for Year 11, in Vietnamese, in her own time after school and helps students in some science classes.

The Languages Other Than English (LOTEs) programme provides both language maintenance strands in Vietnamese, Turkish and Greek, and second language learning strands in French, Beginners' Greek or Spanish to Year 10. Language maintenance is generally compulsory to Year 10 for those whose ancestral language is offered as a LOTE (although large numbers of Vietnamese-speaking students and the non-availability of Vietnamese

Cultures of Schooling

teachers have made it non-compulsory in practice for some years), but studying a second language is not compulsory. While the school as such does not offer languages in Years 11 and 12, it is a site for the Victorian School of Languages, which is held on Saturdays and includes instruction in Vietnamese, Turkish, 'Chinese' and Spanish.

Various social education (social science/humanities) courses throughout the years have 'multicultural' components. The social studies programme in Years 6, 7 and 8 has extension units in multicultural studies and local area studies, for example, but several of the staff said it was more of an ethos throughout the curricula. It was the general studies/humanities programmes in which the bilingual classes first took place. The principal explained that 'personal development' had been taken away from the humanities and given to physical education and home economics staff: 'it will thus include the study of different foods, family relations, . . .'. The home science programme in Year 9, for example, looks at 'multicultural aspects of food and cooking'.

The former bilingual coordinator pointed out that they had had 'cultural studies' programmes in the past, which were quite successful, but she thought that such a concern needed to be integrated into all curricula, rather than be an 'ethnic studies' approach. The language coordinator, on the other hand, thought that the school needed 'ethnic studies. . . . if we are to build up a multicultural society then we should have students studying others' cultures'.

In terms of structural/organizational features — one teacher described the school as 'well-off in that area' — the school has a pastoral care programme and an 'Education in a Multicultural Society' policy. The ethnic aides are not only used in classes as noted above, they are also available to the staff generally, for translation and interpreting in communications with parents and students, and so on. The Centre has had ethnic aides for several years. Parent liaison is assisted by the ethnic aides. Some parents of Vietnamese background attend meetings convened by the Vietnamese ethnic aide, but the Greek Parents' Association, very important in the 1970s, no longer meets. There is, however, a parent 'think tank' convened by the superintendent, and, of course, parent representation on the school council.

Despite the 'community' intent behind the Centre's design, despite a history in the 1970s of encouraging and getting parent involvement (especially amongst the Greek community), and despite the existence of the above organizational features, there wasn't, currently, a great deal of active community support in the secondary school. On the other hand, the primary principal indicated there was more contact with parents in the primary school, and said, for example, that some parents had been vocal in expressing a degree of dissatisfaction with the bilingual programme over recent years, which had a positive effect of increasing accountability. The superintendent (who was the previous secondary principal) said that they got some help from Rotary and other community and youth services, but in terms of parents he said they had 'the usual' problems:

Most parents are working hard. They expect the school to get on with it! ... The points of agreement outweigh those of disagreement despite the popular perception on the part of each group that it is wholly unique. Differences exist and take time.

The current principal, on the other hand, said that there had always been strong support from parents for the teaching of languages — 'there is an insatiable demand'. The Vietnamese teacher claimed that the parents were happy, 'because we are trying to help their children understand more', but that 'it is very hard to get the parents at this school involved'. Last year, however, they had one Vietnamese parent help out in a science class. The Vietnamese aide explained that because parents feel the school is so different, and because they are 'too busy earning money', they don't know much about the school or what students are studying. He has tried to inform them more, but because it is so different 'they don't want to know'. The Turkish teacher said that they had tried to establish a Turkish parents' club two years previously but with no success, largely due, he believed, to the peasant background of the parents. They don't come to such events he explained and only a minority come to parent/teacher nights.

Students interviewed confirmed the view that their parents' work prohibited them from involvement in the school, but added that the barrier of language was also crucial. These students thought that learning their 'own language and culture' was important, and indicated that their choice in studying the mother tongue was more significant than parent pressure. One student stressed the function of having both English and the home language in helping their parents, and that keeping the latter was important because 'when you need to communicate with others you need to know the language very well'.

Several Vietnamese-speaking parents gave much the same rationale. Learning Vietnamese was important because, 'if they speak English at school then they speak English at home and we can't understand the problem'. Others suggested a range of benefits, from reading a Vietnamese newspaper to getting better results. They stressed the language barrier to their involvement in the school, and suggested the need for more ethnic aides to interpret and to inform them about the school.

With regard to the use of new technologies, the school had two computer rooms but, according to one student, these were not used outside computer courses. The language coordinator explained, however, that computers were used in some programmes, but essentially as typewriters — a Turkish class, for example, used them for word processing. She thought they could be used better and was planning greater use. The former coordinator of the bilingual programme said that it was difficult to get into the rooms regularly because they were permanently booked. The principal thought that 'you should grab every new thing that comes along and see what you can make of it', but that they were not being used in mainstream subjects to his knowledge.

Context of the Innovations

The bilingual programme that is the focus of this study of Collingwood Education Centre has two important aspects to its implementation: the long-term history of innovation at the school, and the specific origin of the programme in the Post Primary Bilingual Education Pilot Project, which was a cluster initiative of the Multicultural Education Services within the Ministry of Education, and regional consultants. The LOTEs programme is linked to these aspects but this has a more general history arising from state and federal multicultural policies. It also provided something of the framework and personnel of the bilingual programme.

The school was originally a girls' domestic school, but when the high-rise housing went up in the mid-60s, without the Ministry of Education being warned, it 'burst at the seams'. The current coordinator of the Social Justice Branch in the Ministry of Education, who taught at the school at the time, described how they had to teach in factories and halls and, after a fire, used portable buildings in public parkland. The construction of an Education Centre complex in the mid-70s was a response to the climate of the time — they had had no success in getting students to the Higher School Certificate, and 50 per cent of the student population were of Greek or Yugoslav background — and the Centre was to be an all-purpose community centre, involving students from 'day one' in Kindergarten to when they left. There was a lot of debate about its size (in terms of it being a large, preparatory to Year 12 school) at the time, as there was considerable debate generally, but the main idea had been to establish community involvement. Its design and intention as a 'community school' was, in fact, one of the reasons it was chosen for this project, he said. It was also chosen because it is the starting point for so many new arrivals, and has had 'to grapple with a population that won't sit still' — a phenomenon that really 'hit' the school.

The current Manager of the State Multicultural Education Coordination Unit (which replaced the Multicultural Education Services) also taught at the school then, and confirmed the degree of experimentation going on at the school and generally in the late 1960s and 1970s:

> It was the Ministry's view that attention to inner urban schools was needed, looking at the issue of what was relevant, and so on. A parallel activity was the VSTA [Victorian Secondary Teachers Association] inner urban group who took on the issue of ESL. Collingwood was one of a group ... which created pressure to have ESL acknowledged; it was a grassroots thing. ... Collingwood was one of the characteristic schools related to Housing Commission and migration patterns, and there were mostly Greeks and Yugoslavs. ... ESL wasn't *formally* taught in 1968. Collingwood had the first designated Migrant Ed. teachers, but before that had activities and structures dealing with it internally.

At the same time as being more responsive to the English language needs of NESB students, there was increasing pressure to operate more as a community-based school and to develop collaborative decision-making processes:

> [The school] initiated the Greek Parents' Association, which met Sunday mornings. Up to then it had had nil parent involvement.
>
> A significant element at that time was the Greek kids in senior years; some had made it and were sophisticated, and took on a lot of issues. There was a Greek student group which was active on school council, and assertive about the need to link school and home. Kids had not been allowed to come to school socials, so they made the socials into Greek dances.
>
> The principal . . . was a key person through the critical period of the 1970s. She had a working-class view that working-class schools shouldn't be in the pits and was prepared to take risks. She was enormously supportive of the staff, and gave them decision-making and initiating roles. No other schools operated like this.

There was also increasing interest in introducing mother-tongue programmes:

> There were no languages then — it was a miserable inner suburban girls' school which taught needlework and cooking. The languages started in the early 1970s, due to pressures in the school, built on the perceptions of the kids and parents articulated through teachers. . . . Collingwood was conscious of the need to teach mother tongue, and used whatever means to get Greek speakers to teach at school, . . . but the Yugoslavs were never as keen on keeping their language.

She left the school in the late 1970s, and since then it has undergone massive change — demographic, structural, leadership. The large numbers of students of Greek background 'disappeared almost overnight', replaced by students of Turkish and Vietnamese background. This affected the language plans, she explained, because there were no longer one or two major groups.

The Post Primary Bilingual Education Pilot Project came about through this wider concern with issues of language maintenance, cognitive development and bilingual education, which had begun to receive systemic attention, and the school's concern that it needed to be doing more for the newer waves of immigrant students. This four-year cluster project involved three schools — Collingwood Education Centre, Brunswick East High and Preston Girls' High — constructing bilingual programmes to suit the specific needs of each but under a general umbrella project. The three schools and regional consultants set up a committee and wrote a detailed, researched submission presenting a general rationale and individual programmes.

There had been programmes in transitional bilingual education in a few primary schools for several years, including the Collingwood Education Centre, which had primary programmes since 1981, and this had interested people in doing something at the post-primary level. Several teachers had raised the question of what the school was doing for groups such as the Turkish and Vietnamese. The ex-principal expressed the opinion that the bilingual approach was 'modish' in the early 1980s.

The then languages coordinator, who became the bilingual coordinator, pointed out that 'Collingwood had a history of interest in multiculturalism and language; I don't know why because it wasn't doing much'. She explained that the current Manager of the State Multicultural Education Coordination Unit (then with the Multicultural Education Services) approached her and the principal about setting up the project, and together with the other schools set up a committee and lobbied the Minister and local members — 'a lot of work!' She said they didn't ask for money, but extra staff, and the rest was to be provided from within the school's allocation.

The submission for the umbrella bilingual project sets out in some detail the objectives and rationale of the broader proposal (see Chapter 4). Within this, Collingwood Education Centre's individual proposal was for two further classroom teachers and one programme aide for a post-primary part-bilingual programme in Mandarin, Vietnamese and Turkish with social studies/ humanities as the 'focal points'. This required 1.0 Vietnamese teacher (to teach Years 8–11), 0.5 'Chinese' teacher (Years 8–10) and 0.5 Turkish teacher (years 6–9), with the aim being to double this provision in the third year of the project. The school already had Greek and Turkish bilingual programmes at the primary level and a Greek language programme at the post-primary level.

The proposal delineated different aims: for students of Indo-Chinese background it was to facilitate conceptual development in mother tongue and English and 'prepare them for language-based subjects such as humanities'; for Turkish-speaking students it was to 'build on their strengths in their mother tongue and to ameliorate some of the problems commonly faced by second phase learners' of English. The students of Indo-Chinese background were seen to choose maths and science courses, *regardless of suitability*, because they lack confidence and the appropriate language skills to cope with other subject areas such as humanities and commerce' [original emphasis]. This was seen to be necessary because of the recommendations of the 1985 Victorian *Ministerial Review of Post-compulsory Schooling*, known as the Blackburn Report, that humanities be compulsory in senior years.[1]

Staff, student and parent support had been sought and established — at a curriculum day, by survey and through meetings and representation. The then languages coordinator and the principal were the school's representatives on the proposal committee. The former indicated that it had been a difficult political exercise getting support from local members of parliament and other state politicians. The cluster of schools continued to meet after the project was approved, but each school had quite different programmes, according to the coordinator.

The Innovations in Practice

The bilingual programme ran for two years (1986–7) with some bilingual classes operating in following years. A 'Chinese' teacher could not be found, so only the Vietnamese and Turkish classes were run, but a Vietnamese teacher could not be found until the middle of first term, 1986. The programme involved students of Vietnamese and Turkish backgrounds having two of their general studies (Years 6–9) or humanities periods (Years 10–11) taught in the mother tongue, as well as having three periods in the language maintenance programme, making a total of five in the mother tongue. Science courses and one ESL class became involved later. The Vietnamese classes were to be in Years 8–11, while the Turkish classes were in Years 6–9, these years being chosen because of the concentration of students from those backgrounds at those levels.

The original proposal had all periods of general studies or humanities taught by the bilingual teacher. However, withdrawal of these students for two periods from the mainstream class, normally allotted four or five periods, became the main strategy. Students not of those backgrounds stayed in the mainstream class with the subject teacher. This model, where the two teachers shared a class, was referred to as 'team-teaching', although it did not necessarily involve the teachers together in the same lesson. The Vietnamese teacher also worked as a support teacher in some classes. In science classes, for example, the technical terminology used was almost entirely in English, as was the lesson generally, with Vietnamese being used to explain concepts where necessary.

The Vietnamese teacher was originally to teach fifteen fifty-minute periods — five each for Years 8/9 combined, Year 9 and Year 10 — and have six left for materials development. With the withdrawal method, the bilingual teachers were only used for two of the four or five periods planned. Some of this came to be used up through their acting in support roles in mainstream classes, helping students of their language background while the subject teacher taught the lesson. But because few mainstream teachers took up the offer for help, both teachers had several periods free, which were then devoted to teaching in the language maintenance programme.

The content studied by the bilingual classes depended, of course, on the mainstream subject in which the classes were placed; whether it be in the humanities, sciences or ESL, for example. A Year 8 programme in general studies, for instance, was constructed around units of work adapted from the ESL materials, *Highways*, available in the school:

Unit 1: Aboriginal History
Geography — Uluru and environs

Unit 2: Australian Exploration
Geography — Murray River, Mt Kosciusko, Victoria

Unit 3: Survival in a New Land
Foundation of South Australia, the SA Company
Commerce — companies and shares

Unit 4: The Environment and Conservation
Introduced species, their effect on indigenous flora and fauna
Long term effects

Other humanities classes looked at themes such as myths of origin and world religions, peace studies, causes of war, individuals and nations, and so on. A Year 10 ESL class of Vietnamese-speaking students involved students and both the ESL and Vietnamese teachers watching news programmes and discussing events in both languages. The choice of which classes and subjects were to be included in the bilingual programme depended on the individual subject teacher and whether he or she wished to be involved.

Despite the substantial planning that had gone into the submission stage, a number of problems associated with the implementation of the bilingual programme had been overlooked. Most importantly, the difficulties of timetabling were immense, because each of the four administrative units in the secondary school devised its own timetable according to its own priorities. Two of the units held general studies at the same time, which made things easier there, but lack of uniformity meant that bilingual classes were often provided on an *ad hoc* basis. If students were withdrawn from a class that clashed with other subjects then few students would be willing to forego other subject lessons, and smaller classes resulted. On the other hand, the LOTEs programme was facilitated by blocking on the timetable, although there were still some clashes because some classes were held at the same time as other activities. There was also the timetabling problem of whether students not in the language maintenance classes should be made to study one as a second language. Timetabling was renegotiated each year by the units.

The various administrative units within the school identified the students to take part in the bilingual programme and then required parental permission. In 1987, not all Vietnamese-speaking students could be accommodated in the programme. Class sizes varied considerably, with low numbers particularly in the Turkish classes. A case study of Collingwood Education Centre programmes carried out by Joy Elley for the Commonwealth Schools Commission in 1987 referred to Vietnamese science classes with about twenty students and general studies classes of about five students. One bilingual class was discontinued in 1987 because a number of the students moved from the area.[2]

The Vietnamese and Turkish teachers were, in practice, given a smaller period allowance, of four and three periods respectively, for materials development, which was primarily spent in translating the materials and following the lesson plans prepared by the mainstream teachers, with some planning and discussion.

Apart from the submission for this innovation, the school has outlined its objectives regarding bilingual education and the teaching of languages other than English in several places. The 1988 School Policies handbook stresses conceptual development, competency in mother tongue and English, students' self-esteem and 'pride in both cultures', confidence and motivation. It goes on to say that, in Years 7–12:

> Secondary students receive at least 20 per cent of instruction time in their mother tongue at all levels. This ratio may vary slightly according to the students' needs.

The LOTEs programme is framed in terms of both language maintenance and second language learning, emphasizing linguistic competence, self-esteem and confidence 'by promoting their home culture', promoting 'understanding and tolerance of other people's culture and background', giving students better vocational opportunities, and strengthening 'links between the student and the family and the school and the family'. The LOTEs programme has also produced other documents outlining the cognitive/linguistic, social/psychological and political/economic advantages of learning a LOTE. One also specifies advantages to Collingwood Education Centre — in terms of successful, past performance at Year 12 in mother tongue; the proportion of bilingual students; the reputation of Collingwood Education Centre in LOTEs and bilingual education, having been 'chosen' to participate in the bilingual project; and because of parental support.

The superintendent (who was the former principal) defined the major goal of the bilingual programme as moving students 'towards improved access to those skills which will fit the student to live in Australia and be a decision maker'. The current principal claimed it was 'to value the mother tongue' and enhance concept development, but not at the expense of English learning. The former bilingual coordinator stressed both skills-based and self-esteem goals, and reiterated the differing specific goals of the Vietnamese and Turkish strands — students of the former background needing to be 'pushed' into humanities courses more by providing them with better language and conceptual skills, 'to better prepare Asians for a wider curriculum'. She didn't see any contradictions between trying to meet goals of mainstream skills and esteem of cultural difference, but the superintendent said 'there can be, but not necessarily. To act on the basis of esteem of cultural difference can result in positive gains in the field of access'. The language coordinator stated that the goals of the LOTEs programme were essentially mother-tongue maintenance, and that she hoped that the students also come to understand others. Self-esteem, however, was the first priority, with academic skills following.

The superintendent saw the underlying view of education as one of empowerment: 'it is a world where literacy is determinant of status and wellbeing'. The ex-bilingual coordinator likewise claimed that it was to better prepare students for further education and the outside world, a world of pluralism and work where it was important for students to feel good about themselves; 'different students have different needs and the education system has to address this in programmes or through a general philosophy'. The superintendent didn't know whether he was right or not, but the ex-coordinator asserted that 'you have to believe in what you believe in'.

The bilingual programme was linked to the outside world essentially through its being part of the cluster project. Apart from that, the principal said that it was 'relatively unique to the three schools — post-primary, that is', but linked to multicultural, literacy, social justice and equal opportunity objectives. The former coordinator explained that the cluster met on a regular basis — twice a term — for coordination and sometimes administration and to keep each other informed about progress and problems, which they would share and solve. But there was not a lot of similarity, she added, so they couldn't share methods. Within the school, there were links with the subjects being taught in the bilingual programme — humanities, science and ESL, although these tended to be with the individuals involved rather than the faculties as a whole.

The former coordinator described the curriculum as being devised week-to-week and not consolidated. The Vietnamese teacher elaborated on this by saying that she made her own materials sometimes, but Year 11, for example, used a textbook. When 'team-teaching' was involved, she claimed that she mostly just translated the the English text. It was said also that there was some discussion about teaching strategy, because there were various approaches that could have been used — team-teaching, withdrawal, support, and so on. The former coordinator claimed that all approaches were used, but which ones and how much depended on the bilingual and subject teacher. The Vietnamese teacher commented that she didn't think she had a particular style, but preferred 'the Australian way', where students have their own opinion. She added that the students preferred this too. She used discussion in the current Year 11 class, rather than have them working on their own, because she only had them for one period a week. Likewise, the Turkish teacher claimed that as they only had two periods, it was not enough time to develop activities, so he mostly just explained or discussed things. He said that the students indicated that they preferred that.

The former bilingual coordinator explained that a variety of teaching styles was used because of the different areas worked in. In science, the students in the Vietnamese language class were doing experiments, requiring individual learning and inquiry. But it was said that there was also teacher-centred work. The Vietnamese teacher commented that it was not entirely true that students of Vietnamese background preferred traditional learning styles for cultural reasons; 'they try very hard to learn with the text by themselves, because they don't have the language. When they can discuss in

Vietnamese in class, they like to do so ... ; sometimes they complain that other teachers don't explain enough'.

Student assessment depended on the subject in which the bilingual classes occurred. Broadly, it was continuous and based on homework, assignments, attendance and participation.

The teaching and curriculum styles used in the LOTEs programme were equally mercurial. The coordinator said that topics of study have grammar components, but that these were not that important and they didn't teach a lot of grammar. She added that the Vietnamese students 'think that if you teach grammar then you are a good teacher'. While staff, she said, were aware of the debates over immersion in language experience versus explicit teaching of grammar, there was not a lot of discussion, nor did they change what they did much because this could be unsettling for students. There was no policy on teaching materials, but she explained that there was a dearth of appropriate texts.

Evaluation: The Bilingual Programme

Both in the evaluation carried out at the end of 1986, the first year of the bilingual programme, and in the interviews held for the present study, all those who commented on the bilingual programme spoke of significant outcomes; whether they be in terms of the students' performances and cognitive development, or the professional development of the staff. Yet most also spoke of these benefits being hamstrung by a number of problems, primarily centring around the organizational difficulties involved in administering a programme which demanded a degree of flexibility and whole-school support.

The evaluation carried out at the end of the first year of the secondary bilingual programme in 1986 stressed the experimental nature of the project, and its status as a 'challenge' to the school — staff and students alike. The coordinator commented on 'small but significant gains in the students' progress and learning', and on the '*process* of tolerance, acceptance and learning' involved. The Vietnamese teacher summarized the key problems — the difficulties of team-teaching, a fixed timetable, teaching style, the withdrawal/ support dilemma, and student and staff attitudes.

Revealing that she felt a degree of uncertainty at first, a science teacher recalled she became involved when she realized she had students, especially new arrivals, with severe ESL problems. They had not been sure how to organize it, so they tried a support approach first, with students divided into group activities. She noted a number of benefits, including her own awareness 'of the magnitude of the problems that face ESL students' and the need to change her teaching style. She added that the students underwent 'magical changes':

> They stopped looking confused and bored and became attentive and cheerful. They went from being mute ... [to being] eager to

participate and ask questions. Their comprehension seemed to increase enormously, and they were much more willing to 'have a go' at speaking or writing about things in science.

She noted, however, that there was not enough time to plan and discuss with other teachers. An ESL teacher bemoaned the limited time that can be spent with the Vietnamese teacher in the class, and hoped that her students would be able to have bilingual classes the following year. One the other hand, two general studies teachers claimed 'it involved an incredible upheaval and that the amount of disruption to the mainstream course seemed disproportionate to the value of the programme'. The withdrawal of students from the mainstream class was particularly disruptive, both for students and staff. At the same time, they maintained that the Vietnamese programme was most successful because it filled an immediate need. The Turkish programme was not as useful because most of these students 'were already fairly proficient in English. Therefore there was no noticeable change in their competence, attitude or confidence when they returned to the mainstream class'. They also noted a lack of continuity in the mainstream class, 'as all lessons had to be "one-offs" to accommodate the withdrawn students'. The problem of preparing material in advance was stressed.

A humanities teacher claimed that there was 'a marked improvement in the attitude, comprehension ability, linguistic ability and the overall confidence of the students', and noted that this 'gave the Vietnamese students an advantage over other Asian students in the class who did not have access to the bilingual programme. Another teacher, who generally responded positively to the programme, also said that she was concerned 'that more learning in a mother tongue means less learning of the mainstream language. Can our kids afford not to get as much skill in the English language as we can teach them?'

The Vietnamese students responded very positively to the programme in the 1986 evaluation. One Year 8 student described it as 'very useful, because I can learn more Vietnamese and English. Also it helps me to understand the vocabulary more thoroughly'. A Year 9 student expressed the opinion that having a Vietnamese teacher helps in understanding 'difficult vocabulary' and 'hard phrases', 'rather than having to ask an English teacher for help outside of class'. Another Year 9 student concluded that, 'my writing skills are very poor so I hope that the bilingual classes will continue'.

The transitional nature of the bilingual programme was underlined by a Year 10 student:

> If we want to have good results the most important thing is to have good English. If we want our English to be good, we must not only speak more, read more and have contact with Australian teachers, but we have to know the way of study and we have to understand the vocabulary. But how can I be helped to get good results? I think the only way that can help me to success is the bilingual programme.

Another Year 10 student said that it made 'knowledge go further' and hoped English could be included as a subject in the bilingual programme to help make 'essay writing easier'. The bilingual programme, it was added, was 'the key to open the valuable treasures in the world' and would help students 'to get a beautiful success'. A third Year 10 student claimed that, as a result of the bilingual course, 'I can speak and understand more grammar'. Many of these students voiced the opinion that the bilingual programme would be most useful in science.

Parents seemed to know little about the programme but expressed support for the idea of it when it was explained. One parent said that while he had not known his child had taken part in the programme, he thought it was a good idea and would be happy to participate in it if needed. Also, a guardian claimed to have noticed the improvement in her nephew's understanding as a result of the programme.

Three years later, most concerned still thought that the programme had had positive outcomes. The Vietnamese teacher emphasized the actual benefits to the students: 'because they understand the lessons! They can do their work and feel confident about keeping up'.

Despite the problems of coordination, the social science teacher was equally positive about the bilingual programme. He stressed the aid to conceptual development:

> Bilingual classes aid cognitive development; LOTEs don't . . . ; we need to target groups that find conceptual development difficult. . . . It's needed most in primary grades . . . but it's also needed in secondary years because that's when conceptual development can be a real problem. Kids are moving from concrete to abstract thinking in Year 7, but it's happening much later than it should be. They talk of 'this' war, not 'war' in general. In the transition unit in Years 6, 7 and 8, you can see it happening.
>
> 'Anglo' kids have many of the same problems, but many have parents who at least can discuss with them what's happening on the TV in English, they may have read documents, or know the moral issues of 'Baby Kajal' [about adoption]. The Vietnamese wouldn't know. The linguistic and cultural disadvantage is countered by bilingual education.

He added that, in one case, it was the only way to get two particular students to communicate. An example was also given of one female student who had poor language skills and learning difficulties, and was continually sullen, but as a result of the bilingual programme became very excited in one lesson and kept saying that she had learnt that particular topic.

The secondary principal also thought that the students saw it as useful — 'this is the ultimate test':

Cultures of Schooling

> Where it works, it's brilliant — for example, where [the Vietnamese teacher] can teach physics to kids in Vietnamese. Some kids have to spend six hours a night just translating the physics text book.

At the same time, however, he added:

> I don't know about meeting its objectives. In a short term it had an impact, but it fell short of what they *hoped* to achieve. In terms of learning efficiency, Victorian Certificate of Education results improved, but I don't know if this was because of the bilingual programme.

The Vietnamese teacher thought that there was a change in students' behaviour and motivation, but questioned their motives for staying on at school, 'sometimes I wonder if they stay back because of the bilingual and language classes or because of Austudy' (financial assistance given to disadvantaged students to allow them to continue their education).

The former coordinator believed that the objectives of the programme had been met, but explained that there were no 'measurable educational goals' set, nor did they pre- and post-test. Given that there were no instruments to assess whether students' linguistic and cognitive capacities had improved as a result of the bilingual programme, the claims made to this effect referred to above have to rely on anecdotal evidence. The evaluation carried out in 1986 used no such measures, relying on interviews and statements. Within the programme, the Turkish teacher said that he left student assessment to the 'class teacher', although he occasionally had them prepare written work.

One student claimed that, because in the bilingual class students went over what they had done in the English class, they understood more, and he would like to have bilingual classes if they were still there. Most ESL students in Years 9, 11 and 12 who were surveyed were generally positive about the bilingual programme and most of the students questioned had been in a bilingual class. They stressed the benefits of 'doing the same work as English students but in your own language' and that 'it help us better in our mother tongue'. One or two explained something of how or why it was there: 'To help students who is lack of English or to help the students to understand more about the subject'. Others, however, expressed the opinion that it was 'not useful for our future' or they got 'nothing much' out of it. Two students said they didn't like it because, being withdrawn, they were singled out as 'one nationality'. Another claimed it made no difference to the school because it was only for a year, while another thought it could be better if it continued from year to year.

A number of parents of Vietnamese background who were interviewed knew little about bilingual programme, except that there were senior science classes available, although both the Vietnamese and Turkish teachers believed that parents approved of the programme. The principal, however, said he noted a degree of 'buyer resistance', in that 'some families want their kids to be in English-speaking classes'.

The former coordinator claimed that, if nothing else, it had been a good learning process for students and teachers. A major outcome for her was the professional development of teachers which resulted from the fact that teachers were exposed to situations not otherwise experienced. This, it was asserted, had made many more teachers aware of the language needs of students and of how to meet those needs, and that the 1986 evaluation of the programme showed this.

The superintendent likewise claimed that there was a 'greater sense of relevance of the first language on the part of students' and a 'growth in cooperative working relationships between some staff'. The Turkish teacher agreed that what made it successful was the nature of the staff involved, the majority of whom accepted that it was useful, and that there was a very supportive administration. He also stressed the nature of the clientele, because if it had been more than 50 per cent 'Anglo' then the students would have rejected being pulled out of class.

Despite the positive outcomes expressed by staff and students, the bilingual programme had all but ended by the beginning of 1988, apart from one or two periods of bilingual support in Vietnamese in physics and chemistry classes, and a senior science class held by the Vietnamese teacher in her own time, after school. The bilingual teachers now teach their respective languages in the LOTEs programme, which had absorbed both bilingual strands. The Vietnamese teacher explained that:

> when I first came, there were no Vietnamese classes, so I started only in the bilingual programme. It was very hard to get teachers to agree to work as a team, so I was left with some free teaching time. So I set up some Vietnamese classes, and the students were very happy with that. . . . I became more interested in teaching Vietnamese language, because there were many problems in the bilingual programme. The first year, it was nearly all bilingual. The second year, it was half and half. This year, it is nearly 80 per cent language teaching.

The ex-principal noted further:

> the programme took time to settle down as the language teachers and the humanities/science teachers learned to cooperate. The latter came to appreciate the value of a bilingual approach (gradually) and were less resentful of ceding time. However, this healthy development only lasted for brief periods as hiccoughs were experienced.

The ex-principal suggested that the 'degree of understanding of the programme and its rationale was small and needed a great deal more low key preparation'. This showed, he believed, that the school was not as aware of its cultural context as he had thought. The understanding was 'superficial' but had deepened, he felt, as a result of the programme, 'to the degree that the link between learning and cultural demands is beginning to be made. . . . demands of empowerment override the "sentimental" side of multiculturalism', even if the latter, in granting esteem to cultural differences, was, in itself, 'inherently valuable'. At the same time, he stressed that 'children learn from a position of security and sense of identity. By helping the child maintain the culture of the home we assist in giving the child what he needs for effective learning'. He thought that by the end of its first year, the programme had begun to meet its objectives.

The issue of staff attitudes, however, was a recurring one. A critical lesson for the Vietnamese teacher was that, 'I now know that you need much broader support to make it work'. The ex-principal also identified staff attitudes, and some student resentment, as key problems. He put these down to 'insufficient preparation of both camps'. The Vietnamese aide said that some teachers thought that they would lose jobs as a result of the bilingual programme; others simply didn't see its significance.

The former coordinator suggested that there was no systematic way of supporting programmes like this although systems have a rhetoric of support for multicultural education. She claimed that programmes like this die and are not 'seen through', which she considered a waste of resources. The Vietnamese teacher likewise noted a structural problem, but within the school:

> there is nothing continuous, nothing well planned . . . having to work in team-teaching with different teachers and different groups of teachers all the time is a problem.
>
> The bilingual programme was not linked to other things in the school. The other teachers never came to the bilingual programme; we had to go to them to offer help. The language programme is different, because it is independent. It is fixed in the timetable and you have your own class. You don't have to ask people to team-teach.
>
> . . . Not even the principal can teach people to team-teach. Most teachers think they need more English. They don't understand how bilingual conceptual development and transfer works.

The current principal gave as a critical lesson the general point that a bilingual programme is very difficult to organize in a secondary school, as opposed to a primary school, because of the range of subjects and the staffing and timetable restrictions: 'How do you select the subjects to be taught bilingually? How do you choose teachers?' A lot of time went into recruiting the Turkish teacher, for example, and timetabling problems 'were one of the main reasons it didn't get up. How then do you run a class of five kids if the average class size is twenty-five?' He speculated that perhaps its most important problem was associated with its nature as a pilot project:

The main disappointment is that it was not institutionalized. It is now past its peak; it has lost its impetus. This is possibly due to the way the teachers were given to us, through special arrangements. And they were supposed to have a time allowance for course development.

A social science teacher, 'one of the few' who taught in the bilingual programme, said that:

> it's outrageous that the programme was scrapped because it couldn't be staffed. The bilingual teachers had demands made upon them as LOTEs, maths and science teachers. All this was done on the general allocation, not special funding. They were employed specifically for the bilingual programme and maths, not LOTEs, which they ended up doing.

He added that coordination was difficult — they had to meet every fortnight, in their own time before school — because of overlapping what he and the bilingual teacher did. He often had to 'stop and regroup; two steps forward, one step back, regroup, half an inch forward...'. Having to resource the project from within the school's general allocation rather than special funding made the staffing less flexible.

An organizational problem noted in the 1988 Elley study was that some mainstream teachers resented having to give up part of their allotted time with those students withdrawn for two periods. They felt that they could accomplish less themselves as a result. The necessity of planning jointly and in advance was also demanding, as were the difficulties of team-teaching and having to adjust teaching styles. Both that study and the present study here revealed a high degree of hesitancy on the part of mainstream teachers initially about taking part in the programme, usually due to lack of information. The absence of preparation noted above by the Vietnamese teacher was echoed in the comments of one teacher in 1987, whose initial reaction was, 'what a muddle! Why is this happening so fast without us having time to sort it out properly?' The case study carried out in 1987 suggested that there was a lot of hostility left by earlier, unsuccessful attempts at language teaching, particularly due to tension existing between mother-tongue and second language approaches.[3]

The Turkish teacher mentioned some teacher hostility, but dwelt on practical difficulties: the delivery of material not happening on time; and his own lack of training in the social sciences. On the latter issue, he said that he felt more comfortable with senior science that junior social science, and it required much more work of him. He spent much time going through texts in the library to find things that were useful. The Vietnamese teacher was also in a similar position of lack of expertise in the social sciences, which necessitated a degree of on-the-spot 'retraining'.

Cultures of Schooling

A major change which occurred in the implementation of the programme, was that where bilingual classes had been located initially in the social sciences, with the specific intention in the Vietnamese strand to steer the students towards the humanities, this changed to include more science. This happened largely because the students, the Vietnamese speakers in particular, when surveyed, wished it that way. It also suggests, perhaps, that the teachers are more able to assist students in their areas of expertise. An unintended benefit may be that these teachers can act as role models by functioning in these areas.

The Turkish teacher, however, remarked that he was 'still unsure as to whether it was helping or just confusing the students by introducing terminology in both languages'. He was particularly concerned that it may not be of use to those students who had been here for some time. He felt that the Turkish strand was not as successful as the Vietnamese. The Vietnamese aide, further, stressed the transitional nature of a bilingual programme, and the need to maintain an emphasis on English language learning, by arguing that whilst some students understand the terminology 'even in Year 10 they still can't fill out a form or write properly'. He also made the crucial point that bilingual tuition was needed in subjects like maths, although some staff disagreed, because those subjects also involve cognitive development and manipulation of concepts.

Reasons offered for the premature demise of the programme, given that it was planned to be a four-year project, were several. The former coordinator explained that, in the case of the Vietnamese classes, there were not enough staff, and they were not given any more when it was requested. The Turkish teacher claimed that in his strand it was simply a question of falling numbers. The local area was a 'stepping stone' from which families move when they have enough money. The numbers in his LOTEs classes were also dropping. Last year he had only thirteen students in the Years 7 and 8 class and eleven in Years 9 and 10, whereas four years ago he had twenty-two in Years 9 and 10. In Year 7 this year there were less than ten students of Turkish background. The school therefore made a decision related to numbers to end the Turkish strand, although, he added, 'actually we never talked on this, just all of a sudden it finished'.

The former coordinator maintained that a critical lesson for her was that 'if you believe in something it's worth battling on' and, despite the difficult situations they had sometimes, she thought it had been worthwhile. But, she added, the bilingual programme needed a lot of support from staff to keep going, and it had not become part of the structured provision of the school nor had it come to share the staff expectations of the mainstream subjects. The Vietnamese teacher blamed lack of committed staff, planning, continuity and links to school organization. The current principal suggested that resources, or lack thereof, were a crucial determinant. A social science teacher believed that the school was not prepared to staff the programme but had used the allocated staff for LOTEs and other subjects.

The possibility of the bilingual programme returning was remote. As the Turkish teacher explained:

> the school has stopped talking about bilingual. I don't know what the present administration's thinking is on this. We don't have a co-ordinator any more; nobody wants to do it now. It's just a LOTEs programme.

The former coordinator confirmed that she didn't know if the staff were still willing — and it needed at least one or two to shoulder it. The Vietnamese teacher remarked that, although many of the younger Australian-born Vietnamese-speaking students were coming through with English now, there was still a need for the bilingual programme. There would not, however, be one: 'I would not like to work in the bilingual programme any more. It is too hard for me and I don't think it's worthwhile'. The principal explained:

> We work just year by year. We will do as much as we can with the resources we've got. We know the bilingual is *ideal*, but we will just have to see how far we can afford to approximate to this. We are at the mercy of resources, and, in the secondary section, of the timetable. It is a matter of getting staff with the skills needed who want to teach it, getting the numbers of kids into the classes, and getting the staff to do the timetable hijinks.

Asked if the bilingual programme would still be going if there was greater systems support, one interviewee said, 'probably... in the leadership at the top level of the Ministry there has been a total lack of interest in the post-primary branch of LOTE'. Echoing this, the principal stated that, 'multiculturalism has always been a con, chronically under-resourced; there has been tokenism only, at election times'. Understandably, then, as he noted, while the project had 'put bilingual education on the agenda for the school', it had 'not changed the organization of the school across the board'.

There was a general feeling that the programme could be reproduced as long as the problems which arose were ironed out. Most of these were structural issues, about the difficulties of actually implementing a programme, both within the school and in terms of policy and support from above. The Vietnamese teacher thought that there needed to be continuity, both in having the students continue in the programme from year to year, and in having the same teachers to work with each year. She also thought you needed a committed staff. She then added:

> No. I don't think a bilingual programme can work well here in Australia. It could work well in an underdeveloped country, but not in a developed country, because of the dominance of the mainstream language. It is different in Malaysia or Indonesia, because the

Cultures of Schooling

bilingual programme would be a real bilingual programme, because there are real benefits; here it is just an *ad hoc* programme.

The principal thought it could work in schools with vertical, modular timetables which would be more flexible. He also said that it would 'be better to do away with the uncertainty of knowing how long you'll have the resources for', otherwise it only has an 'add-on' quality. The former coordinator said it needed to be staffed in ways that didn't affect the rest of the school in the competition for resources, and that made it stable and secure. Because of the structure of their school, they had done it 'the hard way'. They had a long-term plan, but this was not implemented because they didn't have enough staff. Such planning was, nonetheless, essential. The opposition that arose could have been dealt with, she thought, through inservicing and 'staff liaison' — this was critical.

The Turkish teacher also thought more whole staff inservicing was needed, so the goals of the progammes were understood by all. This would answer individual objections. Discussions with those that have tried bilingual education, such as them, would help other schools. Staff need to be trained, and students informed and convinced.

Other problems which schools need to address were associated with pedagogy and curriculum. The Turkish teacher, conscious of his own difficulties with social science methodology, stressed the training of teachers. The Vietnamese teacher also emphasized training for team-teaching. Some support in terms of language development would also help.

The social science teacher suggested that bilingual classes are needed mostly in junior grades in the primary school but should be used in such a way that it is followed through from year to year. It need not be fixed, and social science is not the most crucial area, but you could have maths one year and science the next. There is still a need in secondary education, however, because of the conceptual development, particularly in Year 7, when the shift from concrete to abstract thinking is most evident.

Certainly, observation of a Year 10 science lesson, in which an ESL aide supported the teacher, suggested that the need for a Vietnamese aide was still great. Language difficulties existed, which affected the quality of communication between teacher and students, in a class — on evolution and processes of adaptation — where the concepts and language used were quite challenging. These problems were not significantly alleviated by the aide, who targeted individuals with particular problems but could not facilitate conceptual grasp by being able to explain in Vietnamese, which all bar one or two students spoke. The science teacher said he never knew if the students understood. Moreover, the aide had only been in the class for some weeks and it was not guaranteed that he would be there next term. This type of arrangement, reported the science teacher, had been in existence for some years.

The students in the Year 11 physics class, which had the Vietnamese teacher come in to support for one period a week, discussed a lot amongst themselves in her absence, presumably to supply the explanations that she normally provided. The numbers of Vietnamese students in the school meant that she had to spread herself thinly to get to as many as possible — the result being she could only provide support to a smaller number of students (and these had to be senior, given their immediate demands), but only with minimal contact, unless she ran unofficial classes in her own time after school, which she did.

The primary bilingual programmes have experienced difficulties not unlike those of the secondary school. Declining numbers forced the school to change its Greek bilingual programme into a withdrawal language maintenance programme. There is also a difference between the remaining two programmes. The Turkish bilingual programme is a misnomer, explained the primary principal, because it was simply a mainstream class learning only in Turkish; whereas the Vietnamese programme was more a support programme in which the aide participated in several subject areas, using both Vietnamese and English. The earlier emphasis on a more clearly transitional approach had lost something of its force, he indicated.

There had been an initial 'ghettoization' of the Turkish classes because of the lack of a link between Turkish and mainstream staff, but that had apparently been overcome. Commonwealth funding for the programme will run out in the next few years, and the principal indicated that there will have to be a re-evaluation to consider whether the school wants to continue with it. He is worried by the fact that those coming out of the programme are those with the greatest language difficulties. As a result, a number of parents have started to take their children out of the programme. They see English learning as the school's main job. The school has begun to come to grips with this by integrating the programme more across subjects.

The primary principal, despite his reservations, thought that the bilingual approach can work, but needed to give students more exposure to English, and iron out the problems regarding staff attitudes — both bilingual and mainstream teachers — towards the programme. Another model, such as one in which the bilingual teacher had a greater support role in mainstream areas, needed to be considered.

Evaluation: Teaching Languages Other Than English

The LOTEs coordinator thought that the programme met its objectives 'up to a point' — in terms of self-esteem she said 'yes'; in terms of skills, she said that she assesses these as they go along. There was no uniform assessment procedure, however, because of the very different levels of the students. Assessment was generally descriptive, but grades were given if they were wanted. There was no attempt to impose a particular level as a goal because of these differences, and, she added, some didn't need high levels of competence.

Cultures of Schooling

In three ESL classes surveyed, Years 9, 11 and 12, all students said that learning the mother tongue was 'very' (72 per cent) or 'fairly' important. Both the secondary principal and the Turkish teacher spoke of significant parental support for language maintenance programmes in the school. Parents who were interviewed, and who knew little about the bilingual programme, spoke at length of the LOTEs programme. Several agreed that learning Vietnamese was important. One said that they got better results as a consequence, and could, for example, read a Vietnamese newspaper. Another said, however, that the students must be made to understand English to understand the teachers — 'sometimes they explain but they still don't know'.

The LOTEs programme was, however, under a degree of pressure, largely related to changing demographic conditions and the structure of the school whereby grades were broken up into independent administrative units. Languages were offered as composite classes in the transition unit, for example, with the modern Greek class being made up of students from Years 6, 7 and 8. In 1988 this class had fourteen students. On the other hand, numbers in the Vietnamese classes for Years 7–8 and Years 9–10 are over twenty-five, requiring that they be broken up into groups with the help of the Vietnamese aide.

The spanning of two administrative grade units created staffing and curriculum difficulties. The need for another Vietnamese teacher and lack of Vietnamese materials were mentioned by the coordinator as crucial. The Turkish teacher also had to make do with materials he wasn't entirely happy with; in a Year 9 class observed he had students reading old primary readers imported from Turkey which, he said, the students hated.

The availability of languages other than English for those not covered in the language maintenance classes was also said to be in doubt, primarily due to the lack of staff. The coordinator asked, 'what will happen to the students who have studied these languages next year?' The demand by students for second language learning classes was also a problem because most students, outside of the language maintenance strand, didn't want to learn another language, particularly if they were NESB students whose mother tongue was not catered for. The coordinator added that the *raison d'etre* for maintenance courses was often more in terms of keeping students — both of these facts meant that there wasn't 'a philosophy of the value of another language'. She was hesitant about having beginners' Greek, as well, because if it is offered then the Vietnamese 'get upset'.

There is, consequently, some controversy around the LOTEs programme, reflecting a history of conflict and a disagreement over objectives and methodology. The whole LOTEs progamme, as a consequence, was currently being reviewed. One teacher commented that he was not happy with the languages offered and the way they were taught. While he supported language teaching, he said he would prefer to see mother-tongue maintenance shifted to Saturday school, and become the onus of the community rather than the school. He would like to see all students learn at least one of the 'commonly consensual languages' — Japanese, Chinese or French, for example — ones that were internationally useful. He argued that languages such as Turkish were not internationally useful, and that cultural maintenance was not the role of the school. The school's role was, he explained, in the cognitive side of language learning: 'Bilingual education aids cognitive development; LOTEs do not'. He said his 'utilitarian' view was a value judgment, but that 'that's life'.

Further, the Turkish students were good in Turkish, he argued, because it was their home language, but weren't in English, and the English suffers because they were not getting enough instruction in English language. Rather than LOTEs, and given funding constraints, he would like to see more bilingual classes targeted at students who found conceptual development difficult.

He believed that the LOTEs programme was a 'shambles' because staff hadn't thought through what to do with those not in the chosen language groups. They can do beginner courses, but often these were organized to deal with behavioural problems, such as with students of Greek background. These students, who often had poor Greek skills anyway, were isolated in a small class as a way of managing them better. In this way, he added, it was not like maths with a set curriculum. And it was because the agenda of language maintenance programmes was often cultural maintenance, rather than language as a pedagogically useful activity, that he didn't like them: 'they don't teach language'.

Several parents of Vietnamese background commented that, while the Vietnamese programme was good now, it could be improved. One suggested that despite being a preparatory to Year 12 school, there was some repetition in what the children did and there was 'no unity' across the years. The secondary principal claimed that they had always had strong support from parents regarding community languages.

One of the students interviewed expressed the opinion that it was not just important to know your own language, but to strike a balance between that and English. A boy of Turkish background in Year 11 said he went to Saturday school because there were not enough students of Turkish background to have a senior language class. He said 'you have to learn it because otherwise you have to have translators'. A girl of Vietnamese background, however, suggested that she did more language in the LOTEs programme than in the Saturday class, but she thought that LOTEs was boring and Saturday school better. Both these students said there was some parental pressure to do the language, but that it was primarily their choice. They also thought that it was useful in terms of getting jobs, but stressed more helping their parents and functioning in their community. They could not say whether doing LOTEs and the bilingual programme had helped Turkish-speaking and Vietnamese-speaking students do better, but one thought that having lots of languages taught at the school had 'improved it a lot' — attracting more students to the school and giving it a good name.

The Manager of the State Multicultural Education Coordination Unit summarized the long-term problems associated with demographic change at the school — there were no longer one or two major language groups which constituted the vast majority of the student population, as there had been once. This affected LOTEs plans, because it became impossible to service all language maintenance demands. Pressure on the language maintenance provision also adversely affects the provision of second language learning courses, because of the demand for adequate staff and the effects on timetabling. Consequently, the Greek and Turkish LOTEs could probably end within the next few years because of numbers.

The language coordinator said that more time and materials were always crucial to strengthen a programme. Their LOTEs programme was not innovatory, like the bilingual programme, but had clear benefits to schools and society — in terms of maintaining numbers; making students feel that Australia is not such a strange place to live; and the long-term economic benefits for international trade of a multilingual nation.

As far as structural features are concerned, the Manager of the State Multicultural Education Coordination Unit suggested that the Ministry needs to rethink a model for dealing with schools of such linguistic diversity:

> You need a good study first, to establish the needs and abilities of students. But you also need flexibility and mobility, with language teachers moving around within areas to service the range of needs, but also spending time within the school to develop programmes. A few models need to be looked at. ESL have language centres, for example, and Geelong have itinerant ESL teachers who move into schools when needed.
>
> But language is not exactly like that, it has to be ongoing. The system has to accept that if you make a commitment to multiculturalism and the teaching of languages other than English, you make a commitment. You have to maintain *real*, ongoing support.

Evaluation: The School

Of the fifty-one students (out of a possible sixty-six) who returned a 1988 school survey to show where they had gone after school, eight went on to university (most in Arts), thirteen to college, seven to a Technical and Further Education college or an apprenticeship, twelve were working, five were unemployed, and six responses were not clear. About 55 or 60 per cent of Year 10 students stay to Year 12.

The current coordinator of the Social Justice Branch of the Ministry, who had taught at the school, claimed that staff movements had meant that the original idea of the school as a 'community school', had been lost. The objective had been to provide an education which achieved a degree of cohesion across the years of schooling, a true responsiveness to community needs and a high level of parental involvement. Over the years, he claimed, the intimate administration of a 'community school' had been replaced by what he considered to be an impersonal, bureaucratic approach, resulting in a loss of community involvement. Moreover, he believed that the notion of 'community' was fairly static, and did not take into account the groups that would come and go. The size of the buildings, for example, was determined at a time when there was a small Year 11. There had been a resultant loss of administrative and staff commitment, as they became overwhelmed by the demands of a rapidly changing and diverse population. Indeed, one of the chief protagonists, herself of NESB claimed, 'look at me; I made it without LOTEs . . . ; just ESL does it'. The acting principal, in response, suggested that these comments should be seen in context. He pointed out that the school had changed again in recent times.

The deputy principal hammered home the problems associated with a large new arrivals intake, which created the high degree of transience in the student population. In the space of two days, twelve students arrived at the secondary school alone; due, she thought, to a 'family reunion wave'. This is complicated by the fact that that many cannot be fitted into the local language centre, so are enrolled straight into the school with very little or no English. The language centre's class sizes had a maximum of ten, so the school had to take them irrespective of larger classes there. They have to give them ESL provision, but the school, and the students, could not cope. She gave an example of two students of Moroccan background who could not be placed in the language centre. They 'were nice kids but became problems because they had no English and did not even have same-language peers to help them'.

At a broader level, most respondents signalled the difficulties for the school in dealing with the immense problems of cultural diversity. This meant coming to terms with parental expectations and values, particularly within a school which was designed to cater to community needs. Students generally said their parents were happy with the school, but one wrote: 'there not that happy because the teachers don't teach that good', and another that said hers were not happy 'because my study has gone down the mountain'. One student complained that a few teachers were racist, but most indicated a good atmosphere at the school.

The parents spoke generally about the school, saying that they liked the greater freedom, but that this sometimes meant less discipline, which could be bad. They appreciated the greater help the school gave parents, through interpreters, and thought that the school was very accepting of different cultures. But one also commented that schools can be too free, and that they are sometimes 'not serious enough'. Not enough homework and too many excursions were given as examples, and they also explained that they had requested that the school make uniforms compulsory, have stronger discipline, and have a homework policy. The school listened, but 'it moves slowly'.

Servicing both the demographic shifts and the extensive diversity of students, it was said, requires greater thinking through, particularly given the high number of new arrivals at the school. This involves coming to terms with the sociocultural experiences of students. The Vietnamese teacher said:

Vietnamese students are facing a dilemma. In the cultural sense, they don't have enough education or understanding to know the good things about Western culture, and they don't know enough about their own culture to understand it; so they become very materialistic. They try to assimilate in the new culture, but they only imitate the bad things. If you are confident and know about yourself, there is less 'danger' in getting to know another culture.

A curriculum of cultural self-knowledge, suggested by the social science teacher, would go a long way to addressing this problem. He suggested that in response to the complex nature of Australian society and the impact of cultural and linguistic diversity, he would like to see a more thought-through social science programme as well as more bilingual classes, that addressed the needs of students of non-English speaking background:

We overhaul the humanities every four years, and come up with the imperatives of the time, which are urgent, so we change and then find them irrelevant later. With more foresight, and those 'imperatives' on top, we could cover that cultural imbalance, the cultural as well as linguistic disadvantage that groups such as the Vietnamese experience in coming to terms with Australian society.

He believed that they needed an approach that has a moral or ethical side as well as the simple 'Australian studies' that the new Victorian Certificate of Education will make compulsory. Such an emphasis is crucial for understanding what it means to live in our society:

What makes us 'Aussies'? This is important for NESB students — not for a nationalist purpose, but to provide access to information. We often see our society as a *tabula rasa*, but there is something there, the Judaeo-Christian heritage, and so on.

He suggested that the 'stuff on festivals' was an impediment to students' learning, and wanted to see a more critical content. There would be problems with parents, he said, and added that there had been. The human relations course, for example, was 'torpedoed' by parents, and some parents had wanted them to present sexually transmitted diseases as 'God's scourge'. These problems with differing cultural values in the school community were immense, and he claimed they needed consultation nights and greater information given to parents, but in the end, he concluded, teacher professionalism and judgment had to be seen as most important. He insisted that it was important, however, to make it clear that the school was a critical *presenter* of social values, and not simply a *maintainer* of them.

Notes

1. BLACKBURN, J., *Ministerial Review of Post-Compulsory Schooling*, Melbourne, 1985.
2. ELLEY, J., *Collingwood Education Centre: A case study of a school with more than one language other than English program*, Commonwealth Schools Commission, 1988.
3. *Ibid.*, p. 5.

Chapter 7

'A Place in the World':
The Language in Learning Program and the Intensive Language Unit at Cabramatta High School

> A large state high school in the south-western suburbs of Sydney, Cabramatta High has a strong emphasis on language learning, partly the result of having many students enter the school via the Intensive Language Unit established for newly arrived immigrant and refugee adolescents, which is attached to it. As well as the Language in Learning Program, which includes faculties across the school in English language instruction, the school offers five languages other than English: German, French, Vietnamese, Mandarin and Spanish.

The Locality

Cabramatta is located in the south-western suburbs of Sydney, about thirty kilometres west of the central business district. The area is reached by the Hume Highway, the major route to Sydney's expanding south-west, and lined by car dealers, light industry, fast food chains and the occasional red brick Italianate mansion, a monument to the region's history as a Mecca for Australia's new, and not so new, arrivals.

A short distance from the highway, Cabramatta's retail centre is a thriving suburban centre which evinces signs of change and prosperity. Indo-Chinese restaurants and tailors are replacing the milk bars and cafes of a previous wave of inhabitants, and a number of small but new shopping centres have sprung up in recent years.

The district has traditionally been one of low socioeconomic status, with both an English-speaking working class and waves of post-war immigrants finding employment in the surrounding industrial areas. Some of the recent arrivals of Indo-Chinese origin have been more oriented to small business; 'mini-capitalists, with an enormous work ethic', as the principal of Cabramatta High described them. However, 17 per cent of the labour force in the local government area in 1986 was unemployed: twice the state average.

Historically, the area has had large numbers of immigrants from Eastern and Southern Europe, and South America. Recent arrivals from the Indo-Chinese nations, and especially Vietnamese immigrants, now outnumber these older groups. The local immigrant hostel was closed three years ago, but it had, in its latter years, drawn refugees, particularly from South-East Asia, into the suburb. In 1986, 65 per cent of those who lived in Cabramatta were born overseas, while the growth in the number of overseas-born was almost twice that of the total growth. One in five had arrived in the last five years.

Accommodation in the Cabramatta area is largely rented flats, with more houses away from the retail centre. The high proportion of new arrivals, drawn to rented accommodation near the existing facilities, has resulted in a very high population density in the heart of Cabramatta (which means that many local children have to be bussed to schools in the Green Valley district, to the south). But as one teacher said:

> There is quite a lot of real estate activity. In a sense, it is an upwardly mobile area, where people are working hard and struggling to buy their own homes. The shopping centre has become a magnet; that has pushed up prices.

Another teacher said that it is an entry point for many immigrants 'into the Australian dream' of owning a home in the outlying suburbs.

Of the Indo-Chinese who have arrived in the last decade, many in the early 1980s were ethnic Chinese who had business backgrounds. Now many more are ethnic Vietnamese, Khmer and Lao, who have come from a lower socioeconomic or rural background.

Consequently, Cabramatta has an old, established Anglo and Celtic working class; an established immigrant population of European background; an increasingly established Asian community, which includes several wealthy families but which is supplemented by new arrivals of lower socioeconomic origin. There is some geographical division related to ethnicity; West Cabramatta is 'Asian', according to the school principal, resulting in 'some resentment as properties fall into Asian hands'; while in East Cabramatta there are Southern Europeans; and 'on both sides there are remnants of Anglo-Saxons'.

The Cabramatta Community Centre is the centre of much of the local welfare activity. Some community groups, such as people of Turkish background, are clustered around places of worship. There are groups such as the Hong Kong Chinese Association, whose influence is greater than its size as it has a number of well-known people as members; and there are a number of other organizations covering communities such as those of Serbo-Croatian, Indo-Chinese and Spanish-speaking backgrounds. They are, according to one teacher, becoming more skilled at lobbying on issues such as immigration and welfare. Those of Vietnamese background 'have started to flex their muscles in local government, and have a representative on the council', explained the principal. The established groups are seen in other ways; the mayor is of the Italian-speaking community, which is powerful, but diminishing in number. The community of Khmer background, on the other hand, are poorly organized and loose-knit, with little local influence.

As a result of this cultural and linguistic diversity, and primarily because of the highly visible Indo-Chinese communities, Cabramatta — dubbed 'Vietnamatta' by the media and popular culture — has received 'bad press' over the last decade, having a reputation for inter-ethnic violence, Vietnamese 'gangs' and spiralling criminal activity.

The School

All those interviewed at Cabramatta High confirmed that its student population was comparable to the neighbourhood in general. This was the result of a growing but condensed population, which meant that the school had a 'tight' drawing area, with only two feeder primary schools.

There are currently 1192 students at Cabramatta High, with a slight underrepresentation of females, and a large senior school of about 320 students. There has been a slight decline in recent years since a peak of over 1300 students. At the time of the annual census, 1008 students, or 93 per cent of the student population, were of non-English speaking background (NESB). The two largest language backgrounds, other than English, were 'Chinese' (mostly Cantonese) with 282 students, and Vietnamese with 265 students. These were followed by those who spoke Khmer (ninety-eight), Lao (seventy-six), Serbian (seventy-three), Spanish (sixty-seven), Turkish (twenty-eight) and another twenty or so language groups.

This census also registered seventy-one students aged nineteen or over. About eighty of the school's students are enrolled at the Intensive Language Unit attached to the school, whose clients have been 'overwhelmingly South-East Asian' in the last eight years.

Student composition has changed significantly over the years. The principal saw the divisions related to length of residence; an 'Anglo-Saxon working class' here for some time; 'an older ethnic group' of Southern Europeans of 1950s vintage; South Americans and others who started coming in the 1970s; and the 'latest waves' of Asians. Another teacher commented that a dozen years ago Italians were one of the largest language groups in the school, but are now just over 1 per cent. The number speaking 'Yugoslav' languages dropped by a third in three years. Now, over two-thirds of the student population are of Indo-Chinese origin. The numbers of Khmer speakers, for example, has almost doubled within the last year.

Most students from the recently arrived groups, such as the Indo-Chinese, are first generation immigrants; while those of the established groups are more likely to be the children of immigrants. A quarter of all students have been in Australia for less than four years.

Teachers at the school spoke of a large degree of economic hardship amongst many families at the school, but also of the presence of some who had done well. The school has considered a 'needy students' scheme to work out ways of identifying students in need. On the other hand, one deputy commented that 'a lot of people have the impression that it is working class, with a lot of unemployment. This is true, but we do have some who have quite a deal of money through their industrial enterprise'.

Many of those better off are shopkeepers, said one teacher. This is complicated by the fact that some of those who came here with qualifications have not had them recognized; one teacher recounted the story of a mother of Russian-Chinese background who was an engineer in her homeland but is a process worker in Australia. Those of South-East Asian background were either of rural or shopkeeper background in their country of origin, although a few Chinese immigrants were teachers. One teacher said, 'There's a tendency for the Khmer to be unemployed; most are rural', although some may have trades skills such as fabric-cutting. A number of female parents are involved in 'home industry', such as sewing.

Many families, particularly those who came as refugees, live in rented flats, the conditions of which, according to one deputy, were 'not very nice'. Extended families are common amongst families of Southern European or Indo-Chinese background, believed the principal. A large number of pupils of Asian background (about half those of Vietnamese background, for example, according to a Vietnamese aide) are 'detached': that is, living with friends or relatives other than parents. A number of the recently arrived Vietnamese students are considered 'at risk' because of the absence of close family. Some of these were described as 'street kids' by one teacher, and often leave school early.

The principal said that many pupils of Asian background, particularly in senior years, were 'academic oriented' and gave over much of their leisure time to study. Those in junior years 'spend too much time watching videos and TV'. He was concerned about the children of Yugoslav background, who are 'growing away' from their parents and are more 'Australian'; 'the boys drink too much and have accepted the macho image in sport'. Another teacher commented that 'the soccer teams are virtually all Yugoslav'. Boys of South American background were also said be very sport-oriented. Some boys of Indo-Chinese background it was said, go to snooker and pinball parlours. Girls were seen to be much less involved in organized forms of leisure.

The school has a teaching staff of about one hundred, having lost seven in the last year due to a new staffing formula established by the New South Wales (NSW) Department of Education. There are ninety 'establishment' teachers, plus eleven who teach in the Intensive Language Unit. There are four ethnic aides and two part-time community liaison officers: almost thirty ancillary staff in all. Over 40 per cent of the teaching staff are of non-English-speaking background. In the maths staff of thirteen, for example, there is 'a Greek, an Estonian, three Indo-Chinese, a Polish, three Assyrians [sic], two Italians, and one "Yugoslavian" ', according to the headteacher.

The principal expressed a concern that the staff:

> is becoming too slewed toward a non-Anglo-Saxon mix ... resulting in a staff mix so complex that pupils no longer are receiving a role-model message — it is now confusing. I believe in role models. They also need to have them within ethnic communities ... but the pupils need the uniformity for a sense of community and for role models.

Because of 'the importance of the teacher as role model', the principal added, he supported the notion of school-initiated staffing. 'The present staff ethnic mix has resulted in a fragmented professional ethic and confused staff values', he explained.

Despite being a large school, there was not a large turnover of staff; but there had been three principals over a short period. There was, however, a good morale, according to all those interviewed.

The principal said of the management of the school that he tends to 'get out of the office; I like to know everything and have a personal involvement'. There are two deputy principals and weekly executive meetings. He said the style was 'consensus, building on policy, networked through the executive. There's a complex communication network, because of the numbers and size of the school'. One deputy described this system as 'very democratic'; year advisers, for example, were elected by staff and the chair at school meetings rotated. One teacher alleged, however, that 'there is some discussion and then decisions are made anyway', while another believed that 'democratic decision making was a lurk' and was done at the expense of 'educational leadership'. The principal asserted that, far from eschewing a leadership role, he 'might have expected an accusation of a "democratic facade"'. When the second deputy position was created in 1988, there was a division of duties, with each responsible for a number of faculties, programmes and areas. Neither of the deputies was happy with the division and this has been re-organized to allow more overlap. One deputy explained that because the school was large, the principal was not able to 'keep close scrutiny, so the school operates as a collection of faculties. The deputies supervise these'. The faculties, however, were 'fairly autonomous'. The principal emphasized the 'leadership role' of the 'Executive Council', an 'informal body consist[ing] of all executive staff . . . invaluable as a tool for communication, advice, . . . policy evaluation and formulation and inservice of the executive'.

The school's budget, unlike 'smaller working-class Anglo-Saxon schools to the west', is supplemented by the fact that about 90 per cent of parents pay at least part of their children's fees. Parents of Asian background are particularly supportive, the principal explained. Some faculties, such as art, charge fees to buy materials. The budget is topped up by funds for projects from the Disadvantaged Schools Program (a Commonwealth funded programme aimed at improving the quality of education for disadvantaged groups). This comes to over $50,000 each year. The principal said that:

> If one teacher equals about $50,000 — $30,000 plus $20,000 in facilities and materials — then the Disadvantaged Schools Program's funds only equal about one teacher, but the impact of that on our ability to implement policies is enormous. I wish I could get that through to politicians.

He commented that, while the contribution of the Program to school finances is 'minimal', 'its impact on innovation, morale and staff development is of great value'.

Since the Disadvantaged Schools Program (DSP) was established in 1973 the school has received over $300,000, which has been used to purchase computers and other equipment, and to fund various camps and activities, as well as programmes such as the Language in Learning Program. The principal liked the Disadvantaged Schools Program funds because they were long term, and he considered himself a long-term planner; 'you have to look to 1991, and you need funding for the long term'. Funding from the Participation and Equity Program (a Commonwealth funded programme designed to increase the participation of and equality of outcomes for disadvantaged groups) had been 'important but patchy'. They had also received a little funding from the NSW Multicultural Education Coordinating Committee. He also said that he 'squeezes the system' to get what he can, because 'the Lord helps them who help themselves'. Most comes, however, from within the school.

The school has a community relations room, with facilities, for use by community groups, 'but it's virtually never used', said the principal. The school's Parents' and Citizens' Association is small, provides no funds, and attracts 'about half a dozen parents of Anglo-Saxon background', he added. Most staff mentioned the difficulty of getting parents of Indo-Chinese background into the school as a result of language problems, different cultural expectations, and work commitments. A deputy said:

> Parent participation is almost zero. There is a very high distance approval of what goes on. The Asian community will vote with their feet; if they don't like the school, they will go and live with uncle or aunty. The 'volatile races' will let you know if there is something wrong. They don't, so they must think it's OK.

The former coordinator of the Language in Learning Program explained that the school has had most of its contact with community groups through intermediaries such as the Cabramatta Community Centre, which has organized meetings and committees on various issues. Local businesses support things like the multicultural day, and the Hong Kong Chinese Association donated nearly $1,000 to fund a community liaison officer. An Intensive Language Unit teacher said they occasionally get someone like a police officer in to talk about subjects such as the role of police in Australia.

There is a resource centre a few suburbs away, and several consultants — multicultural, English as a Second Language (ESL), and so on — are available. The ESL faculty meets in a cluster of schools, organized by the Intensive Language Unit. The ESL coordinator added that funding for inservicing was virtually cut out, so there was very little of that. The head of the Intensive Language Unit claimed that they had a higher degree of systems support than the school, helped by the fact that she had spent two years at head office, and was somewhat more familiar with 'the protocol'.

The school provides a core curriculum up to the end of Year 10. All subjects are compulsory in Year 7, and while there are electives from Year 8, a core of English, maths, science, history, geography and physical education must be studied. Students are provided with booklets to help them make curriculum choices, and at the end of Year 10 they are counselled at a Beyond Year 10 camp.

Within the school's core curriculum and organization, there is a broad framework for servicing cultural and linguistic diversity. The school's statement of *Educational Aims* stresses academic success and skills for social participation. It includes 'the recognition that the school must always ensure, as far as possible, an equity of education for each student without disadvantage of any kind'.

The *Aims* statement outlines academic, personal and social/cultural aims, with specific objectives in each. The first area emphasizes 'excellence', 'balanced development' and 'positive self-direction', and lays particular emphasis on language instruction. The *Aims* are underlined by an old sense of academic rigour and the values of: 'self-discipline', 'perseverance', 'ability to approach a task methodically' and 'cooperation with peers and staff'; as well as the concern for a 'willingness to learn to think critically'. This sense of excellence is to be realized through the use of extension work for students wherever possible, and an overall concern that work always be structured to be challenging and open-ended. Strategies for pursuing and acknowledging excellence are also listed; in sport, which is also given a high profile, as well as academic endeavour.

Personal aims include fostering self-confidence, particularly for girls, in relation to developing the individual's potential. Social/cultural aims emphasize cooperation, responsibility, tolerance and cultural and multicultural understanding of society. Overarching these concerns is an ethos of preparing students for understanding and participating successfully in Australian society. The purpose of a 'broad education' is to enable students 'to compete, function in wider social networks and cope with technological change'.

A student's self-esteem, the document says, 'is based on an understanding of his or her needs and responsibilities while taking into account the culture and values of the school community'. There is an emphasis on responsibility to the school and the community. A student's potential, for example, is also their 'potential contribution to society'. The social/cultural aims involve the 'student's ability and willingness to work and live cooperatively, responsibly and with mutual respect'.

The 'knowledge and understanding of Australia's history, government, society and culture' are crucial. The 'perception of contemporary Australia as a multicultural society and a tolerance of the variety of cultural backgrounds within it' is framed by 'a wider loyalty to and cooperation with community and country'. There is thus an emphasis on 'encouraging community involvement through individual commitment, e.g., as individuals, within school, within society'. This includes 'positive attitudes to the Law', 'pride in and enthusiasm for this school' and 'serving community or school needs'. To this end, the *Aims* statement points to the development of an 'Australian History across the curriculum' perspective.

While there is no separate multicultural policy as yet (it is currently being formulated), the *Aims* document articulates the way the appreciation of multiculturalism is fostered within this ethos, such that school and community identity is primary. This involves 'engineering by the school of greater social integration through excursions, picnic days, walkathons, etc., where all pupils are asked/told to participate and thereby mix freely with other ethnic groups'. 'Multicultural events', which include 'promoting communication between Aboriginal populations and our school', take place within this framework, such that there is a simultaneous promotion of Australian culture and multiculturalism. Each faculty, in fact, is required to have a 'cultural (e.g., Australian History and Society) and multicultural policy'.

This ethos was elaborated by the principal:

> If you consider pupils as young men and women who have to be given the opportunity to share in a common identity with the school and nation, then these have an importance over ethnic diversity.

Cultures of Schooling

The principal defined his position as one of 'mainstream multiculturalism':

> The role of the school is to maintain meaningful cultural diversity within the broad framework of allegiance to a common Australian way of life. Australian-ness and multiculturalism are not in conflict. There's also a need to give pupils a belief in the importance of their own culture and to maintain it . . . ; this benefits both the school and country. But being a Turk is not counter to Australia and the school.

He related this 'community ethos' and 'sense of service' to his own educational experience of growing up in a private country boarding school and added that 'education is still mostly about individual pupils achieving a place in the world for themselves — satisfying to the self and supportive to the community'. The existence of this 'core culture' required the study of core subjects, including history and geography, 'those social sciences necessary for an Australian identity'. But these needed to be flexible so that they could change with the profiles of students, he added.

This view of the role of the school was shared by other staff. Many supported a philosophy of cultural and linguistic maintenance, but within a strong ethos of the school and nation, and the goal of equipping students for a place in Australian society. One deputy of non-English speaking background said:

> if they're going to assimilate, students need to know how to operate in Australian society. For example, sport; they need it here. They need to learn how the Australian community operates . . . ; multiculturalism is about assimilating.

The other deputy, who was of English-speaking background, expressed the belief that 'the school's role is to foster the "Australianization" process'. A Vietnamese aide commented that it was 'not always good to keep Vietnamese culture. They should mix with the Australians. I want my children to mix; they live here, we can't go back'.

Cabramatta High has a number of specific programmes which are crucial to its servicing of the needs of cultural and linguistic diversity within this ethos. The school has a large ESL faculty of seven staff; all of which are trained in ESL method. They provide separate ESL classes, parallel to English classes, and team-teaching in which ESL teachers work in mainstream classes and are also involved in the Language in Learning Program. The parallel classes constitute about two thirds of the ESL provision, and have about 250 students across the years. The Language in Learning Program services many more.

Attached to the school is the Intensive Language Unit, which, as part of the Commonwealth government's New Arrivals Program, receives refugee and migrant students of secondary school age. The aim of the Intensive Language Unit is to provide the first six months of language learning and to assist in cultural and social orientation before entry to high school. On average, students spend between six months and one year in the Intensive Language Unit. It provides classes in core subjects as well as English language instruction, and has separate classes for students with special needs. Students are slowly integrated into the mainstream curriculum in the high school. There are eleven staff, including nine teachers, of whom seven are permanent. The Intensive Language Unit also employs a part-time counsellor and four bilingual aides.

Both the ESL and Intensive Language Unit staff are important to the school's Language in Learning Program, which is the key focus of this study. The Language in Learning Program involves the use of language-based materials in subjects across the curriculum. These materials are used by mainstream subject teachers alone or jointly with ESL teachers in a team-teaching arrangement. While the school is still developing a language policy, the statement of *Educational Aims* outlines clear concerns in the teaching of English language. This includes 'developing a School Language Policy to guide and consolidate effective student language learning throughout the curriculum', in the areas of reading, writing and speaking. The *Aims* document refers to the necessity of modelling spoken and written language. It also has specific objectives, such as 'increasing staff awareness that the development of expository text reading skills in students is the responsibility of each and every faculty'. To this end it requires the formulation of a writing syllabus in every faculty in which 'a progression of written forms necessary for students' life and future study' is outlined, with 'clear assessment criteria'. It urges staff to exploit 'opportunities for students to use their first language in appropriate learning situations'. The school has a structured reading time, called Redtime, as part of its strategy to foster positive attitudes to reading.

The Languages Other Than English (LOTEs) programme offers study in German, Spanish, Vietnamese, French and 'Chinese' (Mandarin). Italian was taught until very recently, and both Turkish and Serbian have been offered in the past. Cabramatta, in 1984, was one of the first secondary schools in New South Wales to introduce Chinese, funded by the Multicultural Education Coordinating Committee. Chinese was introduced for two reasons, the LOTEs headteacher explained:

> First; in a context where language faculties were 'battling', a large influx of a particular language group can help defend a language faculty. Second; it is not fair to the large Chinese-speaking groups not to introduce their language to the curriculum.

The school had conducted a survey in 1983 which established the predominance of Chinese speakers. The LOTEs headteacher said that it was essentially community pressure which led the school to introduce Vietnamese in 1986. The Vietnamese community liaison officer surveyed parents of Vietnamese background and found there was 100 per cent support amongst them.

Cultures of Schooling

All students have to study languages in Year 7, and do half a year of one European and one Asian language. After Year 7, study of a language is an elective. Most of the languages are offered in senior years.

There is no specialist sociocultural curriculum which addresses the issues of cultural diversity, except where it is built into the mainstream subjects; students may study, for example, 'the Indo-Chinese war in history'. The principal said that he wouldn't support such a specialist programme. When he arrived at the school, there was a programme for combating racism in the school, but he believed it made students more aware of differences. This project, the Racial Equality Project, was intended to explore the problems of racism and prejudice in the school as part of the wider community, and develop strategies which were useful for raising the issues of a diverse society and challenging racism in the school and community. It involved staff and student surveys, and outlined the way the school dealt with these issues or was affected by them. At the time, it was an important part of the school's framework for addressing the needs of cultural diversity, but was met with disapproval by the incoming principal and was terminated within a few months of his arrival. The principal said that 'the material produced was considered inflammatory by the then Regional Director'. It achieved little, believed the principal, and 'had begun to generate staff opposition and negative self-esteem in pupils'. Some members of the school, however, continued, together with the Cabramatta Community Centre, to be involved in a Racial Equality Action Committee, which concentrated on countering the negative image of the area in the media, as one torn by racial conflict.[1]

The school has a student support programme which, as a Disadvantaged Schools Program evaluation makes clear, is seen to be essential because of the cultural diversity of the school. Each Year has a team of three coordinators, which serves both to provide enough staff to meet the pastoral care needs of a large school, and means, according to one deputy, that 'the system gets more people involved as well; it's a great professional development exercise'. There is also a range of activities, funded by Disadvantaged Schools Program money, such as: the 'bush school', where Year 9 students 'rough it'; and a camp, as part of the peer support programme, for Year 7 students, with Year 11 students acting as liaison. The school distributes a New Arrivals handbook for students which outlines the key features of the school and attempts to answer the kinds of questions new students would ask. There is also a welfare committee. A number of those interviewed saw the student support initiatives as some of the most important programmes in the school.

There is a community liaison programme, with two part-time community liaison officers and a bilingual support officer. The senior liaison officer is seen to be particularly valuable to the school, largely because he speaks six Asian languages and dialects as well as English. The school has initiated a number of programmes designed to involve students in the community, such as visiting the elderly; and improving the amount of information given to parents and the community, through preparing notices in 'community languages' and mounting displays in public places. The school works regularly with the Cabramatta Community Centre. It also provides a range of activities such as cultural days and exchange visits to other schools, seen to be an 'institutionalized celebration of multiculturalism' which will engender 'harmony among students and the community'. The community liaison officers are seen to be the link between student support and community liaison in the school, as well as the link between school and home. The importance of the position is seen by the fact that a few years ago, when the school could not get funds for it, staff contributed from their own salaries and organized fund-raising activities to ensure that the school could retain a community liaison officer. The staff handbook exemplifies a sensitivity to diversity by including a pronunciation guide to Vietnamese names.

The school has developed courses in computers, partly because, the principal claimed 'maths is important for Asians'. They have three 'computer rooms', including a 'technology room' for teaching office procedure and legal studies. But they have only just begun looking at basic subjects and have been hampered by having 'to train on the spot'. He has told staff 'they have *carte blanche* to buy appropriate software'. Several staff said they 'are looking at' using computers. The *Aims* statement does, however, stress the need 'to develop an integrated, holistic approach and cross faculty teaching' in technology. The school currently has a Computers across the Curriculum Program, funded by the Disadvantaged Schools Program, which aims to provide staff development and software.

Context of the Innovations

Cabramatta High has had a series of language across the curriculum programmes since 1982: Language across the Curriculum, from 1982 to 1986; the Integrated Language Program in 1987; and the Language in Learning Program since 1988. The school has received continuous Participation and Equity Program and Disadvantaged Schools Program funding for these programmes since 1983. Up to and including 1989 funds, the various programmes have received $72,500. It will receive another $11,500 in the next two years.

The former coordinator of the Language in Learning Program (now on secondment to the Department of Education) explained the history of the current version of the language programme as arising out of a dissatisfaction with the previous programme and with the way ESL was taught:

> The school had been strong in language across the curriculum since 1982. This had been led by the English faculty . . . and was a mainstream thing with an English and humanities approach. From my point of view as an ESL teacher, it assumed a high level English ability and didn't meet the needs of NESB students.

ESL method, on the other hand, 'tended to be pedestrian, grammatical exercises'. ESL involvement in mainstream classes was based on 'language rather than content focused exercises'. He wanted to integrate the best of both approaches: to join the language across the curriculum approach with language learning strategies, thus integrating language learning with content areas. He was an ESL teacher who had been involved in the Transition Education Program and in the Participation and Equity Program. The focus of the Transition Education Program had been to get students out of school into the workforce, but he interpreted it to mean the need to 'transition' students from Years 9 and 10 into higher education. The Participation and Equity Program was intended to increase participation, he added, so therefore schools had to develop strategies for doing this. With this background, the coordinator undertook the development of the Integrated Language Program and the renamed Language in Learning Program.

The Language across the Curriculum Program had introduced the reading time (Redtime) to the school, and encouraged some discussion of the psycholinguistics of reading. The school also had a resource teacher who would assist where necessary, but that was limited, and worked more like ESL 'support'. During the existence of the Language across the Curriculum Program, teachers in the school were grappling with similar problems of students' grasp of English language, and were concerned by the effects this had on their performance. A science teacher had been trying to meet the language needs of her students; 'my methods were very old: nouns, verbs, sentence structure, word lists, . . . but I had the perception that no matter how I was teaching, it wasn't getting through'. She added that 'we couldn't find appropriate material in textbooks because the language was too hard. Often, the language models there were poor; for example, paragraphs were wrong'.

The former Language in Learning Program coordinator, then an ESL teacher, approached her with a scheme for which they obtained Participation and Equity Program funding for language-based materials development (which lasted until two years ago), which they used to provide release time of ten days each for four teachers: themselves and two Intensive Language Unit teachers. Out of this came materials for a Year 9 'Language and Science' course which has run for four years. Later, in 1988, the science faculty ran a separate Other Approved Studies course (school-based courses approved by the Secondary Studies Board) for Year 11, but for one year only. The implementation of the materials was accompanied by separate language-oriented science classes and required the presence of an ESL teacher in the class. They decided to target Year 9 because it was critical in terms of preparation for Year 10 assessment, and there is usually a big intake of students from the Intensive Language Unit in Year 9. They used Participation and Equity Program-funded days to consider how to deal with the Intensive Language Unit intake and concluded that all students in Year 9 needed help with language. The decision to target Year 11 was taken because many NESB students had 'inadequate language skills to achieve in senior science' and needed 'to improve their understanding of scientific concepts'.

Art was also targeted. The current art headteacher explained how the programme was 'in its infancy' when she arrived four years ago, but she 'got involved' because 'the concepts of art are very abstract and needed better communication. The role of art teaching is not vocational. It is aimed at visual self-expression; understanding the world and environment and expressing this'.

The ESL coordinator said that once it was tried out in science, 'where it was successful, we then went across the board'. The language-based materials programme became much more directed towards staff development and involved more staff from across the school than the Language across the Curriculum Program.

Building on this class materials development model, the former Language in Learning Program coordinator began the Integrated Language Program and the Language in Learning Program with a 'retreat' for all staff over a weekend in 1987. About fifty teachers attended the retreat, where they tried out and discussed a range of language activities. There were two inservices in 1987. Later, they gave teachers two days each to write up the materials, which were then trialled. Inservicing continued; they had one consultant talk to the staff on language functions and another talk to science staff about language and science; but this became less important once materials were in use. The former coordinator described the whole process as 'action research'.

During 1987 and 1988, the programme went through a number of stages: consultation with staff and preparation of sample materials; development of materials; trialling of materials and strategies; publication of materials; and programme evaluation. To do anything such as this needed money, the former Language in Learning Program coordinator explained, so the Participation and Equity Program and Disadvantaged Schools Program funds were crucial. They needed casual teachers to allow staff time off to produce materials, and a loading for the coordinator, which was two days a fortnight.

The Intensive Language Unit attached to Cabramatta High, one of six Intensive Language Units in the region, is part of the Commonwealth government's New Arrivals Program. Its main aim is to cater for the needs of newly arrived students of immigrant and refugee status, who cannot be provided for adequately in mainstream schooling and who have great difficulty in coping with the Australian secondary school system.

The Intensive Language Unit was established in 1978 with Commonwealth funds as a 'contingency programme'. According to an Intensive Language Unit teacher, 'because it was regarded as temporary, it was staffed with casuals for the first four years. There was an industrial campaign to get permanency'. One effect of its 'temporary' nature was that the Intensive Language Unit was housed in demountable buildings. The position of headteacher in the Intensive Language Unit was only created as a promotions position three years ago, which meant that there has been mainly peer supervision in the Unit. There has also been a strong emphasis on professional development, 'adapting' teaching methodologies to the needs of students. There is a division made between 'regular' classes and smaller classes of students with special needs, which are primarily those who have suffered from disrupted schooling or are emotionally disabled. Small classes were not established until 1984, however, when there was an industrial dispute over the issue. Classes were of twenty-five students at that stage. Now regular classes have eighteen students, while special needs classes have ten, although the flexibility of the Unit means that it can arrange classes so that those with the greatest difficulties can be placed in classes of only six or seven.

In the beginning, the Unit was isolated from the high school. There has been, however, an increasing degree of collaboration over the years: there are 'school experience' integration programmes, which involve introducing Intensive Language Unit students to the secondary school slowly; the Intensive Language Unit curriculum is more closely related to the school's provisions; the Intensive Language Unit and the ESL staff work together in the Language in Learning Program, and in providing special courses such as supplementary English in the secondary school; informal and formal means are used to communicate information between the two, particularly when Intensive Language Unit students are 'exiting' the Unit and entering the high school.

The Intensive Language Unit is primarily funded through the Commonwealth government, but funds are allocated through the state government. It holds up to eighty-six students. The Unit receives $20 per capita per month, above salaries, which comes to about $6,000 per year, plus an allocation of $2,000 for requisitions.

The Innovations in Practice:
The Language in Learning Program

The Language in Learning Program was described by staff as having a range of aims. The materials being prepared by the former coordinator for publication state them most clearly as:

- to integrate language across the curriculum approaches with language learning strategies
- to integrate language learning with content learning
- to integrate teacher inservice with teaching practice
- to facilitate effective student learning in subject areas.

The former coordinator indicated that part of the process of the programme was refining goals, so these can be seen as the end-point of a period of discussion. His rationale for the programme was to combine the benefits of a

Cabramatta High School

language across the curriculum model with the strategies of ESL teaching. The language across the curriculum approach was based on the principle that 'we learn through using language', and that 'student-centred experiential learning' was 'how' learning occurred. The 'language based' instruction of ESL methodology, however, stressed the use of exercises and materials because 'students need to learn language forms' through 'conscious application'. The former coordinator believed that an 'integrated language' approach would use 'language generative tasks' in a 'structured interaction with texts' because 'we learn from using and attending to language'.

The staff development book he prepared argues that a successful approach needs to blend the 'process writing' approach of the language across the curriculum model, in which students are seen to learn best when they use their own language 'expressively' to create meaning; with the 'genre model', in which the emphasis is placed on the socially powerful forms of writing such as exposition and the explicit teaching of the linguistic structures which constitute these genres. The first approach, he comments, is about the *process* of writing; the second is about the *product* which students need to master for academic success.

This meant training teachers in the use of strategies which, a Disadvantaged Schools Program submission suggests, are 'focused on providing wider opportunities for student language use throughout the curriculum' and 'developing language-based class materials for learning in the content areas'.

Those interviewed did not put the aims of the programme in such a theorized form, but all agreed with the former coordinator that the prime goal was 'more access to academic learning'. A science teacher summarized the aims more briefly: 'to improve language functions, while keeping the work interesting; to improve their science'. She argued that English language was very important for NESB students in particular; 'they need this for themselves, so the wool isn't pulled over their eyes. All kids should be competent at a very high level'. The art headteacher saw the goal specifically as producing a booklet of useful strategies. The former coordinator said that he had shared a practical view of the goals of the programme:

> When I started I had a very technical view of education; if you have a problem, you can fix it by strategies x, y, z, . . . ; a technical view that if you simply structure a task this will solve the problem.

This practical emphasis was symbolized, for the Intensive Language Unit headteacher, by the transfer of the coordination of the Language in Learning Programme from the English faculty to the ESL and Intensive Language Unit staff.

After the initial processes of inservicing staff and preparing materials, the trialling of the materials and implementation of strategies was organized. The ESL coordinator explained:

A lot of strategies came from ESL on pupil-free days. There was a lot of trial and error. . . . Strategies that didn't work were changed, new strategies came fro<Mm our professional development.

In science an ESL teacher comes into some of the classes in a team-teaching arrangement, in which the ESL teacher is involved in directing the lesson; usually when language tasks are central to the lesson. Sometimes the ESL teacher simply provides 'support': answering questions regarding language or monitoring student work. In one lesson, in which a language activity was central to the lesson, the more experienced science teacher directed the lesson while the ESL teacher functioned primarily in a supporting role but took a more central role at the instigation of the subject teacher. In the past, students were often withdrawn from the subject class for specialist help in language.

In Year 11 art, ESL staff team-teach four periods every ten-day cycle, instructing students in essay writing and note-taking. A resource teacher is also used, preparing programmes or coming into the class for several lessons a week. Several staff said the programme was less structured now, because they were more familiar with the strategies. A science teacher explained:

It's less intensive now. We don't withdraw now unless they really need it. Now the focus is more on staff development and getting teachers to use a language approach in their own classes.

She said about 60 per cent of the entire staff are involved in some way in the programme, including, for example, industrial arts and home science.

Students are 'selected' for the programme by formal identification of language needs through the teacher's general perception of a problem. Year 8 science, for example, is ungraded, but at the end of the year students are assessed to determine the level of help needed. Those with greatest difficulties are placed in the special Year 9 Language and Science class. She added that she decided to use an ESL teacher in a top Year 9 class because, while they understood the content, some did not have the English language to convey this understanding. She realized this when she asked them to write a passage explaining 'Why is the sky blue and the sunset red?', and received either mere descriptions or badly expressed explanations, in comparison with one student who had achieved both aspects of the task.

The science teacher commented that the programme's strategies spread into all classes because 'the kids were very enthusiastic; kids from other classes were asking for the worksheets'. The science faculty decided to have as policy staff incorporation of language activities, partly because the new science syllabus is language based.

The integration of the language programme in the content of the mainstream subjects was consolidated by the establishment of a committee which has a member from each faculty, and by the running of whole school inservices. The science staff have furthered their links with the Intensive

Language Unit by participating in a cluster network of schools fed by the Intensive Language Unit, in which they have an input in creating a science programme for Intensive Language Unit students.

The former Language in Learning Program coordinator maintained that, in terms of curriculum, the most important thing was the practical emphasis in the programme. They have tried to give models of a language approach to help teachers, building on what they did in class. The teaching style, therefore, was 'goal based', and more like 'action research', where the teachers 'have to consider what they are doing and the language activities have to be related to the context of what the teacher is doing'. These activities provide opportunities for both teachers and students to reflect on classroom learning.

The materials have two approaches, he explained. The first is a communicative/inductive approach, where the principle is that 'students learn best by doing it then reflecting on it'. The other is the 'text task', which is deductive. The problem with the language across the curriculum 'process' model is that it is 'all induction and no guidance, which is OK for those already with the skills, but not for those without them'.

A science teacher, however, emphasized that students 'do their own work. They do project work and then give talks on it to the class. To start with, they are more directed, especially in the Year 9 language class'. Eventually, it is more based on teachers helping students while they are doing their own work. In the Year 9 class, they are also learning how to take notes. The top Year 9 class, on the other hand, has done report writing. In all cases, she said, it was important to give students a model of the appropriate language, and because the textbooks were often inappropriate, she used students' texts. Art uses a wide variety of texts, but usually modifies the language and presents them on worksheets. They also use a lot of student-centred activity such as group work. The headteacher said the students 'prefer to learn things themselves. They hate chalk and talk; although migrant kids often prefer this because it is non-participatory and non-challenging'.

The materials themselves vary in style. Those being prepared by the former coordinator outline a procedure: selecting a text and its content, concepts and language; considering the task options, such as cloze techniques or flowcharts; determining the activity, based on student needs; preparing the material; and trialling.

In practice, language activities are often a range of classroom strategies useful for immediate purposes, organized around text types, 'language functions' or particular grammatical features. The staff development resource book provides a list of strategies: 'best of' booklets; class essays; sequencing, where passages of writing are cut into strips and reconstructed. Samples of cloze models, cued writing, classification, underlining main points, translating 'in your own words', and so on, illustrate the kinds of tasks set. Tasks can be more specifically related to a grammatical function; one ESL teacher in a science class gave worksheets on conjunctions for use in report writing, which largely consisted of practising items given as a list. Some other materials prepared for

Cultures of Schooling

one science programme virtually constitute a textbook. This uses, for example, a number of poems to provide an alternative depiction of the subject, even if not used in the lesson. Activities which follow from this theme include students writing 'descriptive' sentences or constructing comparisons.

Students are assessed mainly in terms of the subject content. Assessment of the language strategies, when implemented, is usually through small tests or evaluation grids requiring that students rate lessons. On the other hand, diagnostic testing of students is used to establish levels of competency as a way of determining which students, for example, are to be selected for the Years 9 and 11 Language and Science courses. The ESL programme has its own forms of assessment, involving diagnostic testing, and all students are assessed in Year 10. Evaluation of the overall programme is done through staff survey and discussion, and prepared as a necessary part of the submission for Disadvantaged Schools Program funding.

The Innovations in Practice: The Intensive Language Unit

The main functions of the Intensive Language Unit are: to 'provide students with a secure environment'; to provide the opportunity for students to develop their English language proficiency; and to develop an understanding of the NSW education system. Within the objectives of ESL instruction, the Intensive Language Unit seeks: to develop the student's ability to function in a wide range of contexts; to develop listening, speaking, reading and writing skills in all curriculum areas; and to facilitate conceptual development while learning English. One Intensive Language Unit teacher stressed the 'enabling' function of the Unit: 'the Intensive Language Unit's job is to prepare kids for high school, and especially to provide knowledge of Australian society; to develop language skills and to get kids to function in the wider society'. Another said that 'language is the key' to 'equity, access to learning, improving life chances'. Students are assessed for their English language competency and extent of education on enrolment to identify special needs. This may involve testing where appropriate, and is used also to determine class placement.

There are seven classes currently available at the Intensive Language Unit, which include five special needs classes. There are also two classes which are at the stage of preparing students for 'exiting': one to the junior years of secondary school; the other to the later years or to the Adult Migrant Education Service or a Technical and Further Education (TAFE) college.

Each class has a teacher who remains with the class most of the day. Bilingual aides are used in the classroom, with one aide being provided for every two classes. The class follows an intensive language programme which focuses on listening, speaking, reading and writing skills. Students are gradually introduced to a variety of subjects and their language and concepts. The Intensive Language Unit teachers at Cabramatta have a variety of language backgrounds, including English, Arabic, Croatian, Lao, Spanish and Greek.

The Intensive Language Unit has developed a core curriculum, with the aid of mainstream teachers from the receptor schools, which draws on the relevant syllabi to prepare students for mainstream schooling. This began as an action research project and is a very important innovation, according to the headteacher. The core subjects are English, maths, history, science, geography, art, music and careers. The main class teacher is relieved from face-to-face teaching by teachers who teach in some of the core subjects. Thus the Intensive Language Unit uses a methodology which is concerned to have students use language in context and for a range of purposes, which necessarily includes teaching language across the curriculum. Within the core, each teacher develops programmes specific to the needs of the class. The special needs classes focus on basic literacy and numeracy. The predominant approach is a 'language experience' approach.

In the classes where the focus is on exiting to the mainstream, students take part in a School Experience Program or Partial Integration Program, which works on the basis of the 'goodwill' of mainstream teachers and students. Intensive Language Unit students are paired with a student in the secondary school for the School Experience Program and join mainstream classes for a week, to familiarize students with the high school. Counselling follows in which the experience and any concerns of the student are discussed. In the Partial Integration Program, students are integrated for a longer period, usually one term, in mainstream classes for some subjects. In those classes, which are electives, an Intensive Language Unit teacher and a subject teacher team-teach. Students usually stay in the Intensive Language Unit for three terms, but this may be extended to five terms for those with special needs. The 'general readiness' for the mainstream is assessed, said the headteacher, through observation, facilitated by the sharing of classes amongst teachers who all have lots of interaction with the students. There is also formal monitoring through a review committee (which includes an officer from the New Arrivals Program), which 'goes through every class, every child'. There are currently about three hundred students in secondary school who went through Cabramatta Intensive Language Unit, about two thirds of whom went to Cabramatta High. According to one Intensive Language Unit teacher, there are a number of older students 'who really don't fit into the academic curriculum. We are now trying to encourage them more towards Technical and Further Education'.

The bilingual teachers' aides function to help teachers in both the teaching of Intensive Language Unit students and in providing a support role. They are involved in preparing and team-teaching lessons, working in small groups of students and identifying needs. In a support role, they provide information to teachers, identify problems and liaise with parents. According to the Vietnamese aide, they also do a lot of unpaid interpreting. The four aides, one part-time, speak Chinese, Vietnamese, Khmer, Lao and Spanish. The counsellor runs programmes such as social skills (dealing with, for example, experiences of racism) and provides careers information.

The small size of the Intensive Language Unit allows for an environment which is supportive. This is enhanced by organizational elements, such as vertical roll groups and peer support. Year 11 students also come into the Intensive Language Unit to act as reading partners to foster integration with the secondary school. There are a number of other activities (sport, camps, and so on) where Intensive Language Unit and mainstream students are placed together. ESL and Intensive Language Unit staff often prepare units of work together and team-teach.

An Intensive Language Unit teacher said that they develop more of their own materials now rather than use textbooks, and use a more student-centred approach. The headteacher said Intensive Language Unit students tend to be very traditional in their expectations and 'are happier with the teacher at the centre of the information flow. We meet their expectations at first, using a teacherly manner and then become more friendly. We have tremendous group work success'. She added that the students are fascinated about the different learning styles in Australia compared to their homeland and 'love talking about the cultural differences'.

There is also a high degree of professional development, with regular inservices every few weeks, facilitated by the close network established between the six Intensive Language Units in the region. The staff also keep a record of the success or otherwise of lessons, according to one teacher. The links within the school, despite the integration programmes, still tend to be distant and fairly separate, observed an ESL teacher, although this has improved in recent years.

Evaluation: The Language in Learning Program

The high level of staff participation in the Language in Learning Program, between 50 and 60 per cent, is an indicator of its perceived value. All those interviewed spoke highly of its usefulness and outcomes. A science teacher said that 'you can see the kids improving as you go; not from formal evaluation, just from observation. The kids are pleased they are getting more attention, that there are two teachers in the class. Sometimes they come back and ask for help even when they are in Year 10'. One Year 9 student said 'I think my English [has improved] very well in this year' because of the programme, which had also helped her 'get a lot information'. She didn't like the programme in art, however, because it 'is not important'. Another said:

> Before my reading was worse. I hardly understand what I have read. However, now my reading about 300 words per minute and I understand well.

Another believed teachers benefited because they 'are more close to students this way and also get to know them better, what they understand and where improving is needed'. She thought having two teachers was good, but bemoaned the lack of 'time' and 'resources'. A Laotian student also spoke highly of the smaller classes, while another said she learnt 'to write reports in science and speeches in English, science and history. I also learn to write essays in commerce'. One ESB girl pointed out 'it helps not only the people from non-English speaking backgrounds'.

The former coordinator thought that the 'design and conception of the programme', were good; 'there's a clear sense of what the process was'. The principal commented that 'one of the school's successes, which has come from the Language in Learning Programme, has been making all teachers language teachers'. The Intensive Language Unit headteacher commented that while staff were 'exhausted from commitment and energy over the years' and won't attend the multicultural committee meetings, the language committee is very popular. She also saw the build-up of resources as crucial.

In the evaluation 'good news' included the inservicing package being prepared by the former coordinator, positive outcomes were grouped into those relevant to students, teachers and programme. The supportive comments made by students, the former coordinator believed, reflected their involvement and achievement. Students reflected on their learning and achieved 'real communication with teachers'. There was evidence of 'increased task related talk' and 'increased problem solving'.

For teachers, there had been a high level of support for the programme, which resulted in reflection about learning and greater staff interaction. They had developed resources and models for communicating strategies, and 'some strategies in particular have been taken up and developed independently by teachers'.

One teacher commented that the programme 'involves people in looking at the make-up of the school and encourages more commitment in the staff. It produces a good atmosphere . . . and gets everybody to pull together'. It also provided, she said, 'the tools to target what's really wrong with individual students and work with them. You don't write kids off because you don't understand them'.

The staff, however, identified a number of critical lessons, some relating to factors such as lack of money or time to develop materials or inservice further. The ESL coordinator said that 'you need time, time for the staff. It's not done overnight. The science staff took a long time, and they're still making fiddling changes'. The former Language in Learning Program coordinator said that, after some years of the programme, 'there was, this year, more staff involvement, more working as a team'. Staff energies had been dissipated because of the existence of so many committees; 'we "OD'ed" [overdosed] on them, because it was the same people involved all the time, taking up their lunchtimes'.

Several commented, like the ESL coordinator, that there were some staff who still 'don't see the language priority' in their disciplines:

> If teachers are aware of the language needs then it can only serve to benefit, but we need it in writing materials and staff development. There's no long-term impact if it's based on individual philosophies.

Cultures of Schooling

Pointing to the need for all teachers to be knowledgeable about language teaching, one girl, who regarded herself as Uruguayan, said 'if the teacher doesn't know what to do why should we have an extra teacher?'

The art headteacher said that 'maintaining ongoing commitment' was difficult and required more inservicing, particularly for new staff. 'It would be great', she added, 'to take the staff faculty by faculty and inservice them'. Particular faculties, such as maths, were seen to feel that language is not important in their area. The maths headteacher said that the impact on maths of the Language in Learning Program was negligible. An Intensive Language Unit teacher and a maths teacher are now looking at language in maths but it was not seen as a pressing issue, although the headteacher did comment that they have found, in terms of vocabulary, that they have to reduce their explanations to 'the lowest terms'. Further, 'kids won't say if they're having problems with concepts'.

One teacher commented on her own 'inexperience in ESL' as a weak point. Similarly, two ESL teachers commented that, because they were not experts in the disciplines, it was very difficult for them. The former Language in Learning Program coordinator said teacher training was inadequate because teachers didn't understand the language that they used. The practical emphasis of the programme was, in this sense, a problem. He had only been able to move 'from a practical to a critical perspective' because his secondment to the Department had given him time to consider the issues. There 'needs to be greater thinking, a philosophy or a framework': a language policy that is at the same time practical.

> In the end, teachers have to remake curriculum. There's always the problem of context, and teachers have to reinterpret and adapt it. But curriculum guidelines need to be more practical than grand policy statements. We tried to do this in the programme by providing models.

The art headteacher complained that finding resources had been a major problem; 'people do need concrete examples'. They virtually had to make all their materials. Others also commented on 'the lack of models'. At the same time, the former Language in Learning Programme coordinator said that 'you need to get teachers to think about the thinking involved. It's a metacognitive thing'. There was the impression that some teachers felt they'd done enough when the materials were produced:

> But they didn't understand the principles, the deeper whys and wherefores. It became only imitative, not adaptive behaviour. This was still beneficial, but they need to keep going back to the broader question of the students' needs. Teachers have got bits of materials ... but there's no structure to it.

Some staff, he added, thought they had 'the answer' and took up things like cloze activities without going beyond these. Teaching tends to focus on the 'immediate', he said, 'it is done then it is filed, but structuring and supporting communication requires taking time for preparation'. One boy of 'Yugoslavian' background believed 'the teachers aren't putting enough effort in the learning programme'.

Evaluation was an issue the former coordinator identified as one that still had to be taken up. They gave an evaluation to teachers and some students, which produced positive responses, but there remained the problem of assessing student performance. He said that he didn't know whether the programme improved performance: 'art would tell you "yes", but it's a failing in the programme that it has no evaluative mechanism. But everywhere, no-one knows how to measure anything; there has been little consensus or practical guidance'. A science teacher suggested the need for initial testing for language competency. The former coordinator also said that as teacher feedback at this stage was informal — he didn't go into classrooms — there was little way of knowing how the materials were actually being used. He suspected that they were used on an occasional piecemeal basis rather than in a coherent programme.

A report, prepared as a result of a faculty survey, suggested that subjects are still only assessing content, without assessing whether students have acquired the language skills. This report underlined a number of pedagogical issues:

> Many faculties seemed to see the learning of writing as a graduation from word, sentence, paragraph, text, with particular emphasis on word and grammatical accuracy. This means that opportunities for sustained writing are withheld until Years 9 or 10 or even later. Consequently, by Year 11, many students are ill prepared for the demands of essay writing. . . . Does our emphasis on the particles of writing reflect our low expectations of students' language competence?

A language function approach, which concentrates on particular strategies rather than the holistic 'discourse based' approach outlined by the ex-coordinator, which takes on board the overall sense of structure identified by the genre model, means that teachers end up using 'bits' of the approach without locating these in a structured development of writing.

One consequence of the previous language across the curriculum approach meant that, 'most faculties appear to be using descriptive or narrative forms of writing, even when in later years, the texts and required writing for that subject is of a more developed expository form', despite the insight that 'the form of writing affects how its information is organized, what vocabulary is used and even what grammatical structures are used'.

The report recommended greater use of modelling to show students acceptable forms of writing and being explicit about the criteria by which 'appropriate form' is judged. A focus on language functions, to the exclusion of language structures, militates against this. The summary of the negative points in the inservicing material suggests that 'many teachers need a deeper understanding of the use and context of strategies'.

There were some problems initially with targeting students: 'some kids didn't want to be in a separate class; they wanted to be in with the "Aussie kids", to learn to speak like them'. A number of students commented that they 'don't mind' the presence of an ESL teacher in the classroom, but she did 'not really' help them much and they would prefer to do more science than language exercises. This suggests that the purpose of teaching language in science hasn't been clearly demonstrated to the students, or that the concentration on language functions is not seen to be useful but simply an extraneous grammatical exercise. Their opinion was in contrast to the science teacher who thought that the programme was successful 'because we forget about science and teach them language, using the science as examples. The science we teach them in Year 9 is the minimum necessary for Year 9; the language is more important'. The same teacher, however, also said that she would like to see every Year 7 student taught report writing.

Interestingly, none of the parents or students interviewed, and only some of the students surveyed, knew anything about the programme; some even argued that there was no such programme. This was not surprising, according to the former Language in Learning Program coordinator, who argued that, 'as one of the goals of the programmes was to integrate language learning within the content areas ... it was "invisible" to students and parents alike'. He contrasted this with 'language-based materials' approaches and team-teaching contexts which are organizationally separate and therefore highly visible'. One ESB parent spoke more generally about English language teaching in the school, saying that she 'strongly disagreed' with the lack of emphasis on spelling and grammar. Another believed that the time devoted to NESB students in fact retarded the development of ESB students; such programmes were 'a waste of time for Australian students'.

The former Language in Learning Program coordinator said, however, that 'teachers who see its value, see it because it's better than doing things other ways. I began with the idea that there's got to be a better, more efficient way. But then you have to take into account human culture; that's why it's uneven. ... It is effective learning, but it depends on how it's taken up by teachers'. This is why he sees a need for ongoing inservicing that takes a 'philosophical' and 'critical' as well as a practical perspective. A science teacher also saw long term benefits: 'As the kids have a greater command of the language, it could produce a higher standard of science ... and increase the level of self-confident people joining the society'.

There was no doubt amongst the staff as to the continuation of the programme, but several said that the secondment of the former coordinator could mean a loss of 'impetus', and will require the commitment of a keen coordinator to maintain staff support. Most saw it as improving, 'because it is being evaluated', and because the 'bank of resources' is building up across the years. All commented that its successful continuation depended on 'more release time to develop materials', continued funding and ongoing inservicing.

The former coordinator is currently developing the materials for wider use:

> When it's published it will be a self-access thing. This might only serve to contribute to the 'photocopy curriculum', so objectives will have to be clear and explicit. It's a poor substitute for human interaction in inservices; we need to do as much of that as we can.

He had outlined in the most recent Disadvantaged Schools Program submission a long-term plan which involved ongoing language inservice for all staff in all programmes in the school, and implementation and evaluation of a Language in Learning policy.

Evaluation: The Intensive Language Unit

The Intensive Language Unit's *Overview* concludes that the Unit has generally met the basic needs of NESB students. The principal of the high school said that the Cabramatta Intensive Language Unit, with the school, led the way in the region and state in developing a core curriculum for Intensive Language Unit students and in integrating Intensive Language Unit students into the secondary school; he considered it another 'faculty'. There was also a degree of integration of the two staffs, since Intensive Language Unit teachers 'are used in the mainstream and mainstream teachers are used in the Unit. This is good inservicing because it helps us "know about knowing"'. The ESL coordinator commented that she could identify which Intensive Language Unit the students came from, and that the Cabramatta Intensive Language Unit was most successful, largely because of the degree of expertise and stability that the Unit provided for students.

The *Overview* states that,

> as a result of team-teaching, teachers have commented on the value of teaching Intensive Language Unit students with the support of the Intensive Language Unit/ESL teacher. A significant comment has been that the students can 'handle' the work.

A result of this arrangement 'has been the establishment of an ESL (mainstream) team-taught Industrial Arts class in Year 8'. It continues:

> Another significant outcome has been a growing awareness of the needs of 1st. phase students. The mainstream teachers have become aware of the importance of language in their subject and have seen

how a language approach can work. Intensive Language Unit teachers have also become aware of the language demands of High School and developed a better understanding of the context they are preparing their students for.

Accompanying this has been a high degree of professional development and a build-up of expertise. The regular contact between the six Intensive Language Units in the region and the extent of the ongoing inservicing was significant. The Vietnamese aide claimed that the Intensive Language Unit was more organized than when she started there ten years ago; 'they do more for the students . . . ; lessons are more prepared and there's more choice'.

The Unit's 1986 evaluation set out to examine the educational outcomes of those students who had exited the Unit between 1983 and 1986. It was initiated because of a concern that many of its ex-students were 'at risk' within the educational system. It found that 248 of a total of 299 ex-students went on to the four main receptor high schools in the area (most went to Cabramatta High), another thirty-three to other high schools and twelve to the Technical and Further Education system. Over a third stayed on to Year 12. Over a third of the sample came from Cambodia, where there was no formal education system from 1975 to 1979. School Certificate results indicated that while English results were not high, maths results were much higher:

> The overall impression gained from the surveys and interviews is that students exiting from the Intensive Language Unit do settle well into mainstream High School.
> Students appear socially well adjusted and report some success as do teachers. The Intensive Language Unit does fulfil an important pastoral and orientation function.

It found that most students continued at school or found employment. A negative finding was the degree of professional isolation of Intensive Language Unit staff: an aspect that has been somewhat reversed in the last few years by increasing collaboration between the Unit and the school.

One teacher said that the Unit had, overall, 'mixed success' in terms of integration with the high school: 'there is much greater language development, but there are problems in getting real commitment from some high school teachers'. Attempts at greater involvement, however, were not always beneficial: 'in the past there was much more autonomy; now we are more closely tied to departmental guidelines. Now we are more rigidly tied to the high school timetable'.

The Intensive Language Unit headteacher commented that an increasing number of the top English students in the high school were of Asian background. This could be because they've been here longer, she added, but thought that things like the Intensive Language Unit and the Language in Learning Program must have contributed something. Other staff suggested that the Unit had been very successful, given the difficult conditions in which it has had to exist. Problems referred to included the conditions of working in demountable buildings, and having to 'fight' for a telephone. More important was the nature of the clientele: students who had been through and were going through incredible hardship.

Many of these students were illiterate in their first language, sometimes as a result of disrupted schooling, explained the headteacher. The conceptual development of these students then suffers, she added. Because of the shock of dislocation and the alienness of the Australian education system, the Intensive Language Unit had to provide an experience which was as 'comfortable' for them as possible. Many of the staff had felt some frustration because 'the mainstream wouldn't or couldn't support these kids'. She added that some of these students were much older than the norm, and many were those 'who will never be ready to exit. We have quite a few. They may have mild retardation, but tests aren't there to assess these kids adequately . . . what tests do?'

A mainstream teacher also commented on the depths of the learning difficulties and their relation to socioeconomic factors; 'it depends on the starting vocabulary of the children. For example, we went to [another] Intensive Language Unit [in a high socioeconomic status area]. The things they were doing with their bottom class were still above our top class'. Several of those students interviewed spoke highly of the Intensive Language Unit. One qualified his praise, however, by adding that the subjects they did 'were a bit primary-like . . . for beginners'. Another commented that those classes where students of 'mixed ages' were in the same class were the 'main problem'.

In the future, the headteacher would like to see more integration with the high school. Another teacher said of the Unit's future; 'it is as assured as it has been. The Intensive Language Unit is meeting a need, and people are unlikely to stop coming'. He would, however, like to see more involvement earlier in these students' schooling, and much more assessment of students' needs than teaching to a set curriculum. There is also a need, he added, to develop teaching methods further, which 'requires more inservice time, more professional help. Sometimes people reinvent the wheel two or three times'. An important step would be 'to upgrade the status of the teachers' aides who are often qualified as teachers in their own country', and to have more bilingual teaching to aid conceptual development, he believed.

Evaluation: The School

All staff interviewed, along with most students and parents, spoke very positively about their school and indicated that there was a general belief that the school achieved its broad goals: educational success; equipping students with the skills of social access; and sense of community. The principal believed that 'the school leads the region in many areas'. He thought of the whole school as innovatory, but 'where it is most successful it is because it fitted in with the ethos'. He considered most successful the creating of a school identity, which he saw as largely based on the welfare programme, the Language in Learning Program 'as a whole school programme', on computer education and 'on the integration of recent arrivals in the school environment'.

Both the deputies pointed to the welfare system of the school as crucial to its success, and as a particular response to the arrival of students of Asian background: 'I've never been in a school where the demand was so great for the welfare component. In other schools, this level of welfare would be rejected as an intrusion!' The welfare programme 'engenders throughout the school an attitude of a caring school', said one. One believed their success lay with a very 'committed staff', and gave the staff's decision to share the Year adviser role as an example; 'they do three times the work for only one pay'. Several parents noted that they were 'teachers who care'. A Vietnamese student declared 'the special in this school is every teachers to so kind with student [sic]'.

Pastoral care is tied to the academic goals, one deputy said; 'the main consideration of the welfare programme is to assist in the academic development of the child... welfare means learning for "real education": social as well as academic'. Even the senior community liaison officer stated as the major goal of his programme 'to encourage students to carry on to Year 12'. The principal claimed that 'in terms of language in broad terms, one of our successes has been making all teachers language teachers'. The emphasis on English language learning is tied to a uniform commitment to the goals outlined in the *Aims*. The ESL coordinator put it in the following way:

> Everyone is entitled to an equal education. That's what we are trying to give the kids. They are entitled to come out with something, a formal education and also social education. We're not trying to change them into 'acceptable' Australian social beings, but to fit in and be active social participants. The focus is on helping kids gain skills.

These standards are matched by high student aspirations. The ESL coordinator gave an example of a nearby high school with an 'alternative' English language course for Year 11: 'few here would choose it; students here want to be educated, succeed, go to uni, and they do programmes that will get them there. And we would be doing them a disservice if we didn't have high level English'. But, she added, there is a 'low tail', made up mostly of students who arrive in middle secondary years but stay to Year 12: 'they aren't going to do brilliantly in the HSC [Higher School Certificate] but will benefit from an emphasis on communicative competence'. The maths headteacher also spoke of the 'long tail' who balance out the otherwise very high maths results. He also commented on the fact that this year they allowed students to choose the level of maths they wished to do in senior years with no guidance, and they ended up with two Year 12 four-unit maths classes (the highest level) of thirty students, of which only three-quarters are capable, he thought; 'they're almost all Asian kids'. They also ended up with three three-unit maths classes in Year 11 (the highest level in Year 11), again with a lot who, he thought, are not capable; 'they think that if they set their mind to it, they can do it'. High aspirations are matched by an enormous effort on the part of students, particularly of Indo-Chinese background. The school library is always full, according to the librarian, as was the local public library after school. The Cabramatta Community Centre organized a study assistance programme, in which two dozen students, on average, attended special classes in their own time.

The Higher School Certificate results reflect these high aspirations. Fourteen students sat for four-unit maths in 1988 and all scored higher than 72 per cent. Of these students, seven scored 90 per cent or more. At the same time, twenty-eight students sat the lowest level of maths, twenty-one of whom had an overall result in the bottom 10 per cent of the state. There is clearly a bi-polar result within subject areas, but an even higher discrepancy exists between subjects. For example, where only one-fifth of Year 12 sat the lowest mathematics exam, 85 per cent sat the lowest English exam, of which over two-thirds scored lower than 50 per cent. Again, however, a relatively large class, of five students, sat the highest level of English. Also, while the school has a high retention rate to Year 11, at about 75 per cent, over half of the students at Cabramatta High finish in the last 10 per cent of the state in the Higher School Certificate.

Parents of both Indo-Chinese and English-speaking background spoke very highly of the school, one commenting that the principal was 'big on basics'. Both groups, however, referred to lack of discipline and 'respect for teachers' as issues that concerned them, and believed that the school should be more strict. 'The children have too much freedom. They need more guidance. . . . They need to have more respect. . . . They're allowed to answer back! There's too much emphasis on teachers and students being friends.'

The social goals of the school hinge on the creation of a sense of community within the school and a sense of being part of the wider community. Almost all staff, students and parents interviewed testified to the existence of a school identity and a positive atmosphere, and staff stability was pointed to as an indication of good morale. All teachers also commented on the good relations between students and the fact that Cabramatta High was a peaceful and friendly place to teach: 'we must be doing something right because the school is working; it's quiet, the kids are happy'. The principal saw the school's ethos as crucial to this:

> I have no doubt that a policy other than building up identity with a close community would have produced friction that doesn't exist at present. I decided that the more they fragment community the more they increase the risk that the community will tear itself apart.

The school's approach, then, is to avoid 'making an issue' of cultural differences, while also valuing them. The LOTEs headteacher believes that there are few racial problems in the school. I believe this is in part a result of giving value to different cultures through the LOTEs programme. If the school didn't have any Asian languages, the Asian kids would be entitled to think their culture was being put down.

As far as the educational worth of the LOTEs programme was concerned, however, one English-speaking background parent said that 'languages are not worthwhile. One term of Chinese is not enough. . . . I'd love them to learn a second language but the kids are not keen'.

The rationale for introducing languages has often been expressed as the 'promotion of tolerance and racial harmony within the school', particularly for students of Asian background, because of 'the frequent attacks on them and their culture by elements in the community'. Others also recognized ongoing problems of racism and prejudice both within and outside the school; one teacher spoke of past incidents of spitting, but said that NESB girls still saw Australian males as 'predatory', and feared them. One incident in the school involved a complaint by a parent about boys of Asian background 'touching' girls of non-Asian background. The school responded by organizing an assembly for girls advising them 'on how to conduct themselves and being careful about the signs they give boys'. Two parents voiced the opinion that while there were 'never big problems here', there was a 'Yugoslav problem ten years ago. They're a volatile race'.

The downplaying of these incidents in the belief that there is a 'relative absence of racial friction in the school', was explained by a community worker as a 'defensiveness' on the part of staff because of the very poor media image portrayed of the school and area; they felt they had been 'done over' by the press. But she also commented that problems of prejudice had decreased dramatically over the years, although institutionalized racism still existed throughout the entire community. This was partly the result of time and numbers, and partly because of a 'committed staff who work towards defining that multicultural emphasis'. Several students commented that the 'multiculturalism' of the school was its most positive feature, because 'you can learn about other backgrounds'. At the same time, however, about half of the students surveyed thought that the school 'poorly' understood their cultural backgrounds. One girl of Uruguayan background said 'I think they know zilch about my language and what my country has been through in the last few decades'.

Almost all those interviewed, however, claimed the cultural values of the 'Asian' students was the underlying reason for the absence of cultural dissonance. Their perceived respect for the authority of the teacher and eagerness to study were praised repeatedly. The Vietnamese aide recounted how, in her culture, there was a saying: 'the king first, then the teacher, then the family'. At the same time, however, there were subtle indicators of ongoing conflict or, at least, the lack of integration. Several parents, for example, of both English-speaking and Indo-Chinese backgrounds, pointed to the fact that students continued to socialize in their own language groups. Both liaison officers remarked, moreover, that 'staff still complain about how to get on with Asian students, because they keep silent'. One ESB student commented that 'gangs' and 'Asians' were two of the things he didn't like about the school, adding that his parents were 'not very happy, as there are gangs and too many fights'.

The Racial Equality Project intended to bring these issues into debate: issues which were not just those of Cabramatta High. The project officer believed that 'Cabramatta was not unusual. In fact it is one of the better schools'. But by surveying students and staff, the project revealed a degree of prejudice, and a feeling among Indo-Chinese students that they were being discriminated against. The negative reaction to the project from the school administration, a few staff and the Department of Education indicated to him the sensitivity of these issues and the need to address them directly, through a carefully developed sociocultural curriculum. The continuation of the Racial Equality Action Committee, organized through the Cabramatta Community Centre (which now enjoys greater collaboration with the school largely as a result of the Racial Equality Project) suggests that many professionals in the area still wish to address these issues.

Several staff documented the continuing difficulties of working in a school with a high degree of cultural and linguistic diversity. The principal was concerned that some students of Asian background lack the necessary degree of social interaction, 'so they are taking longer to integrate in the Australian community'. This was seen in their language development and the predominance of the first language of their families. This was why the principal stressed the role of English-speaking background teachers in providing role models and helping to create a sense of community. The head of the Intensive Language Unit referred to 'the culture shock' for staff resulting from the rapid population changes in the last eight years, and the continual need for support and staff development.

The avoidance of making cultural difference 'an issue' could, however, also have a problematic side. A community liaison officer said that his major difficulty was how 'to get on with the teaching staff'. While they were aware of the problems of diversity, he said, 'they don't want to get involved'. He contrasted Cabramatta with another of his three schools, in which 'the staff were more accepting' and attended the information meetings he organized with parent groups enthusiastically, providing refreshments. This had resulted in a very successful liaison programme within just six months; about forty Chinese background and sixty Vietnamese-speaking parents attended the regular, language group meetings. He had had some success at Cabramatta, he said, and had twenty-four Russian-Chinese parents — a group notoriously isolated — come to a meeting. This was tremendous, he added, because there were only thirty-five students from that community in the school. To achieve this, however, he had to put in a lot of extra work, including home visiting, which was extra to his work load. Yet the principal was the only teacher to come to the meeting, so he had decided that the best thing for him to do was start talking to teachers individually, or by faculty. Staff had stated their support, but were not actively assisting. Part of the problem, he added, was that faculties don't talk to each other, or share in social activities.

The principal commented that the result of cultural diversity was the challenge to which the school must respond:

> We have to work hard to get the rewards.... Innovation comes from the environment, not the individual. The community cries out for innovation. It's related to needs that don't exist anywhere else. The environment demands innovation and it requires that it be perceptive.

Note

1 RICHARDS, P., *'Mira, Yo No Say Racista...': A Project for Cabramatta High School, draft,* Cabramatta High School, 1986; *Fairfield Advance,* 15th July, 1986.

Chapter 8

'Culture Cocktail':
The English as a Second Language and Languages Other Than English Programmes at Footscray High School

> In an area of rapid demographic shifts, Footscray High School, in Melbourne's inner west, has responded to the needs of its clientele over the last decade by implementing wide-ranging innovation. Within a whole school emphasis on student welfare and diversification of curriculum to meet students' needs, the school has established a large English as a Second Language programme, which includes a compulsory humanities course, and offers Languages Other Than English programmes in Greek, Macedonian and Italian, also compulsory in Years 7 and 8.

Cultures of Schooling

The Locality

Footscray High is located in Spotswood, just south of Footscray proper in Melbourne's west. The suburb is reached by a freeway that skirts the portside areas and crosses the Yarra River via the Westgate Bridge, a symbol of the divide between the eastern and western suburbs, rich and poor, mainstream and immigrant; symbolic, also, because a number of workers, many of immigrant background, were killed when the bridge collapsed during its construction. Severed from the central business district by an industrial belt, Footscray has a curiously suburban feel that belies its relative proximity to the city's edge. A mix of the old and not-so-old, the area nevertheless has a quiet, settled quality which is disrupted by the mass of concrete which is the freeway, dissecting communities in the march of modernity.

The suburb is ringed by large industrial areas, encompassing a range of manufacturing and commercial activities. The local abattoirs, just along the freeway from the school, have recently closed and will be redeveloped. These industries provide much of the employment, and unemployment, in the area. This area is typically working class, and largely of non-English speaking background. In the 1986 census, over 43 per cent of the population of Footscray were born overseas, well over the 25 per cent for the state as a whole. Yugoslavia (8 per cent), Vietnam (7 per cent), Greece (4 per cent) and Italy (4 per cent) were the greatest source of overseas-born — this figure, of course, does not include Australian-born children of immigrants. Over 13 per cent said in the census that they did not speak English well or at all; almost 6 per cent of 5–14 year-olds were in the same category, compared to a state figure of seven-tenths of 1 per cent.

A significant proportion of the population is transient, as new arrivals — primarily Indo-Chinese — gravitate towards cheap rental accommodation, said to be the cheapest in Melbourne. At the time of the census, over 9 per cent of the population in Footscray had been in Australia less than five years, and a remarkable 25 per cent had been in the local government area for less than a year. Perhaps an even greater number are leaving the area, heading for outer suburbs such as Sunshine and Altona once established enough to afford to buy a house. As one teacher explained, 'even the new Asian communities are moving out because they tend to buy houses as soon as possible'. The population of Footscray is expected to fall by about 7 per cent between 1986 and 1991, and further by 2001.

This 'tidal thing', as one teacher described it, meant that there were always families experiencing 'hard times' and 'rebuilding their lives'. The next suburb, Yarraville, was described as 'dilapidated', with a lot of Housing Commission flats and houses, but further south there was better brick-veneer housing. The principal suspected that the 'yuppies', astute about inner city property values, had discovered the cheap accommodation and were beginning to move in. There were a few families in the 'upper echelons' of society, but most residents were workers, pensioners and some self-employed.

There was a number of welfare, community and cultural or sporting groups but the Greek-speaking and Macedonian-speaking communities have had the greatest effects on the area because of their size and length of settlement. The latter, for example, were said to be 'fighting here for recognition at home', and have been organized and vocal. Like Cabramatta in Sydney, this area also has something of a reputation for inter-ethnic conflict — open or submerged — which was referred to by several of those interviewed.

The School

The numbers of students at Footscray had dropped dramatically over the last two to three years; from over 950 to 827 in 1989, to around 760 in 1990, according to the principal. It was the result, primarily, of demographic changes in the larger district, and was reflected in other local schools (except a local private girls' school). This was a phenomenon typical of most inner suburbs of Melbourne, the principal said. He added that the famed drift to private schools may have had a small part in this. There was also an underrepresentation of girls in the school. In 1988, 92 per cent of the student body was of non-English speaking background (NESB).

The overall decline coincided with a rapid rise in the numbers of students of Indo-Chinese background, who were roughly equal in size with the longer established groups of Greek and Macedonian backgrounds, each of which represented around a quarter of the student population. With students of Indo-Chinese background (mostly Vietnamese) now, these three groups make up 75 per cent of the school population. Several years ago, those of Greek and Macedonian background together made up more than this proportion. Altogether there were about thirty languages represented in the school, including students from a variety of Spanish-speaking backgrounds, Arabic and Indo-Chinese language backgrounds. One teacher pointed out that 'Vietnamese' was often used as a general term which included many groups; Lao, Cambodian, Chinese-Vietnamese and 'Vietnamese-Vietnamese', the last of which was the single largest group, with about 20 per cent of the school population. The English-speaking background students made up 8 per cent of the population.

A third of all students were born overseas. The students of Indo-Chinese background were predominantly first generation, while most other groups, particularly those of Greek and Macedonian backgrounds, were second generation. A large number of students, including second generation ones, spoke one language at home and another at school. As further testimony to the language and learning difficulties of these students, in 1988, one-quarter of NESB students had experienced five years or less of schooling in Australia.

Students came from overwhelmingly working-class backgrounds, although one teacher pointed out that many parents of South-East Asian background were middle class in their homeland — professionals or bureaucrats — 'but they are working class here'. About 200 students come from families who were in receipt of welfare payments — the principal presumed these to be mostly single mothers — and about 120 students are on Austudy (Commonwealth financial assistance given to disadvantaged students to enable them to continue their education). The principal added, however, that 'there are also kids who get picked up in a Mercedes': a comment echoed by others.

About a third of the students of Vietnamese background are orphans, and about half, the boys in particular, live with relatives other than parents, or friends. Students of Macedonian and Greek background were seen to be more likely to live in extended families, and 'Anglos' in nuclear families. Housing Commission flats and homes were common. While student backgrounds were generally thought to be very comparable with the surrounding area, the former community liaison officer added that Footscray High, because of its geography, drew from a very wide area. The relatively high turnover of students of Indo-Chinese background also complicates the picture somewhat. The former community liaison officer also said that many of the students' leisure activities took place within the family network. Boys were more involved in weekend activities, according to the principal, and girls more family oriented.

Male students of Macedonian, Greek or Italian backgrounds were 'into soccer'; those of Vietnamese background played table tennis and volleyball, although some have been 'assimilated' and play cricket and Australian Rules football. The student welfare coordinator said that a regional welfare committee in the western suburbs had identified an absence of youth services, and 'while the boys were OK because they had sport, this was a problem for the girls'. Many parents feared for them and would not let them out. The curriculum coordinator said, as a general point, that many students, particularly the new arrivals, are not 'mobile' and had not travelled beyond Footscray or the central business district of Melbourne unless they had relatives elsewhere.

There are seventy-six teaching and twenty ancillary staff at Footscray. Excluding the three part-time ethnic aides, over a third of the teaching staff are of non-English speaking background, although the principal thought it was as high as 50 to 70 per cent of 'names on the list': 'we've always been fortunate in that the mix of staff has always been good. Maybe it's too high; it's more important that they're four-year trained. It's only a help if they speak a language'. The curriculum coordinator said that while there was a good mix of backgrounds amongst the staff, there were few of Vietnamese background. The numbers were skewed towards the settled, European communities.

Research carried out by Marta Rado and others in 1985–6 to examine the feasibility of introducing a Vietnamese language maintenance programme at Footscray, showed 71 per cent of teachers spoke English as their first language. Seventy-seven per cent said they spoke another language, but this was primarily French, Italian or German. All teachers had appropriate qualifications, and a third had specialist training.[1]

There had been enormous staffing changes at the school over the last few years. This suggests, perhaps, something of the difficulties of teaching at a

Footscray High School

school with a large immigrant, working-class population, but it also coincided with demographic shifts and a large number of teachers having taken leave, resulting in an annual departure of as many as twenty to thirty teachers. The result was a new and young staff, many of whom had only been at the school for two or three years. The ESL coordinator, in her fourth year at this, her first, school, had been coordinator for two years. She said that the high turnover had resulted in a 'greater than usual opportunity for promotion' for those who stayed on at the school.

The school's guaranteed recurrent budget comes to around $200,000 (not including salaries), with $160,000 to $170,000 coming directly from state government payments. The curriculum coordinator described the budget as 'deeply stretched due to government cutbacks and demands for greater teacher workloads, such as in ESL (English as a Second Language)'. They also get about $30,000 from the Disadvantaged Schools Program (a Commonwealth-funded programme which aims to improve the quality of schooling for disadvantaged groups by funding specialist initiatives), without which, the principal remarked, they would not have been able to get a computer or the school newspaper programme. The deputy principal pointed out that most of the $30,000 was spent on aides' salaries; only $11,000 was available for programmes that year. The school asks parents for a voluntary $30 levy, said the principal, but they did not get it: a fact he related with the socioeconomic composition of the school population. Nor did they do any fund-raising. The principal said they needed $10,000–15,000 for each faculty to upgrade: it was very difficult.

The school is housed in two 1950s light timber constructed blocks, a few newer brick buildings and six to eight 'relocatable' classroom blocks, and is fronted by an award-winning native garden. Apart from its own 'multipurpose' courts and soccer field, it has the use of the playing fields in an adjacent public reserve. It also has a computer room. According to the principal, Footscray is no better or worse than other state schools with regard to facilities, but 'in relation to a private school we're hopeless'. They had hoped to introduce a language laboratory but it would have meant taking the money away from other programmes.

The school, like all Victorian state high schools, has a school council with its various sub-committees. It also has an administrative committee, a curriculum committee, parent associations, a students' representative council and a staff association. Meeting are held for the whole staff, faculties, the four 'sub-schools' (Years 7/8, 9/10, 11, and 12), Year levels and home groups, and various other committees that are established from time to time, such as the student welfare committee. The *Staff Handbook* sets out a five-stage decision-making model to clarify procedures and structures.

The school has a clear emphasis on 'collaborative decision making'; 'a consultative process' involving staff, students and parents in 'an attempt to reach consensus wherever possible', which is summarized in a 1989 staff questionnaire to establish 'What is Footscray on about?' All staff testified to a management style based on consensus. The principal said that he was, in 1984, the first through the system whereby school councils participate in the selection of principals, a result of the changes in education brought about when the state Labor government came to power in Victoria. He thought there were too many authoritarian principals, and was eager to try 'consensus'. He saw himself as a 'facilitator'. The curriculum coordinator agreed that the consensus style was the reason he came to the school, but felt that it is slow to make change, and time-consuming and problematic when there is a changing staff, as they had. There are also the problems he said, 'over which committee says what'.

In response to its large and diverse NESB population, Footscray has articulated a clear concern both for students' welfare and responsiveness to community needs. The results of a staff survey, 'What is Footscray on about?', reaffirmed a number of principles related not only to 'collaboration and participation'; but also 'care and support'; curriculum 'which caters to a range of abilities, needs and backgrounds'; and equal opportunity and multiculturalism. The school rules, which were given to the students' representative council to review in 1987, are also based on three broad principles: equal opportunity, 'safety', and a caring environment.

The original principle of multiculturalism at the school was that 'at Footscray High we respect, enhance, value and work towards catering for the variety of cultures in the school community'. This has since been changed, as a result of the survey, to 'FHS is a polyethnic school where the staff promote respect for all individuals, their cultures and backgrounds in the curriculum and in relationships between individuals'. Consequently, the school has developed over a number of years a series of initiatives in curriculum and school organization to meet the needs of their students and their policy goals.

The school has a large English as a Second Language (ESL) programme which includes parallel classes (often called withdrawal) in ESL throughout the grades — held at the same time as English classes *and* offered as an elective — and Alternative English programmes at senior level. The ESL faculty also teaches the compulsory humanities course for ESL students in the junior years, and provides some teacher support in mainstream subjects.

The Languages Other Than English (LOTEs) programme offers Greek, Macedonian and Italian; the study of one of which is compulsory in Years 7 and 8, and which become electives from Year 9. Footscray was the first Victorian secondary school to introduce Macedonian as a language. It has been looking at introducing Vietnamese into the LOTEs programme, and in 1985, together with the Australian Vietnamese Women's Welfare Association and the Committee for Introducing the Teaching of Vietnamese into Victorian Schools, initiated the report, *Introducing Vietnamese into Footscray High School*, funded by the Ministerial Advisory Committee on Multicultural and Migrant Education and compiled by Marta Rado and Jennie Oldfield.

Mainstream subjects have developed units relevant to multicultural issues, such as work on migration in Year 8, discussion of racial discrimination in Year 10 social studies, comparisons of different cultures in Year 10 science and Year 9 home economics, and so on. The school has a wide range of school-based and alternative courses.

The school has a community liaison programme involving a community liaison officer, a shared school community development officer and bilingual information officers, parent groups, and three part-time ethnic aides — Greek, Macedonian and Vietnamese — who are available to teachers and provide services for translating and interpreting, in addition to their main task of assisting student programmes in the classroom. The community liaison officer for two years received a financial allowance as well as a period allowance, which allowed her to make contacts with parents and set up formal and informal meetings. This position, however, no longer receives a pay supplement, following the reduction in paid responsibility positions because of falling enrolments.

A large pastoral care programme exists at the school, and includes a student welfare coordinator and committee, an equal opportunity officer, multiple Year level coordinators, 'sub-schools' and home groups, camps, lunchtime activities, a human relations course, and a careers councillor. Years 7 to 10 were organized into three 'sub-schools' in 1986 to facilitate pastoral care and administration, and help create 'a sense of belonging' in the school.

Footscray High has also been involved in one-off programmes such as the *Culture Cocktail* project, whose aim was to produce a video documenting activities in the school which reflected and responded to multiculturalism. A general ethos of understanding and respect is exemplified by the staff handbook, which includes an explanation of the Vietnamese naming system and a guide to pronunciation.

Context of the Innovation

Footscray has a long history of implementing innovatory programmes. In 1983, for example, the school introduced a Transition Education Advisory Committee-funded programme in Year 9 and 10 which included courses in community research and cross-age tutoring. As a Participation and Equity Program school, in 1985 it took part, with four other schools, in the *Culture Cocktail* project. The broad aim was to increase tolerance and understanding across cultures whilst developing the students' video-making skills. The introduction to the report of this project explained that over the last few years the school has attempted to provide curriculum and develop processes which include the experiences of people from a variety of cultures. A 'Multicultural Video Class' became a Year 9/10 elective for the duration of the project, in which at least a half of the students were girls, a third ESL students, and the major ethnic groups given proportional representation. The programme attempted to have the issue of racism 'tackled openly and honestly':

We critically analysed students' seating arrangements in our own room; we asked questions about friendship groupings that corresponded to language groups and we explored territory that is too often regarded as sensitive and therefore avoided.[2]

The school has developed over the years a diverse range of subject offerings. In Years 7 and 8 there is a compulsory curriculum of English, maths, science, humanities, a language, physical education, art and music (with some choice within a couple of the areas). In Years 9 and 10, however, there are compulsory, year-long core subjects (English, maths, science and humanities in Year 9; English and maths in Year 10) and a range of electives organized around a semester timetable. In Year 9, students select eight electives (four per semester), one each from the following areas: creative arts, commerce, computers and personal development; the last of which includes, for example, physical education, home economics and human relations. Students can also choose to do a language, and extra ESL. In Year 10, ten electives (five per semester) are chosen from the above areas, plus science and humanities. They can also choose to study a number of courses at a local technical school in place of two electives offered within the secondary school.

Around seventy semester courses are available in Years 9 and 10, across the various areas, including 'Work Education', 'Community Action', 'Typing', 'You The Consumer', 'Out On Your Own', 'Community Research', 'Cross-Age Tutoring', 'Let's Cook Food From Around The World', 'School Newspaper', and 'Horticulture', as well as the more conventional offerings. Likewise, in Years 11 and 12, there is a large number of alternative courses 'with an emphasis on practical areas', such as 'Catering', 'Photography', 'Mathematics at Work' and 'Secretarial Studies'. Over a third of those available are Group 2 subjects. Under the current Years 11 and 12 credentialling provisions, subjects are grouped into two areas. Group 1 subjects are more high-status, academic courses, geared towards tertiary education. Group 2 subjects, on the other hand, are generally alternative courses designed more for students who do not necessarily wish to enter tertiary study. Many of the latter are not recognized by tertiary institutions for entry into their own degrees or diplomas. This formal distinction will largely be erased with the introduction of the new Victorian Certificate of Education, which is itself based on a wide, diversified curriculum.

The rationale for this variety within the school's curriculum is in terms of 'individual needs'; in particular, the perceived needs of a large and diverse NESB student population, and best serviced by school-based curriculum development:

> Footscray High School provides a curriculum whereby all students achieve success through ... access to a broad-based curriculum ... which caters to a range of abilities, needs and backgrounds.

The staff survey, 'What is Footscray on about?', specifically links the diversification of the curriculum to cultural diversity by stating, under the heading of 'Broad Based Curriculum', that the school needs to 'become more aware of cultural diversity of students by preparing a profile for staff handbook'.

The principal noted, however, that they were changing Years 9 and 10 again, returning to more of a core curriculum approach, 'influenced by external factors such as John Dawkins (Federal Minister for Education) and the Curriculum Development Centre'. (Both the Minister and the federally-funded Curriculum Development Centre promote the idea of a national core curriculum.) The curriculum committee emphasizes the development of:

> curriculum that ensures the equality of educational outcomes . . . [and curriculum] that seeks to provide equal outcomes for girls and for students of all cultural or socioeconomic backgrounds.

It also seeks to develop curriculum that works towards 'the redress of disadvantage and discrimination'.

The concerns of the staff with the broader social success and welfare of NESB students, as well as their academic achievement, is illustrated in a school submission regarding the proposed introduction of new socioeconomic indicators in determining 'disadvantage' in educational resource allocation. The submission argues that the assumption 'that NESB students will be adequately catered for through ESL special staffing' does not recognize 'the specific disadvantage suffered by students as a result of their ethnic backgrounds', nor

> is capable of responding to the specific curriculum needs of ESL students above and beyond the requirements of language acquisition. This assumption totally ignores what schools who deal with large numbers of NESB students knows to be a reality — that NESB students and their families require greater servicing and support in the curriculum, administration and welfare areas and that this servicing goes well beyond ESL services.

The depth and complexity of the migrant experience — the hardships and the expectations — which schools with large NESB populations confront, is best summarized by the following extracts from Year 11 ESL students' writings:

> 1. On the day that I left my country I was very sad because I was leaving my friends, family and the country where I was born. It has been the saddest day of my life so far, and I am sure I will not forget it as long as I live . . . ; deep inside me there was something wanting to explode . . . ; I felt hatred towards my parents because they had decided to come to Australia. At that moment I also felt like running away from there.

2. ... [T]he people's faces ... looked so different from the ones I left in Portugal, because of their way of looking at people. For me it seemed that they knew that I was a new person in that city and it seemed they were making me feel unwelcome.
On that day, I felt that everything was turning black ... ; I was afraid that the new people would be different from me and they wouldn't accept me the way I was.

3. ... I was so happy and emotional about my future and the things that I had to do to face it. This was a free land that I had never dreamt of living in. I thought to myself that I was the lucky one, someone who could live in Australia for the rest of their life, and could grow up and do the things that they wanted.
... My last thoughts were of the things that I had been through, and the things that I would be doing like learning new language, becoming an Australian citizen and being useful to my new home. I wondered what would be waiting for me in this new country.

The principal admitted frankly that the cultural diversity of the school is demanding in terms of time and of 'your power and emotional base', particularly with students 'continually getting into strife'. There are 'punch-ups all the time amongst the boys', and he had intervened in a serious student confrontation during the research, but said there is no discernible pattern to explain conflict. He added that the challenge of cultural diversity 'puts us on notice all the time ... we're walking a fine line'. He believed, however, that most of the problems emanate from outside the school. 'Wog', he claims, is a term used freely by adults in the community. The expression of cultural conflict in the school, he suggested, 'reflects society; it isn't created here' in the school. But, he added that it is 'a red hot issue' and that he feared that the school and its community are 'sitting on a racial time bomb' over which they have little control. The school thus sought to create attitudes that could go back into the community, though he was mindful 'that you can't change the world'. He said, therefore, that he 'has an overall concern with keeping the school together and happy'.

Some parents of 'Anglo-Australian background,' the principal explained, complain that a lot of time is spent on NESB students to the detriment of ESB students. He reported that a Footscray student said just that when he appeared on a programme which looked at the issue of cultural diversity, in an edition of *The 7.30 Report*, a national television current affairs programme, in 1988. But, the principal added, there were no 'huge crises'. The school's emphasis on providing a safe, caring environment is crucial to its smooth functioning, and he believed there was a sense of community there, a view shared by the curriculum coordinator. The principal said he works hard 'to impress toleration of cultural differences' through informal means such as student home-groups and the work of the multiple Year coordinators, as well as through the content of the curriculum, but he admitted this tolerance is, at times, 'very fragile'. One of the problems the school has to deal with was regular 'invasions' from the 'outside', particularly on Mondays when weekend fights are brought into the school.

The language coordinator also testified to the problems of managing cultural diversity. Many students of Macedonian background, for example, assert a strong, traditional identity, which is, in her opinion, a reaction to the Australian influence, 'maybe to do with the underlying racism that everyone says doesn't exist'. She said that there were many examples of implicit and explicit prejudice in the school, from both students and teachers. Much of this was simply name-calling, but she felt it contributed to, for example, Greek-Macedonian tension.

This was linked, she added, to the low self-esteem of students:

> These kids don't see themselves, or others, in a good light — the result of living in the western suburbs. The kids say, 'but mum, no-one cares about us'. I spent half a year with one class on human development skills. What's the point of teaching them English if they couldn't deal with each other?

She also suggested that: 'The racism that the Vietnamese are now experiencing, the Macedonians went through earlier, although they forget that and are as much to blame as others'.

The deputy also commented on 'complaints' made by parent representatives of English-speaking and Greek background on the school council about special language classes or activities for the more recently arrived students of Vietnamese background. The feasibility study for introducing Vietnamese into the LOTEs programme also noted that a significant proportion of teachers and non-Vietnamese students perceived intergroup relations to be poor, although the Vietnamese-speaking students themselves did not admit to poor relations, a reaction the authors of the study describe as a 'defence mechanism' against discrimination.

The ESL coordinator pointed out that, given the school's diversity, it was hard to impress a notion of 'community', particularly on the boys. On the other hand, whilst there were expressions of racism, such as slogans on walls and name-calling, she thought it was 'low key' precisely because the school was so culturally diverse and, in particular, because there were so few 'Anglos'. She admitted, however, that there was some inter-ethnic conflict. Students will, for example, express attitudes such as, 'Greeks are better than Macedonians'. But she, too, was more worried by the 'ghettoization' of newer immigrant students of Asian and Arabic backgrounds. The student welfare coordinator also referred to the 'playground politics' that occurred as the students of Vietnamese background grew in number and challenged the groups of Greek and Macedonian background for the best positions after years of being ousted from the valued areas.

Cultures of Schooling

The principal explained that his way of dealing with the diversity of cultural practices and values in his school was symbolized by the Australian flag on his desk. When critical issues arose that seemed unresolvable he would point to the flag and use it to signify that in Australia, and in his school, there were points of unity: that there were certain laws and rights that were available to all and that all in turn had to respect. This strategy, he said, was particularly useful when questions of gender practices and culture arose. The school's policy of non-sexism, he explained, presented dilemmas in a co-educational school such as his:

> We'll always be in a battle because of these cultural differences. [Parents] will say, for example, 'this is our culture, how dare you'. You have to say, like Mill, 'this is the law, respect it'. The only morality you can pass on the kids in a state school is the law.

He viewed his role, however, not as one trying to change values. In the end, he said, everyone had to accept what the nation itself had accepted; 'This is Australia, a multicultural society', and that went for the newly arrived as well as those longer established. But he admitted that it was a fragile exercise still in the making. It is within this context, of a trend towards curriculum diversification and the increasing cultural and linguistic diversity of students, that the innovations under focus in this case study, the ESL programme and the LOTEs programme were developed.

The ESL provision has expanded over recent years and is offered in all years, but is called Alternative English in Year 12, the official Victorian Curriculum and Assessment Board title. ESL has been provided since the 1970s, according to the current coordinator, but until four or five years ago there was no ESL department with an independent programme as such, 'just a small group of ESL staff acting in support roles', whereby they simply helped out in mainstream classes when required. Students asked for more help with their English language learning, she explained, so the programme was expanded and 'withdrawal' classes became predominant; students were taken out of the mainstream and located in special ESL classes which were run parallel with English classes. About 140 students are now in the programme, up from about fifty in the early 1980s.

Within the LOTEs programme, the school offers Greek, Macedonian and Italian classes. Originally, the principal explained, the school had offered the 'traditional' languages, such as French, which reflected teacher training and availability, and the agreed-upon 'international' languages. When Macedonian, which had been taught in community schools for over a decade, was introduced into the school in 1981, Footscray was the first high school in the state to do so. Now about half a dozen secondary and a dozen primary schools in Victoria were teaching it. Serbo-Croatian was also considered for introduction at the school in 1984, and Vietnamese in 1985, but neither has eventuated as yet.

Both Macedonian and Greek were introduced into the school after lobbying by the respective parent associations in the school, both of which were formed in 1979. In the case of Macedonian, an English/French teacher of Macedonian origin became active in the Macedonian-speaking community after some years of isolation, and helped establish the parents' association, in which the current coordinator's father had been involved. She said that the parents of Macedonian background had 'needed to be led' to get organized. The current coordinator and this teacher had become friends while the former was at university, and had set up a cross-campus organization for students of Macedonian background there. They lobbied to get Macedonian introduced at Monash University. The coordinator explained that parents of Macedonian background wanted the language to be taught to their children 'as an identity thing, which is important', but she had wanted it because she 'had realized that many of them don't have Macedonian or English skills, so we had to start with the first language'.

The Innovations in Practice: The ESL Programme

There are seven teachers in the ESL faculty (6.5 plus 0.5 special needs allowance — an allowance which is given to schools to supplement staff where the school sees fit). This is one down from last year's peak, and teachers from other faculties provide an extra couple of periods to help out because of timetable clashes. There are three ESL classes in each of Years 7, 8 and 12; two in Year 9; three in Year 10; and three in Year 11. From Year 9, ESL includes both classes that are run parallel to the English mainstream and elective classes. Funding is primarily federal, but the programme also receives approximately $1,000, according to pupil numbers, from the school's normal allocation from the state government.

All new arrival students at the school are grouped in three categories of English proficiency: beginners, intermediate and advanced. This is done, according to the coordinator, 'on the basis of long experience' and, where appropriate, on the advice of the intensive language centres from which they have come (these centres provide a six months, or in some cases more, on-arrival course for new immigrants). Those who arrive from other schools or who have been in the country a year or two are tested with an initial assessment task. The ESL faculty has tried to cater for as many students as possible, beyond those in most need, because of the central role of English language proficiency in the academic success of NESB (and indeed all) students, but the coordinator said that they still 'can't cater to all students as we'd like'.

In Years 7 and 8, 'beginners' are automatically withdrawn from LOTEs, English and humanities classes for ESL instruction. The humanities course is incorporated in the ESL class. In Years 9 and 10, students are then allowed to choose to continue in the ESL programme or to join a mainstream English class. However, if the staff feel a student should continue but has chosen not to, the student is 'counselled' as to the benefits of staying in the ESL programme. ESL students can also choose to do extra ESL classes in place of an elective. In Year 11, students can choose to do ESL (ten periods) or ESL support (five ESL and five English). In Year 12, students can do Alternative English (ESL), which is a Group 1 subject, or English B, which is Group 2, as alternatives to Group 1 English, the most 'academic' of the three courses and regarded by many as more adequate preparation for a number of tertiary courses.

The extent of the senior ESL provision at Footscray, rare amongst secondary schools, is an indication of the school's recognition that many of their students, some of whom are arriving in the final years of secondary school, continue to need specialist language instruction in these years. The report on the introduction of Vietnamese to the school comments that 'Vietnamese students like to attend the school especially in Years 11 and 12 because ESL is still offered at these upper levels'.

The goals of the ESL programme were described by the coordinator as 'trying to provide NESB students with the English language skills needed, varying from survival skills to success at tertiary education', as well as pastoral care:

> the whole ESL faculty see pastoral care as part of the job; you are the one they come to first if they have a problem — you just accept it. Informally, this has almost as much weight as the linguistic goals.

She said there can be contradictions between these two sets of goals, and gave the example of a student who had been having problems with his father: 'the ESL teacher spent a lot of time trying to help him', but he 'suffered linguistically' because some of this came out of class time. She explained that there was also a conflict over the role of ESL within the faculty:

> The majority view is that the ESL students will not absorb language in the other classes — they will just sit there and 'drown' . . . and there is a need for the ESL teacher to teach them about life.

But, she declared there was a 'dissenting voice', who believed that ESL support in mainstream classes would be more beneficial to students than withdrawing them into separate ESL classes.

The coordinator, however, was adamant that her experience as an ESL support teacher had demonstrated to her that mainstreaming 'didn't work'. She recognized the need for some support in some classes, and gave the example of a senior science class, but claimed that, in many mainstream classes, NESB students with limited English who need particular attention were distracted from their work by the needs and behaviour of others. 'There are some subjects, she said, 'where the ESL students sit up the back and say nothing — especially in the male-dominated subjects'.

The ESL programme hasn't been greatly modified since the expansion of the provision, except for the fact that one junior ESL class was disbanded because of staffing cutbacks. The students were returned to a mainstream humanities class. The Year 11 course has also been partly modified from a language focus to a 'life skills' focus because, as the coordinator explained, 'some are not "academically inclined". So we introduced "Life Skills", "Work Orientation Skills", and so on, in consultation with the careers teacher'.

It is expected that the introduction of the changes to the Victorian Certificate of Education, in which the division between Groups 1 and 2 will be abolished and a wider range of semester-based courses will be provided, will have great effects from next year, as ESL will be forced to integrate more with mainstream offerings.

The syllabus guidelines drawn up by the ESL staff outline topics covered and texts used in ESL programmes from Year 7 to Year 11. Year 7 'beginners' ESL, which has eleven periods a week, is based on texts such as *Comprehension Through Grammar*, used for two to three periods, and a range of short stories and plays which are read and for which students complete exercises. The Year 8 syllabus states its main aim as being an emphasis on spoken English and also aims, to 'encourage and engender a sense of identity i.e., in belonging and being part of the school'. It also claims to 'link work to their mainstream subjects' and 'facilitate their transition into the "normal" classroom situation'. Grammar is a constant feature of the guidelines, usually in terms of 'tenses, parts of speech, punctuation', and the Year 10 syllabus recommends 'Informal grammar lessons where and when needed'. The amount of time spent on oral and written language is left up to the class teacher.

Year 11 ESL is for ten periods a week, and includes in its aims competency in written and oral English 'to prepare them for Year 12 Alternative English'. The Year 11 ESL 'support class' is for NESB students 'who have been studying English for six years or more and still require some English practice' but who no longer qualify for the main ESL class. Students take five ESL periods a week in addition to their five English periods. The ESL 'support class' constitutes one of the six subject choices and is assessed as a separate subject.

The coordinator and an ESL teacher interviewed agreed that there is no common teaching style. The former said it was 'very individually based'. She described her style as 'informal', adding that 'you just can't use chalk and talk, because the kids see you as more "human" than their other teachers', underlining the intimacy built up in smaller classes. But she believed that repetition and reinforcement are very important in ESL. The coordinator said they have a massive number of resources but write their own if needed: 'we have a syllabus for Years 7–11, but we might throw it out depending on the individuals in the class'. She gave the current Year 11 'beginners' as an example, explaining that 'they're so remedial'. A textbook used with these students, *Get Your Tenses Straight*, focused on the use of tense in extracts of 'authentic English and a series of '"slot-filling" worksheets, mostly based on information-transfer'. The textbook emphasizes that it has no tests, or exercises 'which are difficult to do', and explains to students that while they may not think they are learning anything because they are so 'easy', practising writing 'the right words' will help them remember them.

The links between the ESL staff and the rest of the school tend to be based more on 'informal staffroom requests' for help, but the mere five periods 'left over' after the ESL teachers have subtracted the classes they teach as parallel classes militates against sustained, systematic integration with other faculties. Only three ESL teachers this year had periods left to be able to offer support after their allotted teaching load. (Timetable changes since the time of the interviews 'mean we now have twelve "support" periods', according to the ESL coordinator. This meant that six out of seven ESL teachers could offer one or more periods of 'support'.) One ESL teacher said that the support provision wasn't planned, 'but happened merely because some teachers are underallotted'. The coordinator elaborated that 'another problem [was] the unwillingness of mainstream teachers to allow ESL teachers into their classes'.

There is a local 'ESL network', of primary and secondary teachers, which meets regularly at the local education centre, and the staff have just joined the ESL Teachers' Association. The ESL teacher suggested that the network was mostly concerned with contacting feeder schools and informing students and parents of the ESL programme. The coordinator said that while the regional consultant was helpful, the 'system' itself gave little support, 'but the Victorian Certificate of Education has brought them out of the woodwork — there have been curriculum days, inservices. It has shaken up the Victorian Curriculum and Assessment Board, too'.

In terms of new technologies, an ESL teacher 'road-tested' a number of software packages, bought with Disadvantaged Schools Program money, and wrote a report on them last year. These involved language and grammar exercises, and the coordinator said that they mostly use a video game approach. They also have taught word-processing skills within ESL.

The Innovations in Practice:
Teaching Languages Other Than English

Study of a language other than English is compulsory in Years 7 and 8, except for ESL students, and becomes an elective in Year 9. Footscray offers mother-tongue maintenance programmes in Greek, Macedonian and Italian. Students for whom these are not the first language may learn one, usually Italian, as a second language.

There are, currently, five LOTEs staff — two Greek, one Italian and two Macedonian teachers. Macedonian is taught through to Year 12. The coordinator taught the junior years (and an English class, one Italian lesson and one ESL lesson), while the second Macedonian teacher took the senior years.

There had been a third Macedonian teacher the previous year, who had been 'roped in' but was not interested or trained. Greek is also taught to Year 12, with two classes in each year to Year 9. Italian is taught to Year 10, with two classes in Years 7 and 8 each. All bar the Italian teacher taught some English or ESL lessons.

The LOTEs coordinator claimed that there is some difference in emphasis between teachers, regarding the goals of the programme. One teacher saw the goal more as 'keeping the difference, and it has become a patriotic thing'. She saw the goals as 'double-edged', but because there are students with inadequate skills in both English and the mother tongue, language skills in the first language have to be given priority over a cultural emphasis to overcome the cognitive gap. The course handbooks, which outline curriculum choices for each year, stress both 'spoken and written skills' and learning about the 'history, geography, culture and literature' of the particular language studied. The Year 9 Italian course more explicitly states a language emphasis:

> Students interested in doing Italian are strongly advised to have an understanding of grammatical concepts like:
> - masculine and feminine, singular and plural;
> - nouns, articles, verbs, agreement of adjectives;
> - the present tense;
> - a reasonable amount of vocabulary;

and goes on to describe the subject in terms of using present and perfect tense, studying Italian literature and culture, conversation, comprehension and translation.

The curriculum coordinator, however, thought that the languages staff were strong on a cultural perspective, largely because languages are compulsory in the junior years. This meant that in each class the teachers have to teach to a range of competencies. The LOTEs coordinator also specified this as a challenge and hopes to introduce Macedonian for beginners within the year, if staffing and resource restrictions can be resolved. She indicated that the value and support that the school gives to LOTEs is shown by making them compulsory in the junior years, and the fact that they 'are trying to hang onto languages and ESL' in the face of falling enrolments, which says something of how the school regards the critical role of language as a whole. In the study assessing the worth of introducing Vietnamese to the school, 71 per cent of teachers said that every child should learn a LOTE, and a third of the staff wished to see the LOTEs programme expanded. Eighty-two per cent of teachers questioned then said they would support the introduction of Vietnamese as a subject in the school.

The LOTEs coordinator believed the Macedonian course has been improved over the years simply because they've begun to get over the shortage of materials, which affected that language more than the others. This required an enormous effort to develop materials appropriate to their needs and the

Australian context. Those brought back to Australia were 'too academic, which the kids can't cope with because the standards are generally lower'. They use primary readers, but even they can be too formal. The grammar books are too dry, she added; 'ours are more diagrammatic'.

The LOTEs coordinator thought grammar was very important, and she taught it, but others didn't, which suggested some differences in teaching style. The course handbooks, however, show that, for Years 9 and 10, for example, there is a balanced representation of grammatical exercises and communicative tasks, and written and oral work, throughout each language offered.

Evaluation: The ESL Programme

Both staff and students spoke of the benefits of the ESL programme and the importance of the programme within the school. The coordinator said that a major effect of the programme had been to heighten 'the school's awareness of the problems of ESL students'. The size of the programme, the extra funding it received from the school and the extent of the provision for senior students were all indicators of the school's recognition of the crucial role of ESL and English language proficiency in its students' success, and the extent of their continuing needs. The curriculum coordinator stressed that 'English language is an important component [in the school] and is a barrier to many students' success'. The 1986 report, *Introducing Vietnamese into Footscray High School*, concludes that the school attracts a large number of Vietnamese students, particularly in the final years, 'because ESL is still offered at these upper levels'. The coordinator also believed that 'it's helping to keep the numbers up — many are here for the ESL programme', which is especially important given the general fall in enrolments in the area.

The coordinator said, however, that the programme was handicapped from fully meeting its objectives 'because there are not enough staff' at the school which means they 'can't cater to all student needs'. However, she argued that, for those they did reach, smaller ESL classes made learning 'more enjoyable and accessible for students, because they get more attention'. She referred, in particular, to the ESL camp as a 'raging success', and, as such, as an indicator of the programme's effectiveness in terms of its social goals at the very least.

The language coordinator spoke well of the ESL programme, saying that it was 'very important in the school; they do so much here':

> ESL is great, but they need it far more because the problem is broader than the ESL programme can deal with. Fifty per cent of kids need remediation. Some teachers say ESL is a waste of time, but they are the ones who have the ESL kids in the back of the class and are not aware of them.

An ESL teacher, the 'dissenting voice' referred to by the ESL coordinator, believed that support ESL, or team-teaching, would be a more appropriate method for addressing students' needs in the mainstream areas. While he was alone in his severe criticism of parallel or withdrawal methodology, there were other ESL teachers who, according to the deputy, were 'somewhere in between' the debate between total withdrawal and total mainstreaming. The deputy, herself trained as an English teacher, also didn't like too heavy an emphasis on withdrawal, believing that, 'it is necessary for the early stages, but once the students reach a certain level of oral ability, they should be in normal classes'. She believed that, as a result of withdrawal, the 'migrant students' can suffer a degree of deprivation; 'to some extent we are letting them down. Some would acquire some skills more rapidly in with mainstream classes'. The coordinator, however, preferred to err on the side of caution:

> There are some occasions when you cannot expect ESL kids to cope outside the ESL programme. Yet there are cases where you put an ESL kid into the mainstream and they cope very well. There are no firm guidelines. It depends on how much reading they do, how much they know of the world, as to how they will survive in the mainstream.

The LOTEs coordinator, whose understanding of the needs of NESB students is informed by her own non-English speaking background and by the fact that she was also a student at Footscray High, also believed that the school needed something broader; structured remediation programmes, for example, or something that addressed the needs of all students because of the general shift away from explicit and structured language instruction in English:

> It's all *laissez faire* now. They've abandoned all styles of traditional grammar and spelling, but the new hasn't worked. Now they are going back to basics. You can't just go back to basics, you have to take what worked. Let's look at what went wrong.

She said that, at least 'after ESL, the students have a better grounding in language because it's explained to them', and gave as an example the understanding of things like the past perfect tense. She added, however, that the extent of the language problems in the school meant 'that they do need both withdrawal and language across the curriculum — a mix'. The coordinator commented that they 'place a high priority on the bricks and mortar of language' because this addressed the students' needs; 'the Vietnamese as a group would like to sit there and do grammar all day; anything that's structured. They absolutely adore structure'.

A Year 11 ESL student's comments suggested, however, that the ESL staff, out of necessity, provide some 'language across the curriculum' support, at least informally. He said that 'students could ask the teachers to help them with their language problem from other subject'. In the junior years, the integration of the humanities course into the ESL programme also means that ESL instruction is not just situational English, in which contexts are simulated rather than authentic. While the 'dissenting voice' ESL teacher described this as resulting in 'a watered down humanities course', it meant that the teachers used the language demands of a subject area as the basis of language learning. The ESL faculty have submitted a proposal for teaching the compulsory Australian Studies component of the new Victorian Certificate of Education to ESL students, and this would necessitate the same use of a language across the curriculum approach in one subject.

The debate within the ESL staff about withdrawal and mainstreaming ESL has had a positive effect. According to the deputy:

> There was enormous conflict, but it did raise the level of consciousness in the school about language issues. A lot more people are now aware of the Ministry guidelines in favour of mainstreaming with support, rather than withdrawal.

The coordinator admitted that it had been 'an eye-opening experience' and had increased the school's awareness of the issue. Almost all staff interviewed mentioned this debate in some way or other, indicating its presence as a crucial issue. The LOTEs coordinator, as an ex-pupil, pointed out, however, that after years of ESL and other programmes, there has been no improvement in pupil performance since she was here:

> More are doing the HSC but with not particularly good results. Some are getting into places like the Footscray Institute of Technology, but with inadequate qualifications and fewer academic skills, because of special provisions for NESB students.

On the other hand, the fact that ESL programmes, as a whole, have forced credentialling bodies and tertiary institutions to recognize a different type of English proficiency from NESB students, through such special provisions and through the Alternative English course (a Group 1 subject), can be seen as a gain for these students. This allows them to continue their study, whilst continuing to extend their English, rather than being penalized for having had limited time to achieve an 'acceptable' level of proficiency. The careers teacher referred to the problem some of their students have in having their achievements acknowledged because they do many low status Group 2 subjects:

> There is a need for affirmative action. One of our NESB kids was turned away from FIT [Footscray Institute of Technology] because his English score was too low, even though his other results were good. Philip [Institute], however, accepted him.

The 'dissenting voice' in the ESL staff claimed that the programme did not equip students adequately with the English language skills necessary for educational success and active social participation. He pointed out that three out of nine students passed the Alternative English course in 1987, and two out of fourteen in 1988. The coordinator, however, argued that all their Year 12 ESL students did get into employment or tertiary education last year. In English as a whole in the Victorian Certificate of Education in 1987, while only one student achieved a grade higher than a 'C' in the English (Group 1) exam, a high proportion of students — forty-four out of 103 students — actually did the course. Fifty students sat the English B exam, a Group 2 subject in which assessment is descriptive, for which all but six achieved a 'satisfactory' result.

The 'dissenting voice' ESL teacher noted a number of crucial problems in pedagogy. He suggested that the approach of much of the ESL provision assumed that teachers could simply copy the style of mother-tongue acquisition, ignoring features such as auditory memory. The result was that the Asian kids were locked into an Asian intonation. In his opinion there was no common teaching or curriculum styles, but he believed that some teachers imposed structure by working through exercises from a book, whether they were useful or not.

Of eighteen Year 11 ESL students surveyed, over 60 per cent were of Vietnamese background, but there were four born in Yugoslavia and two Australian-born students of Greek background. All but three had been in Australia for two years or less, but one student had been here for eight years. Most students responded very positively about the ESL programme, highlighting, as the 'best things':

> I like ESL because I can see the teacher each day and talked to her a bout you idea at school.

> The best things are help the students do not scare when they speak in different pronounciation.

> The best thing about ESL Programme are the teachers, because they gave as 10 periods a week that we can learn more and eseyar English.

Students also mentioned: the small classes; the teaching style and the type of activities they did; the fact that they could approach the teachers easily; and the degree of understanding that teachers had for students' cultural backgrounds, problems and needs. One ESL student said that the programme had brought greater diversity to the school because 'kids from other countries can come and learn. If the school didn't have ESL programme there wouldn't be any "wogs" '.

Another wrote of ESL, 'we work with essays, we reed books, we do gramare. On the end of the year we go to a ESL camp'. A student who had been in Australia for four years, however, showed that he had still some language difficulties. He wrote, regarding the best things about the ESL programme, that:

> it a bit easy than english, it gaves students who just come in Australia like me before learning english. the teachers they knew that we doesn't know muche english so they very nice to us at first.

Much of the debate within the staff over ESL stemmed from differing perceptions of goals. The coordinator had stressed pastoral care concerns as virtually equal to language skills, and her position was certainly perceived this way by other staff. The deputy, for example, had highlighted the pastoral care role, as articulated by the coordinator, as a 'point of focus' for immigrant students with difficulties. This emphasis on welfare was no doubt seen to be important for those the coordinator said were 'not academically inclined', and needed life skills and 'survival' English language skills. On the other hand, the dissenting ESL teacher said that teachers needed to work for communicative competence and help kids 'go on as far as possible in academic achievement'. The stated goals of the ESL programme, however, stress the objective of preparing students for the mainstream. The Year 11 ESL 'support class', for example, examines the novels as set down for the mainstream course, and covers several different types of essay structure. It also looks at exam technique and poetry as well as covering oral skills for ESL students, in an attempt to support the mainstream course rather than be separate from it. This necessitates cooperation with the mainstream teachers to ensure parallel development. Likewise, the ESL faculty has established some guidelines for acting in a support role in mainstream classes.

The ESL teacher who was critical of the current provision in ESL believed few ESL teachers were able to fulfil a real pastoral care role. This was partly the result of teachers sharing classes because of timetable clashes, and partly because ESL staff do not have their own rooms. The coordinator agreed that this lack of 'home rooms' reflected on the status of the programme in the school. The ESL teacher who was critical of the programme thought that the goals of ESL had not been thought out within the school's programme. His own view of education was summed up by the student from the School of Barbiana in *Letter to a Teacher*: 'Make us literate or they will always have power over us'.[3] He added that 'you need an ethical/political reason for work with disadvantaged groups, otherwise your own ego is involved'.

He also suggested that from his perspective there was not such a view underlying the ESL programme. 'There is no overall direction. Spontaneity is all. There is never any debate or organization.' Other members of the ESL faculty vehemently disputed the accuracy of these opinions. The school programme and policies, they insisted, included significant statements on pastoral care, personal development, literacy and numeracy. They maintained that these goals were integrated within the context of the ESL programme and they were outraged by what they felt was a misrepresentation of their work.

The dissenting voice stressed that he did not criticize his colleagues personally by his observations, but that what was happening there was in his opinion an example of what was happening in ESL generally. He blamed systemic factors:

> This state had the best programme for NESB students across the board in 1976. There has been a terrible decline in services, only allowed because the more recent waves of Middle-Eastern, Chinese and Indo-Chinese migrants have had little political clout. They wouldn't do it to the Greeks and Italians. Education now runs on the demands of the administration.

He believed that the Department of Education had not prepared current teachers adequately, and most had neither the experience nor the time to understand more about what they were doing, despite 'the best will in the world'. His own position was informed by a number of years spent working as an academic. When he returned to secondary ESL teaching after an absence of some years he suffered 'culture shock', because at Footscray he didn't recognize what was going on: 'it seemed to be an alternate and very second-rate humanities course rather than ESL as such'. He felt that ESL was underwriting smaller humanities classes, which he saw as 'a massive misuse of funds by the Rialto' (the plush building in the centre of Melbourne which houses the Ministry of Education, and symbolizes to a teacher like him the distance between those who make policy and those who teach).

A further problem he believed existed was the resistance to evaluation and assessment:

> We can't have an evaluation because it might be critical of the programme. Any criticism is seen as interfering with consensus. I was once actually told, 'If you can't say anything nice, don't say anything at all'. There is never any discussion. It is never assessed if a kid no longer needs ESL: they no longer need it when we no longer need their numbers. The programme is in no way needs based. They don't know what the needs of the kids are because these are never assessed. No statistics are kept, no-one keeps records.

He claimed that there was no formalized system within the faculty for assessing students, despite the scaled grades they used for reports. Occasionally, he added, students fight to get into mainstream classes, saying they don't want ESL any more, but this doesn't happen much because the ESL classes 'are easy, cosy and undemanding'. One Year 11 student commented that he would like to see an exam for Year 11 ESL so they can be prepared for Year 12. The coordinator, on the other hand, said that the majority of the faculty wanted ungraded and less competitive assessment. The ESL staff did, however, use a fairly detailed checklist for oral reporting to parents, which covered a range of

Cultures of Schooling

writing, reading, speaking and listening skills. The ESL staff also specified the goals for each subject or level in its faculty handbook.

The coordinator thought the best way to strengthen the programme was to have more staff, although she admitted that a shift to more of a support role in mainstream classes was imminent, and that such support was necessary in some areas. She also said that more students needed ESL help. Other teachers have expressed a preference for a wider programme that tackled language more broadly across the curriculum. The curriculum coordinator, however, explained that there were many teachers in the school, particularly in science and maths, who were unable to see themselves as teachers of the English language as well, despite the school having had curriculum days on the language across the curriculum approach; this made a broader across the curriculum approach a long-term goal.

The dissenting voice thought that ESL will decline in coming years, and that ESL teachers will begin to disappear, 'because nobody will fight for the interests of their clients'. LOTEs, he added, had become the new 'hobby-horse'. The Victorian Certificate of Education will necessitate a shift to more of a support role for ESL, particularly in, for example, teaching the compulsory Australian Studies course to NESB students. The ESL staff at the school, reflecting a degree of responsiveness to the system requirements, had decided to respond to the changing direction by submitting a proposal offering a transition ESL programme in the Australian Studies course, which would run parallel with the first of the four units of study with the aim of preparing ESL students for the following units of study.

Across the five years from Year 7 to Year 11, the syllabus guidelines prepared by the ESL staff reflect an intention to move students into the mainstream. In the first years there is a primary concern with communicative skills, but in the middle years there is an increasing emphasis on written skills, with the aim to have students 'very close to the mainstream English' programme, with similar texts, set novels and essay writing. By the end of Year 11, students should be ready for the mainstream curriculum (or the world of work), although the 'mainstream' is seen to be the Alternative English course, not the Group 1 English course:

> Students to become competent with written and oral English and its comprehension to prepare them for Year 12 Alternative English. For those students not intending to do Year 12, they will achieve a standard of English suitable for the workforce or study elsewhere.

Of the Year 11 ESL students surveyed, many said that their parents or guardians were happy with the ESL provision. One boy commented that 'I think that my guardians get out of the ESL programme is they feel like because I can learn more English when I stay in ESL class and have more chance to talk English to other students'.

The deputy commented that parents also approved of the ESL provision at the school and will 'send their kids here in droves because they know we've got a big ESL programme'. Parent involvement in the ESL programme, however, is low. The ESL faculty saw eight parents at the last parent/teacher night, where other faculties saw up to forty. The coordinator said that they tend to leave the school well enough alone. One ESB parent interviewed commented, not on the ESL programme, but on English language teaching at the school generally. She said that English teaching 'left a lot to be desired', and that she was not happy with her own children's results in English. She was neither well-educated nor a good speller, she said, but believed the teachers didn't concentrate on spelling and punctuation enough; 'there's an idea that near enough is good enough'. One teacher, she added, simply handed out sheets and got them to read newspapers. However, she wished to lay the blame not with the teachers so much as the system itself — 'the directives come from higher up . . . ; it's what the Education Department is turning out across the board'. While she was critical of the compulsory LOTEs programme in Years 7 and 8, she added that they learnt more about grammar from doing Italian than from English. These remarks are consistent with the view that a broader language approach is necessary.

The dissenting voice suggested that the programme could be improved, the first requirement being professional debate. Secondly, flexibility was also needed, such as in the past when ESL teachers were supernumerary and had greater autonomy, able to move around the school because, being 'extra' to the staff, they were not tied down by a rigid timetable. But most importantly, there needed to be more assessment of student needs.

Evaluation: Teaching Languages Other Than English

The LOTEs programme was also valued in the school curriculum, having a status reflected in the compulsory study of one language in the junior years. The overwhelming support for LOTEs amongst staff was reported in the feasibility study for introducing Vietnamese. The same study showed that 70 per cent of NESB students desired to know their mother tongue better, reflecting, as did many of the comments of students regarding the value of their parents' heritage, the fact that the study of 'community' languages had played an important part in giving these languages a social value. The deputy commented that 'it allows them to value something about themselves', as well as providing them with a 'pragmatic, transferable skill'. The former community liaison officer likewise stressed that language maintenance facilitated students' learning and enhanced their 'sense of identity and belonging'. The school's respect of others' cultures, through incorporation of LOTEs in the curriculum, fostered a sense of 'security for one's self within one's own culture', which was necessary for interrelating in society.

NESB parents supported a LOTEs programme, even if largely as an 'identity thing', as the LOTEs coordinator and a parent interviewee suggested. The curriculum coordinator also said that, in the school council:

> the maintenance of cultures is very important. If we wanted to drop Macedonian, for example, there would be an uproar. That happened at my last school.

The low status given Macedonian in the Year 12 curriculum across the state (it is a Group 2 subject) has been a cause for concern, particularly because it reflected a political, not an educational, decision. Greek, for example, is a Group 1 subject. But this would be resolved under the new Victorian Certificate of Education as there will not be this division of subjects which affect languages. In the 1987 Victorian Certificate of Education results, of the twenty-three Modern Greek students, eleven students 'failed', while seven received a very low 'pass' mark; only one student achieved an 'above pass' mark. In Macedonian, six of the nine students received a 'pass' mark, and there was one 'above pass' mark.

Many of the comments by the LOTEs coordinator reflected similar pedagogical issues to those faced in the ESL programme. She had specifically viewed the LOTEs programme as serving the needs of students who were not competent in either their first language or English. She saw a need to improve the first language as a way of facilitating the cognitive development and English language proficiency of NESB students. She was trying to teach grammar in her classes, but found that because the students got none of this in their English classes, it was very difficult. A language needs to be taught 'as a language', she said, and teaching the rules of a language is the most efficient way to do this. She believed there was still a place even for rote learning, although others preferred more 'modern' methods with a 'life-skills', rather than academic, emphasis:

> If they have the academic then they have the organizational skills to get on in life. Some think that this should be only for the top 12 per cent of the population, but it should be for all.

She believed that the new Victorian Certificate of Education will, in the long run, force higher standards on teachers because it requires skills of independent research and critical analysis: the skills that academic success requires, that these kids are not currently taught. 'Democratic ideas,' which say that schools should just respect social and cultural differences rather than impose academic criteria on students, maintain NESB kids in their disadvantage, she said. She referred to a special teaching course for teaching in the western suburbs as 'Mickey Mouse' and being more about 'managing them' than teaching the students. She asked, 'who gets the benefits? How do private schools teach? They might innovate but they teach the three R's for the ruling class.' This was a problem, however, for all students at Footscray, she argued, because the 'working-class Anglo kids' were just as ill-equipped; 'If I can do it as a wog, but Australians can't do it, then it's not just a cultural thing. But you have to push them too'.

In relation to LOTEs, she said that students compared their language classes unfavourably with Saturday school all the time, saying they were less strict at the school. One boy of Vietnamese background interviewed, however, said that he would prefer to study Vietnamese at school than on Saturdays. This student, who was learning Greek as a compulsory LOTE, stressed the various benefits of learning a language: 'you learn about other cultures, and how to get along with others, and for travel'. Another explained that 'here you do cultural background as well as the language'. The Vietnamese-speaking boy also said that he would readily study Vietnamese at the school because he would pass easily. He added that most Vietnamese students wanted Vietnamese introduced to the school.

A girl of Macedonian heritage said:

> I didn't want to do it, but my sister pushed me into it because she had really liked it and knew Macedonian well. I'm glad I did it; I love it. I know how to read and write in it now. And I understand better with my family.

She chose to drop Macedonian in her senior years, but primarily because she wanted to do maths and because Macedonian was a Group 2 subject, so 'it's not worth much'. She added that she would probably study it if it was a Group 1 subject. Both she and the boy above expressed very pragmatic views about learning a language. Other students interviewed also spoke positively about doing a language, but none had continued right through. One boy of Macedonian background said he was 'a dead loss' when he did Macedonian and found it irrelevant in Year 8.

An ESL teacher (himself of NESB) remarked, like the LOTEs coordinator, that, primarily, a language had to be pedagogically valuable. Language maintenance on its own was not enough, because 'it doesn't last forever. There is no need to maintain the language just to talk to Granny; she doesn't talk the standard language anyway'. The coordinator pointed out that language maintenance was supported by parents and students often for reasons of identity, and was often taught by some teachers for the same reason. It was also supported by the school in order to maintain numbers of students. She stressed, however, the problems of an emphasis on difference and identity in LOTEs teaching, partly because it can bring into the classroom all the problems of intergenerational and cultural conflict — racism and sexism, for example, which was largely a reaction to the underlying racism in Australia, and the difficulties in 'fitting in'. The deputy had also commented that in her view cultural maintenance was contributing to inter-ethnic tensions and the politicizing of cultural identity.

The coordinator said that, realistically, they couldn't expect everyone to do a language if they didn't want to. Nor did they have the staff to offer that. Because of the demand for language teachers with the boom in 'community languages', she believed that there were real problems in staffing it appropriately. They had, in the past, used teachers with little or no training in language teaching, who may have come from the language background.

As well as staffing, it was hard to get funding for appropriate materials. When she tried to get a 'talking book' programme for the school, for $8,000, she was refused, even though she had researched it and found it very good. At the same time, the Ministry was spending $4 million on a stress management programme, which she described as 'useful' for the Ministry because of all the changes associated with the Victorian Certificate of Education and funding cutbacks. The shortage and inappropriateness of materials meant that the staff have had to prepare a lot of their own resources, relevant to the students' abilities and to the Australian context.

The curriculum coordinator mentioned, further, that 'there is a problem in having languages for beginners and native or home speakers. For the teacher, this can mean just learning how to cope. I'd like to see LOTEs to Year 10, but there are these constraints'. The deputy also commented that 'there is a problem of how to timetable different language levels', rather than simply putting them all into one class. There were not the resources to cater for a variety of language levels, and in the classroom this created many difficulties for the teacher.

The decision not to introduce Vietnamese was partly for these reasons of staffing and resourcing, although different reasons were given by different sources. While the original feasibility study found support for the idea amongst staff and Vietnamese-speaking parents and students, a number of staff said that the Vietnamese students themselves rejected the idea, preferring to study more ESL or mainstream subjects like science or maths. The deputy said that, 'given the curriculum smorgasbord here, a lot of the Vietnamese students have said that they would prefer to do another subject here and do Vietnamese at Saturday school'. A Vietnamese-speaking boy said he would do Vietnamese if it was offered, adding that he thought the school would introduce it as a trial run in Year 11. The curriculum coordinator said that:

> they will get Vietnamese, but it will take time. There are restrictions of funding: the number of language groups and class size. How do you introduce Vietnamese if it means kicking someone out, and what if the Vietnamese teacher can't teach anything else?

While many NESB parents support language maintenance for cultural reasons, many of those whose children are not serviced by the programme are not as supportive. An ESB parent interviewed thought that her children doing Italian 'was a waste of time' because they learnt so little. 'It would be OK', she said, 'if the children continued with it, but they only do it now because it's compulsory'. Students who weren't native speakers, she added, were therefore disadvantaged. Her child chose Italian rather than Greek 'although she didn't want to do a language at all'. This parent thought that, while she was happy for Macedonians to learn Macedonian, having three or four languages created problems for timetabling. She suggested that it would be better if language maintenance was done elsewhere, as in a Saturday school, so that the high school could be more geared towards English and Australian studies.

A parent of Macedonian background commented that he was glad the choice was there, but personally didn't think that learning Macedonian helped his children:

> they speak it OK, so it would be better for them to pick up more courses. If they want Macedonian they can do it at night, after school in an evening college. I'm not going to push it, like some parents do.

He added that, while some parents of Macedonian background would agree with him, a lot would disagree and wanted Macedonian at the school.

Evaluation: The School

The principal felt that, in general, the school met its objectives:

> I have an overall concern with keeping the school together and happy, and I think we do that. The idea is covert — the staff believe in working in a threat-free environment. I believe we meet our objectives. I like to think the kids, and the school, are more settled . . . ; there is a sense of community here. I think we've got the place to function fairly well . . . ; Schools are really only about two things — learning and teaching — the staff here try to achieve this. I say to parents, 'You may not agree with the methods, but you have to agree they do their best'.

Both parents and students spoke very positively of the school's attempts to meet their needs. Students who were highly involved in the school were particularly strong in their views. They pointed to the level of student participation as a key feature and the Students' Representative Council and school council were important in creating a sense of ownership of the school. One commented that, 'we run our school'. Participation, said one, 'can be intimidating, but after a while you feel part of it', especially because, once on a committee, 'the teachers treat you as human'. They also referred to the range of subjects as a benefit, although one boy said he didn't like 'schools not working together', while another agreed that each school having different subjects was a problem, because there was no comparability. One suggested that the new Victorian Certificate of Education may cause further difficulties 'if teachers are going off in a different directions'.

Several of the students interviewed believed that 'if you are willing you'll get [good results]'. One spoke positively about the way the teachers 'pushed' students and also gave extra help; 'this school's pretty good. It provides lunchtime classes, for example'. They, like some of the ESL students surveyed, had high aspirations. Another said that 'the teachers are willing to help if you've got troubles'. A parent interviewed also believed that the school had a 'top staff here, not like any other school', which included the ethnic aides 'who are doing a tremendous job'.

But the principal asked, when it came to evaluating, just how effective the school was, 'what measures do we have?' Student assessment, however, 'is a running sore in the school community', according to the curriculum coordinator. The school policy is that graded assessment should be replaced by descriptive assessment, but parents, surveyed several years ago, made it clear that they wanted grades, and they continue to see this as important. But, the principal added, they will be disadvantaged because the new Victorian Certificate of Education is moving away from final exams determining access to university. He explained that parents take 'the most observable', such as uniforms, and use that as a measure, reading off discipline, learning modes and so on. They see experiments like goal-based assessment as moving away from the type of schooling they know and understand.

The curriculum coordinator said, regarding the meeting of objectives, that 'in educational terms, it is difficult to ascertain — it's a most nebulous subject. While there are catchcries of accountability as the new bandwagon', he believed, this was biased towards the system's needs, not educational goals.

The principal admitted frankly that the school's Victorian Certificate of Education results — which, he said, were the only external measure of the impact to their programme — were not great. This judgment is borne out by an examination of the results. In 1987, of the 500 grades awarded across 106 students at Footscray, just over half were in Group 1 courses, suggesting that slightly more students were choosing these courses than the 45 per cent of 'Group 1 students' in 1984. This could also reflect an expansion in the courses available in Group 1. However, of those 500, over a third of grades were 'unsatisfactory' or below 50 per cent. A quarter of grades were in the 'D' range. Nine 'A's were recorded, and 22 per cent of grades were awarded in the high status, 'core' subjects of mathematics A, chemistry, biology, physics and economics. This reflects the diversified curriculum of the Victorian Certificate of Education generally, and that of the school specifically, which included physical recreation and health, catering, media studies, psychology, two levels of accounting, and advanced typing.

The careers adviser believed that the careers programme had met its objectives, and cited the fact that only two students from last year were unemployed. However, she added that the school's students have for a long time had a pattern of high participation rates in part-time work. She also commented that some of their students had difficulty in getting into tertiary study, especially in institutions such as Footscray Institute of Technology, many of whose courses preferred students from Group 1 rather than Group 2 courses, 'and they're the courses our kids succeed in'. She and other staff saw one of their goals as convincing tertiary institutions of the value of their courses for NESB students.

Apart from the two unemployed, 46 per cent of the ninety-one 1988 students went on to further study at a college of advanced education or an institute and 6 per cent went on to university, while 15 per cent are enrolled at a technical and further education or specialist college. Eighteen per cent are in full-time employment or a traineeship. This compares well with the hundred 1984 Higher School Certificate students; only 20 per cent went to a college of advanced education then, although the university proportion is much the same at 7 per cent; 28 per cent went into full-time employment while 20 per cent were unemployed; 17 per cent returned to study in technical and further education or elsewhere.

A Year 11 student interviewed stated that they had never had an exam before the senior levels, and thought that it would be better if they were assessed more as in other schools. Another said they had to start having 'mini-exams' in Year 11 to begin preparing for their final exams. All those interviewed, however, thought that school was more about 'life' and 'socializing', and mixing with other cultures than getting a job or further study. One saw this as a particular benefit of state over private schools, with the former having more 'freedom'. They didn't think that private schools got better Victorian Certificate of Education results, but did get preferential treatment when going for jobs; 'it's not just private versus public. It's also east versus west. They're more likely to get jobs; it's just an attitude'.

The ESL students surveyed saw school as equipping students for entry into life 'for children to learn something to save them from the street'. One student mentioned 'the way of teaching' as special about his school; 'like Year 9 and 10 do some subjects together'. Another said the teachers were 'nice and honest'. Several, however, offered critical comments on the education provided. One said, 'I don't like way of schooling, students spend lot of time in school and they learn nothing'. He added that his parents were not happy because 'I don't know how to learn by this way of schooling'. Another wrote 'My parents think that this school is not good because I had a better school overseas'. A third commented similarly, 'they are not very happy because based on the school's number of student passing Year 12, which is very few, they think that the school is not very good'.

One of the parents interviewed claimed that a major concern of those of Macedonian background was the apparent lack of strict discipline, and said that this came up as an issue all the time in school council and in the parent association meetings. His only other major concern was that the school had made the parent groups all meet on the same night for its convenience, but that this had resulted in a decline in the number of parents attending. He wanted it to return to nights of each association's own choice.

The student representatives interviewed, in contrast to some other

Cultures of Schooling

interviewees, thought there were no problems of antagonism over cultural differences, and were positive about the experience of cultural diversity. One said that:

> We learn outside the classroom as well, because of the different cultures. . . . The school has a positive atmosphere. . . . Being an ethnic school, not private; private schools are protected from the real world and from socializing. Here there's more freedom.

Another agreed; 'just looking around the yard, it's multicultural'. Several of those surveyed, however, referred to prejudice amongst both students and staff as things they didn't like about the school: 'one thing I don't like is fighting in the school. There are kids fighting about there countrys a there langueges'(*sic*). The Year 11 ESL students were generally guarded over the question of whether the school understood their cultural backgrounds. One student said 'the teachers understand but some students don't they are picking on us and they call us "wogs" '. Another suggested that the school doesn't understand very well, but only because 'they only know what the students told them'.

One teacher explicitly stated that, in fact, supposedly 'democratic ideas' contributed to the ongoing lack of social and educational access of working-class and NESB kids (a Year 11 ESL student, in fact, listed the availability of Group 2 subjects as special things the school has for NESB students). Another teacher suggested that the only way to improve students' self-esteem was not by programmes that tried to make students feel good, but by those which made them literate and enhanced their educational chances. 'Toleration of difference', whether it be cultural or otherwise, can in fact be a toleration of social inequalities.

Caught between all these tensions, there is a high degree of burn-out — at least two staff interviewed were about to leave, including the LOTEs coordinator who had applied for a job as a barmaid on the day of the interview (she has since resigned). There was also a fragmentedness to what teachers did. As one teacher commented:

> The people here are well-meaning, but disorganized, and this shows through to the kids. We blame the kids but it is us . . . sometimes it is the school, sometimes the bureaucratic nature of education. The government doesn't give a shit. It looks good having multicultural programmes but they are not supported. The results come from hard-working staff instead.

But she, as did other staff, testified to the commitment of the staff; 'it will get better because people are trying to hang onto language and ESL. If it fails it will be because of "above". The staff are trying to get the message across, trying to solve their problems, and they are committed'. But they are dealing with these problems under conditions for which they were not trained:

> The Dip. Ed. taught me nothing and most here will tell you that it was useless for here . . . ; you're stretched beyond your limits. . . . Only anthropology, which was an extra to pick up points, helped me see that you have to judge from within a person's culture.

The deputy also related the problems of dealing with arrivals of Vietnamese students in the late 1970s with 'no preparation . . . we had no idea what to expect. No attempt was made even to coach teachers on how to pronounce their names'. The LOTEs coordinator added that the staff even had difficulty in coming to terms with the diversity amongst itself; there was a broad division within the staff based partly on cultural lines — the 'Anglos' and 'ethnics' — and partly on political and educational lines, with disagreements over pedagogy: 'the non-Anglo-Saxons are more traditional'. This had resulted in two virtually separate main staffrooms.

All nine teachers interviewed, however, said that they agreed with a philosophy of cultural and linguistic maintenance, although they differed in what this meant for schools and their role. The principal commented that the question of cultural integration was complex, but added:

> If the definition of multiculturalism is trying to enable each culture to give of its best, then the time is right in this time of falling enrolments, and so on, for ethnic schools, single sex schools, and separate language schools. Saturday schools and dance schools work well. If girls do better on their own, accept it and work on it. NESB parents are not keen on boys and girls together; let's provide it in state schools.

He gave the example of local private girls' school which was maintaining its numbers. On the other hand, he said that language maintenance was difficult and he wasn't sure if it was the school's role as things now stood.

The deputy admitted she used to think that cultural maintenance should be assisted by schools, but she has seen, at this school, the way it 'underpins a lot of the tensions in the school', particularly between the Greek and Macedonian students. It was also reported that one of the ethnic teachers' aides had been 'very political' and fostered a sense of homeland nationalism which it was believed exacerbated unrest. Several teachers referred to the problems associated with cultural maintenance; the language coordinator suggested that there were limits in terms of sexism and racism. The student welfare officer also said there were difficulties when values were in contradiction, and gave an example of a Turkish girl who was to be 'circumcized' — the school spoke to the parents, but she 'disappeared' anyway. The 'dissenting voice' ESL teacher said he rejected both 'melting pot' and 'mosaic', and preferred the notion of 'embeddedness', where one can select 'bits' from different cultures.

All the teachers maintained, in fact, that their personal lives had been profoundly affected by having to work and live amidst such cultural and linguistic diversity. The ESL coordinator admitted it had challenged her, and:

> It has also led me to question the values of other people around me, such as the ones who've never been over the Westgate Bridge. It's taught me to stand up for the school: I'm proud of it. I've learnt to look at other people's values and found that I need to explain to them what it's really like.

The 'dissenting voice' ESL teacher commented on the value of such 'challenges': 'Australianness is now only coming into being; it is not already there. Aboriginality must be central to the Australian identity, and it is only now coming to be so'. He felt that the migrant experience was also of crucial importance to this process. He said that the staff did feel burdened by the level of commitment needed to respond to diversity: 'a lot of them are confused. With the best will in the world, a lot of them don't understand most of the time. To be fair, it is very difficult and takes time'. He believed, however, that everyone was trying their best to address the issue.

The degree of professionalism and commitment, matched by candid insights and an awareness and sensitivity to these issues, is frustrated by lack of time and available resources. The curriculum coordinator concluded, of all attempts to bridge the gap between students' needs and what schools can physically accomplish: 'It takes time. You need time to run with it, and it will be inefficient until it works'.

Notes

1 RADO, M. and OLDFIELD, J., *Introducing Vietnamese into Footscray High School*, MACMME, Melbourne, 1985.
2 PARSONS, H. and PUTMAN, A., *Culture Cocktail*, Footscray High School and Participation and Equity Program School Resource, 1985.
3 SCHOOL OF BARBIANA, *Letter to a Teacher*, ROSSI, N. and COLE, T. (trans.), Penguin, Harmondsworth, 1970.

Chapter 9

Conclusion: Pedagogies for Cultural Difference and Social Access

This concluding chapter summarizes the empirical data, beginning with **The Six Schools**, an overview of the demographic context of the case-study schools. The chapter then takes each of the five areas of investigation specified in the case-study protocol: **Cultural and Linguistic Incorporation, Community Participation, Pedagogy, Assessment** and **Use of New Technologies in Basic Learning**, and draws conclusions based on evidence from all of the schools.

The chapter then moves into a more analytical mode, suggesting three **Models for Negotiating Cultural and Linguistic Diversity in Education**: the old assimilationist project of traditional curriculum, the cultural pluralist model of progressivist curriculum that rose to dominance in Australia in the 1970s and 1980s, and a new self-corrective phase found in evidence in this research which strives to combine a multiculturalism of social equity with a new pedagogy of access, sensitive to cultural and linguistic differences.

Finally, the issue of **Institutionalization of Innovation** is considered — the replicability of the innovations in other contexts and the relative importance of school-based initiative and centralized support.

The Six Schools

The linguistic and cultural diversity of their student populations had transformed quite fundamentally all six schools in this series of case studies. Their common features, moreover, make them typical of one sort of Australian school, but not all. In all six, the vast majority of students (75 to over 90 per cent) are of non-English speaking background (NESB). Given the size of Australia's post-war immigration programme, these numbers are by no means unusual. But, although there would not be a single school in Australia immune from the effects of mass immigration, these schools are representative of conditions in which it would be impossible to do nothing.

The case-study schools, however, do not just share as a common feature absolute numbers of NESB students, but the range and variety of their language backgrounds. In none of the schools was any one language group overwhelmingly preponderant. Usually three or four groups shared roughly equal numbers, with a total of about twenty or thirty language groups represented in each school.

The populations served by the schools were also extraordinarily transient. In Footscray, for example, 25 per cent of the local population has been resident in the local government area for less than one year. Waves of immigration have meant in all six schools that language groups have more or less come and gone, sometimes in the space of just a few years. These have mostly been the 'first stop' suburbs, places where you rent a house before buying one further out in the great suburban sprawls of Sydney or Melbourne.

It is perhaps a little too simplistic to say that all six schools serve lower socioeconomic status or working-class communities, although there is a good deal of truth in this generalization. Many parents work in unskilled wage work, often part-time, or live on some form of social security payment or other. Others have small businesses — shops or clothing manufacturing, for example. This often means working excessively long hours in unpleasant conditions — a far cry from the conventional image of the entrepreneur. The uneven material results of overtime wage work or toiling in a small business are to be found in every school; students' socioeconomic status is in fact quite variable. A degree of class mobility is also at the bottom of the considerable population movement, either to established middle-class suburbs or to the outer-suburban 'mortgage belt'.

All these demographic features profoundly influence the logistics of servicing the schools' constituent communities. So, for example, the once thriving Greek and Turkish Language Other Than English (LOTE) programmes at Collingwood Education Centre will probably have to end in the next few years because of the rapidly changing ethnic composition of the school's local community. The difficulty of schools responding to the vagaries of demographic change, let alone planning even short-term provision, was also illustrated at this school. In just two days during the fieldwork for this research, twelve new arrivals from South-East Asia turned up, on the doorstep so to speak. There was simply no space for them in the local language centre, and until such time as places came available — several months away perhaps — they could only be accommodated in the general classes.

Socioeconomic disadvantage, moreover, overlays cultural and linguistic diversity in such a way that it is hard to isolate different variables in the determination of educational outcomes. In the words of one teacher, 'if I can do it as a wog, but Australians can't do it, then it's not just a cultural thing'. The enormous, inherent challenge of servicing schools in these sorts of areas means that the value of innovation specifically designed to meet the needs of cultural and linguistic diversity is in itself very hard to measure.

In pedagogy, too, all six case-study schools have trodden a similar path in which innovation was broadly along progressivist lines. The challenge of making the school work had meant, over a ten or twenty year period, a revolutionary change in teaching practices in which students' *cultural and linguistic diversity has been incorporated* into the curriculum rather than excluded as academically and socially inappropriate; in which strong attempts have been made to involve the *community* in the running of the school and their children's education; in which *classroom pedagogy* is experiential, involving students in the active making of their own knowledge and relating learning to their linguistic and cultural background and in such a way that the curriculum is demonstrably relevant to their own experience of life; in which *assessment* doesn't condemn NESB students of the basis of culture- or language-biased standardized tests but positively assesses individual development in relation to a task; and in which, *institutionally*, the project of the school and its innovations are shaped through processes of collaborative decision making. In going down these paths, these schools are by no means unique, reflecting rather, a major paradigm shift in all Australian education over the past two decades — a paradigm shift which has implicated every aspect of education, from its epistemological assumptions in the *minutiae* of classroom experience through to systems management structures. In schools like the ones surveyed here, however, the change has been more dramatic than anywhere else. Putting a positive construction on this, these schools have responded most flexibly because they really had to do something. They could not rest on their laurels in the way that 'establishment' schools might. Or, to put it in more negative terms, there was little resistance here to massive change. Said one curriculum administrator, 'where people [parents] are powerless, changes seem to come more easily than where people are more influential'.

Just as important is what these six schools are not. They are definitely not 'establishment' schools, and perhaps, there, other crucial dilemmas face multicultural education — dilemmas with very different dynamics to those found in the case-study schools. To speak anecdotally, in another (as yet unpublished) piece of research by the principal investigators contrasting four totally different schools, one was of similar demographic, institutional and pedagogical complexion to the six case-study schools in this project, and another an expensive, private 'establishment' boys' school. In the latter, a modicum of progressivist pedagogy had tempered an otherwise traditional curriculum in such a way that students would acquire those linguistic-cognitive competencies needed for conventional academic success and then to 'rule the world'. An all-pervasive sense of cultural homogeneity, however, not only erased the significant but unrecognized cultural and linguistic diversity in the school itself, but produced a racism which can only prove unproductive in the outside world in the long run. These boys will be living and working in a world in which, despite their education, cultural and linguistic variety is more likely than commonality to characterize their workforce. In the other school, broadly similar to the six surveyed in this project, attitudinal racism was much less of an explicit problem. Cultural and linguistic diversity was such an unavoidable reality that racism or cultural isolationism was a barely thinkable nonsense. Yet, viewing the education system in structural terms, the linguistic-cognitive outcomes — cultural goodwill and radically progressivist curriculum notwithstanding — were abysmal. There are, in other words, other very important lessons to be learnt about the necessity of multicultural education outside the type of school which is the focus of this case study.[1]

These schools are also not ones that have just recently taken on the challenge of cultural and linguistic diversity. They have all been doing it for a long time. Indeed, they were chosen for this project precisely because they are among the most soundly established and oldest living examples of multicultural education in the Australian context. They are mostly old, inner city schools in areas that were once the poorest, but which are quite steadily becoming gentrified as inner city real estate prices skyrocket. A good number of immigrants in these areas are now doing quite well for themselves. Now, some of the poorest areas are on the outer fringes of Australia's big cities. Whilst most of the schools in these case studies are, in terms of facilities at the very least, enjoying the luxury of declining numbers (even if declining enrolments also produces serious resource gaps and loss of curriculum range and depth), many schools 'out west' in Sydney and Melbourne are bursting at the seams and only just starting to come to grips with the cultural and linguistic diversity of their constituent populations. So, the Turkish language programme at Collingwood Education Centre and Brunswick East High are fine and have been going for a long time. But the Turkish class sizes in these schools are getting smaller all the time and Melbourne's Turkish-speaking community is moving to outer suburban areas where the schools do not as yet teach Turkish.

This project, also, is not about primary school. It is possible to argue that a good deal of the educational good or damage is already done by the time students reach the secondary school. Special programmes catering for linguistic and cultural diversity at the primary level are crucial. At Collingwood Education Centre, the infants/primary part of the school mounted a variety of bilingual programmes that it was not possible to examine in this secondary oriented project. St Mel's Primary school at Campsie, a feeder school to MacKillop Girls', mounts bilingual teaching programmes in the infants years, but aimed at linguistic-cognitive development, rather than cultural self-esteem or language maintenance. From the mid primary school, the focus of LOTEs teaching is on literacy and learning the language in a way specifically compatible to academic success in it as a subject in the secondary school. It is surely not just the endeavours of MacKillop that produced creditable results in that school, but a degree of coordination, intended or fortuitous, with its feeder primary schools. Unfortunately, this project was neither able to examine case-study primary schools nor the critical issue of the match or mismatch of primary and secondary programmes.

Nor was the project an exercise in looking for exemplary innovation. The innovations were those officially deemed to be innovative by the education systems involved in the project. As the wheels of bureaucracy turn slowly, this meant that by the time the researchers got to some of the schools, the innovation that had been the intended object of study had all but vanished. But this itself produced results which have their own intrinsic interest. As often as the data presented the dynamics of successful innovation, they also presented evidence of why innovation is often problematic or vulnerable. Added to this, in all the six case studies, even the ones deemed to be a success and still in operation, there were little or no hard data, especially pre/post innovation control data, to demonstrate the unequivocal success of that particular innovation. Their claim to be exemplary is thus no better than tendentious.

On the other hand, had the researchers gone looking until they found six innovatory schools, all with hard, longitudinal data to demonstrate tangible success, the picture may well have been different. It certainly would have been hard to find schools with a sufficient level of documentation, but they are around. From 1981, for example, De La Salle College, a Sydney Catholic boys' secondary school with a very high proportion of NESB students, instituted a series of major reforms. A structured English literacy programme; the Social Literacy programme, aimed at conceptual development and cultural self-understanding in social science; LOTEs; and an extensive pastoral care programme, were all introduced. By 1988 the serious intercultural conflicts that had plagued the school at the beginning of the decade had gone and Higher School Certificate results for students who had done all their schooling under then new 1980s regime, had improved out of sight. This can be clearly documented.

Nevertheless, whatever different things could have been done in a different sort of project, there are positive and useful results that have arisen from this one. It would be impossible for there not to be some very instructive lessons to be learnt from these schools, just as much as it would have been impossible for them to do nothing about the cultural and linguistic diversity of their students. In all schools, in fact, teachers said that they met the challenge of cultural and linguistic diversity with the support of the hard-won knowledge of practical experience, not book knowledge or adequate tertiary training. It was their experience of being an immigrant or of non-English speaking background, or of having to come to grips with the ineluctable reality of this sort of school, that taught them more than anything else. For this reason alone, their voices are a critically constructive part of this book. 'I don't think of these programmes as innovations', said one principal. 'They simply answer a need.'

Cultural and Linguistic Incorporation

Australian schools, even during the era of assimilation, have always attempted to incorporate students whose languages and cultures are in a minority in the Australian context. This serves to highlight the fact that 'incorporation' can mean quite different things. On the one hand, incorporation can occur in the sense of actively respecting and servicing the difference of minority students (the cultural pluralist model). On the other hand, incorporation can mean bringing minority students into the mainstream by provding them with paths to academic success (the 'ethnic disadvantage' model of specialist teaching). This may well incorporate them successfully, yet also assimilate them culturally (intentionally or unintentionally), by subsuming their 'minority' culture to the demands of the dominant culture. With the rise of progressivism in Australian education in the 1970s and 1980s, there was a very strong trend to the cultural pluralist model of multiculturalism. More recently, there has been a trend to view multiculturalism as a project which centrally involves equitable access, but without the old assimilationist agenda. In education, multiculturalism thus means removing barriers to access to mainstream society/culture in a context which is nevertheless open to cultural diversity and which actively faces the demands of non-discriminatory intercultural communication in the school and the community.

Of the six case-study schools, this latter sense of incorporation was most clearly expressed at Cabramatta High School. 'Education is still about individual pupils achieving a place in the world for themselves', said the principal, 'satisfying to the self and supportive of the community'. In the words of the deputy, 'if they're going to assimilate, students need to know how to operate in Australian society.... They need to know how the Australian community operates; multiculturalism is about assimilating'. This philosophy was very much in evidence in action in the school's programmes, particularly in the Intensive Language Unit, the Language in Learning Programme, an Australian history across the curriculum perspective and the teaching of five LOTEs as full-scale academic languages. A social science teacher at Collingwood said that, just as much as respecting all the differences, it was important to ask 'What makes us Aussies? This is important for NESB students — not for a nationalist purpose, but to provide access to information'.

Still, it would be safe to say that, across all six schools, this philosophy of multicultural education was less in evidence than the cultural pluralist approach of progressivism. This newer approach to multiculturalism was seen by the school personnel to be self-corrective of inadequacies in the cultural pluralist model. A later section of this chapter will deal with this issue in relation to pedagogy in the sense of classroom strategies and their epistemological presuppositions. At this point, the issues are introduced from the point of view of school organization and the overall strategy of granting esteem to difference. The main elements of progressivist cultural pluralism at this level are curriculum diversification and highlighting cultural difference as a mark of respect.

In the past few decades curriculum diversification has become a key measure to serve students whose needs and interests are inevitably various. This trend has been most marked in the secondary school, particularly in the post-compulsory years of schooling where rapidly increasing school retention rates have produced a more diverse student body. Traditional curriculum, with its middle-class, academic and 'Anglo' cultural biases, so the progressivists argue, was simply an exercise in exclusion, of marking cultural and socioeconomic difference as failure, and rationalizing this as individual 'ability'. Diversified curriculum, on the other hand, presents students with a wider range of subject choice, such that every student can work through a programme of study relevant to their individual needs and interests, and appropriate to their social destination. There is simply no point, so the argument continues, in a curriculum which can only hand down a negative verdict upon a large number of students.

Language teaching, as powerfully as any other area of the curriculum, epitomizes the change wrought upon Australian education by curriculum diversification. Whereas twenty years ago, mainstream schools almost only taught French or German or Latin as an academic 'foreign' language, now, as a direct by-product of immigration and multicultural education policies, over twenty major languages are taught in Australian schools. All six case-study schools now teach at least three LOTEs as full subjects, many for all six years of secondary schooling, often with 'relevant' community-based rationales such as linguistic and cultural maintenance.

In the six schools there has also been a proliferation of 'alternative' courses for the 'less academically inclined', sometimes accompanied by restructuring of the curriculum around short 'semesterized' courses and 'vertical' timetabling. 'Food for Living', 'Life Skills' and 'Driver Education' are a few of the dozens of alternative courses offered in the case-study schools. The Interpreting, Translating and Multicultural Studies course, the focus of this project's case study at Burwood Girls' High, was an 'Other Approved Studies' course, to use the parlance of the NSW Department of Education which underlines the otherliness of one end of the diversified curriculum. Typical of all alternative subjects, however, this course was for students less likely to do well in 'academic', externally examined LOTEs and could not count for credit in calculating a student's tertiary entrance score.

The rhetoric of choice, individual and community relevance, and democratically diversified curriculum, it was reported in the case-study schools, had an underside which in some other senses was not so democratic. In effect, it often amounted to a new form of streaming, dressed up in democratic garb.

Once it was 'ability' that slotted a student into an educational and social destiny. Now it's pseudo-choice and pseudo-relevance. Students, all too ready and able to sniff out the truth behind nice-sounding euphemisms, soon realized that 'communications skills' really meant 'vegie English' and 'maths in society' really meant 'vegie maths'. The ESL coordinator at Cabramatta spoke of the alternative English course offered in Year 11 by another nearby high school. 'Few here would choose [such a course] if it was offered; students here want to be educated, succeed, go to uni, and they do programmes that will get them there. And we would be doing them a disservice if we didn't have high level English.' Sometimes the alternative curriculum meant 'dressing up' a subject — making it stand out as an attractive morsel in the curriculum smorgasbord, and making it more palatable by simplifying its contents. Because you were competing with lots of other 'fancy courses', said a teacher at MacKillop, you had to call your language 'let's be bopping', but as soon as you did that, the subject being taught 'kind of slipped back there'.

The problem of curriculum diversification is even more serious when one stands back and views the scene at a systems level. It is the low socioeconomic status, high NESB schools that predominantly get progressivist, diversified curriculum. Meanwhile, the traditional academic curriculum steams on at the other end of the system, in middle-class state schools and private schools. The differences show in the results at the end of schooling, and these are at the bottom of rapidly growing NESB representation in private schools (often at great financial and personal expense to parents) and the proliferation of private ethnic schools, more concerned with 'standards' than cultural and linguistic maintenance.

A self-corrective trend was to be found in all six case-study schools, with a strong trend back to a rationalized core curriculum. This was partly a recognition on the part of education professionals of the difficulties of wholesale diversification and partly based on a growing feeling that if some things were good enough to choose, they were good enough to be compulsory. Almost all students in all six schools undertook compulsory LOTE study for some time during their secondary education. It was also a matter of students voting with their feet. The interpreters' course at Burwood ended as much because students opted for really relevant courses — the ones that are externally examined for hard marks in the Higher School Certificate. Parents also expressed unease about diversified curriculum. In Australia, said one, summing up a frequently reported view, 'it seems to be a bit loose; it doesn't seem to be a straight line. . . . [I]n South America . . . it's a more common curriculum'.

LOTEs were perceived to be an important part of the curriculum, mainly as a matter of economic necessity — exploiting diverse linguistic resources in a multilingual nation highly integrated into the world economy. They were also seen as a part of the curriculum where NESB students could do well and pick up marks. LOTEs did not have an unproblematic place in the diversified curriculum, however. Some had lower status. Macedonian, for example, is still a 'Group 2' subject in the Victorian senior secondary school, which means, in the words of one student, that 'it's not worth much'. Sometimes, moreover, 'community languages' were perceived to be less than serious academic languages when their objectives were mainly maintenance. Too often, one teacher reported, the maintenance rationale was really an issue of identity and the pork barrel politics of community recognition. 'Language teaching has to be pedagogically valuable. Language maintenance on its own is not enough because it won't last forever. There is no need to maintain the language just to talk to Granny; she doesn't talk the standard language anyway.' The relevant-to-the-community rationale is unsustainable, anyway, when there are so many languages to be serviced in so many schools. School already has an onerous responsibility, said another teacher; it could offer languages as subjects for their intellectual worth and for their international usefulness; it could offer bilingual education because it aids cognitive development; but linguistic and cultural maintenance is up to the community.

At the bottom of curriculum diversification is a set of assumptions about the role of individual motivation in education; if students choose something at which they can succeed and that seems interesting to them, education is more likely to be effective than when they are forced to accept and learn what someone else thinks is important for them. In line with this strong affective-motivational orientation, the challenge of cultural pluralism in schools is treated first and foremost as a matter of self-esteem. If only the school incorporated minority students in the sense of valuing their differences, so the progressivist critique of an ethnocentric, traditional curriculum goes, their relationship to the school, and in all probability their academic results, would improve. In any event, the academic results can only follow, once the school's affective house has been set in order.

One of the primary roles of the Arabic language programme at MacKillop, for example, is to enhance self-esteem. The problem had been that some of the girls 'didn't really value their Arabic background'. The school's response is, via the languages programme, for example, to 'make public' this culture and encourage appreciation of it. The Bilingual English and Social Science Program at Brunswick East has as a 'social' rationale that the privileging of 'mother-tongue languages will lead to an increase in the individual and community's self-esteem'. The programme is evidence of 'the respect the school shows for the culture and language of the home and community groups'. An important part of LOTEs teaching at Collingwood was improving self-esteem and confidence by 'promoting their home culture'. The interpreters' course at Burwood was based on a less 'traditional', more 'confidence building' pedagogy for a 'less academic' clientele.

The focus on granting respect to difference as a means of building self-esteem was challenged a number of times. One teacher pointed out that the only way to improve students' self-esteem was, not by programmes that tried to make students feel good, but by those that enhanced their educational chances. 'Toleration of difference', whether it be cultural or otherwise, can in fact be a toleration of social inequalities. Another teacher criticized one of her LOTEs teaching colleagues, who saw their role more as 'keeping the difference, and it has become a patriotic thing'. This was a 'double-edged' objective, because when there are students with inadequate skills in both English and the mother tongue, language skills in the first language have to be given priority over a cultural emphasis, to overcome the cognitive gap.

It was by no means a foregone conclusion, however, that self-esteem was really created by granting public respect to differences. In some cases, there seemed to be a surfeit of confidence in one's cultural difference, but this was not necessarily translated into self-esteem in a broader social context. 'Everyone is in the same boat; it's all wogs versus the world here', said a teacher. The enormous popularity of the play 'Wogs Out of Work' and the cult of Con the Fruiterer on the high-rating prime time television show 'The Comedy Company', are both testimony to a, slightly counter-cultural, but nevertheless confident, assertion of 'wogness'. There is even a personalized car numberplate in Sydney which simply tells the world 'WOG'. In fact, in popular discourse, 'wog' is now as often associated with status and success — flashy red cars and rococo suburban mansions — as it is with social marginality or inferiority.

All this attribution of positive status, however, is not just an exercise in elevating difference, but in measuring the difference in social terms. The problem that led to the demise of the interpreters' course at Burwood was not that it didn't go out of its way to build confidence and capitalize in a very practical way on students' different language backgrounds, but that in broader social terms and within the pattern of senior school credentialling, it had low status. If students were to be esteemed, it was by publicly measurable success in mainstream courses. Similarly, there's not a lot of point in using the teaching of Macedonian as a stepping stone to self-esteem when the education system marks the subject for low status through its credentialling mechanisms. Put more generally, it can be concluded that esteem is a phenomenon of social relation, not a cultural thing that can be readily isolated. If curriculum relevant to cultural difference does not produce the goods in broad social terms, it is a sham even on its own primarily affective terms.

Massive changes had occurred in curriculum and teaching in all of the schools surveyed and the case-study chapters have documented these in detail. What were the results? Were students being incorporated in the sense of gaining access to the mainstream? This is difficult to measure, partly because it was difficult to access hard, comparable pre- and post-innovation data; and partly because the results themselves are ambiguous. At one of the schools, a teacher who had completed her own schooling in the same place some fifteen years earlier said there had been no improvement in pupil performance. Retention rates in the post-compulsory years had increased and more students were getting into colleges because there were more places, but their results were no better. At times, the results seemed extremely poor for the resources and personal commitment of teachers. At other times, when the results were 'average' in relation to the whole student cohort across the system, this, under the circumstances, was a good result. A number of teachers, however, pointed to an unusually large standard deviation even when the results came out to be average. Whilst some students, strongly committed to success (in the culture of the migration process), do extremely well, there is often an unusually long 'tail' of students who do very badly.

Whilst the case for their academic performance remains unproven, in sociocultural terms, all six case-study schools seem to be succeeding. At Brunswick East, for example, the whole cluster of innovations 'had a centring effect; the school has a clear identity and the students know this'. Whilst an ESL co-ordinator at one of the schools could not speak confidently of their academic results, there was a strong pastoral care element to the ESL programme and it is effective 'in terms of its social goals at the very least'. It was frequently reported that racism is a serious problem in the community but that, comparatively, school is a haven from that. In schools which are located in relatively poor neighbourhoods, and with so much cultural diversity, this must be regarded as testimony to the long-term social success of Australian multicultural education.

This is not to imply that the sociocultural question is a closed book in schools, a problem that has been solved. Racism was still a powerful concern, an object of eternal vigilance. In the words of one principal, 'we're sitting on a time bomb'. Tolerance is 'very fragile'. The school has to deal with regular 'invasions' from the 'outside', particularly on Mondays when weekend fights are brought into the school. Except at MacKillop, where the Social Literacy materials were used as a full mainstream social science programme in Year 7, there were no programmes specifically tackling the question of intercultural relations in a context of cultural diversity. The comment was made several times that LOTEs, for example, were a roundabout way of promoting intercultural harmony. Generally negative comments were made about 'ethnic studies' approaches to multicultural education, but repeated calls were made for sociocultural programmes. 'A curriculum of cultural self-knowledge' was essential, said one social science coordinator. Students desperately needed programmes that gave them knowledge and access to a complex Australian society in which the dynamics of cultural diversity were a central and ever-challenging issue.

Some cynicism was expressed about facile approaches to multicultural education which created more problems than they solved. The 'stuff on festivals', to use one teacher's expression, was an impediment to students' learning and an abrogation of the school's responsibility to take seriously the question of cultural self-understanding — to teach sociological and anthropological concepts — and to teach 'serious stuff' about access and participation in the Australian multicultural society. Several systems administrators, reflecting on schools with a less mature approach than the six case-study schools, pointed out that the 'international days' version of multicultural education produced stereotypes that had as much potential to feed into racism as to alleviate it. The issues are trivialized, and then they don't seem to be important. A token on the periphery of school life becomes an alibi to leave them out of mainstream curriculum. 'A lot of what goes on is really tokenistic; "multiculturalism" is used very glibly. Cultural identity in terms of what people wear and eat doesn't mean anything; it's not hitting the mark.' 'Culture', in the words of another person, 'is more subtle and dynamic and should be seen as such'.

Sometimes cultural maintenance, the barely hidden agenda of this sort of multiculturalism, it was reported, is hard to sustain. Communities often try. 'Once migrated, people tend to remember their culture's ways as they were when they left.' Schools have to have a much more sophisticated view of culture; always moving and with contradictory pressures coming to bear on it. One can't simply support the fossilization of culture; 'schools have to be aware of what culture is, well beyond the surface of spaghetti and polka'. The view was expressed that this is a matter of understanding how people are socialized and of teachers understanding their own cultural assumptions and the culture of schooling as a way of dealing with the various cultural and language groups in the school. It's not a matter of preservation of a distanced 'their culture', but a dialogue, a dynamic process of negotiation. 'Culture is always being formed and reformed', said one principal, always being modified in relation to the mainstream and never static. He felt he was not in a position to make decisions about the maintenance or not of other people's cultures. 'Kids are volatile and can't be treated in an authoritarian way . . . ; we have to think with them, alongside them.'

At other times, the project of cultural maintenance was not necessarily even seen to be desirable. It was a good thing, according to one senior administrator, 'so long as it does not infringe upon basic human rights'. Sexism is one hallowed cultural tradition which schools were to work actively against. In the words of a principal, 'parents will say, "this is our culture, how dare you". You have to say, like Mill, "this is the law, respect it".' The contradiction in values was most strikingly highlighted in the case of a Turkish background girl, about to be 'circumcized'. The school spoke to the parents but she 'disappeared anyway'.

Cultural chauvinism, moreover, appeared as the unacceptable underside of many attempts at cultural maintenance. Preserving culture was also reported often to include an element of political antagonism, sometimes anachronistic, and often contributing little that was constructive, in social and educational terms, to late twentieth-century Australia. Sometimes LOTEs teaching and sociocultural programmes become an intended or unintended medium for this. Antagonisms between different Yugoslav language groups, and between students of Greek and Macedonian background, were cited as examples, as was the case of a Vietnamese teacher's aide who attempted to inculcate a sense of specifically *South* Vietnamese (pre-1975) 'culture'.

Multiculturalism and cultural maintenance in some instances did not necessarily appear compatible. Multicultural education was not simply seen to be a management strategy, a process of opening schooling to the unproblematic representation and reproduction of whatever cultures come along. Multiculturalism manifested itself in these schools much of the time as a powerfully value-laden and culturally specific assumption — that in liberal western society, cultural difference is valued, but within a very particular framework of rights and obligations. One teacher defined the relationship between multiculturalism and cultural maintenance very clearly. 'Cultural maintenance can only be effective when you are maintaining more than one culture at a time . . . , otherwise you get a kind of arrogance. What's good here is that obviously we think it's valuable to be Greek *and* Lebanese *and* Turkish *and* Chinese.'

The culture of schooling needs to be recognized and clearly articulated. This seemed to be a difficulty in the case-study schools. Both progressivism and multiculturalism are ostensibly open creeds, but to protest the openness too loudly, is in fact to highlight the cultural specificity of western liberal education and society. The Salman Rushdie affair, cited by one of the administrators, highlighted the fact that the framework of openness and diversity is itself a solidly cultural phenomenon. In fact, the loud rhetorical protests do little service to ethnic communities who really want to know what strange presuppositions this liberal, progressivist education system rests upon. Nor do they help the school establish its own sense of mission. Schools and societies work best when they have a strong sense of shared institutional community. Pretending cultural agnosticism does not help. All schools reported communal and institutional fragmentation to be an important challenge. They also reported a good deal of unease and uncertainty about the word 'multiculturalism'. Repeatedly, they said the term was faddish or ambiguous or the preserve of political opportunists. They just went about their daily business of dealing with cultural and linguistic diversity. The reality of their constituent communities was such, however, that a strong, positive and generally agreed sense of multiculturalism could be the only antidote to fragmentation.

The project of sociocultural education was frequently associated with these sorts of difficulties, and ESL and LOTEs were seen to be the only respectable manifestations of multicultural education. The problem with LOTEs, however, was that their own underlying sociocultural agenda was often as poorly spelt out as sociocultural education ever has been, leaving themselves open to the same range of difficulties.

Community Participation

Community participation has become a catchcry in Australian education over the past two decades. Schools can use a variety of techniques to increase community participation in education. These can range from processes which democratize decision making, to making parents and communities feel part of the social atmosphere of the school. In Victoria, for example, the school councils have a powerful governing role by legislation and parental involvement is sought on school subcommittees, including curriculum committees. In New South Wales, as well, there is a trend to devolution of control of schools to the community. And, in the area of Commonwealth-funded programmes, it is a clear policy of the Disadvantaged Schools Program (five of the six case-study schools were DSP schools) that the community be involved in all aspects of school decision making.

Yet there are tensions between the rhetoric of participation as an ideal and problems including: a community's ability to participate; a potential conflict between community views on the way schools should work and the authoritative position of the school personnel; the time and material resources required to support community participation; a possible threat to teacher professionalism and control of their work; and the fact that the culturally specific liberal ideal of grassroots community participation might well be at odds with many immigrant cultural expectations.

Starting with the most obvious of material realities, it was reported in all six schools that NESB parents are so preoccupied with the logistics of survival, starting a business or working overtime — they are 'too busy making money' — that it is difficult for them to take an active, participatory role in their children's education. Mostly, it was the few 'Anglo' parents, often education professionals themselves, who found their way onto education policy committees, and, often, the Parents' and Citizens'/Friends' Association as well. All too frequently, the type of parent who participated was self-selected and from a privileged minority.

There were also limits, material restraints aside, to the ability and inclination of NESB parents to participate. One Turkish teacher had tried to establish a Turkish parents' club, but with no success. Parents from a peasant background, he said, found Australian education so unfamiliar that 'they don't want to know'. The idea of critically contributing to the running of the school was culturally alien. An aide quoted a Vietnamese saying about the status of the teacher in a hierarchy of social respect — 'the king first, then the teacher, then the family'. The authoritative place of the teacher — as knower and transmitter of knowledge, meant that parents were to respect the teacher just as much as the students should respect the teacher. Teachers had something to give. Indeed, asking for student and parent contribution sometimes produced more community disquiet than support, as it seemed to indicate a looseness, lack of discipline and allowing the students too much freedom to the point where teachers gave up their proper position of respect.

When NESB parents did contribute, moreover, their input was sometimes at odds with the philosophical and pedagogical temper of the school, demanding, for example, the reinstatement of school uniforms, strict discipline and examinations with grades given, and 'more spelling, grammar and punctuation'. When one of the schools diversified their curriculum offering, 'democracy was very hard to achieve', said one interviewee. 'They were a very reactionary body of parents, who were not convinced that the curriculum was appropriate for their daughters.'

A submerged sense of cultural confrontation, perhaps even ingratitude in a system which gives parents such extensive rights, partly underlined the fact in the case-study schools that community participation is a key tenet of a progressivism as a culture. Community participation was found to be not so much a procedure of openness to other people's cultural ideas about education, but itself an element in a very specific culture of schooling. A story is told of a 'teacher unionist in the feminist boiler suit uniform' who addressed a group of Turkish and Italian mothers in one of the case-study schools about their girls taking up traditional male trades such as plumbing or motor mechanics. Far from enlightening the community about the wider employment prospects for their daughters as a result of non-sexist education and employment practices, parents were appalled by the prospect of their children working in jobs which involved work which was as dirty and heavy as the factory jobs in which many of them — the mothers and fathers — still worked. They wanted their daughters to have the middle-class prospects of the evening's speaker, but to dress better.

It was found, moreover, that immigrant groups did not necessarily want school to reproduce their culture, when that culture is defined by the paradigm of pluralist multiculturalism as their 'difference'. Rather, they want access measured in mainstream economic and social terms. This is just as much a cultural thing, born of the migration process itself, as the differences. They often don't expect their home languages to be taught in school as of right. This is not to imply that, once the language are there, it would be possible to take them away. Nor that, once x language is taught, there won't be parents asking for y language. As the process of incorporation gathers a momentum of its own, specialist provision itself becomes the leverage for emerging lobby groups. Still, repeatedly, parents in the case-study schools stressed the primary importance of English and academically prestigious subjects. LOTEs were fine, but only insofar as they were subjects where their children could get high marks.

'Reactionary' maybe, but it would be wrong to dismiss parents' concerns and expectations. Vietnamese parents at one parent evening, although happy about the particular school and appreciative of the presence of a Vietnamese aide as an interpreter, said that the most disturbing things about Australian education were that it did not instil solid moral values such as respect for elders and teachers, and was too weak on the 'hard' academic disciplines such as maths. Read carefully, it seemed from the evidence from the case-study schools that there may well be a lot of truth in this perception — that schools have not projected a solid image of their own values mission (such as the meaning of multiculturalism, projected in a direct, positive sense), and that progressivism has brought with it a slippage in traditional academic rigour, and 'soft', imprecise assessment which is unsatisfying to parents and fails to prepare students for the 'hard' assessment of public matriculation exams. This is not to imply that the parents' view is an immediately acceptable answer. They refer to the only alternative known to them, not being professional educators

— their own experience of schooling. Their reference point may not be relevant to a first world society in the late twentieth century, but their observations, as they emerged in this research, were perceptive and important nevertheless.

Yet it was repeatedly pointed out that a populist vision of democratic control needs to be tempered with a positive reassertion of teacher professionalism. In one school parents 'torpedoed' a human relations course because it dealt with sexually-transmitted diseases. They insisted that the diseases be presented as 'God's scourge'. There was a point, concluded the teacher who told this story, when teacher professionalism had to override community participation. 'The school is a critical presenter of values and not just a maintainer of them.' This conclusion applies just as much to multiculturalism as it does to pedagogy. Multiculturalism is evidently not just an empty vessel, but an overarching principle of social action in Australia. The school has to take an explicit educative stance *vis a vis* cultures which are chauvinistic, reclusive or which breech official institutional and legal stances on issues such as sexism. Equally, insofar as progressivist pedagogy embodies some profound insights into the way socially powerful knowledge is made in industrial societies in the late twentieth century — actively appropriated by critical, inquiring, ever-adaptive minds — it was obvious from the case studies that school communities need informing and educating, rather than unproblematically 'giving them a say'. They need to know, they desperately want to know, about those forms of knowledge and learning that really give access. They only hark back to a supposedly golden past when the present doesn't seem to be producing the goods, or when the way the present is producing the goods has not been convincingly explained to them.

The most developed of the community liaison programmes, at MacKillop Girls' High, undoubtedly proved that much was to be gained from informing parents and actively involving them in their children's school. On the one hand, community liaison educates the school about parents' cultural expectations of schooling. It destroys fanciful notions about what parents want. It trains the school on the inside about what the outside is like.

> The fact the [NESB] children do not do very well at school is not always just an ESL problem; half the time it isn't at all. You can't remove language problems from their social context. So being able to see their problems from the two sides is very useful; . . . it's useful to the teachers because you can contribute both aspects, and it's useful to the parents because you can explain linguistic problems as well as look at cultural problems.

There can be no doubt that the Community Liaison Program at MacKillop played an important part in the creditable academic results achieved by students in that school.

As it transpired from the case studies, for different cultural groups there are different entrees to participation. One of the ironies of the culture of liberalism, working with concepts like 'rights', 'participation', 'control' and empowerment', is that, whatever the practical virtues of getting parents involved, and however much they connote community access, they are themselves culturally alien, even culturally threatening, terms to many people. They work well in the culture of the liberal individual, confidently able to avail themselves of their rights of participation. A principal in one of the Victorian case-study schools made this point clearly: 'very few schools are able to have school councils take an active role, unless they are white and middle class.'

At MacKillop, community liaison had worked because all the parents were visited in the relative security of their own homes, on their own cultural ground. The stance was 'informative' rather than 'empowering'. The cups of tea and coffee established ties of intimacy and bonds of hospitality and obligation which could not have been established in the institutional setting of the school. For the parents at this school, this was the culturally appropriate entree to participation, and possibly even, in the longer term, empowerment. In the words of the community liaison teacher:

> discussion is the important thing, because you don't necessarily change people, but if they understand *why* we are doing something and we understand why they say something — that makes the difference. It's the discussion that's important, not the resolution. But I think the discussion *is* a resolution in a way.

Pedagogy

Surveying Australian syllabus documents and curriculum materials over a period of three or four decades, there has been a revolutionary change in pedagogy. Nowhere is this more pronounced than in the teaching of English and the humanities. The Language Learning Policy at Burwood Girls', for example, spells out the currently fashionable and official 'process' approach to writing. Gone are the emphases on drill and convention of the past. The first principle is 'ownership', a culturally laden principle of knowledge and learning to be sure, in which 'a student has the choice of topic, form and full control of the writing without the constraint of formal grammar and spelling'. The latter is attended to in the 'process' of writing — drafting and editing to make the meaning clear, a process which involves 'conferencing' with teachers and fellow students. No curriculum area has been exempt from the move to an emphasis on process over content. Teaching is now the management of students making their own knowledge rather than the presentation of a defined and rigidly sequenced body of knowledge as it was in the past. Even senior maths, the last bastion of traditional curriculum, one would think, had succumbed to progressivism. A Vietnamese parents' evening at one of the schools was entirely devoted, despite the broader intention of the convenor, to the new Victorian Certificate of Education maths syllabus. The parents were concerned that the syllabus moved away from a definable set of contents — formulae to be memorized and the like — to a problem-solving approach in which the answer and the formulae are less important than the problem-solving skills.

In this project, two main issues emerged: the epistemological presuppositions of progressivist curriculum, and its practical form. The most elementary epistemological principle of progressivism is the centrality of the critical ego in the making of knowledge and learning. Thus motivation and self-esteem are seen to be prerequisites to effective learning, learning how to learn and making one's own knowledge. The Language in Learning Program coordinator at Cabramatta characterized an earlier approach to language across the curriculum at the school which was based on the idea that 'we learn through learning language' and where 'student-centred experiential learning' was the order of the day. Bringing the influence of his own ESL training to bear, he subsequently modified the pedagogical approach away from progressivism somewhat, using exercises and materials, because 'students need to learn language forms' through 'conscious application'. This move to a more explicit and less 'naturalistic' pedagogy is encapsulated in the term 'genre'. Emphasis is placed on the explicit teaching of the linguistic structures that constitute socially powerful forms of writing such as reports. Thus we see an important self-corrective process at work, taking the school's approach to cultural and linguistic diversity beyond progressivism, and even beyond the paradigm espoused in departmental syllabus documents.

As was confirmed in these case studies, the epistemology of progressivist pedagogy is culturally specific. As such, it does not necessarily mesh well with the learning styles of immigrant cultures. At the most obvious level, progressivism recycles the terminology of the market — individual ownership and so on. At its deeper psycholinguistic foundations, knowledge is most powerful when made inductively and then owned by the individual. Education must therefore be experiential, an engagement with students' real life experience. This contrasts sharply with other cultures, including the culture of Australian schooling just a few decades ago, which place a greater emphasis on externalized knowledge as received truth. If the individual has a place in traditional pedagogy, it is to work deductively from received knowledge to one's own experience. To give an example from history or social studies, today in the multicultural curriculum students might actively research their own necessarily various communities. They will be actively engaged by the demonstrable relevance of their task, and the learning outcome will be a skill of process: social science research skills or historical method or whatever. In traditional curriculum, they might have learnt about an historical metanarrative in which they, incidentally, could deductively locate their own experience: the expansion of the British Empire and the colonization of Australia, for example. Of course, effective schooling has always worked both ways. The historical and cultural point here is the overwhelming tendency of Australian schools in the late twentieth century to work one way rather than the other.

The progressivist pedagogy prevailing in the case-study schools privileges ego-centred cultures and allows environment to play a big role. So much now turns on motivation and the critical ego, and students have to bring to bear a cultural inclination to (progressivist) schooling. Process writing, for example, is founded on a principle of naturalism — that language is learnt naturally through purposeful use. This advantages students from print-immersed environments who will happen to see the purpose of literacy much more 'naturally', and who have more 'natural' skills to apply to the task than disadvantaged students. The 'process model', in the words of one teacher, is 'all induction and no guidance, which is OK for those already with the skills, but not for those without them'.

As centrally determined truths are no longer relevant in the progressivist model, curriculum in the case-study schools was school-based. And as progressivist pedagogy is culturally appropriate in a first world country in the late twentieth century, so the principle of the professional teacher in full control of their work is appropriately in tune with the latest systems management theory. 'It's a metacognitive thing', said one informant. Using other people's materials may well be beneficial if the materials are good; this can too easily become 'imitative not adaptive behaviour; they need to keep going back to the broader question of the students' needs'.

But school-based curriculum, however solid its grounding in management theory, was often found to be of dubious quality. Traditionalists claimed that language curriculum without formal content such as grammar had produced a drop in standards. 'It's all *laissez faire* now. They've abandoned traditional grammar and spelling, but the new hasn't worked.' A systems administrator also complained about huge problems of accountability that came with the radical devolution of control of curriculum. The quality of education, particularly in areas that were innovatory or required specialist servicing, was vulnerable to the ability or commitment of individual teachers. At the end of the day, said another teacher, 'there is no overall direction. Spontaneity is all'. Programmes were often found to be eclectic and discontinuous, both in terms of content and linguistic-cognitive order. Animals — basic needs including health and nutrition — Early Man — the Roman Empire, went one of the programmes in this research project. And the best teachers were highly susceptible to burn-out. One teacher saw school-based curriculum as education on the cheap. It was even worth it to the system to spend a fortune on stress management, she said, rather than pour resources into curriculum and materials. Too often, under difficult circumstances, the fallback was onto the photocopier curriculum or pedagogically dubious exercises such as cloze activities.

Cheap maybe, but school-based curriculum appeared to be extremely inefficient. A Melbourne Turkish teacher in one school was struggling with some very old and inappropriate textbooks produced in Turkey, but he was unaware of some excellent materials produced in Sydney. A teacher of Arabic had produced some exquisite calligraphy, which will probably never be seen outside his school. Another Arabic teacher had produced a full set of materials with funds from the Multicultural Education Programme before it was axed, but these had never been published and distributed. The mountain of material produced for the Burwood interpreters' course was sitting in a filing cabinet. In fact, the only innovation destined to see the light of day beyond the school in which it began was the Language in Learning Program at Cabramatta, and this was only because the coordinator had been seconded to the Department of Education to produce the materials as a book. Teachers were extremely proud of the materials they had developed, but this was obviously not something that the systems valued, nor the basis of anything that in the Australian context would be a viable project for a commercial publisher.

One of the great ironies of the field of multiculturalism as portrayed in this project is that LOTE teachers, teaching languages brought into the education system in a spirit of progressivism and pluralism, were often the strongest advocates of traditional pedagogy. Much more than any other group interviewed, they taught formal conventions such as grammar, tested in the manner of traditional examinations, and regarded themselves as the presenters of knowledge rather than the managers of student-centred inquiry. This is obviously not a function of their subject matter since the subject to have gone most dramatically in the other direction was the teaching of English as a foreign language. In fact, the way English is currently taught was frequently cited as a hindrance to effective LOTEs teaching. Students, many LOTEs teachers complained, do not bring with them an ability to think reflectively and explicitly about language structures. Parents and students had an especial respect for LOTEs teachers, and appreciated the fact that students did end up picking up crucial extra marks. In one school, a Turkish teacher taught in an extraordinarily traditional manner, even giving full examinations twice yearly in all years from Year 7. In the final Year 12 external examinations, the Turkish results stood out as the best of all subjects across the school and even students whose results were poor in other subjects scored very well in Turkish.

At another school, a LOTEs teacher spoke of a sort of subtle cultural and pedagogical apartheid between two staffrooms — the NESB staffroom and the 'Anglo, unionist', progressivist staffroom. 'Democratic ideas' which dictate that 'schools should respect social and cultural differences rather than impose academic criteria on students, maintain NESB kids in their disadvantage.' She characterized a special teacher training course on how to teach kids in the western suburbs as 'Mickey Mouse' and 'more on about managing than teaching the students'. 'Who gets the benefits?' she asked. 'How do private schools teach? They might innovate, but they teach the three R's for the ruling class.' Again, this level of debate represents constructive self-correction that is currently taking Australian multiculturalism beyond the difficulties of progressivist pedagogy. The only problem was the toll the debate was taking on individual teachers, on top of the pressure of doing an honest day's work. This woman, a highly qualified anthropology graduate and Macedonian teacher, had applied for a job as a barmaid that morning and has since resigned.

It was regularly claimed that NESB students themselves often have 'more conservative' learning styles. 'The Vietnamese as a group would like to sit there and do grammar all day, anything that's structured. They absolutely adore structure.' Students also voiced their dissatisfaction. 'I don't like the way of schooling students spend lot of time in school and they learn nothing. I do not know how to learn by this way of schooling.' And another student wrote, 'My parents think that this school is not good because I had a better school overseas'. Quite often, however, NESB students found 'the Australian Way' to be more congenial, involving class discussion and the like. Learning style, presumably, is a function of a variety of factors including length of time in Australian schools, level of linguistic competence, and so on.

The match or mismatch of learning and teaching styles was seen to be an important challenge for teachers. Sometimes it was seen as a problem of trying to wean students off 'unacceptable' preferred learning styles. One private school, not part of this project but which the principal researchers have studied recently, consists entirely of full fee-paying 'overseas' students from Asia. Every student in the school qualified for university entrance last year — a unique feat, surely. But the senior staff were concerned that they were not picking up crucial elements in the culture of Australian education and the culture of western industrial society. 'The students are slaves to work, authoritative knowledge and rote learning', said a teacher, 'and this will not serve them well in a western culture that requires creativity, critical engagement and which socializes through sport and leisure'. One could ask cynically, did the school really want to take on all the cultural and pedagogical attributes of Australian schools, including their 'normal' spread of academic results? And why did the staff find the teaching environment 'a dream'? Nevertheless, there are some fundamental aspects of progressivist pedagogy which are culturally very appropriate to advanced technological societies in the late twentieth century.

Teachers in the six case-study schools often agonized over this point.

> I think I failed one class because I tried to teach them using lots of student participation. They didn't like it. . . . They think they do more work when it is teacher-centred. But, as the new V[ictorian] C[ertificate] of E[ducation] is more student-centred, they have to be pushed more toward that style if they are going to succeed.

A teacher in a new arrivals Intensive Language Unit explained how they met this challenge. The students tend to be very traditional in their expectations and 'are happier with the teacher at the centre of the information flow. We meet their expectations at first, using a teacherly manner and then become more friendly. We have tremendous group work success.' Students become fascinated by the different learning style in Australia compared to their homeland and they 'love talking about the cultural differences'.

This project involved lesson observations, the collection of programmes and materials used in the classroom, and an examination of students' written work. Unfortunately, however, the globally-oriented case-study approach did not allow the necessary space to capture and portray the details of classroom interaction which make up effective or ineffective pedagogy. Case-study methodology captures structural dynamics well — institutional factors at the level of the whole school or the whole system which determine the adequacy of servicing of linguistic and cultural diversity. It was thus possible to trace processes of incorporation and community participation. These are tangible and easily described by the case-study participants. Not so the more subtle and pervasive issues of epistemology and pedagogical form. These are much less visible, located deep in the unconscious of conventional wisdom. Frequently the interviewers found themselves leading the interviewees into the realm of 'interesting discussion', things about which they felt uneasy but which they had rarely really considered in depth. It also became obvious that a lot of goodwill, commitment and sheer overwork was foundering on poor or inappropriate pedagogy. The elements of this failure have been outlined here, but to make a detailed linguistic-cognitive map of how this happens would be another research project.

Assessment

Assessment performs a dual function in schooling: promotion from one class to another and final school credentialling; and diagnosis of teaching/learning. Assessment is frequently accused of being a process of ranking which reconstructs differential performance and achievement as reflecting inferior or superior ability. For example, low ranking in the 'majority' language early in a student's school life can affect later educational participation, self-esteem, and so on.

Assessment was by far the weakest point in the innovations examined in the case-study schools. In line with the progressivist critique of traditional assessment, tests were rarely used and reporting was often descriptive only. There was a strong sense that students should not be told they were failing, but rather that they should be assured by being given something at which they could succeed so they could feel positive about doing their best. Rather than fail at LOTEs, for example, students at Burwood Girls' could do the Interpreting, Translating and Multicultural Studies course, at which they could succeed and thus gain self-esteem. But the danger in this sort of school, and with this sort of assessment, is to 'lower one's expectations' and 'do what is reasonable'.

The problem of lack of 'hard' assessment had serious implications for programme evaluation as well. When there are no rigorous procedures for student evaluation, schools can't evaluate programmes. This was a serious methodological problem for this research project. And it is a disastrous problem for the schools. No-one knew whether what they were doing was working beyond a sense of 'doing the right thing' and the programme seeming to 'work' in the teachers' 'professional judgment'. Teachers do indeed have a 'feel' for what's happening. Teacher professionalism is a positive reference point, but as much as anything it can involve projection, wishful thinking and flying by the seat of one's pants.

In the case of one programme, an exasperated teacher reported,

> we can't have an evaluation because it might be critical of the programme. Any criticism is seen as interfering with the consensus. I was once actually told 'if you can't say anything nice, don't say anything at all'. There is never any discussion. It is never assessed if a kid no longer needs ESL; they no longer need it when we [the ESL faculty] no longer need their numbers. The programme is in no way needs based. They don't know what the needs of the kids are because they are never assessed. No statistics are kept; no-one keeps records.

Even information on the final school credential, virtually the only point of valid society-wide comparative assessment and evaluation, is difficult to access. Most problematically, this is not available longitudinally. Anecdotal evidence suggested that the revolution in pedagogy and the assumption of the multicultural mantle over a period of several decades had not produced a significant improvement in educational results and social outcomes in some schools. There is no way for the schools or researchers to know whether this is true or not. In all probability there is neither unequivocal improvement nor unequivocal decline.

The sorts of assessment employed in many of the innovations made it even less possible to isolate 'hard' results attributable specifically to the innovation. The only programme evaluation was linked to specialist funding and submission-writing skills, and this usually presented little more than a proof of the existence of activity. This was only compounded by the nature of the goals of some of the programmes. These are intrinsically hard to evaluate, being all too often vague, unmeasurable, problematic or tendentious. How does one evaluate a programme that sets out to elevate self-esteem, in such a way that meaningful comparisons might be made with other schools, other localities, other types of programme? What is self-esteem anyway, and can the elements of an innovation plausibly be causally linked to the innovation itself?

Use of New Technologies in Basic Learning

A few things were happening in this area in the case-study schools, but nothing that could be considered a significant innovation. A teacher was developing a Vietnamese word processing package at MacKillop. Computers were used in ESL teaching at Footscray. At the systems level there was a project in Victoria aiming to use computers extensively in distance LOTEs learning, and a quite remarkably comprehensive guidebook to multilingual typesetting programmes.

Models for Negotiating Cultural and Linguistic Diversity in Education

Cultural and Linguistic Incorporation

Incorporation in the old sense of assimilation is neither desirable nor viable. Nor can multicultural education successfully incorporate via cultural pluralist strategies such as curriculum diversification and unproblematically granting esteem to difference. Indeed, incorporation itself is not a useful descriptor of the most effective, 'proactive' multicultural processes. Both assimilation and cultural pluralism imply incorporation in its usual passive sense: immigrants passively submitting to the dominant culture or the passivity of immigrant cultures being allowed to do their own things in their own spaces. Multicultural education, to be effective, needs to be more active. It needs to consider not just the pleasure of diversity, but more fundamental issues that arise as different groups negotiate community and the basic issues of material life in the same space — a process that equally might generate conflict and pain.

Incorporation, even in its passive sense, implies the existence of a dominant culture. Yet this dominant culture needs to be transformed by multiculturalism: the languages it privileges, the symbols it refers to, the future it envisages for its offspring, and so on. Such a multiculturalism would simultaneously involve structural incorporation for immigrants (access to the mainstream) and openness to cultural and linguistic diversity. The one cannot happen without the other. Respect for difference rings hollow when, institutionally, the programme catering for difference does not actively and demonstrably promote social access. Tolerance of difference rings hollow when the dominant culture is itself inflexible to cultural transformation and regeneration.

The task of multicultural education is thus much more challenging than mere incorporation. If it is successful, it will inevitably transform the mainstream. Its fostering of universal rights and values will profoundly influence cultures of everyday life. This includes making institutional space for cultural and linguistic variety. Citizens of the next century will require facility based on linguistic-cognitive skills and cultural knowledge, with which to operate effectively in a world with multilayered identities and affiliations — ethnic, national, regional, global. For both longer established and more recently arrived residents, this will be an ongoing need. Multicultural education will have to come to grips with the dynamic of a new epoch — constant flux, decentring and the necessity continually to negotiate difference.

Practically, what does this imply? With populations that are extraordinarily transient, it is not possible, for example, to teach all languages. It is possible

Pedagogies for Cultural Difference and Social Access

CULTURAL & LINGUISTIC INCORPORATION

Traditional curriculum; Assimilationism. 1940s to 1960s	Progressivist curriculum; Cultural pluralist version of multiculturalism. 1970s and 1980s	Self-corrective phase: Equitable multiculturalism; Post-progressivist curriculum Late 1980s+
• Incorporation to core culture in this case meant the dominant 'Anglo' version (with Celtic undertones). With economic and cultural links to the 'Motherland' perceived to be important, Australian education socialized students in values and skills to service that link. Minorities, such as Aborigines and NESB immigrants had to submerge and transform their own sense of destiny and lifestyle to this.	• Core culture comes to respect aspects of minorities' cultures (traditions, customs etc.) and attempts to address access and equity issues: securing an equitable share of resources. A diverse population (a recognition of immigrant lifestyles and 'seeing' indigenous peoples) requires new strategies for servicing schools, etc. These are the 'ethnic disadvantage' and cultural pluralist models of incorporation. Passive connotations to incorporation in its impact on the mainstream.	• Beyond the passive connotations to the term 'incorporation', the core dominant culture is transformed by multilayered allegiances. A flexible, multiskilled citizenry is international in its economic and cultural orientation; markets are internationalized through deregulation and there is an increasingly mobile international labour and skills market. Growing recognition of Australia's possibly pivotal place in Asian regional cooperation.
• Minority cultures subsumed by assimilation to the dominant culture.	• Respecting and servicing cultural differences; access to the dominant culture — but the fundamental character of the dominant culture remains unchanged.	• Social fabric transformed by cultural and linguistic diversity; necessity for all citizens to be able to negotiate life and work in a society with multiple layers of identity and affiliation.
• Marginalization of minority languages and cultures by neglect.	• Structural marginalization of issues of multiculturalism as cultural self-esteem or 'ethnic disadvantage'. 'Ethnic-specific' servicing.	• Equitable access to Australian society through education. Core skills plus Australian Studies: including diversity in a liberal-democratic society.
• Chauvinism and systemic processes of dominance by dominant culture.	• Self-esteem programmes and cultural maintenance programmes for linguistic/cultural minorities. Tokenism on the margins of curriculum. Access programmes that fail to define or refine the dominant culture.	• Access programmes including overarching framework of liberal society (rights, values etc.; e.g., the culture of schooling) — a social identity that allows for diversity within the limits of liberal-democratic society. Esteem achieved through enhancing life chances.
• Subsuming of cultural and linguistic minorities.	• Cultural relativism.	• Multiculturalism as a positive, value-laden thing. Toleration, basic principles of human rights have a definite cultural content. Clear, positive articulation of the culture of schooling.

Cultures of Schooling

CULTURAL & LINGUISTIC INCORPORATION (cont.)

Traditional curriculum; Assimilationism. 1940s to 1960s	Progressivist curriculum; Cultural pluralist version of multiculturalism. 1970s and 1980s	Self-corrective phase: Equitable multiculturalism; Post-progressivist curriculum Late 1980s+
• No multicultural education. Focus on all students, in undifferentiated way.	• Multicultural education has a focus on minority students: e.g., cultural self-esteem, mainstream skills.	• Education for cultural and linguistic pluralism has focus on all students: epistemology of pluralism (effective intercultural communication) plus linguistic/cognitive skills for life-long learning in a society constantly subject to technical and cultural change. Specialist educational strategies (e.g., ESL) will be needed, but to achieve common educational objectives.
• No specialist strategies to meet the demands of cultural and linguistic diversity.	• Multiculturalism a strategy to rectify educational disadvantage for groups of minority cultural/linguistic background.	• Multicultural education is a basic social and economic necessity.
• Comprehensive curriculum.	• Diversified curriculum.	• Reconstructed core curriculum, e.g., LOTEs and multicultural Australian Studies as compulsory.
• Fixed, centralized curriculum.	• A relativism of curriculum diversification. Choice, relevance, needs. A new streaming in pseudo-democratic garb. Suspect quality of the progressivist end of the diversified curriculum.	• Core linguistic-cognitive skills for participation in a society of increasing technological automation and complex social interconnectedness; rights and values of universal applicability plus epistemological and social skills to live with cultural and linguistic diversity.
• National development goals that appear singular and uncontested.	• Relevance, choice and diversity of lifestyles; possible sense of national and school fragmentation.	• A universal core in terms of values and rights in a multicultural society; yet emphasis on flexibility and creativity.
• Welfare/charity for immigrant minorities.	• Ethnic-specific servicing.	• Mainstreaming multiculturalism in such a way that the core culture and institutions are transformed.

to validate the principle — but not to legislate the necessity — of certain programmes in which structural and cultural incorporation complement each other. Schools should promote bilingual programmes as a fundamental element in linguistic-cognitive development, particularly at the early childhood stage. They should offer as wide a range of languages as possible, so long as they have equal institutional status and are seen to be as pedagogically serious as science or maths or history. Indeed, Australian society is now such, and its international intertwinement such, that compulsory LOTEs learning is in order.

Ironically, the most do-able and most critical part of multicultural education is that which is currently least and worst done. The sociocultural dimension of multicultural education is not concerned to teach the 'other' to like themselves — trying to engender self-esteem like this is a patronizing exercise anyway — but to enable each student in the investigation of how they have become a cultured being and how they relate to others. As the century draws to a close, this will become a lot more than just a humanitarian frill in a liberal education. It will be a sheer economic necessity. The boundaries of nationhood are falling in a unified Europe. Multiple layers of regional affiliation — from feeling Welsh to feeling European — have diminished the significance of boundaries of nationality. In the same way, the Australian economy has to find bonds of complementarity in the world at large and in particular in its region. This will inevitably lead to greater cooperation with Asia. Nor will migration slow down. As unusually high as Australian immigration has been by international standards, a pattern has been established over the past half century which is unlikely to be reversed. Without a strong and positive multiculturalism as national sociocultural policy, this could lead to disaster. And all our cultures will be constantly exposed to the cultures of others in a global network of media ownership. The technologies for the transmission of culture will be such, and the culture market so thoroughly internationalized, that anything other than a multicultural worldview will be irrelevant and marginalized by history. And to sell cultural and manufactured products successfully on this international market, people will have to understand the dynamics of cultural reception extremely well. Schools, perhaps more than any other social site, have a lot to do. It will be a difficult challenge, not simply to revel in the pleasure of difference as has been the extent of much multicultural education in the past, but to establish a new social epistemology, to prepare students for the negotiation of life, including its pain and conflicts, in a decentred and ever more rapidly shifting world, whilst at the same time maintaining cohesive sociality as a core value.

Community Participation

Effective school management and community participation involves interaction in which parents and the broader community play a significant role in

Cultures of Schooling

school life, whilst, at the same time, teacher professionalism is maintained and a mutually educative dialogue is established between school and community about the role and function of schooling in late twentieth-century industrial society. The only problem is that this is a time- and energy-consuming process. It requires additional staff, which means additional expense. This is a small

COMMUNITY PARTICIPATION		
Traditional curriculum; Assimilationism. 1940s to 1960s	Progressivist curriculum; Cultural pluralist version of multiculturalism. 1970s and 1980s	Self-corrective phase: Equitable multiculturalism; Post-progressivist curriculum. Late 1980s +
• Parents deliver children into the care of the state. Schools present basic skills and homogeneous 'Anglo'-centred cultural literacy.	• Diversity of backgrounds and lifestyles challenges the traditional role of the school. School now has to negotiate its role and be responsive to economic restructuring. Openness tends to lead to fragmentation of school identity and mission; threats to teacher professionalism, etc.	• A mechanism to reforge school identity is now needed. Schools need to be explicit about their socializing role and the core values of the culture of schooling, as well as re-establishing teacher professionalism.
• Institutional correctness and benevolence.	• Community participation. But differential ability to participate and difficulties with the liberal-democratic culture of participation, rights, control, etc.	• Mutually educative dialogue between school and community in which teacher professionalism is maintained yet schools are accountable to communities.
• Traditional structures of schooling and curriculum non-negotiable.	• Multiculturalism and the culture of schooling are ostensibly empty vessels. Creates difficulties for school identity and sense of mission. Yet hidden agenda: the culture of liberal-democratic society.	• Negotiation between the culture of schooling and community expectations.
• Authoritarian relations with community.	• Populist conception of democratic participation.	• Culturally appropriate means of introducing communities to culture of schooling. Democracy as a long-term programme based on knowledge, dialogue, accountability.
• A single entree to participation: the dominant curriculum and management styles of the traditional school.	• A single entree to participation: the culture of liberal-democratic rights.	• Different entrees to participation established in intercultural school-community communication.

investment, however, in relation to potential returns, harnessing parents' positive support in the schooling of their children.

Pedagogy

Successful pedagogy reflects both the living hand of cultural tradition (cueing into culturally specific learning styles) and the particular social, linguistic and cognitive requirements of the future in a rapidly changing industrial society. This is an historically unique demand to be put upon education as a public institution and is pivotal in the articulation of private and public rites of passage or socialization. Pedagogy for 'minority' students will be most effective when it is clear about the core social, linguistic and cognitive requirements of an advanced industrial society, yet when it is also sensitive to the differential pedagogical techniques necessary to achieve that end. At the same time as addressing this core, successful multicultural education will be open to community cultural diversity in its curriculum content and social and behavioural objectives. Pedagogical strategy is an essential issue in this twofold endeavour: initiation to the core linguistic, cognitive and employment requirements of late twentieth-century society, yet sensitivity to the local, the culturally specific and the particular.

As important as it is to cue into culturally specific learning styles in order to teach new ones most effectively, the dominant pedagogical paradigm itself should not be seen as given and uncontested. Progressivism may well be potent as a technique, and culturally relevant to life in the late twentieth century, but in its more unrestrained guise in disadvantaged schools it often unhelpful in failing to be explicit about knowledge and in failing to explain and justify its own epistemological appropriateness. The answer, perhaps, is curriculum which is more authoritative in its content and principles of organization, yet not authoritarian as a medium of instruction. It is perhaps an irony that immigrants' critique of individualist epistemology, their sense of the power of socially received knowledge and paradigms of learning, is in some ways truer to industrial society — a more broadly interconnected system of social order than has ever before existed in human history — than the conceit of progressivism that knowledge is a matter of individual perspective. It might also help explain why some immigrant groups have a peculiar cultural resource which sets them, despite all their particular educational handicaps, educationally beyond many members of the longer established English-speaking background population.

What then, needs to be done in a practical way? One clear finding of this research is that rigorous, materials-based inservice training is needed. School-based curriculum is enormously inefficient and teachers learning on the job is an *ad hoc* way of schools facing the challenge of cultural and linguistic diversity. There is also a great need to elevate the science of teaching. School-based curriculum development has also meant a degree of amateurization of curriculum to the best that can be done in circumstances where one also has to teach

PEDAGOGY

Traditional curriculum; Assimilationism. 1940s to 1960s	Progressivist curriculum; Cultural pluralist version of multiculturalism. 1970s and 1980s	Self-corrective phase: Equitable multiculturalism; Post-progressivist curriculum. Late 1980s +
• Singular cultural and economic goals require rote learning and authoritarian pedagogy	• Pace of change increases; fixed knowledge less important than creativity, motivation, versatility. Education now process-oriented: openness to constant change and life-long learning. Paralleled by increasing cultural and linguistic diversity which means no fixed truths of cultural literacy.	• Pedagogy based on core linguistic/cognitive skills, yet premium placed on technical and cultural creativity. Skills-based education, but also clear overarching social/educational philosophy. Education should aim at a new cultural literacy with common objectives for all students, both broader than older versions of the sociocultural project of multiculturalism in aiming at theory/abstraction about the nature of culture and diversity and narrower in terms of basic skills and knowledge foundations. Creativity and adaptability still critical, so return to core of learning does not imply 'back to basics' strait-jacket. This task needs to be located in a combination of professional development and a variety of excellent, authoritative materials to choose from.
• Core subjects and overt streaming.	• Diversified curriculum and covert streaming.	• Core and diversified curriculum of equal status.
• Authoritarian pedagogy.	• Pedagogy based on individual motivation.	• Authority in structure of task and effective mastery. Exercise of choice and creativity in application, reapplication, adaptation, etc.
• Monolingualism or 'foreign' language learning for the 'academically inclined' elite.	• 'Community' model of LOTE teaching: maintenance and self-esteem.	• Multilingualism a norm and necessity. All language learning equal status and intellectual seriousness.

Pedagogies for Cultural Difference and Social Access

PEDAGOGY (cont.)		
Traditional curriculum; Assimilationism. 1940s to 1960s	Progressivist curriculum; Cultural pluralist version of multiculturalism. 1970s and 1980s	Self-corrective phase: Equitable multiculturalism; Post-progressivist curriculum. Late 1980s +
• Nationalism around a single ethnic group.	• Fragmentation, e.g., around 'relevant' ethnic studies.	• Theory of cultural becoming; the facts of cultural diversity. Equitable initiation to core linguistic, cognitive and employment requirements, yet sensitive to experiences based in the local, the culturally specific and the particular.
• Product or content orientation.	• Process orientation.	• Process as management technique and as basis for operationalizing curriculum; explicit product (content of curriculum) as a basis for more effective and accessible teaching/learning, clearer educational accountability, as a basis for negotiating educational change etc.
• Knowledge based on objectified, externalized content. Object of knowledge: the 'facts'.	• Knowledge a function of the critical ego. Motivation and experience as key elements in learning. Object of knowledge: openness to change, processes of problem solving.	• Both authoritative knowledge possible and students active learners, shapers of their own understandings. Critique as a crucial skill in a diverse society undergoing rapid change.
• Fixed, content-centred learning.	• Student-centred learning.	• Definite contents to skills and standards of socially powerful knowledge, yet students as active inquirers.
• Inflexible 'standards' and decontextualized, meaningless 'rules'.	• 'Anything goes' relativism according to 'needs', 'relevance'.	• Core linguistic/cognitive requirements, cultural literacy.
• Singular pedagogical technique.	• Pedagogy relativizes knowledge, skills, differential outcomes.	• Variant specialist pedagogies; singular ends.
• Failure of minority students, less academically affluent students etc. through boredom and irrelevance.	• Failure through pseudo-democratic streaming mechanisms and relativizing socially powerful knowledge, diffused in a plethora of ostensibly relevant forms of knowledge.	• Hard, core skills plus specialist areas of interest and knowledge.

Cultures of Schooling

PEDAGOGY (cont.)		
Traditional curriculum; Assimilationism. 1940s to 1960s	Progressivist curriculum; Cultural pluralist version of multiculturalism. 1970s and 1980s	Self-corrective phase: Equitable multiculturalism; Post-progressivist curriculum. Late 1980s +
• Pedagogical formalism.	• 'Naturalism'.	• Rigorous, skills-based inquiry.
• Bias to deductive reasoning.	• Bias to inductive reasoning.	• Productive and balanced interplay of deduction from received theory/knowledge and induction in experiential learning.
• Centralized curriculum. Teachers as transmitters of received, official knowledge and values.	• School-based curriculum. Teachers as professionals, makers of curriculum, and managers of open classroom processes. Yet, ironically, problems of quality, standards, curriculum vulnerable to the ability or commitment of teachers, programmes tend to be eclectic or discontinuous, duplication and wastage of energy, etc.	• Centralized models of curriculum in the form of exemplary materials in conjunction with professional development programmes. Aim to raise professional status of teaching and science of teaching. Return of structure, skills, rigour to curriculum, yet allowance for creativity, openness, active student inquiry.
• Insensitivity to match/mismatch of teaching/learning styles.	• Insensitivity to match/mismatch of teaching/learning styles.	• Match/mismatch of teaching/learning styles as a critical educational concern.

and be a guardian to students. In a revived science of teaching, progressivism provides insights into educational management, operationalizing the pedagogical process, harnessing motivation, and so on. At the same time, it is time to be more explicit about the content of culturally powerful knowledge and culturally powerful ways of knowing.

Assessment

'Soft' forms of assessment are often weak in their capacity for comparability, in failing to report accurately on results as they lead to the final school credential for entrance to higher education, in being often unclear and ambiguous, and involving, as they frequently do, a devaluing of the assessment process to the point where it loses much of its meaning. Notwithstanding the critique of the effect and reliability of standardized testing and IQ tests on 'minority' students, assessment is crucial. Teachers need assessment tools of broad

ASSESSMENT		
Traditional curriculum; Assimilationism. 1940s to 1960s	Progressivist curriculum; Cultural pluralist version of multiculturalism. 1970s and 1980s	Self-corrective phase: Equitable multiculturalism; Post-progressivist curriculum. Late 1980s +
• IQ and other standardized tests. A method of using education to stratify society, 'blind' to cultural and linguistic diversity and pronouncing on 'ability' or lack of 'ability'.	• Critique of traditional testing: not useful to measure students, whose starting points and aspirations are different, by a common measure. Move to describing behaviour and individual development. Since education a process, cultural literacy fluid and curriculum is diversified, there is nothing fixed to test. Assessment more subjective and behaviour-based.	• The extent of diversity itself increasingly demands benchmarks to ensure that difference is not a mask of segmentation. Concrete, national evaluation tools are needed to ensure that schools are reaching their objectives in socially measurable terms in order not to be unfair to individuals. Performance indicators needed to measure effectiveness of innovation. Measurement impacts productively back on curriculum and not the fate of individual students.
• Rigid system of placement; culturally and linguistically loaded IQ and standardized test.	• Subjective, descriptive, behaviour-based assessment.	• National assessment frameworks to ensure finetuning of curriculum, quality control, measurable success in achieving equal outcomes.

comparability for diagnostic purposes. Meaningful parent participation requires clear and accurate assessment and reporting procedures for the purposes of accountability. Students need accurate feedback on their work. Education systems need comparable results for final school credentialling and to determine entrance into post-secondary education. Assessment, therefore, needs to be designed to be sensitive to cultural differences, not foreclosing possibilities in the fashion of standardized tests or IQ tests, yet reporting to teachers, parents, students and systems in ways which are accurate and ensure comparability.

What needs to be done on the assessment front? Sophisticated forms of assessment are sorely needed for the purposes of diagnosis and for comparability. Parents really do need to be told honestly whether the education their children are receiving, in broad social terms, will produce outcomes commensurate with their aspirations.

The problem of assessment in integrally related to the problem of curriculum. Without a clearly defined linguistic, cognitive and cultural core, schools have no generalizable things to assess. The project of assessment is now coming back onto the agenda of schools, as part of the historical

Cultures of Schooling

self- corrective process. The problem is to avoid the 'rort' that was traditional, standardized testing. At the programme evaluation level, meaningful performance indicators are needed, and at the level of the individual student, clearly specified assessment criteria are required, which: measure linguistic skills; identify the attainment of cognitive objectives (levels of abstraction, critical engagement and so on); evaluate levels of cultural literacy necessary for access and participation in the multicultural society; and assess the practical and theoretical skills necessary for joining the workforce in a highly technological society and as an autonomous, responsible and responsive worker.

Use of New Technologies in Basic Learning

The use of new technologies in basic learning can involve learning in traditional ways (but more efficiently whilst incidentally gaining familiarity with new tools), or new ways of learning, packaging knowledge or presenting curriculum which would not otherwise be presented. In other words, new technologies in basic learning can mean both more efficient ways of teaching the 'basics' using traditional pedagogy, and new ways of knowing in which, for example, memory and note-taking are less important than an ability to access information storage, use spelling programs, draft and edit on a keyboard and so on.

Institutionalization of Innovation

Innovation only happens in favourable institutional circumstances. The remarkable thing about the six schools that were the subject of this investigation was not so much the profundity of change at a grassroots level in response to cultural and linguistic diversity, but that the institutional climate had been such that this amount of change could occur. Sophisticated and proactive centralized policy, occurring in the historical context outlined in Chapter 2, can enjoy much of the credit for the thorough infusion of multicultural education at the case-study schools. One of the greatest ironies of both multiculturalism as social policy and progressivism as educational policy, however, is that, rhetorically, they devolve the focus of control and the practical initiation of activity, but that, in historical reality, they were both initiatives from a very creative and forward-looking centre.

Australia's immigration history is unique amongst first world countries, and this helps to explain the success and creativity of centralized policy. The proportionate numbers and the diversity of immigrants set Australia apart. So do the settlement policies over four decades, always anticipating permanent settlement. Whether it be through assimilation or the various refinements of settlement policy that have led to today's multiculturalism, Australia has for some decades accepted a reality which many other first world countries are now finding forced upon them. The supposed 'guestworkers' are really there for good. In demographic terms alone, Australia already represents a uniquely advanced urban pluralism which will be the destiny of many other 'first world' countries as they move into the twenty-first century. Minority languages are geographically dispersed and, usually three or four major minority language groups enjoy equal numbers in any one location. Canadian-style bilingualism or specialist servicing of immigrant enclaves in just not possible in this sort of society.

Education has been a critical site in the large-scale absorption of immigrants. And there, devolution of control and diversification of servicing have been cornerstones of multicultural education. In some ways this is a sophisticated and humane management technique. No more Taylorism or Fordism of the production line which breaks the work process down into its most elemental units and deskills the vast majority of workers. Teachers are more in control of their own professional environments; communities have a say in their children's education; students contribute in the government of the school. Democracy, choice, relevance. If Weber were alive in the late twentieth century, he would have to rethink his theory of bureaucracy. Bureaucratic intransigence there still is; hierarchy there still is; inequality of socioeconomic outcome there still is. But bureaucracy also encourages diversity, responsibility, autonomy, creativity, negotiation, consensus.

This book has tried to explain the dynamics of all this — how cultural and linguistic diversity has been a catalyst to rethinking the whole way education is managed and delivered. In larger historical terms it describes lessons of a politics which some would call postmodern, lessons which are only now beginning to be learnt in the Soviet Union and which China evidently still has to learn — that the most effective way of enlisting commitment in highly technological industrial societies is to nurture the culture of liberal civil society and that this is done by devolution of control and the active recognition of communal diversity.

Yet, modern management practices are a two-edged sword. They are all-consuming (committees, negotiations, consultations) to the point of personal exhaustion and to the point of attrition where the blandest of commonsense must prevail. Teachers' control of their working environment shifts the burden of responsibility for curriculum onto them and increases workloads to the point of burn-out. The promise of the democratic rhetoric has not borne fruit either in the quality of teachers' lives or in significantly improved patterns of educational results. These difficulties are compounded by the ever increasing pace of change. Sometimes it seems like change for change's sake, changing the acronym to appear to be doing something new, abandoning an imperfect, incomplete project to start another afresh. A succession of funding arrangements and schemes passes by with bewildering rapidity: the Multicultural Education Program, the Participation and Equity Program, the National Advisory and Consultative Committee on Multicultural Education, to name just a few. The current Australian Advisory Council on Languages and Multicultural Education, up and running to administer National Policy on Languages funds last year, may not last beyond next year. Sometimes, well intended but unsustained handouts are more disruptive than helpful. A lot of resources are simply wasted. Said one principal of a now-defunct innovation we were investigating as part of this project, 'it was one of those one-off things. We do those very well in Australia; we get a wonderful programme and then the funding disappears'.

This is by no means a finished story. However far Australia's demography has taken it down new historic paths, the problems are not solved, and a new pattern of difficulties and contradictions is unfolding. The education system is now in another major self-corrective phase. If this book has been critical of the cultural pluralist version of multiculturalism and the progressivist version of pedagogy, it has not been to denigrate the historical achievements of these complementary movements, but to highlight in the foreground the most promising incipient developments in Australian multicultural education.

Throughout the world, people are experiencing a state of permanent cultural flux. The French Bicentennial parade was shown on Australian television, a broadcast bought from a Canadian television network. America was 'represented' by a Southern USA all black gymnastic band; Britain was 'represented' by a dance group with umbrellas who were showered by a fire engine and kept ostentatiously sneezing in the wet. La Marseillaise was sung by the black American opera singer, Jessye Norman. The Canadian commentators were lost for words. 'It's not national; it's not French; it's not even European. It's fragmented, a collage.' In a year when one would expect France to be celebrating the birth of the modern liberal-democratic nation, the parade foretold the decline of the nation and the rise of a pluralist, liberal civil society in which bonds of community are more local and bonds of economy are more international.

In this crisis of flux, there seems to be no centre. How can there be ethos or community when the core itself is not defined? How can you deal with the immigrant minorities when you don't know yourself? In redefining nation, Australia is particularly advanced. In multicultural education, Australia perhaps has most to offer in a revived sociocultural education.

Note

1   KALANTZIS, M., COPE, B. and NOBLE, G., *The Economics of Multicultural Education*, (Unpublished report), Office of Multicultural Affairs, Canberra, 1989.

Bibliography

A. **History of Australian Immigration**

BAKER, L. and MILLER, P. (eds), *The Economics of Immigration*, DILGEA, Australian Government Publishing Service, Canberra, 1987.
BETTS, K., *Ideology and Immigration*, Australian University Press, Melbourne, 1976.
BIRRELL, R. and BIRRELL, T., *An Issue of People: Population and Australian Society*, Longman Cheshire, Melbourne, 1981.
BIRRELL, R. and HAY, C. (eds), *The Immigration Issue in Australia*, La Trobe University, Melbourne, 1978.
BOTTOMLEY, G. and DE LEPERVANCHE, M. (eds), *Ethnicity, Class and Gender in Australia*, George Allen and Unwin, Sydney, 1984.
BURNLEY, I., et al. (eds), *Immigration and Ethnicity in the 1980's*, Longman Cheshire, Melbourne, 1985.
CASTLES, S., LEWIS, D., MORRISSEY, M., BLACK, J., *Patterns of Disadvantage among the Overseas Born and their Children*, Centre for Multicultural Studies, University of Wollongong, 1986.
CASTLES, S., COPE, B., KALANTZIS, M., MORRISSEY, M., *Mistaken Identity: Multiculturalism and the Demise of Nationalism in Australia*, Pluto Press, Sydney, 1988.
COLLINS, J., 'Immigration and Class: the Australian Experience', in BOTTOMLEY, G., and DE LEPERVANCHE, M. (eds), *Ethnnicity, Class and Gender in Australia*, George Allen and Unwin, Sydney, 1984.
COLLINS, J., *Migrant Hands in a Distant Land: Australia's Post-War Immigration*, Pluto Press, Sydney, 1988.
DAY, L. and ROWLAND, D., *How Many More Australians: The Resource and Environmental Conflicts*, Longman Cheshire, Melbourne, 1988.
DOUGLAS, D. (ed.), *The Economics of Australian Immigration*, Proceedings of the Conference on the Economics of Immigration, 1982.
EVANS, M. and KELLY, J., 'Immigrant's Work: Equality and Discrimination in the Australian Labour Market', *Australian and New Zealand Journal of Sociology*, 22, pp. 186–207, 1986.
HUGO, G., *Australia's Changing Population: Trends and Implications*, Oxford University Press, Melbourne, 1987.
JAKUBOWICZ, A. and CASTLES, S., 'The Inherent Subjectivity of the Apparently Objec-

tive in Research on Ethnicity and Class', *Journal of Intercultural Studies*, 5, pp. 5–25, 1986.

JAKUBOWICZ, A., MORRISSEY, M., PALSER, J., 'Ethnicity, Class and Social Policy in Australia', Report No. 46, Social Welfare Research Centre, University of New South Wales, Kensington, 1984.

JUPP, J. (ed.), *The Australian People*, Angus & Robertson, 1988.

KUNZ, E., *A Continent Takes Shape*, Collins, Sydney, 1971.

KUNZ, E., *Displaced Persons: Calwell's New Australians*, Australian National University Press, 1988.

MARKUS, A. and CURTHOYS, A., *Who are our Enemies? Racism and the Working Class in Australia*, Hale and Iremonger, Sydney, 1978.

MORRISSEY, M., *Migrants and Labour Market Programs*, Centre for Multicultural Studies, University of Wollongong, 1985.

MILNE, F. and SHERGOLD, P., *The Great Immigration Debate*, Federation of Ethnic Communities Councils of Australia, 1984.

NORMAN, N. and MEIKLE, K., *The Economic Effects of Immigration on Australia*, CEDA, Sydney, 1985.

PRICE, C. (ed.), *Australian Immigration: A Bibliography and Digest*, No. 5, Australian National University, Canberra, 1981.

STRONBACK, C.T., 'Immigration as a Source of Skills', *Australian Quarterly*, 58 (2), pp. 183–91, 1987.

VIVIANI, N., *The Long Journey: Vietnamese Migration and Settlement in Australia*, Melbourne University Press, Melbourne, 1984.

WILTON, J. and BOSWORTH, R., *Old Worlds and New Australia*, Penguin, Melbourne, 1984.

WITHERS, G., 'Migrants and the Labour Market: the Australian Evidence', OECD, *The Future of Migration*, Paris, 1987, pp. 210–233.

B. Key Immigration Reports

AUSTRALIAN COUNCIL ON POPULATION AND ETHNIC AFFAIRS, *Multiculturalism for all Australians*, Australian Government Publishing Service, Canberra, 1982.

AUSTRALIAN ETHNIC AFFAIRS COUNCIL, *Australia as a Multicultural Society*, Australian Government Publishing Service, Canberra, 1977.

AUSTRALIAN INSTITUTE OF MULTICULTURAL AFFAIRS (AIMA), *Evaluation of Post Arrival Programs and Services*, Melbourne, 1982.

AIMA, *Reducing the Risk: Unemployed Migrant Youth and Labour Market Programs*, Melbourne, 1985.

AIMA, *Migrants, Labour Markets and Training Programs: Studies on the Migrant Youth Labour Force*, Melbourne, 1986.

AIMA, *Report of Commonwealth, State and Territory Ethnic Affairs Offices on Migrant Unemployment*, Melbourne, 1986.

AUSTRALIAN POPULATION AND IMMIGRATION COUNCIL, *A Decade of Migrant Settlement, Report of the 1973 Immigration Survey*, Australian Government Publishing Service, Canberra, 1976.

BUREAU OF LABOUR MARKET RESEARCH, *Migrants in the Australian Labour Market*, Australian Government Publishing Service, Canberra, 1988.

COMMISSION OF INQUIRY INTO POVERTY, *Welfare of Migrants*, Australian Government Publishing Service, Canberra, 1975.

Bibliography

COMMITTEE TO ADVISE ON AUSTRALIA'S IMMIGRATION POLICES (CAAIP) Secretariate, *Understanding Migration*, Australian Government Publishing Service, Canberra, 1987.
CAAIP, *Immigration, A Commitment to Australia*, (The FitzGerald Report), Australian Government Publishing Service, Canberra, 1988.
DEPARTMENT OF IMMIGRATION AND ETHNIC AFFAIRS, (DIEA) *Migrants in the Labour Market*, Canberra, n.d.
DIEA, *Australian Immigration — Consolidated Statistics*, No. 13, Canberra, 1983.
DIEA, *Don't Settle for Less: Report of the Committee for Stage 1 of the Review of Migrant and Multicultural Programs and Services*, Australian Government Publishing Service, Canberra, 1986.
GALBALLY, F., *Review of Post-Arrival Programs and Services for Migrants*, Australian Government Publishing Service, Canberra, 1978.
IMMIGRATION ADVISORY COUNCIL COMMITTEE ON SOCIAL PATTERNS, *Inquiry into the Departure of Settlers from Australia*, Australian Government Publishing Service, Canberra, 1973.
OFFICE FOR MULTICULTURAL AFFAIRS (OMA), *National Agenda for a Multicultural Australia*, Australian Government Publishing Service, Canberra, 1989.

C. History Of Education and Multicultural Education in Australia

BARCAN, A., *A History of Australian Education*, Oxford University Press, Melbourne, 1980.
BULLIVANT, B. (ed.), *Educating the Immigrant Child: Concepts and Cases*, Angus and Robertson, Sydney, 1973.
BULLIVANT, B., *The Pluralist Dilemma in Education, Six Case Studies*, George Allen and Unwin, Sydney, 1981.
BULLVANT, B., *Cultural Maintenance and Evolution*, Multilingual Matters, Clevedon, England, 1984.
BULLIVANT, B. (ed.), *The Ethnic Encounter in the Secondary School: Ethnocultural Reproduction and Resistance*, Falmer Press, Basingstoke, 1987.
CLAYDON, L. et al., *Curriculum and Culture: Schooling in a Pluralist Society*, George Allen and Unwin, Sydney, 1977.
CONNELL, R.W. and WHITE, V., 'Child Poverty and Educational Action', *Poverty, Education and the Disadvantaged Schools Program Project, Report 2*, Macquarie University, 1988.
COPE, B. and ALCORSO, C., *A Review of Australian Multicultural Education Policy, 1979-1986*, a commissioned background paper for the National Advisory and Consultative Committee on Multicultural Education, NACCME Commissioned Background Papers Series No. 9, Canberra, 1987
DE LACY, P. and POOLE, M., *Mosaic or Melting Pot?* Harcourt Brace Jovanovich Group, Sydney, 1979.
D'URSO and SMITH (eds), *Changes, Issues and Prospects in Australian Education*, University of Queensland, Brisbane, 1981.
FALK, B. and HARRIS, J. (eds), *Unity in Diversity: Multicultural Education in Australia*, Australian College of Education, Carlton, Victoria, 1983.
FALK, B., *'Slogans, Policies and Practice in Multicultural Education in Australia'*, NACCME Discussion Paper No. 2, Canberra, 1985.

Bibliography

Foster, L., 'The Politics of Educational Knowledge: From Migrant to Multicultural Education', in Browne, R. and Foster, L. (eds), *Sociology of Education*, Macmillan, Melbourne, 1983.

Foster, L. and Stockley, D., *Multiculturalism: the Changing Australian Paradigm*, Multilingual Matters, Avon, England, 1984.

Foster, L. and Stockley, D., *Australian Multiculturalism: A Documentary History and Critique*, Multilingual Matters, Avon, England, 1988.

Hannan, B., *The Location of Multiculturalism in the Development of Australian Education*, NACCME Research Paper No. 5, n.d.

Hannan, B. and Spinoso, G., *A Mediterranean View of Schools*, BRUSEC, Hodiga, Richmond, Victoria, 1982.

Harrold, R., *The Evolving Economics of Schooling*, Deakin University Press, Deakin University, 1985.

Kalantzis, M. and Cope, B., 'Multiculturalism and Education Policy', in Bottomley, G. and de Lepervanche, M. (eds), *Class, Gender and Ethnicity*, George Allen and Unwin, Sydney, 1984.

Kalantzis, M., Cope, B. and Hughes, C., 'Pluralism and Social Reform: A Review of Multiculturalism in Australia Education', *Thesis Eleven*, No. 10/11, 1985, pp. 195–125.

Keeves, J. (eds), *Australian Education: Review of Recent Research*, Allen and Unwin, Sydney, 1987.

McRae, D., *Teachers, Schools and Change*, Heinemann, Melbourne, 1988.

National Advisory and Co-ordinating Committee on Multicultural Education, *Education in and for a Multicultural Society: Issues and Strategies for Policy Making*, Department of Education and Youth Affairs, Canberra, 1987.

Phillips, D. and Houston, J. (eds), *Australian Multicultural Society*, Dove Communications, Blackburn, Victoria, 1984.

Rawson, D. and Neale, R. (eds), *Equality of Opportunity Reconsidered*, Academy of the Social Sciences in Australia, Canberra, 1985.

Wyatt, T. (ed.), *Indicators of School Effectiveness*, Reporting on Education Progress Bulletins, Directorate of Special Programs, NSW Department of Education, 1988.

Wyatt, T. and Ruby, A. (eds), *Indicators in Education: Papers from the First National Conference*, Australian Conference of Director-General of Education, Sydney, 1988.

D. Sociology of Education and Multicultural Education in Australia

i) Issues of Disadvantage

Ainley, J. et al., *Staying at High School in Victoria*, ACER, Hawthorn, Victoria, 1984.

Ainley, J. et al., *Patterns of Retention in Australian Government Schools*, ACER, Hawthorn, Victoria, 1984.

Bradley, D. and M., 'Problems of Asian Students in Australia', Department of Education and Youth Affairs, Canberra, 1984.

Brown, S., *Non-English Speaking Background Girls and Education — an annotated bibliography*, VCPS, Melbourne, 1984.

BROWNE, R. and FOSTER, L., *Sociology of Education*, Macmillan, Melbourne, 1983.
BIRRELL, R., 'The Educational Achievement of Non-English Speaking Background Students and the Politics of the Community Languages Movement', in BAKER, L. and MILLER, P. (eds), *The Economics of Immigration*, DILGEA, Canberra, 1987.
BOTTOMLEY, G. and DE LEPERVANCHE, M. (eds), *Ethnicity, Class and Gender*, George Allen and Unwin, Sydney, 1984.
BULLIVANT, B., *Getting a Fair Go: Case Studies of Occupational Socialization and Deceptions of Discrimination in a Sample of Seven Melbourne High Schools*, Human Rights Commission, Canberra, 1980.
BURGESS, R. et al., *The Educational Needs of Non-English Speaking Background Girls in Secondary Schools in NSW*, Social Policy Unit, NSW Ministry of Education, 1985.
COMMONWEALTH DEPARTMENT OF EDUCATION AND YOUTH AFFAIRS, *Immigrant and Refugee Youth in the Transition from School to Work*, Australian Government Publishing Service, Canberra, 1983.
CONNELL, R., ASHENDEN, D.J., KESSLER, S. and DOWSETT, G.W., *Making the Difference: Schools, Families and Social Division*, Allen and Unwin, Sydney, 1982.
COPE, B. and POYNTING, S., 'Class, Gender and Ethnicity as Influences on Australian Schooling: An Overview', in COLE, M. (ed.), *The Social Contexts of Schooling*, Falmer Press, Basingstoke, England, 1989.
DEPARTMENT OF IMMIGRATION AND ETHNIC AFFAIRS, *Family, Work and Unemployment: A Study of Lebanese Settlement in Sydney*, Australian Government Publishing Service, Canberra, 1984.
DWYER, P. et al., *Social Division, Economy and Schooling*, Deakin University, Victoria, 1985.
EDUCATION COMMISSION OF NSW, *Research in Multicultural Education*, Sydney, 1984.
HENRY, C. and EDWARDS, B., *Enduring a Lot: The Effects of the School System on Students of Non-English Speaking Backgrounds*, Human Rights Commission, Canberra, 1986.
HORVARTH, B., *An Investigation of Class Placement in new South Wales Schools*, NSW Ethnic Affairs Commission, Sydney, 1986.
KALANTZIS, M. and COPE, B., 'Why We Need Multicultural Education: A Review of the "Ethnic Disadvantage" Debate', *Journal of Intercultural Studies*, 1988, Vol. 9, No. 1, pp. 39–57.
KALANTZIS, M. and COPE, B., 'Aspirations, Participation and Outcomes: From Research to a Curriculum Project for Reform', in FORSTER, V., (ed.), *Including Girls: Curriculum Perspectives on the Education of Girls*, Curriculum Development Centre, 1988. pp. 37–46.
MARJORIBANKS, K., *Ethnic Families and Children's Achievements*, George Allen and Unwin, Sydney, 1980.
MARSH, C., 'Access and Success of School Children from Non-English Speaking Backgrounds', Office of Multicultural Affairs, Policy Option Paper, Canberra, 1988.
MATTHEWS, J., *Education Needs of Young Refugees*, ICRA, Sydney, 1988.
MEADE, P., 'Comparative Educational Expectancies of Students of Non-English Speaking Migrant Origin and Students with Australian-born Parents', Brisbane CAE, Brisbane, 1984.
MISTILIS, N., 'Destroying Myths: Second Generation Australians' Educational

Bibliography

Achievements', Centre for Migrant and Intercultural Studies, *Mimeo*, Australian National University, 1986.
QUALITY OF EDUCATION REVIEW COMMITTEE, *Quality of Education in Australia*, Australian Government Publishing Service, Canberra, 1985.
STURMAN, A., 'Immigrant Australians and Education', *Australian Education Review* No. 22, Australian Council for Educational Research, Victoria, 1985.
TSOLIDIS, G., *'Education Voula: A Report on Non-English Speaking Girls and Education'*, Victorian Ministry of Education, Melbourne, 1986.
WATSON, I., *Double Depression*, Allen and Unwin, Sydney, 1985.
WILLIAMS, N.P., 'Research on Poverty and Education 1979–1987', Poverty, Education and the Disadvantaged Schools Program, Macquarie University, 1988.
WILLIAMS, Y., *Participation in Education*, ACER, Melbourne, 1987.
YOUNG, C. et al., *Education and Employment of Turkish and Lebanese Youth*, Australian Government Publishing Service, Canberra, 1980.

ii) Key Debates in Curriculum and Multicultural Education in Australia

AIRD, E. and LIPPMAN, D. (eds), *English is their Right*, Australasian Education, Croydon, Victoria, 1983.
BETTONI, C., 'Maintenance as New Learning? Italian in Schools', *Babel*, 7, 2/3, pp. 25–33, 1981.
BETTONI, C., 'Italian Language Attrition: A Sydney Case Study', in CLYNE, M. (ed.), *Australian Meeting Place of Languages*, ANU Press, Canberra, 1986.
BOOMER, G., *Negotiating the Curriculum*, Ashton, Sydney, 1982.
BOOMER, G., 'The Helping Hand Strikes Again? An Exploration of Language, Learning and Teaching', Address to the International Symposium on Language in Learning, University of Queensland, July, 1988.
CAHILL, D., *A Greek-English Bilingual Program: Its Implementation in Four Melbourne Schools*, Language and Literacy Centre, Philip Institute of Technology, 1984.
CALLAGHAN, M. and ROTHERY, J., *Teaching Factual Writing*, DSP Metropolitan East, Sydney, 1988.
CAMBOURNE, B. et al., 'Process Writing with English and Non-English Speaking Children in Kindergarten Classes: A Report on Research in Progress', Centre for Studies in Literacy, University of Wollongong, n.d.
CATHOLIC EDUCATION OFFICE OF VICTORIA, *Diversity*, Special Issue: Languages Other Than English, Vol. 6, No. 2, 1988.
CAROSI, P., *Practical Aspects of Community Languages*, Inner City Education Centre, Sydney, 1988.
CHAN, M., 'A Report on Chinese Language Education in NSW: A Case Study', Mimeo, 1983.
CHRISTIE, F., 'Curriculum Genres — Towards a Description of the Construction of Knowledge in Schools', University of New England, Armidale, 1989.
CHRISTIE, F. et al. (eds), *Writing in Schools: Study Guide*, Deakin University Press, Geelong, 1989a.
CHRISTIE, F. et al. (eds), *Writing in Schools: Reader*, Deakin University Press, Geelong, 1989b.
CHRISTIE, F. (ed.), *Literacy for a Changing Word*, Australian Council for Educational Research, Melbourne, 1990.

Bibliography

CLYNE, M., *Multilingual Australia*, River Seine, Melbourne, 1982.

CLYNE, M. (ed.), *Australia — Meeting Place of Languages*, ANU Press, Canberra, 1986.

COPE, B., 'A Textbook Case: Teaching Australian History, from Assimilation to Multiculturalism', *Agora*, Vol. 23, No. 2, 1988 pp. 21–27. Reprinted in *Teaching History*, Vol. 22, No. 2, 1988, pp. 16. 20.

COPE, B. and KALANTZIS, M., 'Cultural Difference and Self-Esteem: Alternative Curriculum Approaches', in KENWAY, J. and WILLIS, S. (eds), *Hearts and Minds: Self-Esteem and the Schooling of Girls*, Department of Employment, Education and Training, Canberra, 1988, pp. 151–166.

DRURY, H. and GOLLINS, S., 'The Use of Systemic Functional Linguistics in the Analysis of ESL Student Writing and Recommendations for the Teaching Situation', *Australian Review of Applied Linguistics*, Vol. 9, No. 2, pp. 209–236, 1986.

EGGINS, S. et al., 'Writing Project Report 1987', *Working Papers in Linguistics*, No. 5, University of Sydney, 1987.

FOSTER, L. et al., 'Evaluating Bilingual Education', *Multicultural Australia Papers*, No. 29,. CHOMI, Richmond, Victoria, 1984.

GARNER, M. (ed.), *Community Languages, Their Role in Education*, River Seine, Melbourne, 1981.

GRANT, A., 'Defining Literacy: Common Myths and Alternative Readings', *Australian Review of Applied Linguistics*, Vol. 9, No. 2, pp. 1–22. Edward Arnold, London, 1986.

HALLIDAY, M.A.K., *An Introduction to Functional Grammar*, Edward Arnold, London, 1985.

HODGE, A. et al., 'Multicultural Innovations in Secondary Schools', Multicultural Centre, Sydney College of Advanced Education, 1984.

HOUSTON, C., 'English Language Development Across the Curriculum', *Australian Review of Applied Linguistics*, Vol. 10, No. 1, 1987.

KALANTZIS, M., COPE, B., SLADE, M., *Minority Languages and Dominant Culture: Issues of Education, Assessment and Social Equity*, Falmer Press, Basingstoke, 1989.

KALANTZIS, M., 'Issues in the Education of Girls of Non-English Speaking Background', A position paper for the New South Wales Department of Education's Work Opportunities for Women Project, Sydney, 1986.

KERR, A., 'The Case For and Against Bilingual Education', in PHILLIPS, D. and HOUSTON, J. (eds), *Australia's Multicultural Society*, Dove Communications, Blackburn, Victoria, 1984.

KNAPP, P., 'The Politics of Process', *Education*, April 17, 1989.

KRESS, G., *Learning to Write*, Routledge and Kegan Paul, London, 1982.

KRINGAS, P., 'The Role of Ethnic Schools in a Multicultural Society', in PHILLIPS, C. and HOUSTON, J. (eds), *Australian Multicultural Society*, Dove Communication, Blackburn, Victoria, 1984.

LEWINS, F. and KRINGAS, P., *Why Ethnic Schools? Selected Case Studies*, ANU Press, Canberra, 1981.

LEWINS, F., 'Ethnic Schools and Multiculturalism in Australia', in BROWNE, R. and FOSTER, L. (eds), *Sociology of Education*, Macmillan, Melbourne, 1983.

MCLEAN, B., *Languages Other Than English in the Primary School — Six Case Studies*, Australian Government Publishing Service, Canberra, 1982.

Bibliography

MARTIN, J., 'Literacy in Science: Learning to handle text as technology', in CHRISTIE, F. (ed.), *A Fresh Look at the Basics: The Concept of Literacy*, 1990.

MILLS, J., 'Bilingual Education and Australian Schools: A Review', *Australian Education Review Number* 18, ACER, Hawthorn, Victoria, 1982.

NORST, M., 'Ethnic Schools: Where Are They and What are They Likely to Be?' *Journal of Intercultural Studies*, 3, 2, pp. 6–16, 1982.

PAINTER, C., *Learning the Mother Tongue*, Deakin University, Geelong, Victoria, 1985.

PRIDE, J., *Cross Cultural Encounters: Communications and Miscommunications*, River Seine, Melbourne, 1983.

RADO, M., 'Bilingual Materials and Their Use', in PHILLIPS, D. and HOUSTON, J. (eds), Australian Multicultural Society, Dove Communications, Blackburn, Victoria, 1984.

RADO, M. et al., *English Language Needs of Migrant and Refugee Youth*, Australian Government Publishing Service, Canberra, 1986.

REID, I. (ed.), *The Place of Genre in Learning: Current Debates*, Typereader Publications No. 1, Centre for Studies in Literacy Education, Deakin University, Geelong, Victoria, 1988.

ROTHERY, J., 'Writing to Learn and Learning to Write', *Working Papers in Linguistics No. 4*, University of Sydney, 1986.

SECANSKI, J., 'Reform in the Ethnic Schools: the Multicultural Model', Paper No. 5. AIMA Conference, *Ethnicity and Multiculturalism*, 1980.

SKELTON, K., 'Identifying Issues and Implementing Strategies', *Combatting Prejudice in Schools Project No. 1*, CHOMI, Richmond, Victoria, 1985.

SKELTON, K., 'Language Issues', *Combatting Prejudices in Schools Project No. 12*, CHOMI, Richmond, Victoria, 1987.

E. Systems Documents

i) Overviews of Policy

ATCHISON, J., *Position/Chopping Block Paper on Historical Development of Multicultural Education Policy up to 1985*. NACCME (Draft).

BRENTNALL, R. and HODGE, A., *Policies on Multicultural Education in Australia: An Overview*. Education Commission of New South Wales, Sydney College of Advanced Education, Multicultural Centre, 1984.

BULL, K. and TONS, J., *Multicultural Education: From Practice to Policy*, Education Department of South Australia, 1985.

CAHILL, D. et al., *Review on the Commonwealth Multicultural Education Program*, Commonwealth Schools Commission, Canberra, 1984.

COPE, B. and ALCORSO, C., *A Review of Australian Multicultural Education Policy 1979–1986*, a commissioned background paper for the National Advisory and Consultative Committee on Multicultural Education, NACCME Commissioned Background Papers Series No. 9, Canberra, 1987.

FALK, B., 'Slogans, Policies and Practice in Multicultural Education in Australia', *Discussion Paper No. 2*, National Advisory and Consultative Committee on Muticultural Education, Canberra, 1985.

HARRIS, J., *Study of Insertion Classes under the Commonwealth Ethnic Schools Program*, Canberra, 1984.

KALANTZIS, M. and COPE, B., 'Multiculturalism and Education Policy', in BOTTOMLEY,

Bibliography

G. and de LEPERVANCHE, V. (eds), *Class, Gender and Ethnicity*, George Allen and Unwin, Sydney, 1984.

ii) National

CAMPBELL, W.J. et al., *A Review of the Commonwealth English as a Second Language (ESL) Program*, Commonwealth Schools Commission, 1984.
CAMPBELL, W.J. and MCMENIMAN, M., *Bridging the Language Gap: Ideals and Realities Pertaining to Learning English as a Second Language (ESL)*, Commonwealth Schools Commission, Canberra, 1985.
CAHILL, D. et al., *Review of the Commonwealth Education Program*, 1984.
COMMONWEALTH DEPARTMENT OF EDUCATION, *Report on the Survey of Child Migrant Education in Schools of High Migrant Density in Melbourne*, Australian Government Publishing Service, Canberra, 1975.
COMMONWEALTH DEPARTMENT OF EDUCATION, *Towards a National Language Policy*, Australian Government Publishing Service, Canberra, 1982.
COMMONWEALTH SCHOOLS COMMISSION, *Schools in Australia: Report of the Interim Committee for the Australian Schools Commission*, Australian Government Publishing Service, Canberra, 1973 (Karmel Report).
COMMONWEALTH SCHOOLS COMMISSION, *Education for a Multicultural Society*, Australian Government Publishing Service, Canberra, 1979 (McNamara Report).
COMMONWEALTH SCHOOLS PROGRAM, *Report on the Commonwealth Ethnic Schools Program*, Australian Government Publishing Service, Canberra, 1983.
COMMONWEALTH SCHOOLS PROGRAM, *Participation and Equity in Australian Schools: The Goal of Full Secondary Education*, Australian Goverment Publishing Service, Canberra, 1983.
COMMONWEALTH SCHOOLS PROGRAM, *Girls and Tomorrow: The Challenge for Schools*, Australian Government Publishing Service, Canberra, 1984.
COMMOMWEALTH SCHOOLS PROGRAM, *Quality and Equality: Commonwealth Specific Purpose Programs for Australian Schools*, Australian Government Publishing Service, Canberra, 1985.
COMMONWEALTH SCHOOLS PROGRAM, *In the National Interest: Secondary Education and Youth Policy in Australia*, Canberra, 1987.
COMMONWEALTH TERTIARY EDUCATION COMMISSION, *Learning and Earning: A Study of Education and Employment Opportunities for Young People*, Australian Government Publishing Service, Canberra, 1982.
DAWKINS, J., *Strengthening Australia's Schools*, Australian Government Publishing Service, Canberra, 1988.
LO BIANCO, J., *National Policy on Languages*, Commonwealth Department of Education, Australian Government Publishing Service, Canberra, 1987.
MIDDLETON, M. et al., *Making a Future: The Role of Secondary Education in Australia*, CSC, Canberra, 1988.
MINISTERIAL REVIEW OF POST-COMPULSORY SCHOOLING, *Report*, Volumes 1 and 2, Canberra, 1985.
MULTICULTURAL EDUCATION CO-ORDINATION COMMITTEE, The Teaching of Community Languages — Position Paper 2, Canberra, 1983.
NATIONAL ADVISORY AND CONSULTATIVE COMMITTEE ON MULTICULTURAL AND MIGRANT EDUCATION, *Education In and For a Multicultural Society: Issues and Strategies for Policy Making*, NACCME, Canberra, 1987.

Bibliography

OFFICE OF MULTICULTURAL AFFAIRS, *A Fair Go, A Fair Share: Access and Equity for a Multicultural Australia*, Department of the Prime Minister and Cabinet, Australian Government Publishing Service, Canberra, 1987.

QUALITY OF EDUCATION REVIEW COMMITTEE, *Quality of Education in Australia: Report of the Review Committee*, Australian Government Publishing Service, Canberra, 1985.

SENATE STANDING COMMITTEE ON EDUCATION AND THE ARTS, *A National Language Policy*, Australian Government Publishing Service, Canberra, 1984.

iii) New South Wales

EDUCATION COMMISSION OF NEW SOUTH WALES, *Research in Multicultural Education*, Education Commission of New South Wales, Sydney, 1984.

NEW SOUTH WALES DEPARTMENT OF EDUCATION, *Aboriginal Education Policy*, Support Document No. 1, 1982.

NEW SOUTH WALES DEPARTMENT OF EDUCATION, *Our Multicultural Society*, 1983.

NEW SOUTH WALES DEPARTMENT OF EDUCATION, *Community Language Education*, A Support Document to the Multicultural Education Policy, 1983.

NEW SOUTH WALES DEPARTMENT OF EDUCATION, *Mutlicultural Education Policy Statement*, 1979.

NEW SOUTH WALES DEPARTMENT OF EDUCATION, *Mutlicultural Education Policy Statement*, 1983.

NEW SOUTH WALES DEPARTMENT OF EDUCATION, *Ethnic Affairs Policy*, 1984.

NEW SOUTH WALES DEPARTMENT OF EDUCATION, 'A Study of Class Placement and Student Backgrounds', unpublished report by Division of Management Information Services, 1984.

NEW SOUTH WALES DEPARTMENT OF EDUCATION, *Community Languages in NSW Primary Schools*, Multicultural Education Centre, 1985.

NEW SOUTH WALES DEPARTMENT OF EDUCATION, *'Me No Good, Miss', Self Esteem and Social Skills Strategies for Students of Non-English Speaking Backgrounds*, Liverpool Region, 1985.

NEW SOUTH WALES DEPARTMENT OF EDUCATION, *Equality of Outcomes and Issues Paper*, Disadvantaged Schools Program, 1986.

NEW SOUTH WALES DEPARTMENT OF EDUCATION, 'Memorandum to Principals: The Establishment of School Councils', 23 February, 1987.

NEW SOUTH WALES DEPARTMENT OF EDUCATION, *State Language Policy: Issues for Discussion*, 1988.

NEW SOUTH WALES DEPARTMENT OF EDUCATION, *Multicultural Education Centre — Initiative Outline*, 1988.

NEW SOUTH WALES DEPARTMENT OF EDUCATION, *The Fair Discipline Code*, 1989.

NEW SOUTH WALES DEPARTMENT OF EDUCATION, NSW Ethnic Schools Grant Program 'Guidelines 1987'.

NEW SOUTH WALES DEPARTMENT OF EDUCATION, Multicultural and Aboriginal Education: NSW Guide to Structures and Services, 1985.

SYDNEY CATHOLIC EDUCATION OFFICE, Ethnic Backgrounds of Students in NSW Catholic Schools, Sydney, 1978.

SYDNEY CATHOLIC EDUCATION OFFICE, Purposes and Outcomes for Catholic Schools, 1983.

Bibliography

iv) Victoria

GARNER, N. and VIEWER, M., 'Otherwise It Could Go On Forever, Language, Science and Second Language learners', Education Department of Victoria, 1982.
LO BIANCO, J. *A Language Action Plan*, Victorian Department of Education, 1988.
LOCK, S., *Second-language Learners in the Classroom: Some Considerations*, Victorian Education Department, 1983.
TSOLIDIS, G., *Educating Voula: A Report on Non-English Speaking Girls and Education*, Ministry of Educating, Melbourne, NESB, 1986.
VICTORIAN ASSOCIATION FOR MULTICULTURAL EDUCATION, *Multicultural Education 1978 Policy Statement*, CHOMI Reprints, No. 305, Melbourne, 1978.
VICTORIAN EDUCATION DEPARTMENT, *Curriculum Development and Planning in Victoria: Ministerial Paper Number 6*, 1984.
VICTORIAN EDUCATION DEPARTMENT, *Curriculum Frameworks P—12: An Introduction*, 1985.
VICTORIAN EDUCATION DEPARTMENT, *The Implementation of Bilingual and Community Language Programs in Primary Schools*, 1983.
VICTORIAN EDUCATION DEPARTMENT, *The Teaching of ESL in Primary and Postprimary Schools of the Education Department of Victoria*, 1984.
VICTORIAN EDUCATION DEPARTMENT, *Social Education P—12: A Preliminary Statement*, 1984.
VICTORIAN ETHNIC AFFAIRS COMMISSION, *Language Use in Australia: Information Paper No. 3*, Victorian EAC, East Melbourne, 1989.
VICTORIAN ETHNIC AFFAIRS COMMISSION, *School Attendance — First and Second Generation — Appendix 1*, n.d.
VICTORIAN MINISTERIAL ADVISORY COMMITTEE ON MIGRANT AND MULTICULTURAL EDUCATION, *Ethnic Schools in Victoria: A Discussion Paper*, n.d.
VICTORIAN MINISTERIAL ADVISORY COMMITTEE ON MIGRANT AND MULTICULTURAL EDUCATION, *Education for a Multicultural society: A Kit for Educators*, Clearing House on Migration Issues, Richmond, Victoria, 1981.
VICTORIAN MINISTERIAL ADVISORY COMMITTEE ON MIGRANT AND MULTICULTURAL EDUCATION, *Non-English Speaking Background Girls and Education: An Annotated Bibliography*, Melbourne, 1984.
VICTORIAN MINISTERIAL ADVISORY COMMITTEE ON MULTICULTURAL AND MIGRANT EDUCATION, *Education in, and for, Multicultural Victoria: Policy Guidelines for School Communities*, Draft mineo, 1986.
VICTORIAN MINISTRY OF EDUCATION, *Taking Schools Into the 1990s, A Proposal from the Ministry Structures Project Team*, 1986.
VICTORIAN STATE BOARD OF EDUCATION and MINISTERIAL ADVISORY COMMITTEE ON MULTICULTURAL AND MIGRANT EDUCATION, *A Language Policy for Victorian Schools*, 1986.
VICTORIAN STATE BOARD OF EDUCATION and MINISTERIAL ADVISORY COMMITTEE ON MULTICULTURAL AND MIGRANT EDUCATION, *The Place of Community Languages in Victorian Schools*, 1984.
VICTORIAN STATE BOARD OF EDUCATION and MINISTERIAL ADVISORY COMMITTEE ON MULTICULTURAL AND MIGRANT EDUCATION, *The Place of Languages other than English in Victorian Schools: Report for the Minister of Education*, 1985.

Index

Aborigines 2, 13n, 26, 28, 94, 97–9, 155, 214, 239
Academic Results 4, 7, 11–2, 36, 47, 57, 66, 88, 90, 104–5, 123–4, 132–4, 142, 174, 177, 200–1, 205–6, 210, 219, 223–5, 230, 234–5, 237
Adult Migrant Education Service 119, 166
Arabic Language and Background 2, 30, 41–3, 45, 48, 51–3, 56–7, 60–2, 69–70, 72, 74, 76, 78, 80–1, 84, 89–90, 93–4, 99, 119, 167, 183, 191, 223, 233–4
Art 90, 98, 153, 161, 164–5, 167–8, 170–1, 188
Asia 26, 28, 41, 117, 149, 235, 241
Asian Immigration 2, 28
Asian Languages and Background 2, 32, 43, 53, 61, 70, 93, 95, 118, 121, 126, 129, 132, 149–54, 158, 174, 176–9, 182–4, 191, 201, 203, 216
Assessment and Evaluation 6, 12, 34, 47–8, 82, 84, 86–8, 90, 98, 102, 110, 128, 131, 134, 141, 164, 166–7, 171, 174–5, 203, 210–11, 217, 224, 229, 234, 236–7, 246–8
Assimilation 1–4, 15–8, 24, 28, 156, 220, 238, 248
Australian Advisory Committee on Languages and Multicultural Education (AACLAME) 4–5, 27, 249
Australian Broadcasting Commission 23–4
Australian Citizenship Act 20

Australian Institute for Multicultural Affairs (AIMA) 20, 23
Australian Second Language Learning Program (ASLLP) 26, 30, 62
Austudy 54, 134, 184

Bicentennial 29
Bilingual Education 10, 34, 75–82, 86–90, 116, 118–9, 121–2, 124–44, 175, 218, 223, 238, 249
Blackburn Report (1985) 78, 126
British Isles 41, 61, 250
Brunswick East High School 5, 68–91, 125–6, 218, 223, 225
Brunswick Secondary Education Council (BRUSEC) 71
Burwood Girls' High School 5, 92–115, 221–4, 231, 234, 236

Cabramatta High School 5, 103, 148–80, 183, 220, 222, 232, 234
Calwell, A. 1
Cambodia 174
see also Khmer
Campbell Report (1984) 47
Cantonese 94, 99–101, 103, 105, 110, 113, 117, 150
Casuarina High School 99–100
Catholic Education Office (CEO) 5, 30, 44–5, 55, 58–9, 65, 67
Centre for Educational Research and Innovation (CERI) 4–6, 10
Centre For Multicultural Studies (CMS) 5, 65

Index

Chinese Languages and Background 2, 61, 73, 94–5, 100–1, 103, 105, 108, 110, 112–3, 117, 122, 126–7, 142, 149–51, 154, 157, 167, 178–9, 183, 203, 227
Chipman, L. 28
Class, Social 22, 34
  see also Middle Class; Ruling Class; Socio-economic Status; Working Class
Claydon, L. 71
Collingwood Education Centre 5, 76–8, 116–47, 216, 218, 220, 223
Commerce/Economics 65, 126, 169, 188, 210
Commonwealth Child Migrant Education Program 17–9
Commonwealth Department of Education 23
Commonwealth Employment Service 112
Commonwealth New Arrivals Program 156, 161, 167
Commonwealth Schools Commission 19–21, 25, 49, 97, 128
Community, Sense of 72, 74, 82, 88, 120–1, 145–6, 152, 155–6, 175–9, 185–6, 190, 209, 212, 220, 227, 230–1, 238, 241, 249–50
  see also National Identity
Community Languages 22–3, 26, 30, 32, 36, 45, 71, 75, 77, 81, 103, 120, 143, 158–9, 205, 208, 223
  see also Language and Cultural Maintenance; Languages Other Than English
Community Languages Policy (NSW) 30
Community Liaison 41–2, 44, 46, 48–60, 66–7, 122, 154, 157–9, 176, 179, 187, 230–1
  see also Community and Parent Participation
Community and Parent Participation 6, 11–12, 31, 44, 49, 51–4, 58, 60, 65, 70–2, 74, 82, 85, 96, 112, 120, 122–3, 125–6, 144–5, 154, 179, 193, 205, 211, 217, 229–31, 241–2
  see also Community Liaison; Management, School; School Councils
Constitution, Australian 15
Core Curriculum 21, 48, 61, 65–6, 154, 156–7, 167, 173, 188–9, 222
Croatian see Serbo-Croatian
Cultural Pluralism 4, 10–1, 13, 17, 19, 21–2, 24–5, 28–9, 44, 74, 89, 130, 220–1, 223, 229, 238, 248, 250
Cultural Homogeneity 1–2, 21, 29, 218
Culture, Theory and Definition 21–2, 36, 83, 226
Curriculum Development and Planning in Victoria (Ministerial Paper No. 6) 77, 79
Curriculum Development Centre 37, 189
Curriculum Diversification 31, 34–5, 37, 46–50, 97–8, 221–2, 228, 233, 238
  see also Other Approved Courses; Progressivism; School-based Curriculum

Dawkins, J. 189
De la Salle College, Ashfield (NSW) 219
Department of Immigration 19, 110
Disadvantage 4, 11, 17–22, 35, 72, 97, 189, 206, 217, 220, 233–4, 239–40, 243
  see also Class, Social
Disadvantaged Schools Program (DSP) 19, 44, 49–50, 52, 55–6, 58–9, 67, 71, 119, 153, 158–9, 161, 163, 173, 228
Dutch Language and Background 2, 94

Economic Development 2–3, 11, 25–6, 28, 144, 222, 241
Education and Cultural and Linguistic Pluralism (ECALP) Project 4–6, 10
Education In, and For, a Multicultural Victoria 29
Education Interpreter Service 29
Employment 42, 70, 94–5, 110–1, 118, 144, 149, 151, 182, 210–1, 216
  see also Class, Social; Middle Class; Socioeconomic Status; Unemployment; Working Class

263

Index

English, June 71
English (subject) 31, 45, 59, 62, 64–5, 72, 75–82, 84, 87, 89–90, 101, 104, 106–7, 132, 136, 143, 154, 157, 159, 163, 167–9, 172, 174, 176–7, 186–8, 192–5, 200–2, 204–5, 222, 229, 231, 234
English as a Second Language (ESL) 23–4, 26, 28–30, 45, 52, 55–6, 58, 72–3, 89, 96, 101, 120–1, 124, 127, 130–1, 134, 144, 154, 156–7, 159–60, 162–4, 166, 168, 170, 173, 186, 188–9, 192–6, 198–205
English as a Second Language Policy (NSW) 30
Equitable Multiculturalism 220, 238–50
Ethnic Aides 29, 74, 80, 102, 119, 121–3, 126, 140, 142, 152, 157, 166–7, 175, 184–5, 187, 210, 213
Ethnic Disadvantage Debate 3–4
Ethnicity 20–2, 24, 32, 34
Ethnic Schools 20, 22–3, 222
    see also Saturday School; Victorian School of Languages
Ethnic Studies Policy (NSW) 30

Federation of Ethnic Communities Council of Australia (FECCA) 25–6
Filipino Background 41, 53, 60
First Generation Migrants 4, 41, 109, 118, 151, 183
    see also Immigration; Second Generation
FitzGerald Report (1988) 27–8
Footscray High School 5, 181–214, 216
Footscray Institute of Technology (FIT) 200, 210
Frameworks (Victoria) 37
Fraser, M. 19–20, 22–3, 25, 28
Freeman, G. 71
French Language and Background 2, 32, 43, 45, 48, 62–4, 99, 119, 121, 142, 157, 184, 192, 221, 250
Funding 21–6, 30, 37, 44, 49–50, 52–3, 55–7, 59, 65, 67, 71, 76–8, 96, 100–1, 103, 113, 119, 126, 153–4, 157–62, 173, 185–7, 193, 203, 208, 249–50

Galbally Report (1978) 19–25
Gender 34, 58, 98–9, 150, 152, 155, 178, 184, 189, 191–2, 194, 213, 229
    see also Sexism
Genre Theory 163, 171, 232
Geography 61, 64–5, 154, 156, 167
German Language and Background 2, 23, 32, 99, 157, 184, 221
Grammar 31–3, 62, 64, 84, 89, 98–9, 102–3, 106–7, 131, 133, 160, 165, 171–2, 195, 197–9, 201, 205–6, 228, 231, 233–5
Grassby, A. 18–20, 24
Greek Language and Background 2, 23, 69–70, 72, 74, 76, 83–5, 89–90, 94–5, 99–100, 103–5, 113, 117–9, 121, 124–5, 141–4, 152, 167, 182–4, 186–7, 191–3, 196–7, 201, 203, 206–7, 209, 213, 216, 226–7

Hannan, B. 71
Hawke, R.J. 19, 23, 28
Higher School Certificate (HSC) — NSW, 100, 104, 106, 108–9, 111, 176–7
Higher School Certificate (HSC) — VIC, 88, 211, 219, 222
History 29, 32–3, 46, 60–1, 64–5, 73, 90, 98–9, 154–5, 158, 167, 169, 220, 232, 241
    see also Humanities
Home Science/Economics 122, 125, 164
Housing 41–2, 69, 93, 95, 117, 124, 149, 151, 182, 184
Humanities 121–2, 126–30, 135, 137, 146, 159, 186, 188, 193, 195, 197, 199, 203, 231
Hungarian Language and Background 2, 94

Immigration 1–4, 15–16, 18, 27–30, 41–2, 69, 94–95, 117, 124, 149–51, 182–3, 189–90, 216, 248
    see also Refugees
Immigration (Education) Act (1971) 15
Incorporation 6, 10–11, 54, 217, 220–7, 229, 236, 238–41

Index

Indo-chinese *see* Asian Languages and Background
Industrial Arts 164, 173
Industrial Society 1, 230, 235, 241–3, 248–9
see also Liberal Democracy
Innovation 6, 46–8, 50, 71–2, 88, 124, 180, 187, 217, 219–20, 248
see also Institutionalization of Innovation
Inservicing 31, 37, 59, 112–4, 140, 154, 161–5, 168–70, 172–5, 243
Institutionalization of Innovation 66–7, 89, 113–4, 136, 138, 173, 175, 177, 203–4, 248–50
see also Innovation
Integration 2–4, 15, 17–19, 28
Intensive Language Centres/Units 55, 73, 117, 144–5, 151–2, 154, 156–7, 160–3, 165–8, 173–5, 193, 217, 220, 235
Italian Language and Background 2, 30, 41–5, 48, 53, 60–1, 69–70, 72, 76, 79, 84–5, 89–90, 94–5, 99–100, 102–5, 110, 112–13, 119, 150–2, 157, 182, 184, 186, 192, 196–7, 203, 205, 209, 229

Japanese Language and Background 23, 28, 142
Jupp Report (1986) 23–4

Karmel Report (1973) 21–2
Karmel Report (1985) 78
Khmer Language and Background 94, 149–51, 167, 183
Knight, T. 71
Korean Language and Background 60, 94

Labor Party 18–20, 22–4, 28, 33
Language Across the Curriculum 45, 56, 65, 73, 78, 98, 100, 141, 157, 159–73, 199–200, 204, 232
Language and Cultural Maintenance 22–3, 25–7, 36, 77, 82–3, 101–2, 121, 123, 125, 127, 129, 141–2, 156, 165, 184, 193, 196–7, 205–9, 213, 219, 221, 223, 226–7, 229
Language Functions 103, 161, 163, 171–2
Languages Action Plan (Victoria) 29
Languages Institute of Australia 26
Languages other than English (LOTES) 26, 29–30, 45, 48, 61, 63, 67, 70, 72, 75–7, 79, 82–6, 88–90, 106, 110, 116, 121, 123–5, 127–9, 131, 133, 135, 137–9, 141–4, 157–8, 178, 186, 191–3, 196–8, 204–9, 216, 219–22, 227, 229, 234, 241
Lao Language and Background 94, 149–50, 167, 169, 183
Latin 32, 35, 221
Lebanese Background 2, 23, 41–3, 46, 53, 57, 60, 62, 73, 84, 94–5, 227
Leadership 6, 37, 74, 107, 125, 139, 152–3
see also Management, School
Liberal Party 19
Liberal Democracy 11, 27–8, 34–6, 227–8, 231, 241, 249–50
see also Industrial Society
Literacy 26, 31–2, 35–6, 65, 110, 129, 166–7, 175, 202, 212, 219, 233
Lo Bianco, J. 25, 29, 71
Lucas, J. 71

Macarthur Institute of Higher Education 105, 110
Macedonian Language and Background 2, 88, 183–4, 186–7, 191–3, 196–7, 206–7, 209, 211, 213, 222, 224, 226, 234
McGowan Report (1981) 47–8
Mackellar, M. 19
MacKillop Girls' High 5, 40–67, 218–19, 222, 225, 230
McNamara Report (1979) 20–1
MacPhee, I. 19–20
Macquarie University 96
'Mainstreaming' 24–5
Mainstream Society 11, 24–5, 27, 83, 101–2, 139, 156, 220, 226, 229, 238
Mainstream Subjects and Classes 23–4,

265

Index

29, 45, 56, 72–3, 78, 90, 121, 123, 127, 129, 132, 137–8, 141, 156–8, 161, 164, 167–8, 173–5, 186, 192–6, 199, 202–4, 208, 224–6
Management, School 7, 11, 34, 44, 57–8, 60, 74, 79, 87, 96–7, 101, 118–20, 125, 128, 130–1, 135, 137–9, 142, 144, 152–3, 164, 168–9, 185–6, 228, 249
  see also Community and Parent Participation; Leadership; School Councils
Mandarin Language 100, 105, 113, 126, 157
Mathematics 47, 85, 88, 90, 98, 101, 119, 126, 137–8, 140, 143, 152, 154, 167, 169, 174, 176–7, 188, 204, 207–8, 210, 222, 229, 231, 241
Methodology 4–10, 236
Middle Class 35, 74, 95, 117, 183, 216, 221–2, 229, 231
  see also Class, Social; Ruling Class; Socio-Economic Status; Employment
Middleton, M. 46
'Migrant Vote' 18–9, 150
Monash University 193
Multicultural Education Policy (NSW) 30, 98
Multicultural Education Program 20, 23, 25–7, 71, 113, 234, 249
Multicultural Education Service 76, 124, 126
Multiculturalism 2–4, 15, 18–22, 24–9, 33, 35–7, 73, 135–6, 139, 144, 155–6, 159, 178, 186–7, 192, 220, 226–7, 229–30, 234, 238, 241, 248, 250
Multicultural Perspectives to the Curriculum Policy (NSW) 30
Music 98, 119, 167, 188

National Aboriginal Languages Policy 26
National Accreditation Authority for Translators and Interpreters (NAATI) 100, 104–5, 110–11
National Advisory and Consultative Committee on Multicultural Education (NACCME) 24, 249

National Agenda for a Multicultural Australia (1989) 28
National Identity 3, 16–18, 21–2, 27–9, 32–3, 37, 146, 155–6, 191–2, 214, 220, 238, 241, 250
  see also Community, Sense of
National Language Conference (1982) 26
National Languages Policy (1984) 25
National Policy on Languages (1987) 5, 25–7, 62, 71, 78
New South Wales Board of Senior School Studies 104, 108–9, 160
New South Wales Department of Education 5, 16, 30, 96, 98–100, 152, 159, 170, 179, 221, 234
New South Wales Multicultural Education Coordinating Committee (MECC) 50, 62, 65, 100, 153, 157
New Technologies 6, 12, 96, 119, 123, 153, 159, 185, 196, 237, 248

Office of Multicultural Affairs (OMA) 24, 27
Oldfield, J. 186
Organisation for Economic Cooperation and Development (OECD) 4–6, 10
Other Approved Studies (OAS) Courses — NSW 92, 98, 100, 102, 104, 107–11, 160, 221

Parent Participation see Community and Parent Participation
Parent-Teacher Meetings 7, 51, 59, 74, 85, 100, 104, 112, 122–3, 179, 205
  see also Community and Parent Participation; Community Liaison
Participation and Equity Program (PEP) 23, 71, 96–102, 108, 113, 119, 153, 159–61, 187, 249
Pastoral Care see Student Welfare
Physical Education 66, 122, 154, 188
Polish Language and Background 2, 41, 94, 119, 152
Portuguese Language and Background 69, 94
Post Primary Bilingual Education Project 76–8, 124–6, 129–30
Preston Girls' High School 76–8, 125–7

Index

Process Writing 32, 35–6, 98–9, 107, 114, 163, 165, 231, 233
  see also Progressivism
Progressivism 31–37, 46, 62, 64, 84, 98, 106–7, 109, 114, 206, 217–18, 220–3, 227, 229–36, 243–6, 248, 250
  see also Process Writing

Racism 2–4, 17, 25, 27–28, 36, 57, 73, 86, 120–1, 145, 158, 168, 178–9, 187, 189–91, 207, 212–13, 217, 219, 225
Rado, M. 71, 76, 184, 186
Reformism 18–21, 23–4, 26
Refugees 1–2, 28, 41, 54, 151, 156, 161
  see also Immigration
Retention Rates 89–90, 97, 100, 109, 134, 144, 177, 221, 224
Ruling Class 206–7, 234
  see also Class, Social; Middle Class; Socioeconomic Status
Russian Language and Background 2, 43, 94
Russian-Chinese Background 151, 179
Ryan, S. 97

St Mel's Primary School 218–9
Saturday Schools 61, 89, 108, 142–3, 207, 213
  see also Ethnic Schools; Victorian School of Languages
School-based Curriculum 31, 37, 62, 80, 98, 105, 130, 160, 187–8, 195, 221, 233, 243
  see also Curriculum Diversification; Other Approved Courses; Progressivism
School Certificate (NSW) 66, 174
School Councils 7, 74, 85, 122, 185–6, 191, 211, 227
  see also Management, School
Sciences 88, 90, 98–9, 101, 121, 123, 126–8, 130–1, 133–5, 137, 140, 154, 160–1, 163–7, 169, 172, 187–8, 194, 204, 208, 210, 241
Second Generation 1, 4, 41, 66, 94, 110, 118, 139, 151, 183
  see also First Generation Migrants
Self-esteem 11, 22, 33, 35–6, 50, 63, 65–6, 78, 82, 97, 100, 102, 110–11, 114, 129, 136, 141, 155, 158, 191, 205, 212, 218, 223–4, 232, 236–7, 241
Serbo-Croatian 2, 41, 94, 117–19, 124, 150–2, 157, 167, 171, 178, 192, 226
Sexism 27, 36, 192, 207, 213, 226, 230
  see also Gender
Snedden, B. 17, 19
Social Literacy Project 45–6, 65–6, 219, 225
  see also Sociocultural Curriculum
Social Mobility 2–4, 42, 69, 95, 149–51, 216, 218
Social Science/Studies 29, 32–3, 59, 65–6, 72–3, 75–82, 84, 87, 98–9, 103, 112, 121–2, 127–8, 137, 140, 146, 156, 187, 219, 225, 232
Sociocultural Curriculum 23, 26–7, 29–30, 45, 65, 73, 122, 128, 146, 156, 158, 179, 186, 225, 227, 232, 241, 250
Socioeconomic Status 4, 19–22, 57, 66, 69–70, 117, 120, 149–50, 175, 185, 216–8, 221–2, 249
  see also Class, Social; Employment; Middle Class; Ruling Class; Unemployment; Working Class
South and Central American Background 2, 41, 60–1, 94, 149, 151–2, 222
South East Asian see Asian Language and Background
Spanish Language and Background 2, 41, 43, 45, 48, 52–3, 61, 99–100, 105, 121–2, 150, 157, 167, 183
Special Broadcasting Service (SBS) 20, 23–4
Spinoso, G. 71
Staffing 29, 43, 55–7, 74, 77–8, 89, 95, 97, 103, 105, 113–14, 127, 135, 138, 140, 142, 152, 159–62, 184–5, 195, 198, 204, 208
State Language Policy (NSW) 30
State Multicultural Education Coordination Unit (SMECU) — Victoria 29, 76, 124, 126, 143–4
Strathfield Girls' High School 94
Student Welfare 56, 59, 83, 119, 122, 158, 176, 186–7, 189–90, 194, 202, 209, 219, 225

267

Index

Sudanese Background 42–3, 56
Sydney Road Community School 71
Syrian Background 62, 66, 152

The Teaching of Languages Other Than English in Victorian Schools 78–9
Teacher Training 13, 45, 74–5, 96, 120, 134–7, 163, 212–13, 219, 243
Team-Teaching 79–81, 101, 121, 127, 130–1, 136–7, 140, 156–7, 164, 167–8, 172–3, 199
Technical and Further Education (TAFE) Colleges 103, 119, 144, 166–7, 174, 211
Tertiary Entrance 12, 35, 88, 104, 108, 144, 160, 188, 194, 200–1, 210–11, 221, 235, 246–7
Traditional Pedagogy 6, 31–7, 63–4, 84, 106–7, 109–10, 114, 130, 154, 213, 218, 221–3, 228–9, 231–6, 247–8
Transition Education 101, 160, 187
Turkey 2, 83, 233
Turkish Language and Background 26, 69–70, 72, 74, 76, 78, 80, 83–5, 88, 90, 94, 99–102, 105, 108, 110, 113, 117–23, 125–30, 132, 138, 141–4, 150, 157, 216, 218, 226–9, 233–4

Unemployment 42, 53, 60, 69, 93, 95, 97, 144, 149, 151, 182, 210–11
  see also Class, Social; Employment; Welfare; Working Class
Uruguayan Background 53, 60, 170, 178

Victorian Certificate of Education (VCE) 84–5, 88, 134, 146, 188, 195–6, 200–1, 204, 206, 208–11, 231, 235

Victorian Curriculum and Assessment Board 192
Victorian Department of Education 203, 205
Victorian Ministerial Advisory Committee on Multicultural and Migrant Education (MACMME) 71, 186
Victorian Ministry of Education 5, 24, 71, 124, 144, 200, 203, 208
Victorian School of Languages 119, 122
Victorian Secondary Teachers Association (VSTA) 124
Vietnamese Language and Background 2, 41–5, 48, 52–4, 61–2, 69, 74, 84–5, 94, 99–101, 103, 105, 108, 110, 113, 117–23, 125–30, 132–3, 135, 137–43, 145–6, 149–51, 156–7, 159, 167, 176, 179, 182–4, 186–7, 191–2, 194, 197, 199, 201, 205, 207–8, 213, 226, 228–9, 231, 235

Welfare 18–20, 22, 24, 28, 69, 95, 103, 112, 117–18, 150–1, 183–4, 216
  see also Unemployment
Whitlam, G. 18, 20
Working Class 41–2, 69–70, 94, 117, 125, 149–51, 153, 182–5, 207, 212, 216
  see also Class, Social; Employment; Socioeconomic Status; Unemployment
Writing K-12 (NSW) 98, 107

Yin, R.K. 8
Yugoslavia 182, 201
  see also Serbo-Croatian

FEB 11 1992
DISCHARGED

DEC 18 1991
DISCHARGED

DISCHARGED
NOV 8 1994

DISCHARGED

DISCHARGED

DISCHARGED